CREDIBILITY ASSESSMENT

CREDIBILITY ASSESSMENT

SCIENTIFIC RESEARCH AND APPLICATIONS

Edited by

DAVID C. RASKIN

CHARLES R. HONTS

JOHN C. KIRCHER

AMSTERDAM • BOSTON • HEIDELBERG • LONDON
NEW YORK • OXFORD • PARIS • SAN DIEGO
SAN FRANCISCO • SINGAPORE • SYDNEY • TOKYO

Academic Press is an imprint of Elsevier

Academic Press is an imprint of Elsevier
The Boulevard, Langford Lane, Kidlington, Oxford, OX5 1GB
525 B Street, Suite 1800, San Diego, CA 92101-4495, USA

First published 2014

British Library Cataloguing in Publication Data
A catalogue record for this book is available from the British Library

Library of Congress Cataloging-in-Publication Data
A catalog record for this book is available from the Library of Congress

ISBN: 978-0-12-394433-7

For information on all Academic Press publications
visit our website at store.elsevier.com

Printed and bound in China

14 15 16 17   10 9 8 7 6 5 4 3 2 1

Working together
to grow libraries in
developing countries

ELSEVIER   Book Aid International

www.elsevier.com • www.bookaid.org

Dedication

We dedicate this book to our friend and colleague Murray Kleiner, whose scholarship expanded our understanding of polygraph science and applications.

Contents

Foreword xi
Preface xv
Contributors xxi

1. Strategic Use of Evidence During Investigative Interviews: The State of the Science
MARIA HARTWIG, PÄR ANDERS GRANHAG, TIMOTHY LUKE

Introduction 3
General Findings on Deception and its Detection 4
Eliciting Cues to Deception: Strategic Questioning Approaches 7
SUE: Theoretical Principles 9
Translating Psychological Theory into Interview Tactics 15
Meta-Analytic Review of SUE Research 23
Summary and Concluding Remarks 30
References 31

2. Credibility Assessment at Portals
CHARLES R. HONTS, MARIA HARTWIG

Overview of the Problem 39
The US Government's Response to the 9-11 Attack 39
Unique Aspects of the Portal Setting 43
Related Scientific Literature 47
A Science-Based Approach to the Portal Screening Problem 54
Eliciting Cues to Deception, Guilt, and Malintent: The Psychology of Investigative Interviewing 56
Consequences for Portals 57
References 58

3. Validity of Polygraph Techniques and Decision Methods
DAVID C. RASKIN, JOHN C. KIRCHER

Introduction 65
Common Characteristics of All Comparison Question Tests 66
Comparison Question Tests 67

Utah Probable-Lie Test   69
Utah Directed-Lie Test   78
Overall Validity of Comparison Question Tests   79
Methods for Determining Test Outcomes   85
Comparison of Scoring Methods   94
Applied Issues   117
Summary and Conclusions   122
Acknowledgments   123
References   123

4. Countermeasures and Credibility Assessment

CHARLES R. HONTS

Introduction   133
Spontaneous Countermeasures   137
GS Countermeasures   139
Information Countermeasures   140
SP Countermeasures   143
Pharmacological Amnesia: A New Countermeasure Threat?   147
Possible Solutions to the Problems of Countermeasures   148
Current Anti-Countermeasure Training   149
A Theoretical Description of the Mechanism of Effective Countermeasures   151
The Future of Scientific Research on Countermeasures?   154
References   155

5. Detecting Deception Using Ocular Metrics During Reading

DOUGLAS J. HACKER, B. BRIAN KUHLMAN, JOHN C. KIRCHER,
ANNE E. COOK, DAN J. WOLTZ

Introduction   161
Physiological and Psychological Bases of Pupil Dilation   164
Evoked Pupillary Responses During Deception   172
Using Reading Behaviors to Detect Deception   174
How Ocular Metrics During Reading can be Used to Detect Deception   183
Laboratory Experiment 1   188
Laboratory Experiment 2   195
Field Study 1   199
Field Study 2   203
Conclusion   207
References   210

6. The Neural Basis of Deception and Credibility Assessment: A Cognitive Neuroscience Perspective
RAY JOHNSON JR., PH.D.

Introduction   219
The Neurocognitive Approach   220
Functional Neuroimaging Techniques   222
Methods for Assessing Causal Relations between Brain Activity and Cognition   228
Early CNS studies   229
Toward a Cognitive Description of Deception   231
Neurocognitive Studies of Deception   238
Forensic Applications   280
Future Directions   284
Conclusions   288
References   289

7. Theories in Deception and Lie Detection
ALDERT VRIJ, GIORGIO GANIS

Introduction   303
An Abstract Theoretical Framework for Deception and Lie Detection   305
A Brief History of Lie Detection   307
Physiological Lie Detection   310
Non-Verbal Lie Detection   319
Verbal Lie Detection   336
Functional Magnetic Resonance Imaging-Based Lie Detection   345
Comparison of Physiological, Non-Verbal, Verbal, and Brain Activity Lie Detection   354
Interviewing to Detect Deception Through Non-Verbal and Verbal Cues   356
Conclusions   361
References   362

Index   375

Foreword

This unique and important volume edited by Drs. Raskin, Honts, and Kircher provides a scholarly portal into the scientific basis for credibility assessment. The editors are uniquely experienced in this area and have had long and productive research careers dedicated to improving the methods used to detect deception in the field by conducting laboratory and field research. Through their scholarship and persistence, the scientific study of deception has survived and prospered. This volume goes well beyond a summary of their important contributions. The chapters provide scholarly and critical overviews of the literature with objective conclusions regarding the effectiveness of specific methods. The chapters also provide documentation that some methods, which have been assumed to be useful, are ineffective. The volume forces the reader to re-evaluate the literature and to distinguish between data-based findings and speculations.

Credibility assessment, as a research area, is not a single discipline. It is inclusive of a variety of disciplines applying a broad range of methods and technologies. For example, protocols testing aspects of credibility have measured facial expressivity, eye movements and blinks, subjective experience, memory retrieval, reaction time, brain activity, and peripheral physiology. Research assessing credibility is not pragmatic and not agnostic to theory. Approaches to evaluate credibility have been dependent on psychological theories related to memory, motivation, and emotion and neurophysiological models of how the brain and autonomic nervous system function.

As detailed in this volume, the experimental method can be useful in evaluating methodologies that have been used to detect deceptive behaviors. From the well-documented chapters we learn four important points: 1) physiological indicators are, in general, more effective than behavioral observations in detecting deception, 2) expert lie "catchers" tend to overstate their effectiveness, 3) protocols that manipulate the structure of the questions, consistent with psychological principles related to emotion regulation and information

retrieval, are most effective, and 4) when deception is a low probability occurrence, the cost-benefit ratio of screening may be too costly and disruptive.

The scientific investigation of deception is controversial in both the public
and the academic arenas. The public press has frequently demonized technologies proposed to "extract" information from passive participants, while
other forms of media, including television, have overstated the effectiveness
of some methodologies to drive plots and attract viewers and sponsors. This
pro-con debate of the effectiveness and the ethics of technologies to detect
deception in the media has been paralleled in the scientific community. These
controversies have been costly to both a refinement of the science detecting
deception and the application of science-based methods in the field.

For several decades the scientific community has aggressively reacted when
confronted with data demonstrating the effectiveness of polygraphic and
interview techniques in detecting deception. Often the critical scientists in
their own research have accepted variables, such as psychiatric diagnostic
categories, which are less reliable than indices detecting deception in well-
conducted studies. In both realms, passions and beliefs often take precedence
over data. These arguments, often vitriolic and amplified by passionate
beliefs, have led to confusion in the applied arena. This confusion has led to an
acceptance in the field that academic scientists cannot provide the validated
methods that are needed. Functionally, this has created a void between the
availability of validated tools and the need to detect deception in the private
and government sectors. At times, this void has been filled by unproven and
untested methodologies. In spite of, or perhaps due to, these well-publicized
disagreements, unvalidated methods and techniques to detect deception continue to be used in both private and government sectors. The proliferation of
untested methodologies has resulted in a functional disconnect between the
science and practice of credibility assessment.

The current volume is a timely contribution that reframes the debate regarding the use and effectiveness of methods proposed to detect deception by
providing an up-to-date evaluation of research. In addition, the expert critical
evaluations, research rationales, and theoretical justifications for the various
approaches described in each chapter provide a hint for the future. Informed

by the scholarship of this volume, researchers will develop new approaches to study deception that will merge measurement technologies, context manipulations, and variations in interview structure.

Stephen W. Porges, PhD
Professor of Psychiatry, University of North Carolina at Chapel Hill

Preface

A dozen years have passed since the publication of Murray Kleiner's seminal work *Handbook of Polygraph Testing*. The events of September 11, 2001 and heightened concerns about national security and terrorism have resulted in increased efforts to improve existing techniques for the assessment of credibility and develop new techniques for implementation in field settings. We are all aware of the massive expansion of costly government programs, such as the establishment of the Department of Homeland Security and Transportation Security Administration programs for screening airline passengers. However, many concerns have been voiced by scientists and the Government Accountability Office about the scientific basis for such programs and their effectiveness for identifying individuals who plan to harm people, property, and society.

Along with the increased concerns for credibility assessment in national security, there is renewed interest in the use of credibility assessment in criminal investigations. Innocence Projects around the United States have shown that inaccurate credibility assessments by law enforcement officers may lead to false confessions with serious consequences for individuals and society. Scientists and some governments have responded to the Innocence Project data with efforts to improve credibility assessments in criminal investigation.

This emphasis on credibility assessment also raised public awareness and interest in methods for credibility assessment. An unfortunate side effect of this increased interest is the proliferation of television shows and popular media that purport to use scientifically-established techniques to test the credibility of individuals regarding personal matters and anecdotes. These programs typically misuse established methods or rely on methods that have a questionable scientific basis, including observations of facial expressions and gestures and voice stress analysis. Some of the more prominent abuses are drawn from the techniques that are described and evaluated by the scientific experts who have contributed to this volume.

When we were invited to update the Kleiner handbook, the publishers accepted our suggestion that the coverage be expanded to cover the numerous and controversial developments that had not been addressed in a single volume. Thus, we assembled a group of leading scientific experts from the United States and the European Union to describe and analyze the major techniques for credibility assessment and the utility and problems associated with each. These comprise the first six chapters, and the final chapter attempts to integrate and reconcile the empirical data and the various hypotheses that have been put forward to explain how and why credibility assessment is accomplished.

The opening chapter by Hartwig and Granhag begins with a review of the literature that describes commonly-held misconceptions about behavioral cues to deception and highlights the inability of laypersons and law enforcement personnel to accurately assess the credibility of suspects. The authors provide a detailed description of an improved method of questioning known as the strategic use of evidence (SUE) technique for interviewing suspects by planned questioning and strategic disclosures of incriminating evidence. The research indicates that the SUE approach increases the accuracy of credibility assessments, which may provide the basis for improving the current problematic investigative methods generally practiced by law enforcement investigators.

Honts and Hartwig address the challenge of assessing credibility at portals that control entry to countries, public transportation, and public events and facilities. The governments of the United States and many other countries have devoted major resources to developing new technologies for credibility assessment at portals, including machine- and human-based systems. This critical review of these approaches finds them sorely lacking in theoretical foundation and empirical validation. After providing a science-based perspective on the deceptive context of credibility assessment at portals, they describe existing scientific theory and research that may be relevant for that context, and they outline an approach for theory development and scientific validation in this area.

Raskin and Kircher describe current methods and uses of polygraph techniques for the detection of deception. Following a brief overview of the basic principles of polygraph tests, they provide a detailed description of the most widely applied technique for physiological detection of deception, the comparison question test (CQT), and the major analytic methods for determining the outcomes of such tests. Following an analysis of the scientific research and validity of the CQT, they present findings indicating that the diagnostic reliability and validity of polygraph tests compare favorably to commonly-used medical diagnostic procedures and exceed the accuracy of generally-accepted psychological diagnoses. They provide an extensive description and evaluation of current methods for rendering decisions and conclude with a discussion of major issues concerning uses of polygraph tests, including their accuracy on psychopaths and victims of crimes, confidential tests for defense attorneys, and government uses of polygraph examinations.

Honts addresses the use of countermeasures against credibility assessment tests where examinees are frequently motivated to attempt to manipulate and distort the results. This chapter focuses on polygraph tests because there is a relatively large scientific literature concerning polygraph countermeasures and polygraph tests are widely applied in criminal investigation and national security settings. Honts describes a taxonomy of polygraph countermeasures and uses that taxonomy to organize the existing literature. Although published studies show that some countermeasures are effective in laboratory studies, it appears that hands-on training is needed for a person to defeat the polygraph. Current methods to deter or detect polygraph countermeasures are inadequate, and Honts proposes a theoretical model to explain the mechanism of effective countermeasures in the hope that theory-driven research may lead to the development of improved methods to detect and deter their use.

Hacker and his colleagues present a novel approach to detect deception. This methodology is based on a combination of the pupillary response and eye movements to detect deception to simple statements. They describe two laboratory and two field studies in which participants read and respond to three types of statements: relevant to a mock crime they committed, relevant to a crime they did not commit, and neutral. This procedure requires considerably less time than other commonly-employed methods of deception detection. Detailed measures of eye movements and fixations and pupil responses during reading were subjected to discriminant analyses. Overall, more than 85% of cases were classified correctly in the laboratory studies, and 78% of cases were classified correctly in one of the field studies. However, the other field study indicated that the test may not be effective with poor readers. The results indicate that further developments in the measurement of pupillary responses and eye movements during reading may become an exciting new tool for the detection of deception.

Johnson provides a comprehensive review and critical analysis of the relatively recent use of central nervous system (CNS) measures to detect deception. Although all behavioral, cognitive, and emotional measures for credibility assessment arise from brain activity, until recently little was known about the neural basis of deception. This chapter describes how research in the new discipline of cognitive neuroscience aims to unify psychology and neurobiology and may reveal the neurocognitive basis of the complex function of deceiving. Johnson describes the use of powerful new brain-imaging techniques, both electrophysiological and hemodynamic, to observe where and when different brain areas are activated in persons who are engaged in deception. Despite the fact that this research began little more than a decade ago, many new and important insights have emerged concerning the cognitive and brain processes during deception that are instantiated in the brain. The chapter provides an exceptionally comprehensive and integrated review concerning the existing basic and applied neurocognitive studies.

The final chapter by Vrij and Ganis attempts the difficult task of providing a synthesis and theoretical integration of detection of deception using physiological responses, observable behavior, analysis of verbal behavior, and measurements of brain activity. They give a brief history of lie detection and the accuracy of various lie detection tools to analyze physiological responses, behavior, speech, and brain activity. They propose and describe theoretical rationales for each approach: anxiety and orienting response for physiological lie detection; anxiety, guilt, and cognitive load for behavior;

cognitive load and trying to make a convincing impression or memory for verbal behavior; and response inhibition or memory retrieval conflict monitoring for brain activity. The reader will note that the difficulty of achieving this goal results in views and analyses that are sometimes in conflict with the material and views presented in the earlier chapters of this volume. This lack of a complete consensus is a testimonial to the complex and varied types of deception and the long-standing controversies about the methods, results, and interpretations of research on credibility assessment. Such differences of opinions are inherent in the nature of scientific theory and discovery.

We hope that this volume fosters greater understanding of the advantages and disadvantages of the various techniques being developed and applied for detection of deception. Scientific advancement in this area should decrease miscarriages of justice produced by flawed investigative techniques and lead to the use of scientifically-validated techniques in the expanded, expensive, and controversial national security and anti-terrorism programs.

David C. Raskin
Charles R. Honts
John C. Kircher

Contributors

Anne E. Cook   Educational Psychology Department, University of Utah

Giorgio Ganis   Psychology Department, University of Plymouth

Pär Anders Granhag   Department of Psychology, University of Gothenburg and Norwegian Police University College

Douglas J. Hacker   Educational Psychology Department, University of Utah

Maria Hartwig   Department of Psychology, John Jay College of Criminal Justice, City University of New York

Charles R. Honts   Department of Psychology, Boise State University

Ray Johnson Jr., Ph.D.   Department of Psychology, Queens College/City University of New York

John C. Kircher   Educational Psychology Department, University of Utah

B. Brian Kuhlman   Educational Psychology Department, University of Utah

Timothy Luke   Department of Psychology, John Jay College of Criminal Justice and The Graduate Center, City University of New York

David C. Raskin   Psychology Department, University of Utah

Aldert Vrij   Psychology Department, University of Portsmouth

Dan J. Woltz   Educational Psychology Department, University of Utah

Strategic Use of Evidence During Investigative Interviews: The State of the Science

Maria Hartwig[*], *Pär Anders Granhag*[†], *Timothy Luke*[**]

[*]Department of Psychology, John Jay College of Criminal Justice, City University of New York,
[†]Department of Psychology, University of Gothenburg and Norwegian Police University College,
[**]Department of Psychology, John Jay College of Criminal Justice and The Graduate Center, City University of New York

OUTLINE

Introduction	3	Translating Psychological Theory into Interview Tactics	15
General Findings on Deception and its Detection	4	Questioning Tactics	18
Accuracy in Deception Judgments	5	Disclosure Tactics	20
Cues to Deception	6	Meta-Analytic Review of SUE Research	23
High-Stakes Lies	7	Method	24
		Selection Criteria	24
Eliciting Cues to Deception: Strategic Questioning Approaches	7	Literature Search	25
		Coding Procedure	25
SUE: Theoretical Principles	9	Analyses	26
Psychology of Self-Regulation	9	Results	26
Self-Regulatory Differences Between Liars and Truth-Tellers	11	Discussion	29
Liars' and Truth-Tellers' Information Management Strategies	11	Limitations	29
		Conclusions	30
Empirical Research on Counter-Interrogation Strategies	14	Summary and Concluding Remarks	30
		References	31

Credibility Assessment
http://dx.doi.org/10.1016/B978-0-12-394433-7.00001-4

INTRODUCTION

Judging veracity is an important part of investigative interviewing. The aim of this chapter is to review the literature on a technique developed to assist interviewers in judging the veracity of the reports obtained in interviews. More specifically, the purpose of this chapter is to provide an overview of the research program on the Strategic Use of Evidence (SUE) technique. The SUE technique is an interviewing framework that aims to improve the ability to make correct judgments of credibility, through the elicitation of cues to deception and truth. As such, it is not a general framework that will accomplish all goals relevant to interviewing and interrogation. However, as will be shown in this chapter, the SUE approach can help an interviewer plan, structure, and conduct an interview with a suspect in such a way that cues to deception may become more pronounced. As will be described, the SUE technique relies on various forms of strategic employment of the available information or evidence. While the SUE technique was originally developed to plan, structure, conduct, and evaluate interviews in criminal contexts, the theoretical principles apply to interviews and interrogations in other contexts, including those in which the goal is intelligence gathering.

We will first provide an overview of the core findings from a vast body of research on human ability to judge truth and deception. This overview will serve to contextualize the research on the SUE technique and illustrate the ways in which the technique departs from many other lie detection techniques. After reviewing basic work on judgments of truth and deception, we will turn to the fundamental principles on which the SUE framework is based. We will describe the central role of counter-interrogation strategies (i.e., the approaches suspects adopt in order to reach their goal during an interview), and we will review both theoretical and empirical work on the topic of counter-interrogation strategies.

Subsequently, we will describe research on how to translate the basic theoretical principles into interview tactics. That is, we will describe research on strategic questions that aim to produce different responses from truthful and deceptive suspects. We will also review approaches to disclose the information in varying forms to produce cues to concealment and deception. Finally, we will offer the first meta-analysis of the available SUE research, in order to provide a quantitative synthesis of the literature to date.

GENERAL FINDINGS ON DECEPTION AND ITS DETECTION

For about half a century, psychologists have conducted empirical research on deception and its detection. There is now a considerable body of work in this field (Granhag and Strömwall, 2004; Vrij, 2008). In this research, deception is defined as a deliberate attempt to create false beliefs in others (Vrij, 2008). This definition covers intentional concealments of transgressions, false assertions about autobiographical memories, and false claims about attitudes, beliefs, and emotions. Research on deception focuses on three primary questions:

- How good are people at detecting lies? That is, with what accuracy can people distinguish between true and false statements?
- Are there cues to deception? That is, do people behave and speak in discernibly different ways when they lie compared with when they tell the truth?
- Are there ways in which people's ability to judge credibility can be improved?

Most research on deception detection is experimental (Frank, 2005; Hartwig, 2011). An advantage of the experimental approach is that researchers randomly assign participants to conditions, which provides internal validity (the ability to establish causal relationships between the variables, in this context between deception and a given behavioral indicator) and control of extraneous variables (e.g., the personality of the subject). Importantly, the experimental approach also allows for the unambiguous establishment of ground truth – definite knowledge about whether the statements given by research participants are in fact truthful or deceptive. In this research, participants are induced to provide truthful or deceptive statements. These statements are then subjected to various analyses, including coding of verbal and non-verbal behavior. This makes it possible to examine objective cues to deception – behavioral characteristics that differ as a function of whether the person is lying or telling the truth. Also, the videotaped statements are typically shown to other participants serving as lie-catchers, who are asked to make judgments about the veracity of the statements.

Accuracy in Deception Judgments

Across hundreds of studies on human lie detection ability, people average 54% correct judgments. This is not impressive, considering that guessing would yield 50% correct. Meta-analyses show that accuracy rates do not vary much from one setting to another (Bond and DePaulo, 2006). Furthermore, people do not seem to have insight into when they have made correct or incorrect judgments – a meta-analysis on the accuracy–confidence relationship in deception judgments showed that confidence was poorly correlated with accuracy (DePaulo *et al.*, 1997).

That lie detection is associated with a high error rate is stable across groups: another meta-analysis on judgments of deception showed that individual differences in deception detection ability are vanishingly small (Bond and DePaulo, 2008). Despite this pattern, some have proposed the existence of a small number of exceptionally skilled lie-catchers, referred to as lie detection "wizards" (O'Sullivan and Ekman, 2004). However, there has been no peer-reviewed research published in support of the ideas of wizards, and various critical arguments have been raised about the plausibility of their existence (Bond and Uysal, 2007; for a response, see O'Sullivan, 2007).

A common belief is that people who face the task of detecting deception routinely in their professional lives (e.g., law enforcement officers and legal professionals) may, due to training and/or experience, be capable of achieving higher accuracy rates than other people (Garrido *et al.*, 2004). For example, when law enforcement officers are asked to quantify their capacity for lie detection, they self-report accuracy rates far above those observed for lay people (Kassin *et al.*, 2007). Even though their belief may sound plausible, the literature does not support it. In fact, reviews of the existing studies show that presumed lie experts do not achieve higher lie detection accuracy rates than lay judges (Bond and DePaulo, 2006; see also Meissner and Kassin, 2002, for a review of the literature using signal detection theory). However, as can be expected, legal professionals' decision making differs in some ways from that of lay people. Typically, law enforcement officers are more suspicious and they are systematically prone to overconfidence in their judgments (Meissner and Kassin, 2004).

In sum, the literature on human lie detection accuracy shows that people's ability to detect lies is mediocre. This is a stable finding that holds true for a variety of groups, populations, and settings.

Cues to Deception

Why are credibility judgments so prone to error? Research on behavioral differences between liars and truth-tellers may provide an answer to this question. A meta-analysis covering 1338 estimates of 158 behaviors showed that few behaviors are related to deception (DePaulo et al., 2003). The behaviors that do show a systematic covariation with deception are typically only weakly related to deceit. In other words, people may fail to detect deception because the behavioral signs of deception are faint.

Lie detection may fail for another reason: people report relying on invalid cues when attempting to detect deception. Lay people all over the world (Global Deception Research Team, 2006), as well as presumed lie experts, such as law enforcement personnel, customs officers, and prison guards (Strömwall et al., 2004), report that gaze aversion, fidgeting, speech errors (e.g., stuttering, hesitations), pauses, and posture shifts indicate deception. These are cues to stress, nervousness, and discomfort. However, reviews of the literature show that these behaviors are not systematically related to lying. For example, the widespread belief that liars avert their gaze is not supported in the literature. Moreover, fidgeting, speech disfluencies, and posture shifts are not diagnostic signs of lying, either (DePaulo et al., 2003). In other words, it may be that people rely on an unsupported stereotype when attempting to detect lies.

Recently, a meta-analysis investigated whether lie detection fails primarily because of the minute behavioral differences between liars and truth-tellers or because people's beliefs about deceptive behavior do not match actual cues to deception (Hartwig and Bond, 2011). The results showed that the principal cause of poor lie detection accuracy is lack of systematic differences between people who lie and people who tell the truth. In other words, lie detection is prone to error not because people use the wrong judgments strategies, but because the task itself is very difficult. We will return to remedies for this problem shortly.

High-Stakes Lies

Some aspects of the deception literature have been criticized on methodological grounds, in particular with regard to external validity (i.e., the generalizability of the findings to non-laboratory settings; see Miller and Stiff, 1993). The most persistent criticism has concerned the issue of generalizing from low-stakes laboratory situations to those in which the stakes are considerably higher. Critics have argued that when lies concern serious matters, liars will be more emotionally invested and aroused, leading to more pronounced cues to deception (Buckley, 2012; Frank and Svetieva, 2012). There are several bodies of work addressing this issue. In a previously mentioned meta-analysis of the literature on deception judgments (Bond and DePaulo, 2006), researchers compared hit rates in studies where senders were motivated with only trivial means to studies in which people told lies under far more serious circumstances (e.g., Vrij and Mann, 2001). There was no difference in judgment accuracy between these two sets of studies. However, an interesting (and possibly problematic) pattern emerged – when senders told lies under high-stakes conditions, lie-catchers were more prone to false alarm, meaning that they more often mistook truth-tellers for liars. It seems that higher stakes may put pressure on both liars and truth-tellers to appear credible, and that perceivers misinterpret signs of such pressure as indications of deceit.

ELICITING CUES TO DECEPTION: STRATEGIC QUESTIONING APPROACHES

The research reviewed above shows that people have a difficult time telling lies from truths, primarily because the behavioral signs of deception lies are so subtle, if they exist at all. In other words, liars do not automatically "leak" cues to deception that can be observed. Instead, the research suggests that in order to make more accurate judgments of deception, lie-catchers must take an active role to produce behavioral differences between liars and truth-tellers (Hartwig and Bond, 2011; Vrij and Granhag, 2012).

That systematic questioning may produce cues to deception is the premise of pre-interrogation interview protocols such as the Behavioral Analysis Interview (BAI). The BAI is outlined in the influential Reid manual of interrogation, and has been taught to hundreds of thousands of professionals who conduct investigative interviews and interrogation in the course of their work (Inbau *et al.*, 2005, 2013; Vrij, 2008). The BAI is a system of questioning that includes a number of so-called behavior-provoking questions, which are thought to result in different verbal and non-verbal responses from interviewees. For example, liars are assumed to be more uncomfortable than truth-tellers, giving rise to non-verbal signs of discomfort such as posture shifts, grooming behaviors, and lack of eye contact. As described above, these cues have not been shown to be valid signs of lying in the deception literature (DePaulo *et al.*, 2003). Proponents of the BAI claim that the approach has received empirical support and that it can produce hit rates above 80% (Buckley, 2012). However, the study referred to as support for the BAI used a sample of statements where ground truth was established in only two out of 60 cases, which makes the results difficult or even impossible to interpret (Horvath *et al.*, 1994). Furthermore, there was no control (i.e., non-BAI) condition. More recently, Vrij *et al.* (2006b) subjected the behavior-provoking questions of the BAI to an empirical test using statements for which ground truth was appropriately established. Their result did not support the BAI – in fact, the outcome was directly opposite to the patterns predicted by the BAI. Also, a recent series of studies found that the reasoning underlying the BAI does not go beyond common sense beliefs about deception (Masip *et al.*, 2011, 2012). In sum, despite its widespread use, the deception literature casts doubt on the validity of the BAI as a lie detection tool.

During the last decade, researchers have proposed and tested a number of alternative methods of eliciting cues to deception through strategic questioning (Levine *et al.*, 2010; Vrij and Granhag, 2012). These methods have in common that they emphasize cognitive rather than emotional differences between liars and truth-tellers. That is, they assume liars and truth-tellers may differ in the amount of mental load they experience, and/or in the way that they strategize and plan their statements. For example, the cognitive load approach posits that lying is more mentally demanding than telling the truth, because liars face a more difficult task (Vrij, 2008; Vrij *et al.*, 2006a, 2012). The cognitive load approach suggests that by imposing further cognitive load, liars, who are presumably already taxed by lying, may show more signs of cognitive load than truth-tellers. In support of the cognitive load hypothesis, empirical studies demonstrate that when liars and truth-tellers produce their story under mentally demanding conditions (e.g., by being asked to tell their story in reverse order), the behavioral differences between liars and truth-tellers are more pronounced (Vrij *et al.*, 2008). Another line of research, the unanticipated questions approach, assumes that liars prepare some, but not all aspects of their cover story. This approach suggests that by asking liars unexpected questions about their cover story, their responses may be less detailed, plausible, and consistent (e.g., Vrij *et al.*, 2009). For a detailed discussion of strategic questioning approaches, see Vrij and Granhag (2012).

SUE: THEORETICAL PRINCIPLES

In line with the strategic questioning approaches reviewed briefly above, the SUE technique is based on the idea that there are cognitive differences between liars and truth-tellers. Specifically, the SUE approach posits that liars and truth-tellers employ different strategies to convince. These strategies are referred to as counter-interrogation strategies (Granhag and Hartwig, 2008). Before we describe the research on counter-interrogation strategies, we will elaborate on the fundamental theoretical principles from basic psychological research that underlie the SUE technique.

Psychology of Self-Regulation

The SUE approach is anchored in the basic psychology of self-regulation (for comprehensive reviews, see Carver and Sheier, 2012; Forgas *et al.*, 2009; Vohs and Baumeister, 2011). In brief, self-regulation theory is a social cognitive framework for understanding how people control their behavior to steer away from undesired outcomes and toward desired goals. In the present context, the desired goal for both liars and truth-tellers is to convince an interviewer that their statement is true. In general, people formulate goals, and use planning and self-regulatory strategies in order to reach desired goals. While some self-regulatory activity occurs automatically and without conscious awareness or thought (Bargh and Chartrand, 1999), other situations activate conscious, deliberate control of behavior. The SUE technique focuses primarily on conscious strategies to reach goals. Psychological research shows that self-regulatory strategies are evoked by threatening situations, especially ones in which one lacks knowledge about a forthcoming aversive event (Carver and Sheier, 2012). In line with self-regulation theory, it is reasonable to assume that liars and truth-tellers will view an upcoming interview as a potential threat – the threatening element being the possibility that one might not be believed by the interviewer. Importantly, not knowing how much or what the interviewer knows may add to this threat.

A person attempting to avoid a threat and reach a particular goal will, under normal circumstances, have a number of self-regulatory strategies to choose from (Vohs and Baumeister, 2011). The common objective of these strategies is to attempt to restore and maintain control in order to steer oneself toward the desired outcome. Generally, these strategies can be reduced to two basic categories: *behavioral strategies* and *cognitive strategies*. An example of a behavioral strategy is to attempt to physically avoid the aversive event altogether, and an example of a cognitive strategy is to focus on the less-threatening aspects of the aversive event. Both types of strategies may be employed in an interview context. For example, suspects may decide to remain completely silent during interrogation (a behavioral control strategy), or they can view the situation as a chance to persuade the interviewer that they are telling the truth (a cognitive control strategy).

The SUE framework focuses primarily on cognitive control strategies. Self-regulation theory suggests that there are several types of cognitive control (Fiske and Taylor, 2008). For suspects in interview settings, several cognitive control strategies may be relevant: *information control*, which is the sense of control achieved when one obtains information about the threatening event, and *decision control*, which refers to the sense of control achieved when one makes a decision about to how to behave in the forthcoming event (Averill, 1973).

Self-Regulatory Differences between Liars and Truth-Tellers

As argued above, lying and truth-telling suspects are similar in the sense that an interview presents a goal (being perceived as a truth-teller) and a threat (being perceived as a liar). However, liars and truth-tellers differ in at least one important way, which pertains to the critical information they hold. That is, liars are per definition motivated to conceal certain information from the interviewer. For example, they may conceal information about their involvement in a transgression or they may hold on to general information about other people's identities and actions that they are motivated to keep the interviewer ignorant about. The primary threat for liars is thus that the interviewer will come to know this information. Hence, it makes sense for liars to view this information as an aversive stimulus. To be clear, the threat is not necessarily the information in itself, but that the interviewer may come to know the truth about this information. In contrast, a truth-telling person does not possess information that they are motivated to conceal. Thus, truth-tellers have the very opposite problem: that the interviewer may not come to know the truth. In sum, both liars and truth-tellers may plausibly perceive an interview as an event that activates goals; therefore, they will employ self-regulatory strategies to reach their goals. Critically, because liars and truth-tellers differ in concealment of critical information, they can be expected to adopt different strategies with regard to information.

As noted above, decision control strategies are attempts to gain control over a situation by making decisions about how to act. Translated to lying and truthful suspects in the context of an interview, decision control strategies primarily revolve around information management – simply put, what information to include in one's account (Hartwig *et al.*, 2010). Below, we will first focus on the information management strategies of liars and then provide an overview of principles underlying truth-tellers' strategies.

Liars' and Truth-Tellers' Information Management Strategies

We previously noted that the primary threat for liars is that the interviewer will come to know the information they are attempting to conceal (e.g., their involvement in some crime under investigation). In order to avoid this outcome, liars must balance multiple risks in order to convince the interviewer.

They must suppress the critical information, to manage the risk that the interviewer will know the truth. However, in order to appear credible, a liar has to offer some form of account in place of the truth. Offering false information to conceal one's action (e.g., claiming that one never visited place X) entails another risk – if the interviewer has information that the suspect indeed visited this place, the suspect's credibility is in question. Striking the appropriate balance between concealing incriminating information and offering details in order to appear credible is a crucial consideration for liars.

Generally speaking, liars must make a number of strategic decisions about what information to avoid, deny, and admit during an interview. This decision-making perspective draws on work by Hilgendorf and Irving (1981), who proposed a theoretical model to explain people's decisions to confess or deny in interrogations, in turn derived from Luce's (1967) classic work on decision making in risky situations. Although Hilgendorf and Irving (1981) primarily sought to understand why people choose to confess, the model extends to broader aspects of behavior during interviews. The basic assumption of the model is that interviewees, in particular those who are motivated to conceal certain information, must engage in a complicated decision-making process. For example, they must make decisions about whether to speak or remain silent, whether to tell the truth or not, what parts of the truth to tell and what parts to withhold, and how to respond to questions posed during the interview. According to the model, decisions are determined by (1) perceptions of the available courses of action, (2) perceptions concerning the probabilities of the occurrence of consequences attached to the available courses of action (i.e., subjective probabilities), and (3) the utility values associated with these courses of action. For a full description of the model and its implications, see Hilgendorf and Irving (1981) and Gudjonsson (2003).

When it comes to the critical information that must be concealed, there are two broad strategies to manage these facts: a suspect could either choose *avoidance* (e.g., when asked to freely provide a narrative, avoid mentioning that he/she visited a certain place at a certain time) or *escape* (i.e., denial) strategies. For example, in response to a direct question, a suspect could deny that he/she was at a certain place at a certain time. Interestingly, psychological research shows that avoidance and escape strategies are very basic forms of behavior in response to threatening stimuli. Specifically, research on aversive conditioning shows that these strategies are fundamental responses that apply to both humans and animals (Carlson and Buskist, 1996; for a discussion of the neuropsychological mechanisms of avoidance and escape responses, see Cain and LeDoux, 2008).

Turning to truth-tellers, we have already pointed out that they differ from liars in terms of concealment – in contrast to liars, they are not facing an information management dilemma in which critical information must be suppressed and false information must be proposed. As a result of this, we can expect that truth-tellers will employ rather simple strategies by being forthcoming. That is, they may believe that if they simply convey the truth, the interviewer will believe them. This may sound like a naïve and overly simplistic prediction, but it is important to understand such a belief can be explained by a number of basic social psychological theories. First, the mindset of a truth-teller may be influenced by the belief in a just world (Lerner, 1980). In brief, this theory postulates that people have a fundamental trust in the fairness of the world and that they believe that people receive outcomes that they deserve (for a meta-analytic review of the theory, see Hafer and Bègue, 2005). For example, people generally believe that good things happen to good people and that bad things happen to bad people (but not the other way around). The belief in a just world may influence a truth-teller to believe that if they tell the truth, they will be believed simply because they deserve it (Feather, 1999). Second, research on social cognition suggests that people harbor an illusion of transparency (Gilovich et al., 1998; Savitsky and Gilovich, 2003). This is a general tendency to overestimate the extent to which internal processes are evident in behavior. For example, a person who is very nervous about a public speech may overestimate the extent to which the audience can perceive this nervousness. Experimental research shows that people overestimate the transparency of their inner states in a number of situations (Vorauer and Clade, 1998). Of particular relevance for this context, research on guilty and innocent crime suspects suggests that innocent people display an illusion of transparency. Kassin and Norwick (2004) found that innocent (versus guilty) suspects were more prone to waive their Miranda rights and agree to be interrogated. Innocent suspects' actions were accompanied by the argument that they had nothing to hide because of their innocence and that if they simply spoke to the interrogator, he/she would "see" that they were telling the truth (for more on the so-called phenomenology of innocence, see Kassin, 2005).

Empirical Research on Counter-Interrogation Strategies

In the program of research on SUE, there have been a number of empirical tests of the theoretical principles discussed above. This research has mapped liars' and truth-tellers' counter-interrogation strategies. Recall that these strategies are the courses of actions described by interviewees in order to convince an interviewer that they are telling the truth. In the typical study on counter-interrogation strategies, some participants are induced to commit a mock crime, which they are then asked to deny involvement in. Other participants engage in some innocuous activity and hence will be truthfully denying the mock crime. In relation to the interview, these participants are asked (1) whether they had a strategy to convince the interviewer that they were not involved in the crime and (2) if yes, what this strategy was.

Based on the reasoning outlined above, it is possible to propose a number of predictions regarding the counter-interrogation strategies of liars and truth-tellers.

(1) Since lying entails strategic decision making, liars will often report a plan or strategy before entering an interview.
(2) In terms of specific strategies, liars will (if given the opportunity) avoid disclosing critical information.
(3) If liars are deprived of the avoidance alternative, they will turn to escape responses (i.e., faced with direct questions, their strategy will be to deny holding the critical information). As for truth-tellers, previously discussed theory predicts that they will be less likely to express a plan or a strategy to convince. When they do express specific strategies, these will primarily be strategies of being verbally forthcoming.

The empirical data on counter-interrogation strategies support the predictions above. The available studies consistently show that liars are more likely than truth-tellers to strategize prior to an interview. For example, in the sample reported by Hartwig *et al.* (2007), the majority of liars (60.5%) reported a strategy prior to being interviewed, while far fewer truth-tellers did so (37.5%). In line with the expectations from theory, liars' strategies were dominated by information management strategies, such as providing a simple and streamlined story, and avoiding or outright denying incriminating information (Hartwig *et al.*, 2010). Hines *et al.* (2010) also found that liars reported planning prior to an interview, and that the strategies they employed revolved around monitoring and controlling critical information (see also Colwell *et al.*, 2006). Further in line with predictions, the principal strategy reported by truth-tellers (in those cases when they reported having a strategy) was to tell the truth like it happened (Strömwall *et al.*, 2006). Importantly, this pattern of strategies has been replicated for people with extensive experience of interrogation: in a study mapping criminals' counter-interrogation strategies, participants reported using aversive and avoidant strategies when deceiving (Granhag *et al.*, 2009).

TRANSLATING PSYCHOLOGICAL THEORY INTO INTERVIEW TACTICS

In the sections above, we have reviewed the basic principles on which the SUE technique is based. In particular, we have elaborated on the different approaches that liars and truth-tellers employ in order to reach the goal of convincing, and how these approaches can be expected to result in different counter-interrogation strategies. We now discuss the research on how these differences in counter-interrogation strategies can be translated into interview tactics that produce different verbal accounts from liars and truth-tellers.

As mentioned earlier, the SUE approach exploits the available information/evidence to highlight differences in liars' and truth-tellers' counter-interrogation strategies. In order to explain how this can be accomplished, we will describe the first test of the SUE principles (Hartwig *et al.*, 2005). This study employed a mock crime paradigm, in which participants were randomly assigned to be either guilty (i.e., liars) or innocent (i.e., truth-tellers). Liars were instructed (one at a time) to go to a nearby store and to find a briefcase in the corner of that store. They were instructed to open the briefcase and take a wallet that was placed in the briefcase. Truth-tellers were instructed to go to the same store and to look for an object in the same corner. The situation was arranged in such a way that truth-tellers had to move the briefcase in order to look for the relevant object (however, they did not steal the wallet).

There were several pieces of information collected: (1) there was a witness outside the store who saw participants enter the store, (2) there was a store clerk who observed the participants in the corner of the store, and (3) there was evidence that the participants had handled the briefcase, as their fingerprints were found on it. Note that this information was true for both liars and truth-telling participants (i.e., the information suggested, but did not conclusively prove, that the participants may have been involved in the theft). All participants were subsequently informed that there had been a theft and that they would be questioned about their recent actions. Liars and truth-tellers were both told that their goal was to convince the interviewer that they were not involved in the theft, but they did not receive any further information.

There were two types of interviews. In one condition, the available evidence (the two witness reports and the fingerprint evidence) was disclosed in the beginning of the interview, after which the interviewer posed questions about the subjects' actions and whereabouts. In this early disclosure condition, truth-tellers and liars provided similar accounts, which tended to incorporate the evidence without admitting to the theft. For example, both liars and truth-tellers tended to say that they had indeed been in the store and that they had handled the briefcase while searching for an object (recall that this was true for some, but not all suspects). Lie-catchers who viewed these videotaped interviews could not tell the difference between true and false accounts – their accuracy in detecting lies was at chance level. In a second condition (the SUE condition), the evidence was withheld until the end of the interview. While the evidence was withheld, the interviewer asked a number of questions. First, they prompted subjects to provide a free recall of their actions during the day. Second, they asked a number of specific questions that addressed the evidence, but did not disclose that the interviewer possessed this evidence. For example, subjects were asked to describe the locations they had visited during the day, whether they had visited the store in question, and if so, what part of the store. Further, they were asked whether they had been in the corner of the store, whether they had seen a briefcase, and whether they had handled this briefcase.

The purpose of these specific questions was to highlight the difference in strategies between liars and truth-tellers (i.e., to highlight truth-tellers as forthcoming and liars' strategies of avoidance and denial). In this interview condition, the difference between the statements given by liars and truth-tellers was marked. In response to the free recall prompt, liars showed clear signs of avoidance strategies: they frequently refrained from mentioning the store, and without exception avoided mentioning the briefcase. In contrast, truth-tellers' responses to the free recall prompt suggested forthcoming approaches: they frequently volunteered information relating to the evidence, such as having been in the corner of the store and having been in contact with the briefcase. For the specific questions, further signs of differences in strategy between liars and truth-tellers were obtained: truth-tellers' responses were in line with the evidence (e.g., when asked whether they had been in the corner of the store, truth-tellers agreed that they indeed had), while liars' responses tended to be inconsistent with the evidence (e.g., when asked whether they had seen a briefcase, many liars denied). The cue that appeared when suspects were questioned strategically about the evidence was labeled statement–evidence consistency, which reflects discrepancies or contradictions between the suspects' account and the evidence. Lie-catchers who saw the interviews conducted in the SUE manner were significantly more accurate than chance in distinguishing between true and false statements.

Granhag (2010) has argued that the SUE technique is best described as consisting of a *strategic level* and a *tactical level*. The strategic level is the more abstract, and contains the case-independent and general principles underlying the SUE technique. The tactical level is the more concrete, and contains a package of different case-dependent and specific tactics. These specific tactics include *question tactics* and *disclosure tactics* (Granhag, 2010). These tactics are important both for the planning of the interview and during the actual interview. Importantly, all these tactics are derived from the conceptual framework underlying the SUE technique (the strategic level).

Questioning Tactics

The example above illustrates a number of fundamental aspects of strategic questioning in the SUE model. First, in order to highlight differences in strategy between liars and truth-tellers, the relevant information possessed by the interviewer must be withheld (Granhag and Hartwig, 2008). That is, when liars are unaware or unsure about what the interviewer knows, their strategies of avoidance and denial become evident in their verbal behavior.

Second, different types of questions yield different cues to deception when the evidence is withheld. Broad, open-ended questions that invite free recalls tend to produce differences in omissions between liars and truth-tellers. That is, as illustrated by the example above, truth-tellers are likely to volunteer information (even potentially incriminating information such as being at the scene of a crime, plausibly because the information is not perceived as incriminating to them), while liars tend to avoid disclosing such information. For more specific questions (e.g., "were you in place X on day Y?"), liars can no longer employ avoidance strategies – the nature of these questions forces liars to either admit or deny. As discussed previously, there are theoretical reasons to expect that liars' strategies in response to specific questions about critical information will be colored by escape/denial responses. In a study examining the effects of various forms of questions using a SUE approach, Hartwig *et al.* (2011) compared cues to deception in response to broad, open questions to those elicited by more specific, closed-ended questions. Indeed, the results showed that while free recall prompts led to omissions in liars' statements, specific questions led to blatant signs of dishonesty in the form of contradictions with the facts (i.e., statement–evidence inconsistencies). These cues were more pronounced and more noticeable than the omission cues. Much has been written about potential problems with using closed-ended questions during investigative interviews (for an overview of the general literature on investigative interviewing, see Bull *et al.*, 2009), but in this particular context, it seems that specific questions of a strategic nature may be powerful instruments in producing signs of deception. It should also be noted that specific questions about the evidence serve the purpose of systematically exhausting alternative explanations that a guilty suspect may have for the existence of the evidence (Granhag and Vrij, 2010).

Third, a series of SUE studies (e.g., Hartwig *et al.*, 2005, 2006, 2011; Jordan *et al.*, 2012) shows that the more incriminating the information is that the interviewer probes about, the more pronounced liars' escape and denial strategies tend to be. This makes sense if one recalls that liars construe the information to be concealed as an aversive stimulus – put simply, they aim to stay away from that information. In a recent study (Hartwig *et al.*, 2011), liars and truth-tellers were sent to the far corner of a library to commit either a mock crime or a benign act. In order to reach the relevant location, participants had to pass by several different "check points." For example, after entering the library, they passed by an information desk, after which they reached a reference section, followed by a group of tables close to a window (where both groups of participants were to complete their mission). The specific questions addressed these different check points (e.g., "In the library, did you pass by an information desk?," "Did you see a group of tables by a window?"). Interestingly, liars' escape responses became more pronounced the closer the questions came to addressing the most critical information. For example, while some liars admitted to being in the library, fewer admitted to passing by the reference section and even fewer admitted to being by the group of tables where the mock crime was carried out.

In practice, how would an interviewer go about eliciting both avoidance and denial strategies from liars? That is, how would one plan and pose a line of questions that produces omissions and contradictions with facts from liars, and forthcoming accounts from truth-tellers? One possible way in which omissions and contradictions about a given piece of evidence can be elicited is to use a line of questioning with a funnel-like structure. At the top of the funnel are the broadest possible questions, consisting of invitations to provide information freely about the events or action in question. Closer to the bottom of the funnel, there are questions about the critical information held by the interviewer. Although this questioning method is not the only tactic that can elicit omissions and contradictions, it is one that has begun to be examined in recent SUE research (Luke *et al.*, in preparation).

It may be useful to know that training in SUE principles and techniques to plan and implement a line of questioning using the funnel approach can be effective in improving the accuracy of truth and lie judgments. In a training study, Hartwig *et al.* (2006) taught a group of law enforcement students how to use the SUE approach and then tested their performance during an interview where the aim was to determine whether a suspect was guilty or innocent of a mock crime. Their performance was compared with a group of participants who had not received the SUE training. The trained group differed from the untrained group in a number of important ways. First, the trained group was more likely to withhold the evidence during questioning. That is, the untrained group disclosed evidence at earlier stages than the trained group. Second, as recommended by the SUE approach, the trained group asked more specific questions about the background information, without disclosing it. Importantly, the trained group produced far more statement–evidence inconsistencies from liars than did the untrained group. Finally, the trained interviewers obtained an 85% hit rate in distinguishing between truths and lies – a remarkable accuracy given that hit rates tend to be around chance level (Bond and DePaulo, 2006), with exceedingly small deviations (Bond and DePaulo, 2008). The untrained interviewers' accuracy rate was not significantly different from chance performance. One might wonder whether the poor performance in the untrained control group was due to their lack of experience in interviewing. This does not seem like a plausible explanation: a study using a similar paradigm found that highly experienced interrogators (with an average experience of conducting interrogations of 21.7 years) who were not trained in the SUE approach also performed at chance level when questioning lying and truth-telling suspects (Hartwig *et al.*, 2004).

Disclosure Tactics

In some situations, an interviewer may want to disclose parts (or all) of the information at hand to the interviewee. This obviously does not apply to all cases – for a number of reasons, an interviewer may be unwilling or simply prohibited to do so due to the sensitivity of the information held (e.g., in intelligence-gathering contexts). The following section deals with those situations in which the interviewer has decided that there may be reasons to disclose the evidence. What could such reasons be? Most obviously, if an interviewer has conducted a line of questioning using the funnel structure described above, it is plausible that liars may have offered statements that violated facts. For example, after a series of increasingly specific questions about his/her whereabouts, a liar might have denied being in city X, while the interviewer has factual information (e.g., travel records) suggesting that he/she indeed was in that city. Disclosing the information about the travel records could then serve to start a discussion about the cause of these discrepancies in the subject's statement. Also, recent research indicates that such an approach may cause the subject to be more forthcoming in subsequent interviews (Luke, *et al.*, in preparation).

Research on the SUE framework has examined both the timing and manner of evidence disclosure. That is, when is it ideal to disclose the information, and how (i.e., in what form) should this information be presented to produce the most diagnostic outcomes? Starting with the timing issue, a series of studies have manipulated the point at which the information is disclosed to the subject during interviewing. These studies consistently show that early disclosure of information is inferior to late disclosure, because the early disclosure assists the deceptive interviewee to incorporate the information into his/her account (e.g., Clemens *et al.*, 2010; Hartwig *et al.*, 2005, 2006, 2011; Jordan *et al.*, 2012). Simply put, early disclosure helps liars produce plausible denials (for a quantitative synthesis of this work, see below). More recently, research has examined other variations in timing (foreshadowed by Hartwig, 2005), such as drip-feeding of the available information (i.e., disclosure of one piece of information at a time throughout an interview). The results of these studies are mixed. Dando and Bull (2011) found that disclosing the evidence either in a drip-feeding manner or at the end of the interview was more effective in detecting liars than disclosing the same evidence early. They also found that disclosing the evidence in a drip-feeding fashion was more effective than disclosing the evidence late. Unfortunately, Dando and Bull (2011) did not examine verbal cues to deception, so on the basis of their results, it is difficult to know the effects of the varying disclosure tactics on liars' and truth-tellers' statements. In contrast, Sorochinski *et al.* (2013) found that withholding the evidence to the end (i.e., late disclosure) produced more pronounced verbal differences between liars and truth-tellers in the form of statement–evidence inconsistency, compared with when the same evidence was released in a drip-feeding manner. In line with many other studies, early disclosure of information produced the weakest cues to deception. In sum, while it is clear from past research that disclosure of information in a late rather than early stage of an interview is more effective in producing cues to deception, more research is needed in order to resolve the issue of other evidence disclosure tactics such as drip-feeding.

As for the manner in which the evidence is disclosed, recent SUE research has offered a promising framework that may assist interviewers in strategic disclosure of evidence. In order to understand these strategic disclosure methods and their effects on suspects' statements, it must first be recognized that a given piece of information can be framed, or presented, in a number of different ways. For example, CCTV camera footage showing a person at Grand Central Terminal in New York City can, in its most straightforward way, be presented just as such (e.g., "We have CCTV footage showing that you visited Grand Central in New York recently"). However, the same piece of information can also be presented in a more general way (e.g., "We have information that you visited New York recently"). Granhag (2010) introduced the so-called Evidence Framing Matrix in order to illuminate how pieces of information can be framed when they are presented during an interview. This matrix has two dimensions. The first dimension is the source of the information, which can vary from vague to precise. That is, how do we know what it is we know? Using the previous example, the source of the information (CCTV footage) can be presented either as a precise statement (the CCTV footage itself) or as a more general statement (e.g., "information"). The second dimension is the framing of the evidence itself (i.e., what is it that we know), which can vary from general to specific. For example, the interviewer can state that they know that the suspect has been in Grand Central Terminal or they can choose to present this information in a more general way (e.g., that the suspect has been in the midtown area of Manhattan; or even more generally, that he/she has been in New York City).

How is this Evidence Framing Matrix to be used? The ultimate purpose of the matrix is to structure evidence disclosure in a way that presents further difficulties for liars to present credible statements. In order to understand how this can be accomplished, recall the counter-interrogation strategies used by liars. Their aim is to conceal critical information and their strategies revolve around ways to accomplish this – primarily through aversive strategies such as avoidance or denial. Imagine that a liar, who indeed did visit Grand Central but is motivated to conceal this information, has produced an account in which he/she denies being in the New York area altogether. If he/she is presented with the most vague, general framing of the evidence ("We have information that you have actually been in New York"), he/she may revise his statement to include the information being presented, but still aim to conceal the visit to Grand Central (e.g., "Now that you mention it, I did visit New York, but I forgot to tell you because I was never in Manhattan – I only went to Brooklyn"). If he/she is then presented with more precise information about the nature of evidence (e.g., that there is evidence that he/she indeed was in Manhattan), he/she may be forced to revise his statement yet again. The point is, simply put, to "make more" out of each piece of information by presenting it in an increasingly specific form.

Generally speaking, the idea behind the Evidence Framing Matrix is thus to further exploit the concealment strategies of liars in order to produce changes or revisions in their story (labeled within-statement inconsistencies). In a recent test of the Evidence Framing Matrix, Granhag *et al.* (2013b) tested the prediction that it may be more beneficial to begin with a general, vague framing of the evidence and its source, and gradually proceed to more specific, precise framings. The results showed support for the prediction: when the evidence was presented in an incremental fashion (going from general/vague to specific/precise framing), the deceptive subject indeed revised his/her statements to make them fit with the evidence as it was presented. This positive finding was replicated in a recent study by Granhag *et al.* (2013a). Further research on the Evidence Framing Matrix is needed, but the available research suggests that it may be a useful tool to shed light on how a given piece of information can be presented to an interviewee.

META-ANALYTIC REVIEW OF SUE RESEARCH

Above, we have discussed the theory behind the SUE technique, as well as how it translates into particular interview tactics. But how effective is the SUE approach at discriminating between truths and lies? Thus far, no quantitative synthesis of the results of SUE research has been conducted. Here, we present the first meta-analytic review of the literature on SUE. The objective of this meta-analysis is to comprehensively summarize the results of research on the late disclosure of evidence technique. The newer tactical components of the SUE approach, such as the Evidence Framing Matrix, have not been subjected to enough empirical examination to warrant a meta-analytic review. The late disclosure of evidence, however, has been subjected to nearly a decade of empirical investigation. Given the number of studies that have been conducted, a quantitative synthesis of the literature is not only justified, but it may potentially provide further insight into the extent to which this particular SUE tactic is effective.

There are two primary purposes for pursuing this objective: an *applied purpose* and a *theoretical purpose*. From an applied perspective, this review is useful for assessing the effectiveness of the SUE approach's late disclosure technique. From a theoretical perspective, this review serves to evaluate the theory underlying the SUE approach. As previously discussed, the SUE approach is built on the premise that innocent and guilty suspects adopt different strategies in order to maintain their credibility in interviews. As statement–evidence consistency attempts to quantitatively capture the verbal strategy of a suspect, synthesizing the differences between innocent and guilty suspects' statements across studies will provide an evaluation of how suspect strategies differ.

Method

Selection Criteria

In order to be included, studies had to be experiments that manipulated the disclosure of evidence in the context of an interrogation or interview. More specifically, studies had to involve at least two disclosure methods: a non-SUE evidence disclosure technique and a late disclosure (SUE) technique. A non-SUE disclosure technique entailed a technique that either disclosed the evidence from the outset of the interview or, in the case of studies in which the interviewers were participants, disclosed in any method selected by the interviewer. A late disclosure technique entailed techniques that disclosed the evidence after specific questioning in a scripted interview, and in studies in which interviewers could freely question subjects, experimental conditions in which interviewers were trained with SUE tactics were included. Studies also had to experimentally manipulate the innocence or guilt of participants within a transgression paradigm. The interview subjects had to be research participants. The interviewers in the studies could either be members of the research team or they could be participants. Studies had to report a quantitative measure of statement–evidence consistency. In addition, we considered examining quantitative measures of omissions of critical information during the free recall phase of the interview, but only a limited number of studies reported such a measure. Therefore, we deemed it inappropriate to conduct a meta-analysis using that dependent variable.

Literature Search

In order to obtain studies, we conducted a search of electronic databases, including EBSCOhost and Google Scholar, using the following search terms and combinations of the terms: "strategic use of evidence," "strategic questioning," "deception detection," "lie detection," "interrogation," and "interviewing." Additionally, we searched the reference lists of reviews in the fields of deception detection and interviewing, and we contacted known authors in the field and attempted to obtain any unpublished manuscripts relevant to this review. When necessary, we contacted the authors of studies in order to obtain necessary data that were not presented in the report.

Coding Procedure

In order to calculate summary effect sizes, we recorded the mean and standard deviations for statement–evidence consistency and sample sizes for each experimental condition. When available, we recorded the reported effect size for the difference in statement–evidence consistency between innocent and guilty suspects in the non-SUE and SUE conditions; if an effect size was not reported, we calculated the effect size from the means and standard deviations. As statement–evidence consistency was coded using a variety of methods across the studies, we calculated all effect sizes such that a positive effect indicated that guilty suspects' statements were more inconsistent with the evidence. All effect sizes were calculated as a standardized mean difference d. For each study, we recorded the following features: publication year, type of publication, population of interviewees, location the study was conducted, and whether the interviewers were members of the research team or were participants.

Analyses

In order to assess the differences in the statement–evidence consistency in the statements of innocent and guilty, we used a random effects model to compute a summary effect size, confidence interval, and Q statistic for the following comparisons: (1) comparing the statement–evidence consistency of innocent and guilty suspects when evidence is disclosed using non-SUE techniques, and (2) comparing the statement–evidence consistency of innocent and guilty suspects when the evidence is disclosed late. A comparison of these two summary effect sizes will serve as an assessment of the effectiveness of the late disclosure of evidence in eliciting statement evidence inconsistencies. As noted above, effect sizes were calculated as a standardized mean difference d. For each comparison, if there was significant heterogeneity, we planned to conduct a moderator analysis using the following coded features of the studies: type of publication, population of interviewees, location the study was conducted, and whether the interviewers were members of the research team or were participants.

Results

From results of the database search, six reports met the selection criteria. We obtained two additional manuscripts from an author in the field. One manuscript was under preparation at the time of this review (Granhag *et al.*, 2013b) and another was in press but is now published (Sorochinski *et al.*, 2013). Thus, in total, eight reports (reporting a total of eight studies) met the selection criteria and were included in the review (as indicated by an asterisk in the References section of this chapter). From these studies, we extracted a total of 16 effect sizes for synthesis.

Seven of the eight reports were peer-reviewed journal articles and one report was a manuscript that had been submitted for publication. Three of the eight studies were conducted in North America and five were conducted in Europe. Four of the eight studies used exclusively undergraduates as suspects and four used samples other than undergraduates. Only one study that met the selection criteria used interviewers who were not part of the research team. Descriptive statistics for each included study are presented in Table 1.1.

Across all eight studies, there were a total of 599 participants who served as suspects. Of those 599 suspects, 300 were interviewed using the SUE technique (144 innocent suspects and 156 guilty suspects) and 299 were interviewed with non-SUE techniques (148 innocent suspects and 151 guilty suspects). A summary of sample sizes and effect sizes for each study is presented in Table 1.2.

The meta-analysis of the difference in statement–evidence consistency between innocent and guilty suspects' statements when subjected to a non-SUE technique yielded a summary effect size of $d = 1.06$ [95% confidence interval (CI): 0.70–1.43]. This effect size is relatively large, indicating a strong tendency for guilty suspects to make statements that contradict the evidence, even when confronted with the evidence from the outset of an interview. There was significant heterogeneity in effect sizes, $Q(7) = 14.08$, $p = 0.039$.

TABLE 1.1 Characteristics of Studies Included in the Meta-Analysis

Study	Location	Suspect population	Interviewers
Hartwig et al. (2005)	Europe	Undergraduates	Researchers
Hartwig et al. (2006)	Europe	Undergraduates	Participants (police recruits)
Clemens et al. (2010)	Europe	Children	Researchers
Granhag et al. (2013a)	Europe	Mix of undergraduates and community members	Researchers
Jordan et al. (2012)	North America	Undergraduates	Researchers
Luke et al. (2012)	North America	Community members	Researchers
Sorochinski et al. (2013)	North America	Undergraduates	Researchers
Granhag et al. (2013b)	Europe	Mix of undergraduates and community members	Researchers

TABLE 1.2   Summary of Studies Included in the Meta-Analysis

Study	Innocent suspects	Guilty suspects	Effect size (*d*)	95% CI
Hartwig *et al.* (2005)				
Non-SUE	12	15	0.50	−0.27 to 1.27
SUE	13	16	1.10	0.32 to 1.89
Hartwig *et al.* (2006)				
Non-SUE	21	20	1.31	0.64 to 1.99
SUE	20	21	2.74	1.89 to 3.60
Clemens *et al.* (2010)				
Non-SUE	21	21	0.85	0.22 to 1.48
SUE	21	21	1.26	0.60 to 1.92
Granhag *et al.* (2013a)				
Non-SUE	32	32	1.85	1.27 to 2.44
SUE	32	32	2.88	2.18 to 3.58
Jordan *et al.* (2012)				
Non-SUE	15	18	1.24	0.49 to 1.99
SUE	12	18	2.17	1.26 to 3.08
Luke *et al.* (2012)				
Non-SUE	13	12	1.51	0.62 to 2.40
SUE	11	13	2.96	1.80 to 4.12
Sorochinski *et al.* (2013)				
Non-SUE	13	12	0.65	−0.16 to 1.46
SUE	14	14	1.61	0.76 to 2.46
Granhag *et al.* (2013b)				
Non-SUE	21	21	0.55	−0.07 to 1.17
SUE	21	21	0.72	0.09 to 1.34

Thus, we proceeded to conduct the planned moderator analyses. As only one study used interviewers who were not members of the research team, we deemed it inappropriate to conduct a moderator analysis for that variable. The moderator analyses for the location of study and population of suspects yielded no significant results (all $p > 0.05$).

The meta-analysis of the difference of statement–evidence consistency between innocent and guilty suspects' statements when evidence was disclosed late in an interview yielded a summary effect size of $d = 1.89$ (95% CI: 1.26–2.52). Although the 95% CIs overlap, this summary effect size for the effectiveness of the SUE technique is substantially larger than the summary effect size for non-SUE techniques. This summary effect size indicates that there is a strong tendency for guilty suspects to make statements that contradict the evidence when it is disclosed late in the interview. This tendency greatly exceeds the tendency for guilty suspects to make statements that contradict the evidence when evidence is disclosed early. There was significant heterogeneity of effect sizes, $Q(7) = 35.55$, $p < 0.001$. Therefore, we conducted the planned moderator analyses. Again, we did not conduct a moderator analysis to investigate if there were differences in effect sizes as a function of whether the interviewers were part of the research team, as there was only one study in which non-researchers were used as interviewers.

Discussion

The results of this meta-analytic review strongly support the predictions of the SUE approach: guilty suspects have a tendency to make statements that contradict evidence and this tendency is amplified when they are questioned while uninformed about the evidence against them. The summary effect sizes suggest that the late disclosure of evidence nearly doubles the magnitude of this tendency by guilty suspects. This effect was not attenuated by any of the tested moderators, despite the fact that there was significant heterogeneity in the effect sizes.

Limitations

Although this meta-analysis included all the known relevant studies pertaining to the late disclosure of evidence technique of the SUE approach, we tested a relatively small number of moderators. This somewhat limits the explanatory power of the analysis. However, because this meta-analysis did not include a very large number of studies, the appropriate data may not exist to test the moderating effect of certain variables. For instance, to date, only one study testing the SUE approach has made use of interviewers who were not members of the research team. Although using researcher interviewers assists in standardizing interview procedures and increases internal validity, it limits the generalizability of the results. Additional research using non-researcher interviewers will be necessary in order to test if the effectiveness of the SUE approach is impacted when the interviewers are not researchers. The single study that used police recruits as interviewers produced some of the largest effect sizes in the literature, so it may be possible that the laboratory studies in which researchers have conducted scripted interviews have, in fact, underestimated the effectiveness of SUE tactics in eliciting statement–evidence inconsistencies. As only one study using non-researcher interviewers exists, however, it is impossible to conduct an appropriate meta-analytic test of this possibility.

Conclusions

Overall, the results of this meta-analytic review are supportive of the SUE approach. Considering the relatively large summary effect sizes that this review yielded, it appears that there is a strong tendency for guilty suspects to make statements that contradict known facts, compared with innocent suspects. This tendency, even when the evidence is disclosed to the suspect from the start of the interview, produces a large effect size for statement–evidence consistency as a cue to distinguish between innocent and guilty suspects. When evidence is withheld from the suspect, this tendency to contradict the evidence becomes even greater. Indeed, when evidence is withheld from the suspect, the statement–evidence consistency cue's power to discriminate between innocent and guilty suspects is several times greater than that of the strongest cue to deception found by DePaulo *et al.* (2003) (i.e., a global impression of cooperativeness, $d = -0.66$).

SUMMARY AND CONCLUDING REMARKS

As we have discussed in this chapter, the SUE technique consists of a theoretical level of reasoning regarding the state of mind in which liars and truth-tellers approach an interview. This theoretical level is anchored in foundational social cognitive theories of self-regulatory behavior. The theoretical reasoning translates into predictions about different counter-interrogation strategies employed by liars and truth-tellers, which in turn translate into predictions about different patterns of verbal behavior during an interview. The SUE technique also consists of a number of specific, concrete tactics for how to structure, plan, and pose questions in order to produce cues to deception in the form of discrepancies with facts (i.e., statement–evidence inconsistencies). Further, the technique offers recommendations for when and how to disclose the relevant information in order to produce revisions in deceptive subjects' accounts (i.e., within-statement inconsistencies). Thus, the SUE framework provides useful practical tools for interviewers and also strengthens researchers' theoretical understanding of the behavior of interviewees.

The research on the SUE technique differs in important ways from much of the research on deception conducted during the twentieth century. First, it suggests that lie detection should go beyond mere passive observation of the behavior of targets. Instead, lie-catchers need to take an active role in order to create the basis for more accurate judgments of truth and deception. Relatedly, the SUE approach emphasizes the strategic nature of deception and its detection. That is, it views lie detection as a game, in the sense that it involves the mutual use of strategies. Second, the majority of the earlier work on deception has reinforced the conclusion that cues to deception are weak, and lie detection is difficult. We do not deny that this is often the case. However, the SUE approach provides constructive guidelines for how to remedy for this by eliciting stronger cues to deception.

The research program on SUE is, as most research, a work in progress. There are numerous questions left to explore regarding the effects and effectiveness of various strategic interview tactics. Although much work remains to be done, thus far the SUE framework has been shown to be a scientifically sound and effective method of eliciting cues to deception across a range of populations and settings.

REFERENCES

An asterisk before a reference indicates inclusion in the meta-analysis.

Averill, J.R., 1973. Personal control over aversive stimuli and its relationship to stress. Psychological Bulletin 80, 286–303.

Bargh, J.A., Chartrand, T.L., 1999. The unbearable automaticity of being. American Psychologist 54, 462–479.

Bond Jr., C.F., DePaulo, B.M., 2006. Accuracy of deception judgments. Personality and Social Psychology Review 10, 214–234.

Bond Jr., C.F., DePaulo, B.M., 2008. Individual differences in judging deception: accuracy and bias. Psychological Bulletin 134, 477–492.

Bond Jr., C.F., Uysal, A., 2007. On lie detection "Wizards." Law and Human Behavior 31, 109–115.

Buckley, J.P., 2012. Detection of deception researchers needs to collaborate with experienced practitioners. Journal of Applied Research in Memory and Cognition 1, 126–127.

Bull, R., Valentine, T., Williamson, T., 2009. Handbook of Psychology of Investigative Interviewing: Current Developments and Future Directions. Wiley-Blackwell, Chichester.

Cain, C.K., LeDoux, J.E., 2008. Brain mechanisms of Pavlovian and instrumental aversive conditioning. In: Handbook of Behavioral Neuroscience. Elsevier, Amsterdam, pp. 103–124.

Carlson, N.R., Buskist, W., 1996. Psychology: The Science of Behavior, fifth ed. Allyn & Bacon, Boston, MA.

Carver, C.S., Scheier, M.F., 2012. A model of behavioral self-regulation. In: Van Lange, P.A.M., Kruglanski, A.W., Higgins, E.T. (Eds.), Handbook of Theories of Social Psychology, vol. 1. Sage, Thousand Oaks, CA, pp. 505–525.

*Clemens, F., Granhag, P.A., Strömwall, L.A., Vrij, A., Landström, S., Hjelmsäter, E.R.A., Hartwig, M., 2010. Skulking around the dinosaur: eliciting cues to children's deception via strategic disclosure of evidence. Applied Cognitive Psychology 24, 925–940.

Colwell, K., Hiscock-Anisman, C., Memon, A., Woods, D., Michlik, P.M., 2006. Strategies of impression management among deceivers and truth-tellers: how liars attempt to convince. American Journal of Forensic Psychology 24, 31–38.

Dando, C.J., Bull, R., 2011. Maximising opportunities to detect verbal deception: training police officers to interview tactically. Journal of Investigative Psychology and Offender Profiling 8, 189–202.

DePaulo, B.M., Charlton, K., Cooper, H., Lindsay, J.J., Muhlenbruck, L., 1997. The accuracy–confidence correlation in the detection of deception. Personality and Social Psychology Review 1, 346–357.

DePaulo, B.M., Lindsay, J.J., Malone, B.E., Muhlenbruck, L., Charlton, K., Cooper, H., 2003. Cues to deception. Psychological Bulletin 129, 74–118.

Feather, N.T., 1999. Judgments of deservingness: studies in the psychology of justice and achievement. Personality and Social Psychology Review 3, 86–107.

Fiske, S.T., Taylor, S.E., 2008. Social Cognition: From Brains to Culture, first ed. McGraw-Hill Higher Education, Boston, MA.

Forgas, J.P., Baumeister, R.F., Tice, D.M., 2009. The psychology of self-regulation: an introductory review. In: Forgas, J.P., Baumeister, R.F., Tice, D.M. (Eds.), Psychology of Self-Regulation: Cognitive, Affective, and Motivational Processes (The Sydney Symposium of Social Psychology 11). Psychology Press, New York, pp. 1–17.

Frank, M.G., 2005. Research methods in detecting deception research. In: Harrigan, J.A., Rosenthal, R., Scherer, K.R. (Eds.), The New Handbook of Methods in Nonverbal Behavior Research. Oxford University Press, New York, pp. 341–368.

Frank, M.G., Svetieva, E., 2012. Lies worth catching involve both emotion and cognition. Journal of Applied Research in Memory and Cognition 1, 131–133.

Garrido, E., Masip, J., Herrero, C., 2004. Police officers' credibility judgments: accuracy and estimated ability. International Journal of Psychology 39, 254–275.

Gilovich, T., Savitsky, K., Medvec, V.H., 1998. The illusion of transparency: biased assessments of others' ability to read one's emotional states. Journal of Personality and Social Psychology 75, 332–346.

Global Deception Research Team, 2006. A world of lies. Journal of Cross-Cultural Psychology 37, 60–74.

Granhag, P.A., 2010. The strategic use of evidence (SUE) technique: a scientific perspective. Presented at the *High Value Detainee Interrogation Group (FBI) Research Symposium: Interrogation in the European Union*, Washington, DC.

Granhag, P.A., Hartwig, M., 2008. A new theoretical perspective on deception detection: on the psychology of instrumental mind-reading. Psychology, Crime and Law 14, 189–200.

Granhag, P.A., Strömwall, L.A., 2004. The Detection of Deception in Forensic Contexts. Cambridge University Press, Cambridge.

Granhag, P.A., Vrij, A., 2010. Interviewing to detect deception. In: Granhag, P.A. (Ed.), Forensic Psychology in Context: Nordic and International Approaches. Willan Publishing, Cullompton, pp. 75–93.

* Granhag, P.A., Rangmar, J., Strömwall, L.A., 2013b. Small cells of suspects: eliciting cues to deception by strategic interviewing. Manuscript in preparation.

* Granhag, P.A., Strömwall, L.A., Willén, R.M., Hartwig, M., 2013a. Eliciting cues to deception by tactical disclosure of evidence: the first test of the Evidence Framing Matrix. Legal and Criminological Psychology 18, 341–355.

Gudjonsson, G.H., 2003. The Psychology of Interrogations and Confessions: A Handbook (Wiley Series in the Psychology of Crime, Policing and Law). Wiley, Chichester.

Hafer, C.L., Bègue, L., 2005. Experimental research on just-world theory: problems, developments, and future challenges. Psychological Bulletin 131, 128–167.

Hartwig, M., 2005. Interrogating to detect deception and truth: effects of strategic use of evidence. Doctoral Dissertation. Deptartment of Psychology, Göteborg University.

Hartwig, M., 2011. Methods in deception detection research. In: Rosenfeld, B., Penrod, S.D. (Eds.), Research Methods in Forensic Psychology. Wiley, Hoboken, NJ, pp. 136–155.

Hartwig, M., Bond Jr., C.F., 2011. Why do lie-catchers fail? A lens model meta-analysis of human lie judgments. Psychological Bulletin 137, 643–659.

Hartwig, M., Granhag, P.A., Strömwall, L.A., 2007. Guilty and innocent suspects' strategies during police interrogations. Psychology, Crime and Law 13, 213–227.

Hartwig, M., Granhag, P.A., Strömwall, L.A., Doering, N., 2010. Impression and information management: on the strategic self-regulation of innocent and guilty suspects. Open Criminology Journal 3, 10–26.

* Hartwig, M., Granhag, P.A., Strömwall, L.A., Kronkvist, O., 2006. Strategic use of evidence during police interviews: when training to detect deception works. Law and Human Behavior 30, 603–619.

Hartwig, M., Granhag, P.A., Strömwall, L.A., Vrij, A., 2004. Police officers' lie detection accuracy: interrogating freely versus observing video. Police Quarterly 7, 429–456.

* Hartwig, M., Granhag, P.A., Strömwall, L.A., Vrij, A., 2005. Detecting deception via strategic disclosure of evidence. Law and Human Behavior 29, 469–484.

Hartwig, M., Granhag, P., Stromwall, L., Wolf, A., Vrij, A., Hjelmsäter, E., 2011. Detecting deception in suspects: verbal cues as a function of interview strategy. Psychology, Crime and Law 17, 643–656.

Hilgendorf, E.L., Irving, B., 1981. A decision-making model of confessions. In: Lloyd-Bostock, M.A. (Ed.), Psychology in Legal Contexts: Applications and Limitations. Macmillan, London, pp. 67–84.

Hines, A., Colwell, K., Hiscock-Anisman, C., Garrett, E., Ansarra, R., Montalvo, L., 2010. Impression management strategies of deceivers and honest reporters in an investigative interview. European Journal of Psychology Applied to Legal Context 2, 73–90.

Horvath, F., Jayne, B., Buckley, J., 1994. Differentiation of truthful and deceptive criminal suspects in behavior analysis interviews. Journal of Forensic Sciences 39, 793–807.

Inbau, F.E., Reid, J.E., Buckley, J.P., Jayne, B.C., 2005. Essentials of the Reid Technique: Criminal Interrogation and Confessions. Jones & Bartlett, Sudbury, MA.

Inbau, F.E., Reid, J.E., Buckley, J.P., Jayne, B.C., 2011. Criminal Interrogation and Confessions, fifth ed. Jones & Bartlett Learning, Burlington, MA.

* Jordan, S., Hartwig, M., Wallace, B., Dawson, E., Xhihani, A., 2012. Early versus late disclosure of evidence: effects on verbal cues to deception, confessions, and lie catchers' accuracy. Journal of Investigative Psychology and Offender Profiling 9, 1–12.

Kassin, S.M., 2005. On the psychology of confessions: does innocence put innocents at risk? American Psychologist 60, 215–228.

Kassin, S.M., Norwick, R.J., 2004. Why people waive their Miranda rights: the power of innocence. Law and Human Behavior 28, 211–221.

Kassin, S.M., Leo, R.A., Meissner, C.A., Richman, K.D., Colwell, L.H., Leach, A.M., La Fon, D., 2007. Police interviewing and interrogation: a self-report survey of police practices and beliefs. Law and Human Behavior 31, 381–400.

Lerner, M.J., 1980. The Belief in a Just World: A Fundamental Delusion (Perspectives in Social Psychology). Plenum Press, New York.

Levine, T.R., Shaw, A., Shulman, H.C., 2010. Increasing deception detection accuracy with strategic questioning. Human Communication Research 36, 216–231.

Luce, R.D., 1967. Psychological studies of risky decision making. In: Edwards, W., Tversky, A. (Eds.), Decision Making. Penguin, London, pp. 334–352.

* Luke, T.J., Hartwig, M., Brimbal, L., Chan, G., Jordan, S., Joseph, E., Osborne, J., Granhag, P.A., 2012. Interviewing to elicit cues to deception: improving strategic use of evidence with general-to-specific framing of evidence. Journal of Police and Criminal Psychology 28, 54–62.

Masip, J., Barba, A., Herrero, C., 2012. Behaviour Analysis Interview and common sense: a study with novice and experienced officers. Psychiatry, Psychology and Law 19, 21–34.

Masip, J., Herrero, C., Garrido, E., Barba, A., 2011. Is the Behaviour Analysis Interview just common sense? Applied Cognitive Psychology 25, 593–604.

Meissner, C.A., Kassin, S.M., 2002. "He's guilty!": investigator bias in judgments of truth and deception. Law and Human Behavior 26, 469–480.

Miller, G.R., 1993. Deceptive Communication (Sage Series in Interpersonal Communication). Sage, Newbury Park, CA.

O'Sullivan, M., 2007. Unicorns or Tiger Woods: are lie detection experts myths or rarities? A response to On lie detection "Wizards' by Bond and Uysal. Law and Human Behavior 31, 117–123.

O'Sullivan, M., Ekman, P., 2004. The wizards of deception detection. In: Granhag, P.A., Strömwall, L.A. (Eds.), The Detection of Deception in Forensic Contexts. Cambridge University Press, Cambridge, pp. 269–286.

Savitsky, K., Gilovich, T., 2003. The illusion of transparency and the alleviation of speech anxiety. Journal of Experimental Social Psychology 39, 618–625.

* Sorochinski, M., Hartwig, M., Osborne, J., Wilkins, E., Marsh, J., Kazakov, D., Granhag, P.A., 2013. Interviewing to detect deception: when to disclose the evidence? Journal of Police and Criminal Psychology. Epub ahead of print. doi: 10.1007/s11896-013-9121-2.

Strömwall, L.A., Granhag, P.A., Hartwig, M., 2004. Practitioners' beliefs about deception. In: Granhag, P.A., Strömwall, L.A. (Eds.), The Detection of Deception in Forensic Contexts. Cambridge University Press, Cambridge, pp. 229–250.

Strömwall, L.A., Hartwig, M., Granhag, P.A., 2006. To act truthfully: nonverbal behaviour and strategies during a police interrogation. Psychology, Crime and Law 12, 207–219.

Vohs, K.D., Baumeister, R.F., 2011. Handbook of Self-regulation: Research, Theory, and Applications, second ed. Guilford Press, New York.

Vorauer, J.D., Claude, S.D., 1998. Perceived versus actual transparency of goals in negotiation. Personality and Social Psychology Bulletin 24, 371–385.

Vrij, A., 2008. Detecting Lies and Deceit: Pitfalls and Opportunities, second ed. Wiley, New York.

Vrij, A., Granhag, P.A., 2012. Eliciting cues to deception and truth: what matters are the questions asked. Journal of Applied Research in Memory and Cognition 1, 110–117.

Vrij, A., Mann, S., 2001. Telling and detecting lies in a high-stake situation: the case of a convicted murderer. Applied Cognitive Psychology 15, 187–203.

Vrij, A., Mann, S., Fisher, R., 2006b. An empirical test of the Behavior Analysis Interview. Law and Human Behavior 30, 329–345.

Vrij, A., Fisher, R., Mann, S., Leal, S., 2006a. Detecting deception by manipulating cognitive load. Trends in Cognitive Sciences 10, 141–142.

Vrij, A., Leal, S., Mann, S., Fisher, R., 2012. Imposing cognitive load to elicit cues to deceit: inducing the reverse order technique naturally. Psychology, Crime and Law 18, 579–594.

Vrij, A., Mann, S., Fisher, R., Leal, S., Milne, B., Bull, R., 2008. Increasing cognitive load to facilitate lie detection: the benefit of recalling an event in reverse order. Law and Human Behavior 32, 253–265.

Vrij, A., Leal, S., Granhag, P.A., Mann, S., Fisher, R.P., Hillman, J., Sperry, K., 2009. Outsmarting the liars: the benefit of asking unanticipated questions. Law and Human Behavior 33, 159–166.

2

Credibility Assessment at Portals

Charles R. Honts[*], *Maria Hartwig*[†]

[*]Department of Psychology, Boise State University, [†]Department of Psychology, John Jay College of Criminal Justice, City University of New York

OUTLINE

Overview of the Problem	39	Related Scientific Literature	47
		Physiological Approaches	*51*
The US Government's Response to		*Consequences for Portals*	*53*
the 9-11 Attack	39		
Screening Passengers by Observation		A Science-Based Approach to	
Techniques (SPOT)	*39*	the Portal Screening Problem	54
Future Attribute Screening Technology		Eliciting Cues to Deception, Guilt,	
(FAST)	*42*	and Malintent: The Psychology of	
Unique Aspects of the Portal Setting	43	Investigative Interviewing	56
Deceptive Context	*43*		
Low Target Base Rate	*44*	Consequences for Portals	57
Time Pressure	*47*	References	58

Credibility Assessment
http://dx.doi.org/10.1016/B978-0-12-394433-7.00002-6

OVERVIEW OF THE PROBLEM

The critical need for accurate credibility assessment was highlighted by the tragic events of 11 September 2001 (hereinafter 9-11). All 19 of the 9-11 terrorists told lies to US Government officials at portals on at least three occasions: when they applied for a visa for entry into the United States, when they entered the United States, and when they boarded the doomed flights. Had even one of those terrorists been detected in his deception, the 9-11 tragedy might have been avoided. The need for accurate credibility judgment is further highlighted by recent news reports indicating that the security situation in our airports and other portals is little improved over their 9-11 status.

Accurate credibility assessment is a basic need for many of the critical missions of federal, state, and local governments, as well as for many private sector activities. The events of 9-11 make this all too apparent. Accurate credibility assessment is vital every time individuals present themselves for entry into a country, apply for positions of public trust, board public transportation, enter public facilities, enter places where large numbers of people gather, or come under investigation for criminal acts. The failure to detect deception in any of these settings can lead to disastrous consequences for public safety and security.

THE US GOVERNMENT'S RESPONSE TO THE 9-11 ATTACK

Screening Passengers by Observation Techniques (SPOT)

In 2003, the Transportation Security Administration (TSA) adopted a program called SPOT (Transportation Security Administration, 2006) for use in American airports. TSA later reported that the selection of SPOT as a primary airport screening tool was a professional judgment and was not based on a systematic evaluation of possible alternatives or a cost–benefit analysis (Government Accountability Office, 2009). In the SPOT program, behavior detection officers (BDOs) attempt to detect high-security-risk individuals by observing overt passenger behavior that may indicate stress or deception. The behaviors targeted in the observation process are not described in the public literature, but include body language and facial microexpressions (Perry and Gibley, 2011). SPOT was adopted despite the fact that no study in the peer-reviewed scientific literature even suggests that accurate credibility assessments can be made from unstructured, *in vivo* observations of body language and microexpressions. In fact, prominent behavioral scientists consistently express strong skepticism that judgments of credibility can reliably be made on the basis of demeanor (body language) cues (Bond and DePaulo, 2006; Granhag and Strömwall, 2004; Hartwig and Granhag in Chapter 1 of this volume; Vrij, 2008; see also Vrij and Ganis in Chapter 7 of this volume).

With SPOT, it appears that BDOs attempt to assess passengers by casual observation of behavioral cues that include facial microexpressions (Government Accountability Office, 2009; Wilber and Nakashima, 2007). There are several problems with this:

- As noted above, most scientists are skeptical that deception can be detected from body language cues.
- A review of scientific research does not support the notion that microexpressions reliably betray concealed emotion (Porter and ten Brinke, 2008).
- Whereas brief facial activity may reveal the purposeful manipulation of a felt emotion (Porter and ten Brinke, 2008), the problems of interpreting such manipulation renders the approach problematic for practical purposes. This conclusion is not controversial in social psychological science; regulated emotion is not necessarily indicative of deception, but may instead indicate efforts at self-presentation, in which communicators engage regardless of veracity (DePaulo, 1992). The basic premise is motivational; both deceptive and truthful communicators strive to be seen as honest, and will employ purposeful control and manipulation of demeanor to achieve this goal.
- The microexpression approach equates deception with manipulated emotion. This conceptual confusion obscures the fact that most forensically relevant lies are not lies about feelings, but about actions in the past, present, or future.
- There is no evidence that observers, trained or not, can reliably detect microexpressions from real-time *in vivo* observations.

In conclusion, the use of microexpressions to establish credibility is theoretically flawed and has not been supported by sound scientific research, even in highly controlled settings (Weinberger, 2010).

Regarding the efficacy of the SPOT program as a whole, no empirical validation is available where ground truth (i.e., whether the credibility judgment made was in fact accurate or not) is known with certainty. Therefore, at this point we do not know the discriminatory power of the program and if it is skewed towards a particular form of error (false positives or negatives). The reported results from TSA's initial trial of the SPOT program at 40 US airports (Wilber and Nakashima, 2007) are based on field data that do not allow definite conclusions about hit rates to be drawn. However, they show disappointing figures, consistent with the large literature showing that interpretation of non-verbal behavior produces poor accuracy in credibility judgments (Vrij, 2008; see also Vrij and Ganis in Chapter 7 of this volume). Early in the rollout of SPOT, the TSA reported that more than 40,000 people were referred for additional screening. Of those 40,000, only 300 were arrested (Wilber and Nakashima, 2007). This indicates that the confidence one can have that detection by the SPOT system is correct is no greater than 0.0075. Another way of looking at this is that the likelihood that the SPOT is wrong when it flags someone as of interest may be as high as 0.9925. This indicates that by 2007 the TSA may have falsely accused or at least inconvenienced 39,700 innocent travelers. Moreover, given that the correct detections did not include a single terrorist and were only persons with banned substances, outstanding warrants of various sorts, or fraudulent documentation (transgressions with base rates that must be much higher than terrorism), it seems likely that the SPOT program has also made a significant number of false-negative errors.

Despite the lack of supporting data, SPOT has been expanded to 161 airports employing approximately 3000 BDOs and costing the taxpayers of the United States about $212 million annually (Perry and Gilbey, 2011). In 2010, the Government Accountability Office (2010) reported that the program had screened approximately 2 billion (2×10^9) passengers and made 152,000 secondary referrals to law enforcement, who in turn made 1100 arrests. Yet, SPOT had not detected a single terrorist. Although one might argue that SPOT may serve some function as a deterrent, the GAO's own data indicate that at least 16 individuals with terrorist involvement have traveled through eight SPOT airports on 23 occasions. None were detected by BDOs (Government Accountability Office, 2010).

Future Attribute Screening Technology (FAST)

Through a decision and policy process that is anything but transparent, the Department of Homeland Security (DHS) sponsored a research and development effort called FAST (Weinberger, 2010). The FAST program is designed to detect malintent in security screenings at portals. FAST uses a set of technically sophisticated instruments that focus on a vast array of measurements, the majority of which are known to be reliable and valid cues to psychophysiological arousal, and a minority of which are less well established measurements, such as facial activity. At the heart of these measurements is the idea of *malintent*. Malintent is a new and poorly defined psychological construct designed to capture the notion that a person passing through a portal has the intent to commit some transgressive act at an unspecified time. For FAST to be effective, at least two untested hypotheses must be true. The first hypothesis is that a person with a mental state of malintent will produce unique physiological and overt behavioral cues (facial microexpressions) that remote instruments can detect and classify as malintent. The second hypothesis is that a malicious state of mind produces a set of behavioral and physiological cues that differ from those of a non-malicious state of mind. In particular, the notion of malintent suggests that it can be shown to be a psychological state with observable expressions that differ from deception about past events and other physiologically arousing states (e.g., fear, anger, grief, disgust, frustration, etc.).

Syntheses of large quantities of research on cues to deception show no clear behavioral differences between those who did and did not commit a transgression in the past (e.g., DePaulo *et al.*, 2003). It is highly likely that predicting malintent (future behavior) is far more difficult than detecting past behavior. The notion that intention or mere thoughts might give rise to such behavioral differences is a conceptual leap that brings the program closer to science fiction than science – a fact often noted in the media (Weinberger, 2011). Moreover, the FAST program description (Department of Homeland

Security, 2010) does not specify the state of mind hypothesized for those with malicious intent. Is it a negative or positive state of mind? Is it arousal at the thought of the prospective act of terrorism? How would such arousal differ from other forms of arousal that can be expected to occur naturally in the context of portals in those with no malintent? None of these questions are addressed or answered in any of the currently available documents on FAST.

UNIQUE ASPECTS OF THE PORTAL SETTING

Clearly, there are documentary and database aspects of security screening in portals settings; this chapter is not concerned with those procedures. Rather, we are concerned with procedures designed to determine if a person is lying to the gatekeeper and/or if a person is attempting to pass the portal with malintent. Assessing credibility at portals presents several unique problems that are neither addressed nor considered in traditional research on credibility assessment.

Deceptive Context

Virtually all research conducted on credibility assessment has focused on the problem of detecting deception concerning statements about acts that took place in the past. For example, money is missing from a safe, and suspects are questioned and assessed on the credibility of their statements when they deny the theft of the money. For the guilty, there is fear of discovery and the associated episodic memories of the criminal act and the sequelae. For the innocent, there is fear that he/she will not be believed in his/her truthful statements. The innocent face consequences that are equivalent to those faced by the guilty, and they are fully aware that they face such potential consequences.

The deceptive context at a portal is quite different from the above situation. At the portal, the innocent person has not been accused of any crime. It is doubtful that most innocent people approaching border or transportation portals feel anything near the equivalent of the emotional response felt by a falsely accused suspect in a criminal investigation, although admittedly the truthful person at a portal may well feel some anxiety about the screening process. However, it seems likely that for most innocent individuals, approaching a portal is a necessary inconvenience that may cause aggravation, but little fear of true jeopardy. This is quite different from an innocent person falsely accused of a crime. The deceptive context for the guilty is also different from the traditional situation. At a portal, the target person may not, as yet, have committed a malicious act. The target with malintent wants to pass the portal so that he/she can commit a transgression in the future (i.e., he/she has malintent). The person may or may not have false credentials, but if he/she intends to commit transgressions in the future, that is the central nature of the deception and the focus of credibility assessment. To date, little research has addressed credibility assessment in the deceptive context presented by portals. It is simply not clear whether research done in a criminal/investigative context will generalize to the portal situation.

A useful portal screening system must also be sensitive to another complication of the deceptive context. There may be many levels of deception and/or concealment at the portal. Consider persons presenting themselves at the border for entry to the United States. Deception/concealment could vary from a person with false credentials who wants to enter the country to commit terrorism, to someone who is smuggling drugs, to someone who intends to immigrate illegally, to someone who is bringing in contraband for personal use, to someone who has some undeclared purchases. While these are all of interest, detection of the first category is clearly of most importance. It would be highly undesirable to have a system that detects the deception of the last category and assumes that person is a member of the first category.

Low Target Base Rate

Base rates refer to the relative frequency with which a target appears in the sample. Terrorist targets at portal screenings are very rare. This inevitably means that without a perfect credibility assessment discriminator (i.e., perfect sensitivity and perfect specificity) there will be a substantial number of errors, almost all of which are false positives. Since discriminatory perfection is very unlikely, any system for portal credibility assessment must account for and accommodate a substantial number of false-positive errors in a manner that addresses operational needs, while at the same time being acceptable to the general public who innocently present themselves at these

TABLE 2.1   Conditional Probability Analysis for the Detection of Malintent for One Day of US Air Travel with Universal FAST Screening

	FAST outcome		
Reality	Malintent	No malintent	Total
Has malintent	151	25	176
No malintent	246375	1513449	1759824
Total	246526	1513474	1760000

portals. Honts (1991) provided an extended discussion of base rates in the context of national security employment screening. The base rate problem in national security employment screening is a formidable one, but the problem with portals is far worse. To illustrate this problem, consider the statistics. According to the Research and Innovative Technology Administration of the US Department of Transportation (http://apps.bts.gov/xml/air_traffic/src/index.xml), 642 million people boarded airplanes in the United States during the 12 months preceding March 2012. That averages 1.76 million travelers per day. If we assume the base rate of travelers with malintent is one hundredth of 1% (0.0001), then on any given day 176 people would be traveling with malintent of the level that the DHS needs to detect. Let us also assume that although the early laboratory studies estimate the accuracy of FAST at 70% (Weinberger, 2011), it may eventually achieve accuracy rates that approximate those of national security screening polygraph tests used to detect deception about past events, which is about 86%. In our opinion, this is an extremely generous assumption. Moreover, given that FAST is based on physiology and not casual observation, FAST is almost certainly more accurate than SPOT. Using those assumptions, Table 2.1 presents a conditional probability analysis for one day of air travel in the United States where everyone was required to be screened with FAST. Of the 176 malintent travelers, 151 of them would be detected. However, 246,375 travelers without malintent will also be flagged as having malintent. Although FAST would have succeeded in reducing the pool of potential malintent passengers by almost an order of magnitude, it is not at all clear what would happen to the 246,375 travelers who would be incorrectly flagged as having malintent. Several layers of extremely accurate subsequent tests would be necessary to reduce this pool of malinent suspects to some manageable level.

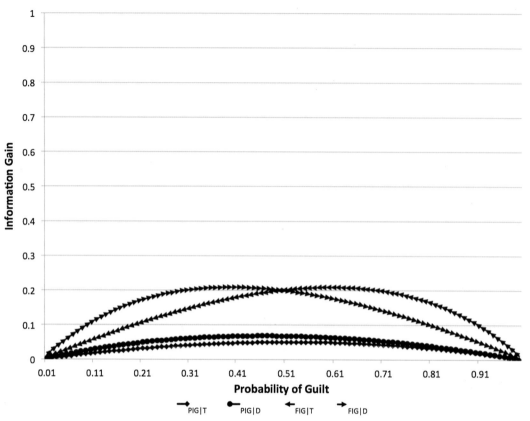

FIGURE 2.1 Information gain curves for professional deceptive (PIG|D) and truthful (PIG|T) decisions and for FAST deceptive (FIG|D) and truthful (FIG|T) decisions.

Another way to look at this problem would be to ask the following: given the assumed capability of FAST, across what range of base rates would it perform better than trained observers? The Information Gain Index (IGI; Wells and Olson, 2002) provides such a statistic. Honts and Schweinle (2009) adapted the IGI for analyzing deception detection situations. We used the Honts and Schweinle formulae to calculate IGI for FAST with the current estimate of 70% accuracy. The results of our IGI analysis of FAST are illustrated in Figure 2.1. Our IGI analysis indicates that as compared with professionals (police officers and immigration personnel), deceptive outcomes for FAST are significantly better only with base rates of deception between 0.26 and 0.39 inclusive. Truthful FAST outcomes provide significantly more information than professionals only with base rates of deception between 0.39 and 0.86 inclusive. The IGI value for FAST deceptive outcomes peaks at a value of 0.21 with a base rate of 0.39. The IGI value for FAST truthful outcomes peaks at a value of 0.21 with a base rate of 0.60. Since the base rates of deception in a FAST context are undoubtedly extremely low, the performance of FAST is expected to be extremely poor. As compared with data on the validity of polygraph tests in forensic settings, this is very poor performance. Using field validity estimates for the comparison question polygraph test and a model that does not include the inconclusive category (Honts, 2004), we calculated that the IGI for polygraph deceptive outcomes peaks at an IGI value of 0.68 with a base rate of 0.16, and truthful outcomes peaks at an IGI value of 0.64 with a base rate of 0.82.

Time Pressure

Credibility assessments at most portals have to be made under extreme time pressure, seconds to minutes. Such time pressure eliminates any methods that require subject/instrument preparation or significant time for analysis. Essentially, the time pressure in this setting means that the process may have to be fully automated and computer based.

RELATED SCIENTIFIC LITERATURE

As described above, little or no scientific efforts have been devoted to the unique aspects of the portals problems. The main challenge for the future is to establish lines of research that investigate the particular psychological problems in portals, including pitfalls and constructive guidelines for practitioners who face the problem of assessing credibility in this setting. Later, we offer some suggestions on directions for such future research. However, empirical investigation does not need to start from scratch; there is a significant body of theoretical and empirical work of relevance for the psychological challenges of credibility assessments in portals settings. We review research pertaining to the psychology of lying and lie detection, and the psychology of interviewing and interrogating for the purpose of assessing credibility.

Research on interpersonal deception (i.e., purposeful attempts to create false beliefs in another) and assessments of credibility has been an active area of scientific study for decades. The literature has approached the question from two angles. First, there is research on the social psychology of deception that focuses on deception in everyday life. This body of work investigates the prevalence of deception in human relations, the types of deception that occur between people, and the motivations for deceiving others. A central finding is that lying is ubiquitous in everyday life. People lie to one another consistently and frequently, in general on an everyday basis. Moreover, most lying does not carry much emotional consequence for the deceiver; people typically do not report feelings of guilt or other negative effects solely due to acts of lying (DePaulo et al., 1996). Social psychological research on deception thus starkly clashes with common morality (and with many theories of moral philosophy, see Bok, 1989), which prescribes that deceiving is immoral and undesirable. Although lying as a social phenomenon is beyond the scope of this chapter, the prevalence of lying and misrepresentation in everyday life has a critical consequence to the disadvantage of lie-catchers in any setting, including the portal setting. Due to so-called proceduralization (Fiske and Taylor, 2008), tasks that are repeated consistently can be expected to be executed automatically and seamlessly with few visible traces of effort and load (DePaulo et al., 2003). In other words, since lying is a common behavior in social life, most people are skilled at deceiving due to repeated execution of this task, and the stereotypical image of lying as tainted by task complexity and negative emotion is often simply incorrect.

A second body of research is the applied psychological study of deception in criminal and forensic contexts. In the forensic context, deception primarily occurs for the purpose of covering up and getting away with various transgressions (Granhag and Strömwall, 2004; Vrij, 2008). In contrast to deceiving in everyday life (DePaulo et al., 1996), the forensic context may be more directly relevant for the problems of portals, where high-stakes conditions with severe consequences of failure exist for both the deceiving person and for the lie-catchers (Mann et al., 2004). Moreover, the forensic context is relevant because deceiving occurs for the primary goal of successfully evading the consequences of transgressions. This body of work has mapped human deception detection accuracy by presenting true and false statements to various groups, including presumed lie experts such as police officers, judges, and customs officers, who are asked to make veracity assessments of the statements. Importantly, the consistent finding from such research is that even professionals who face the task of assessing veracity on an everyday basis are mediocre at this task. Hit rates of such credibility assessments are similar to those obtained by lay people and fall around the level of chance (Bond and DePaulo, 2006; DePaulo and Pfeifer, 1986; Garrido *et al.*, 2004; Hartwig *et al.*, 2004; Meissner and Kassin, 2002; Vrij, 2008). This suggests that neither the training nor the experience of professional lie-catchers is sufficient to improve lie-catching ability (Hogarth, 2001). Simply put, people, including professional lie-catchers with extensive experience of assessing veracity, would achieve similar hit rates if they flipped a coin. The main difference between legal professionals and lay people is that the former have significantly higher levels of confidence regarding their ability to detect deception. Given the hit rates near chance, such high levels of confidence are unwarranted. Some researchers have argued, with little empirical support for the proposition, that certain people possess an ability to detect deception (so-called "lie detection wizards"). However, research on individual differences in recognizing detection has not provided support for the existence of such abilities, and has found that differences between people in the ability to detect true and false statements are minute (Bond and DePaulo, 2008).

The poor deception detection accuracy obtained by professionals and lay people can be explained by two factors pertaining to cues to deception. First, surveys show that people, including presumed lie experts, have stereotypical and incorrect ideas about the characteristics of deceptive behavior (Akehurst *et al.*, 1996). The most commonly assumed cue to deception is that liars are gaze aversive (i.e., they look away more than truth-tellers). People also frequently associate deception with fidgeting and cues to nervousness, such as stuttering and other speech disturbances (Strömwall *et al.*, 2004). In general, people believe that those who provide deceptive statements are nervous and uncomfortable, and plagued by feelings of guilt, anxiety, and arousal. People apparently fail to realize that deceivers might not experience these negative emotions, and that even if those who provide deceptive statements experience such negative arousal and anxiety, overt manifestations of such states can be purposefully suppressed. It is also important to note that in contexts in which the consequences of being judged as deceptive are potentially severe, such as portals, even people who provide truthful statements in the face of scrutiny and suspicion might experience a certain degree of anxiety and arousal. Such anxiety and arousal might stem from appraisal of suspicion itself and from anxiety regarding the consequences of being misjudged as deceptive (Vrij, 2008).

A second explanation for people's poor ability to detect deception is that there are not many differences between deceptive and truthful demeanors. Research has examined truthful and deceptive behavior extensively, and found that deceptive and truthful demeanors are similar; the small differences that have been found can be detected only on an aggregated level in which hundreds of deceptive and truthful people's behaviors are compared (Sporer and Schwandt, 2007). Contrary to expectations, liars are not more gaze aversive and do not engage in fidgeting, self-manipulations, or posture shifts (Vrij and Mann, 2001). Liars are somewhat more tense and give a slightly more negative impression, they tend to be less forthcoming (DePaulo et al., 2003), and liars tend to make somewhat fewer subtle hand movements (Vrij, 2008), indicating that deceptive behavior is, if anything, less fidgety.

Hartwig and Bond (2011) conducted a series of meta-analyses to test these two proposed explanations for the finding that accuracy of credibility judgments is near chance. They used the framework of Brunswik's lens model – a model used to understand human predictions of criteria that are probabilistically related to cues. The results show that the primary reason for poor lie detection accuracy is the weakness of objective cues to deception. That is, in order to improve lie detection accuracy, the most effective route seems to be to enhance the behavioral differences between liars and truth-tellers. Later in this chapter, we discuss recent research that attempts to accomplish this.

Despite the stable finding that behavioral displays have little diagnostic value for credibility assessments, including those indicating arousal and anxiety, manuals directed at an audience of professional lie-catchers continue to assert the value of such cues for lie detection (Inbau et al., 2001). Unfortunately, even some academics contribute to the myth of the value of emotional cues. They argue that while much non-verbal behavior may be subject to purposeful manipulation by the communicator, some very brief facial displays of emotions, so-called *microexpressions*, might actually be indicative of deception (Ekman, 2001). The assumption is that some displays of emotion precede conscious awareness, hence are not subject to purposeful suppression or distortion by the communicator. Even if this notion were true, which is a matter of scientific disagreement (Weinberger, 2010), it does not solve the problem of the interpretation of the source of the emotion. If a person displays a fleeting expression of fear, what does this mean? That the person is afraid that his/her malicious intent will be detected, or that he/she experiences fear due to scrutiny, suspicion, and the appraisal of negative consequences of wrongly being judged to be deceptive? The only potential of this approach seems to be in cases where the denial of a certain emotion is the sole content of the lie (e.g., denying that one is experiencing disgust when one actually is disgusted). In broader conceptualizations of deception, including lies to cover up transgressions that are common in interpersonal and legal settings (Vrij, 2008), such cues are not likely to be diagnostic. In general, the empirical evidence offered in support of the diagnosticity of such expressions of emotions is scarce and from other sources it is far from convincing (Porter and ten Brinke, 2008). It is problematic that this approach has been implemented in portals settings (Hoffman, 2008) since there is little or no evidence to support the claim that microexpressions are diagnostic of the types of deception that occur in these contexts, and the theoretical foundations for the approach concerning relevant acts of deception are weak.

Physiological Approaches

The use of physiological measures for the detection of deception in forensic contexts has a long history of application and research (see the volume edited by Kleiner, 2002). When addressing a single transgression in the forensic context, it can be argued that the physiological approach in the form of the polygraph can produce high rates of accurate classification (see Raskin and Kircher in Chapter 3 of this volume). However, such accuracy is achieved in the context of a narrowly focused target in a highly controlled environment with a standardized set of procedures. It takes more than an hour to conduct a polygraph test. Moreover, the limited available research suggests that as one moves away from the focused context of a single transgression, the accuracy of the polygraph drops (National Research Council, 2003). A study by Honts et al. (2008) examined the ability of the Test for Espionage and Sabotage (TES) to detect malintent in the context of a mock portal situation. They reported better-than-chance performance discrimination that was comparable to the application of the TES in other settings, but less accurate than in forensic polygraph applications. Unfortunately, the use of traditional polygraph technology in real portal situations is essentially impossible because of the time constraints and the need for trained polygraph examiners and equipment. Finally, although established as empirically accurate in the context described above, the polygraph and its ability to detect deception are not well understood theoretically, which imposes limitations on predicting the settings and populations to which the existing results can be generalized.

Earlier in this chapter, we mentioned the FAST effort that had been supported by the DHS. One of the authors of this chapter (M.H.) attended the FAST demonstration in September of 2008 as a representative of the Portals Committee of the US Government's Credibility Assessment Research Summit. We continue to share the Portals Committee's (Honts et al., 2009) concerns about apparent lack of theoretical support for FAST. The most critical limitation of the FAST program, a limitation that indeed makes the technological sophistication irrelevant, is the lack of a psychological theory or model of the concept of malintent from which clear predictions about how and which overt behaviors may emerge. The program explicitly focuses on the detection of malintent, which is a psychological construct different from guilt (which arguably includes guilty intent and guilty action), and from the more subtle form of deceptive self-presentations that occur in everyday social interactions (DePaulo et al., 2003). At a minimum, an empirical explication of the overt and covert sequelae of malintent in a portal situation would seem to be a prerequisite task for the development of such as system, but apparently attempts to identify such sequelae were to be made after the construction of the detection device rather than before. In response to questioning about these limitations, the rationalizations offered for the FAST program at the time of the 2008 demonstration were unsatisfactorily circular. When asked about the patterns of behavioral cues the system would use as classification criteria for malintent, the demonstrators referred to the ongoing empirical study for such patterns. Surely, suggestions on behaviors related to malintent must not emerge from a theoretical and empirical vacuum? In our opinion, the FAST approach was atheoretical and empirically premature.

A reasonable approach to the use of physiological measures for portal screening for malintent first needs to provide a clear theory-based definition for the

concept of malintent. Such an approach must distinguish the unique characteristics of malintent from deception and other psychological states likely to
be encountered in the portal situations. Once the concept has been sufficiently
defined through theory, it could then be operationalized through experimental
manipulations and contrasted with deception and other related psychological
states in an effort to show that the concept has validity and is in fact distinct
from other concepts. If a distinct concept of malintent were developed, then
research should be used to demonstrate generalizability across relevant groups
of persons and settings. Only then would it make sense to define appropriate
discriminative dependent variables and begin designing testing equipment for
application. We realize that this is a big effort that would require considerable time and money. However, the probability that such an effort would be
successful is higher than relying upon blind data collection to serendipitously
happen upon the exact set of dependent variables that will validly discriminate
malintent, and also be generalizable across persons, places, and times.

Consequences for Portals

What does the extant body of research imply for credibility assessments
in portals settings? Most importantly, it tells us that deception is not readily detected from demeanor. We can expect that portals professionals who
attempt to establish veracity by observing behavior from a distance, or who
briefly interact with individuals and observe their demeanor while they
speak, will achieve essentially chance hit rates (Bond and DePaulo, 2006).
That such portals professionals are confident in their ability to assess veracity from demeanor should not be taken as evidence of deception detection
skills. Research has established a near-zero correlation between confidence
and accuracy of these judgments (DePaulo *et al.*, 1997), and found that legal
professionals err on the side of overconfidence (Elaad, 2003; Kassin *et al.*,
2007). It should be emphasized that the shortcomings discussed here are not
specific to professional decision making. It is the task of assessing veracity
from demeanor that is difficult due to the factors mentioned above: people's
proficiency at providing false statements, the similarity of the emotional
and cognitive processes of innocent and guilty people, and the possibility
for both truth-tellers and liars to purposefully control behavioral displays to
give credible impressions.

One might wonder if it is possible to inform people, including those who face the task of making these credibility assessments in the context of portals, of the findings from scientific research on deceptive and truthful demeanor cues, thereby eliminating stereotypical views of deceptive demeanor, such as reliance on non-diagnostic gaze aversion, and replacing flawed decision-making criteria with more productive ones. Such attempts have been found to be largely ineffective and sometimes even counterproductive (Bull, 2004; Frank and Feeley, 2003; for criticism of such training programs, see Docan-Morgan, 2007). There are several explanations for the finding that such information about more diagnostic cues to deception does not aid lie-catchers and sometimes even hampers them. First, it is possible that decision making regarding the veracity of another's statement is not based simply on conscious and declarative knowledge of actual indicators of deceit. These decisions may partly be based on global, intuitive impressions of the other (DePaulo and Morris, 2004), suggesting that awareness of distinct, reliable cues to deception might not take lie-catchers very far. In line with this reasoning, Hartwig and Bond (2011) found that people do not rely on the behavioral cues that they self-report in surveys. Instead, it seems that judgments about deception are largely driven by intuitive processes that operate partly or wholly outside the realm of conscious awareness. Second, it is possible that being asked to replace one's existing decision criteria with another prescribed set of criteria is confusing and causes a form of overload, leading to decreased performance rather than improvement as a function of the information. The seemingly unavoidable conclusion is pessimistic: credibility assessments based on passive observation of demeanor seem to be inherently inaccurate.

A SCIENCE-BASED APPROACH TO THE PORTAL SCREENING PROBLEM

We propose three primary strategies for future empirical research on the psychology of malintent:

(1) Scholars should approach malintent from theory in order to provide a framework for understanding the psychological nature of the concept. For a related theoretical discussion of the nature of true and false intentions, see Granhag and Knieps (2011). For a discussion of the distinction between false intent and malintent, see Granhag (2010).

(2) Research should experimentally manipulate malintent to establish how individuals with and without malintent think, feel, and act in the context of portal screenings. Experimental control provides ground truth (unequivocal knowledge of which individuals are guilty of malintent and which are not), the control of the circumstances, and the possibility of establishing causal links between variables.

(3) Research should attempt to collect field data on cases where ground truth on malintent can be established with a satisfactory degree of certainty to map cues to malintent in naturalistic portals settings. However, it should be noted that such data are inferior in several important aspects to laboratory data on malintent, particularly with respect to the establishment of ground truth. While it might be possible to establish the existence of malintent with a satisfactory degree of certainty (by receiving feedback about an individual's actions after a screening), finding comparable data on lack of malintent might be more difficult. In essence, establishing the absence of malintent in non-laboratory contexts is inherently problematic. The failure to receive feedback about transgressions after screening does not unequivocally establish the absence of such malintent during screening. It might be that such acts were committed but not discovered or it might be that malintent was present in the portal setting but not realized. Thus, the proper role for collecting field data in this context is to establish the generalizability (or lack thereof) of the results of well-controlled experiments, rather than for the primary description of the phenomena. It may be necessary to push the limits of ethically acceptable experimental paradigms to accomplish this goal by conducting what might be classified as field experiments or quasi-experiments. Readers are referred to the study by Ginton *et al.* (1982) for an example of a field quasi-experiment of the polygraph.

ELICITING CUES TO DECEPTION, GUILT, AND MALINTENT: THE PSYCHOLOGY OF INVESTIGATIVE INTERVIEWING

The passive observation of individuals' demeanor is not the only approach to portal screening. Individuals may be selected for further security screening, including baggage examination and individual interviews. This is a more promising avenue for detecting malintent in portals. The possibility that physical examinations will reveal further cues to malintent contributes to this. However, even with regard to the primarily psychological scrutiny of individuals, detecting malintent in interactive settings is markedly more promising (as compared with passive observation of demeanor). Emerging research has shown that it might be possible to elicit more reliable cues to deception by interacting with the targets of scrutiny (for a comprehensive overview of this research, see Vrij and Granhag, 2012). Such research has moved away from the emphasis on the emotional components of deceiving and instead focuses on the particular cognitive challenges for deceivers. For example, research has shown that cues to deception increase in magnitude if liars and truth-tellers are asked to engage in cognitively challenging tasks (Vrij *et al.*, 2006, 2008). Further, lie-catchers who are presented with such statements achieve higher hit rates with no proneness for judgment bias (i.e., a tendency to make excessive truth or lie judgments; Vrij *et al.*, 2008). The explanation is that deceiving in certain respects might be more cognitively demanding than truth-telling and adding further cognitive load presents more problems for an individual who is already engaged in a demanding task (see Vrij and Ganis in Chapter 7 of this volume).

As described earlier, deceiving and truth-telling share some similar tasks, including the suppression of undesirable demeanor in favor of credible demeanor (DePaulo, 1992; Sporer and Schwandt, 2007). However, liars face unique cognitive burdens in that they must make decisions about what untruthful information to provide, what truthful information to hide, and they must provide statements that are internally consistent and also consistent with information external to the statements (Vrij *et al.*, 2006). Consistent with the emphasis on the cognitive challenges lying presents and consequent demands in terms of information management, it has been found that exploiting liars' conservative and evasive strategies concerning information yields cues to deception, and lie-catchers informed of such strategies and how to exploit them achieve significantly higher hit rates (Hartwig *et al.*, 2005, 2006). Other lines of research have also attempted to exploit liars' strategies by posing unanticipated questions to which liars are unlikely to have prepared responses (Vrij *et al.*, 2009).

It thus seems possible to elicit more reliable cues to deception via various forms of strategic interview techniques that exploit the strategies and challenges specific to liars. In contrast to this, empirical data consistently demonstrate that commonly employed tactics to elicit cues to deception do not capitalize on these possibilities. Instead, in line with the commonly held belief that liars experience and display negative emotion and nervousness, law enforcement personnel and others who regularly question people to assess credibility focus on such cues with chance-level performance (Meissner and Kassin, 2002; Vrij *et al.*, 2007). Apart from ethical concerns, it has been clearly established that various forms of pressure and anxiety-inducing tactics do little to aid the decision maker in interviews and interrogation, and tactics that hinge on such pressure are counterproductive (Gudjonsson, 2003; Kassin, 2008).

CONSEQUENCES FOR PORTALS

Much of the literature on the active elicitation of cues to deception and truth in the context of interviews is relevant for portals, as it pertains to the general psychology of deception and credibility. It is, however, important to highlight that similar to research on non-interactive credibility assessments, little or no scientific research has focused on the specific psychological characteristics of portals, including the element of prospective credibility assessments. At this point, empirical research on strategies and behavior of individuals with and without hostile and malicious intent is lacking. Consequently, we propose several tracks of importance for future research. Experimental research modeled after the characteristics of portal screenings should examine the nature of deceptive and truthful behavior in this setting. In particular, for credibility assessments in interactive situations, it is of most relevance to focus on the verbal aspects of such behavior. Research should thus focus on cognitive differences in the tasks of those who deceptively and truthfully deny transgressions and malintent (Vrij *et al.*, 2008), on the characteristics of their verbal strategies and consequent differences in the characteristics of verbal content (Strömwall *et al.*, 2006), and on pathways to exploit such differences between those with and without malintent for the purpose of assessing credibility (Vrij and Granhag, 2012).

Finally, a note of caution is warranted. Due to recent terrorism-related concerns of threats to national security, and the need to protect borders, infrastructure, and key areas against such threats, there have been multiple reports in the media about the development and implementation of techniques to aid decision makers' and professionals' credibility assessments in the context of portal screenings. Given the scarcity of sound scientific research on the theoretical and empirical aspects of credibility assessments and malintent in these settings, the vast majority of these enterprises must at this point be treated as scientifically premature. Scientific theories and empirical evidence must come first, technical tools and implementation later. Technological inventions based on flawed principles and concepts (or none at all), and lacking support in the form of empirical evidence, will not aid the cause of national security – they will drain resources and may provide only a false sense of security. These concerns further emphasize the need for the development of a solid body of theoretically sound literature supported by experimental and field data on credibility assessments, deceptive behavior, and malintent in portal screenings.

REFERENCES

Akehurst, L., Köhnken, G., Vrij, A., Bull, R., 1996. Lay persons' and police officers' beliefs regarding deceptive behaviour. Applied Cognitive Psychology 10, 461–471.

Bok, S., 1989. Lying: Moral Choice in Public and Private Life. Vintage Books, New York.

Bond, C.F., Jr. DePaulo, B.M., 2006. Accuracy of deception judgments. Personality and Social Psychology Review 10, 214–234.

Bond, C.F., Jr. DePaulo, B.M., 2008. Individual differences in judging deception: accuracy and bias. Psychological Bulletin 134, 477–492.

Bull, R., 2004. Training to detect deception from behavioral cues: attempts and problems. In: Granhag, P.A., Strömwall, L.A. (Eds.), The Detection of Deception in Forensic Contexts. Cambridge University Press, Cambridge, pp. 251–268.

Department of Homeland Security, 2010. Future Attribute Screening Technology. Powerpoint Presentation, 28 July. Available from http://epic.org/privacy/fastpresentation.pdf.

DePaulo, B.M., 1992. Nonverbal behavior and self-presentation. Psychological Bulletin 111, 203–243.

DePaulo, B.M., Morris, W.L., 2004. Discerning lies from truths: behavioral cues to deception and the indirect pathway of intuition. In: Granhag, P.A., Strömwall, L.A. (Eds.), The Detection of Deception in Forensic Contexts. Cambridge University Press, Cambridge, pp. 15–40.

DePaulo, B.M., Pfeifer, R.L., 1986. On-the-job experience and skill at detecting deception. Journal of Applied Social Psychology 16, 249–267.

DePaulo, B.M., Charlton, K., Cooper, H., Lindsay, J.L., Muhlenbruck, L., 1997. The accuracy–confidence relation in the detection of deception. Personality and Social Psychology Review 1, 346–357.

DePaulo, B.M., Kashy, D.A., Kirkendol, S.E., Wyer, M.M., Epstein, J.A., 1996. Lying in everyday life. Journal of Personality and Social Psychology 70, 979–995.

DePaulo, B.M., Lindsay, J.J., Malone, B.E., Muhlenbruck, L., Charlton, K., Cooper, H., 2003. Cues to deception. Psychological Bulletin 129, 74–118.

Docan-Morgan, T., 2007. Training law enforcement officers to detect deception: a critique of previous research and framework for the future. Applied Psychology in Criminal Justice 3, 143–171.

Ekman, P., 2001. Telling Lies: Cues to Deceit in the Marketplace, Politics and Marriage. Norton, New York.

Elaad, R., 2003. Effects of feedback on the overestimated capacity to detect lies and the underestimated ability to tell lies. Applied Cognitive Psychology 17, 349–363.

Fiske, S.T., Taylor, S.E., 2008. Social Cognition: From Brains to Culture, first ed. McGraw-Hill Higher Education, Boston, MA.

Frank, M., Feeley, T., 2003. To catch a liar: challenges for research in lie detection training. Journal of Applied Communication Research 31, 58–75.

Garrido, E., Masip, J., Herrero, C., 2004. Police officers credibility judgments: accuracy and estimated ability. International Journal of Psychology 39, 254–275.

Ginton, A., Daie, N., Elaad, E., Gen-Shakhar, G., 1982. A method for evaluating the use of the polygraph in a real-life situation. Journal of Applied Psychology 67, 131–137.

Government Accountability Office, 2009. Aviation security: a national strategy and other actions would strengthen TSA's efforts to secure commercial airport perimeters and access controls. GAO-9-399. US Government, Washington, DC. Available from http://www.gao.gov/assets/300/296404.html.

Government Accountability Office, 2010. Aviation security: Efforts to validate TSA's passenger screening behavior detection program underway, but opportunities exist to strengthen validation and address operational challenges. GAO-10-763. US Government, Washington, DC. Available from http://www.gao.gov/products/Gao-10-763.

Granhag, P.A., 2010. On the psycho-legal study of true and false intentions: dangerous waters and some stepping stones. Open Criminology Journal 3, 37–43.

Granhag, P.A., Knieps, M., 2011. Episodic future thought: illuminating the trademarks of forming true and false intentions. Applied Cognitive Psychology 25, 274–280.

Granhag, P.A., Strömwall, L.A., 2004. The Detection of Deception in Forensic Contexts. Cambridge University Press, Cambridge.

Gudjonsson, G.H., 2003. The Psychology of Interrogations and Confessions: A Handbook (Wiley Series in the Psychology of Crime, Policing and Law). Wiley, Chichester.

Hartwig, M., Bond, C.F., 2011. Why do lie-catchers fail? A lens model meta-analysis of human lie judgments. Psychological Bulletin 137, 643–659.

Hartwig, M., Granhag, P.A., Strömwall, L.A., Vrij, A., 2004. Police officers' lie detection accuracy: Interrogating freely versus observing video. Police Quarterly 7, 429–456.

Hartwig, M., Granhag, P.A., Strömwall, L.A., Vrij, A., 2005. Detecting deception via strategic disclosure of evidence. Law and Human Behavior 29, 469–484.

Hoffman, J., 2008. How faces share feelings. Nature 452, 413–413.

Hogarth, R.M., 2001. Educating Intuition. University of Chicago Press, Chicago, IL.

Honts, C.R., 1991. The emperor's new clothes: application of polygraph tests in the American workplace. Forensic Reports 4, 91–116.

Honts, C.R., 2004. The psychophysiological detection of deception. In: Granhag, P.A., Strömwall, L.A. (Eds.), The Detection of Deception in Forensic Contexts. Cambridge University Press, Cambridge, pp. 103–123.

Honts, C.R., Schweinle, W., 2009. Information gain of psychophysiological detection of deception in forensic and screening settings. Applied Psychophysiology and Biofeedback 34, 161–172.

Honts, C.R., Hartwig, M., Kleinman, S.M., Meissner, C.A., 2009. Credibility Assessment at Portals: Portals Committee Report. Final Report of the Portals Committee to the Defense Academy for Credibility Assessment/US Defense Intelligence Agency.

Honts, C.R., Pittman, F.A., Pittman, J.V., McBride, S.T., Anderson, A.B., Christiansen, A.K., 2008. A new paradigm for the study of deception detection at portals. Paper presented at the Association for Psychological Science annual meeting, Chicago, IL 23–25 May.

Inbau, F.E., Reid, J.E., Buckley, J.P., Jayne, B.C., 2001. Criminal Interrogations and Confessions, fourth ed. Aspen, Gaithersburg, MD.

Kassin, S., 2008. False confessions: causes, consequences, and implications for reform. Current Directions in Psychological Science 17, 249–253.

Kassin, S., Leo, R., Meissner, C., Richman, K., Colwell, L., Leach, A., La Fon, D., 2007. Police interviewing and interrogation: a self-report survey of police practices and beliefs. Law and Human Behavior 31, 381–400.

Kleiner, M. (Ed.), 2002. Handbook of Polygraph Testing. Academic Press, San Diego, CA.

Mann, S., Vrij, A., Bull, R., 2004. Detecting true lies: police officers' ability to detect suspects' lies. Journal of Applied Psychology 89, 137–149.

Meissner, C.A., Kassin, S.M., 2002. "He's guilty!": investigator bias in judgements of truth and deception. Law and Human Behavior 26, 469–480.

National Research Council, 2003. The Polygraph and Lie Detection. National Academies Press, Washington, DC.

Perry, M., Gibley, A., 2011. The screening of passengers by observation techniques programme: analysing the issues. Aviation Security International 17, 12–13.

Porter, S., ten Brinke, L., 2008. Reading between the lies: identifying concealed and falsified emotions in universal facial expressions. Psychological Science 19, 508–514.

Sporer, S.L., Schwandt, B., 2007. Moderators of nonverbal indicators of deception: a meta-analytic synthesis. Psychology, Public Policy, and Law 13, 1–34.

Strömwall, L.A., Granhag, P.A., Hartwig, M., 2004. Practitioners' beliefs about deception. In: Granhag, P.A., Strömwall, L.A. (Eds.), The Detection of Deception in Forensic Contexts. Cambridge University Press, Cambridge, pp. 229–250.

Strömwall, L.A., Hartwig, M., Granhag, P.A., 2006. To act truthfully: nonverbal behavior and strategies during police interrogation. Psychology, Crime and Law 12, 207–219.

Transportation Security Administration, 2006. Train police officers to spot terrorist related activity: TSA designs and tests curriculum to train police officers to spot terrorist-related activity. Department of Homeland Security, Transportation Security Administration press release 6 April. Available from http://www.tsa.gov/press/releases/2012/04/06/train-police-officers-spot-terrorist-related-activity.

Vrij, A., 2008. Detecting Lies and Deceit: Pitfalls and Opportunities, second ed. Wiley, New York.

Vrij, A., Granhag, P.A., 2012. Eliciting cues to deception and truth: what matters are the questions asked. Journal of Applied Research in Memory and Cognition 1, 110–117.

Vrij, A., Mann, S., 2001. Telling and detecting lies in a high-stake situation: the case of a convicted murderer. Applied Cognitive Psychology 15, 187–203.

Vrij, A., Fisher, R., Mann, S., Leal, S., 2006. Detecting deception by manipulating cognitive load. Trends in Cognitive Sciences 10, 141–142.

Vrij, A., Mann, S., Kristen, S., Fisher, R., 2007. Cues to deception and ability to detect lies as a function of police interview styles. Law and Human Behavior 31, 499–518.

Vrij, A., Mann, S., Fisher, R., Leal, S., Milne, R., Bull, R., 2008. Increasing cognitive load to facilitate lie detection: the benefit of recalling an event in reverse order. Law and Human Behavior 32, 253–265.

Vrij, A., Leal, S., Granhag, P.A., Mann, S., Fisher, R.P., Hillman, J., Sperry, K., 2009. Outsmarting the liars: the benefit of asking unanticipated questions. Law and Human Behavior 33, 159–166.

Weinberger, S., 2010. Intent to deceive? Nature 265, 412–415.

Wells, G.L., Olson, E.A., 2002. Eyewitness identification: information gain from incriminating and exonerating behaviors. Journal of Experimental Psychology: Applied 8, 155–167.

Wilber, D.Q., Nakashima, E., 2007. Searching passengers' faces for subtle cues to terror. The Washington Post 19 September, D1.

3

Validity of Polygraph Techniques and Decision Methods

David C. Raskin*, *John C. Kircher*[†]

*Psychology Department, University of Utah, [†]Educational Psychology Department, University of Utah

O U T L I N E

Introduction	65	Methods for Determining Test Outcomes	85
Common Characteristics of All Comparison Question Tests	66	Numerical Scoring	86
		Seven-Point Scale	86
Comparison Question Tests	67	Three-Point Scale	87
		Spot Scoring	88
Utah Probable-Lie Test	69	Evidentiary and Investigative Rules	89
Test Structure and Administration	70	Two-Stage Rules	89
Interpretation of the Results	74	Empirical Scoring System	90
Numerical Evaluation	74	Computer Scoring	92
Computer Interpretations	77	CPS Algorithm	92
		OSS-1	93
Utah Directed-Lie Test	78	OSS-2	93
Overall Validity of Comparison Question Tests	79	OSS-3	94
Accuracy of the PLT in the Laboratory	80	Comparison of Scoring Methods	94
Accuracy of the PLT in the Field	81	Procedures	95
The Polygraph Compared with Other Diagnostic Techniques	84	Datasets	95
		Data Quantification	97

Credibility Assessment
http://dx.doi.org/10.1016/B978-0-12-394433-7.00003-8

63

Scoring Systems   98
Data Transformations   98
Number of Charts   99
Single-Issue Decision Rules   99
Two-Stage Rule for Multiple-Issue
Tests   100
CQs   101
Results   *101*
Single-Issue Examinations   101
Multiple-Issue Examinations   103
Discussion   *107*
Scoring Systems   107

Effect Size   109
Validity of Results   111

Applied Issues   **117**
Decision Making   *118*
Personality Factors   *119*
Confidential Tests for Defense
Attorneys   *119*
Testing Victims   *121*
Government Use of Polygraphs   *122*

Summary and Conclusions   **122**

References   **123**

INTRODUCTION

This chapter describes the most widely applied technique for physiological detection of deception, the Comparison Question Test (CQT), and the various analytic methods for determining the outcomes of such tests. It includes an analysis of the scientific research and validity of the CQT, compares the diagnostic reliability and validity of polygraph tests to other commonly used psychological and medical tests and diagnostic procedures, provides a detailed examination and analysis of current methods for rendering decisions, and concludes with a discussion of some of the major issues concerning uses of polygraph tests.

An earlier review of polygraph techniques (Raskin and Honts, 2002) discussed the basic requirements of a psychological test for assessing the credibility of an individual and evaluated the extent to which various polygraph techniques satisfy the general requirements of a psychological test. They began with the early Relevant–Irrelevant Test (RIT) and covered historically important comparison question tests, including the more recently developed CQT variation known as the Directed-Lie Test (DLT). For each technique, they described and evaluated the basic test protocols, including the question structure, the pretest interview, the development and review of the questions to be asked, the sequence of question presentation, and the methods for evaluating the outcomes. For more information about these topics, see Raskin and Honts (2002).

The basic principles underlying all polygraph tests for the assessment of credibility (detection of deception) are psychophysiological in nature. The test is based on the well-established "fight-or-flight" phenomenon. That is, a physical or psychological threat will automatically elicit a complex set of physiological reactions manifested as changes that are readily measured with a polygraph instrument (Thompson, 2000). These physiological changes include increases in palmar skin conductance and blood pressure, and decreases in respiratory activity and peripheral circulation (Stern *et al.*, 1980).

The various polygraph techniques generally rely on one or more psychological constructs as the causes of these physiological changes, such as fear of detection, enhanced attention, information processing, orienting reflexes, conflict, and arousal (Podlesny and Raskin, 1977; Raskin, 1979; see also Vrij and Ganis in Chapter 7 of this volume). However, the assessment of the underlying causal nature of the physiological responses is a separate scientific question from determining the accuracy of a test. Contrary to criticisms raised by the report from the National Research Council (2003), it is quite possible to have a test validated as accurate for its specified purpose (internal and criterion validity) without having a complete understanding of the underlying theoretical constructs or construct validity (Shadish *et al.*, 2002).

COMMON CHARACTERISTICS OF ALL COMPARISON QUESTION TESTS

All CQTs begin with a pretest interview. The interview usually involves obtaining verbal or written consent from the subject to administer the test. Basic biographical information is obtained, such as personal data and a brief health history. The issues to be covered by the test are discussed, including the specific allegations, and the subject's version of the events is obtained. This interaction is usually followed by the examiner providing some type of description of the relevant psychophysiology, including how and why a person will react physiologically when engaging in deception and when answering truthfully. The physiological transducers are attached to the subject, and the examiner may conduct a demonstration test to accustom the subject to the recording procedures and convey to the subject that attempts to deceive will be accompanied by clear physiological changes, whereas truthful answers will not produce such changes.

All CQTs require the subject to answer direct questions concerning involvement or knowledge of a crime or incident. Questions are formulated so that the subject will answer "Yes" or "No" and are reviewed in detail with the subject during the pretest interview. The relevant questions (RQs) typically embody a major aspect of the incident, and other questions are included for various purposes that depend on the type of test format employed (see below).

All polygraph techniques assume that the measured physiological reactions are automatic (autonomic) and will occur with greater strength to the questions that are most important to the individual (e.g., an RQ that is answered deceptively). However, it is generally accepted by psychophysiologists that there is no "specific lie response" or pattern of reactions that is peculiar to deception (Podlesny and Raskin, 1977; Raskin, 1979). That is to say, an inspection of the physiological responses of an individual to a particular question cannot provide the sole basis for concluding that the subject's answer was deceptive or truthful.

A variety of factors may cause subjects to react with greater strength to questions about crimes of which they are suspected than to the innocuous neutral questions. Serious accusations, the emotional impact of the questions (e.g., if they mention the death of a spouse or friend), the nervousness of the individual, the thought processes and images evoked by the content of the questions, distrust of the examiner, or anger and disgust concerning the accusation (e.g., sexual abuse of one's own child) may cause autonomic reactions to RQs even when they are answered truthfully. In the absence of a properly constructed test protocol, neither polygraph examiners nor psychophysiologists are able to distinguish with any reasonable accuracy such reactions from those that occur as a result of deception.

COMPARISON QUESTION TESTS

CQTs are the most commonly used and generally applicable techniques for the investigation of criminal cases. They are also used in civil litigation, post-conviction assessments, and most frequently by government and law enforcement agencies for pre-employment and periodic examinations in national security settings.

The CQT assesses credibility concerning actions or events about which the subject has direct knowledge or experience and a clear memory (Raskin, 1986b). In most cases, the RQs can be worded in simple, concrete terms that allow an unambiguous interpretation of their meaning. An RQ that is ambiguous or requires the subject to draw conclusions or make interpretations can cause problems in making inferences about truth or deception, regardless of the actual guilt or innocence of the person tested.

Lack of clear memory for an event (from intoxication, trauma, or other causes) may render a subject unsuitable for a test. Also, RQs should not attempt to directly assess a subject's state of mind during the incident or the subject's interpretation of the meaning of such acts or events. However, motives, intentions, or legal conclusions may sometimes be inferred from the content and the meaning of the questions that the examiner and subject discuss during the pretest interview. For example, the subject accused of rape should not be asked "Did Mary voluntarily have sex with you on June fifth?" Instead, he might be asked, "Did you use physical force or threat to get Mary to have sex with you on June fifth?" The subject's veracity in denying a rape can be directly inferred from the test outcome on the use of physical force or threat. However, it is necessary for the examiner to discuss and define the meaning of *physical force* and *threat* in terms of the allegations and descriptions provided by the accuser. A similar approach should be used when a parent or caretaker is accused of touching a child's genitals. The examiner should distinguish between normal child care, such as washing, and touching of a sexual nature. The term *for sexual purposes* is then added to the question. The subject should never be asked, "Did you rape …" or "Did you sexually abuse …." These terms are unsuitable because they require the subject to draw a legal conclusion.

The CQT typically employs between two and four RQs in a sequence of 10–12 questions that includes other types of questions. The nature and purposes of the other questions vary according to the type of technique and the purposes of the examination. The methods for conducting the pretest interview and evaluating test outcomes vary for different techniques.

Comparison questions (CQs) are designed to provide the innocent suspect an opportunity to become more concerned about questions other than the RQs, thereby causing the innocent suspect to react more strongly to the comparison than to the RQs. If the subject does react with greater strength to the CQs, the result is interpreted as truthful. Conversely, stronger reactions to the RQs are interpreted as indicating that the subject was deceptive to the RQs. The lack of a specific lie response is circumvented by the procedure of drawing inferences about truth or deception by comparing the relative strength of this subject's reactions to relevant and CQs.

UTAH PROBABLE-LIE TEST

To increase the internal and empirical validity of the CQT, in 1970 Raskin and his colleagues at the University of Utah reconceptualized it within the framework of current concepts of psychological science and psychophysiology (Podlesny and Raskin, 1977; Raskin, 1979, 1986b). They subjected it to rigorous scientific testing in laboratory and field contexts (for a review, see Honts *et al.*, 2005). The Utah Probable-Lie Test (PLT) is the first polygraph technique developed by psychologists who explicitly incorporated basic knowledge and principles from psychological science and psychophysiology into the pretest interview, question structure, recording methods, and evaluation methods (Handler and Nelson, 2009). Research has consistently shown it to have high reliability and validity (Ad Hoc Committee on Polygraph Techniques, 2011; Krapohl, 2006).

There are numerous variants of the CQT as described by the US Government (Department of Defense, 2006). As research and analysis have demonstrated that the Utah tests are the most accurate of all CQTs (Ad Hoc Committee on Polygraph Techniques, 2011; Krapohl, 2006), we provide a detailed description and evaluation of the Utah CQT examination procedures. The Utah PLT begins with a detailed pretest interview that usually requires approximately one hour. Prior to meeting the subject, the examiner becomes familiar with the case facts by reading incident reports and/or meeting with the relevant investigators or attorneys. At the outset of the pretest interview, the subject is informed of the purpose and issues of the examination, is given a full advisement of legal rights, and gives written consent to undergo the examination. This formal advisement of rights, even when not required by law, creates a serious, professional atmosphere that blunts the argument of the "friendly polygrapher" advanced by polygraph critics (see below).

The examiner should electronically record the entire examination, including the advisement of rights, and the subject should be informed at the outset that such a recording will be made. A complete recording provides a record for later review, as well as protection for the subject and the examiner if any questions are subsequently raised about the manner in which the examination was conducted and its specific contents. The recording is necessary for a thorough, independent evaluation of the examination and for training polygraph examiners.

Test Structure and Administration

The pretest interview is a low-key approach designed to obtain information from the subject without pressure or confrontation. As such, it is an investigative psychological interview rather than an interrogation. The examiner does not lecture the subject or provide morality examples or personal anecdotes. The examiner never challenges the subject's version of the events during the pretest interview. The interview begins by obtaining basic biographical information from the subject, including a brief medical and psychiatric history designed to uncover any serious physical or mental problems that might affect the validity of the test. The examiner then discusses the allegations or issues of the test, and encourages the subject to freely describe and relate any events or knowledge that may be important for the examiner to know. This provides an opportunity to obtain the subject's description of the incident and to clarify any ambiguities or misunderstandings that might interfere with a valid test. The pretest interview helps to reduce the subject's general anxiety, and assists in establishing an atmosphere of professional objectivity and trust.

The examiner then places the polygraph transducers on the subject and provides a general explanation of the psychophysiology that underlies the polygraph test. A rationale is provided as to why people show strong involuntary physiological reactions when they are deceptive and do not exhibit such reactions when they are truthful. Offe and Offe (2007) demonstrated that failure to provide this explanation and rationale substantially decreases the accuracy of the test. A demonstration (stimulation) test is then performed to convince the subject that the polygraph is effective at detecting deception and verifying truthfulness. This usually takes the form of a number test in which the subject is asked to choose a number between

3 and 6, to disclose the number to the examiner, and to deny having chosen any of the numbers 1 through 7 while recordings are made with the polygraph.

After completing the number test, the subject is informed that the examiner now knows the individual characteristics and pattern of the subject's physiological reactions during deception and truthfulness, and that there should be no problem on the test as long as the subject is completely truthful to every question. The subject is also told that any deception to any question on the test will produce even larger reactions than the reaction on the number test because such deception is more serious. Number tests have been shown to increase the accuracy of the polygraph test and should be used with all polygraph tests (Bradley and Janisse, 1981; Kircher *et al.*, 2010; but see contrary results by Elaad and Kleiner, 1986).

The specific wording of each question is then reviewed and discussed with the subject to ensure that no ambiguities are present in the RQs and the subject can answer with an unequivocal "No" or "Yes." The probable-lie questions are then introduced. Probable-lie questions deal with acts that are similar to the issue under investigation. However, they are more general in nature, deliberately vague, and cover long periods of time in the life history of the subject. Virtually every criminal suspect has difficulty in unequivocally answering them with a truthful "No." An example of a probable-lie question in an examination regarding a robbery is "Prior to 2010, did you ever take something that did not belong to you?" The PLT includes two or three CQs that are reviewed with the subject after the RQs have been discussed and reviewed, and they are presented in a manner designed to encourage the subject to answer them with a denial. A typical introduction of the CQs by the examiner during the pretest interview is as follows:

> Since this is a matter of a theft, I need to ask you some general questions about yourself in order to assess your basic character with regard to honesty and trustworthiness. I need to make sure that you have never done anything of a similar nature in the past and that you are not the type of person who would do something like robbing that Quick Mart and then would lie about it. Therefore, I need to ask you some questions for that purpose. So, if I ask you, "Before age 27, did you ever do anything that was dishonest or illegal?" you could answer that "No," couldn't you?

Most subjects initially answer "No" to the probable-lie questions. If the subject answers "Yes," the examiner asks for an explanation. The typical response is a minor admission, such as lying about taking some trivial item at an early age. The examiner then responds by saying, "Well, that was when you were a child and didn't know better. You never did anything like that when you were older and knew better, did you?" Most subjects then answer in the negative and the question is used in its original form or reworded to "Other than what you told me, before age 27 did you ever do anything that was dishonest or illegal?" If the subject makes further admissions, the examiner continues to minimize and discourage admissions until a "No" answer is obtained. The goal is to get to the denial as quickly as possible.

The manner of introducing and explaining the probable-lie questions is designed to pose a dilemma for the subject. It leads the subject to believe that admissions will cause the examiner to form the opinion that the subject is dishonest and is therefore guilty. This discourages admissions and maximizes the likelihood that the negative answer is untruthful. However, the manner of introducing and explaining the probable-lie questions also leads the subject to believe that deceptive answers will result in strong physiological reactions during the test and will cause the examiner to conclude that the subject was deceptive to the relevant issues concerning the robbery. In fact, the converse is true.

There are two forms of the Utah PLT. The version shown in Table 3.1 is used when there is a single allegation to be assessed. The sequence includes three RQs (R1, R2, R3), three probable-lie questions (C1, C2, C3), and three neutral questions (N1, N2, N3). The first two questions (I, SR) are buffers designed to habituate the reactions that normally occur to the question that is presented first and to the first presentation of a question that embodies the relevant issue of the test. The introductory question also serves to reassure the subject that there will be no surprises. The reactions to these buffer questions are not evaluated.

The other version, shown in Table 3.2, is employed when there are multiple aspects or allegations to be tested. This format is very flexible and can accommodate almost any set of issues in a case. Owing to its flexibility, it is also

TABLE 3.1 Utah PLT Single-Issue Question Sequence

Question type	Text
I. Introductory	Do you understand that I will ask only the questions we have discussed?
SR. Sacrifice relevant	Regarding allegations that you robbed the Quick Mart last night, do you intend to answer all of the questions truthfully?
N1. Neutral	Do you live in the United States?
C1. Probable lie	During the first 27 years of your life, did you ever take something that did not belong to you?
R1. Relevant	Did you rob the Quick Mart at Fourth and Main last night?
N2. Neutral	Is your name Rick?
C2. Probable lie	Prior to 2011, did you ever do anything that was dishonest or illegal?
R2. Relevant	Did you use a gun to rob the Quick Mart at Fourth and Main last night?
N3. Neutral	Were you born in the month of November?
C3. Probable lie	Before age 27, did you ever lie to get out of trouble or to cause a problem for someone else?
R3. Relevant	Do you know where the money missing from the Quick Mart is now?

TABLE 3.2 Utah PLT Multiple-Issue Question Sequence

Question type	Text
I. Introductory	Do you understand that I will ask only the questions we have discussed?
SR. Sacrifice relevant	Regarding the counterfeit money, do you intend to answer all of the questions truthfully?
N1. Neutral	Do you live in the United States?
C1. Probable lie	During the first 27 years of your life, did you ever take something that did not belong to you?
R1. Relevant	When you paid with that money at the Quick Mart, did you know it was counterfeit?
R2. Relevant	Do you know where more counterfeit money is right now?
C2. Probable lie	Prior to 2011, did you ever do anything that was dishonest or illegal?
R3. Relevant	Were you involved in printing that counterfeit money?
R4. Relevant	Do you know the location of the plates that were used to print that counterfeit money?
C3. Probable lie	Before age 27, did you ever lie to get out of trouble or to cause a problem for someone else?
N2. Neutral	Is your name Rick?

very useful for single-issue tests. It has the advantage of bracketing each pair of RQs with surrounding CQs for purposes of numerical scoring (see below).

Just before beginning data collection, the subject is instructed not to move around or talk during the asking of questions, except to answer each question simply "Yes" or "No" and to answer every question truthfully. The examiner also instructs the subject that if anything else comes to mind during the test, it should be mentioned right after the question sequence is asked. The questions are presented at a rate of one question every 25–35 seconds while physiological activity is recorded on the polygraph charts. The sequence is repeated at least three times. The neutral questions and CQs, and possibly the RQs, are rotated through their respective locations across repetitions of the question sequence to prevent subjects from producing anticipatory reactions because they expect the questions to be presented in a particular order. If the results are not conclusive after three repetitions, two additional repetitions may be administered.

After each presentation of the question sequence, the examiner asks the subject if there were any problems and discusses any concerns that the subject expresses. The examiner then reviews the relevant and probable-lie questions to ensure that the RQs are clear and straightforward and the CQs remain salient. If the subject makes an admission to a probable-lie question or provides additional information that changes the meaning of a RQ, this is discussed and appropriate adjustments are made in the affected questions. The subject should not be given any information about the physiological reactions observed to the specific questions nor provided any indication of how the subject is doing until the test has been completed and the results have been analyzed. Throughout the examination, the polygraph examiner's demeanor and behavior must be professional and objective. If the subject feels that the examiner is not competent or is biased, the accuracy of the test may be compromised.

Interpretation of the Results

Numerical Evaluation

The outcome of the Utah PLT is numerically evaluated by comparing the relative strengths of physiological reactions to RQs and CQs. This analysis is performed using a method of numerical evaluation that was originally developed by Backster (Weaver, 1980) and modified by the US Government (Swinford, 1999; US Army Military Police School Polygraph Branch, 1970). The Utah group further modified the scoring system based on scientific research conducted at the University of Utah (for a discussion of the basic approaches and differences in results obtained with these three systems, see Weaver, 1980, 1985).

Numerical evaluation begins with an inspection of the polygraph charts to form an impression of their overall quality and the range of reactivity in the various physiological measures. Against this background, comparisons are then made of the relative strengths of reactions to the RQs and CQs. Starting with the first RQ (R1), a score is assigned for each of the physiological parameters (respiration, electrodermal activity, blood pressure, and peripheral vasomotor activity). Respiration is scored first because it alerts the evaluator to the possibility that large, deep breaths occurred prior to or shortly after the onset of the question, which could have produced large changes in the other physiological measures associated with that test question. Scores for each physiological channel can range from –3 to +3, depending on the direction and magnitude of the observed difference in the reactions elicited by the RQ and the CQ.

For the single-issue sequence in Table 3.1, each RQ is compared with its preceding CQ. For the multiple-issue sequence in Table 3.2, each RQ is compared with the stronger reaction produced by one of the two bracketing CQs. If there is an artifact or distortion in the physiological recording for the CQ, another CQ is used for assigning that score. Occasionally, the subject answers "Yes" to a CQ even though the reviewed answer was "No." Research has shown that inclusion of this CQ in the numerical evaluation has no adverse effect on the accuracy of outcomes (Honts et al., 1992). The procedure of choosing the stronger reaction from the surrounding CQs has also been validated by field research (Honts, 1996; Raskin et al., 1988). However, recent data indicate that choosing the stronger reaction may lead to an unacceptable number of false-negative results with some scoring methods (see below).

If the observed reaction is stronger to the RQ, a negative score is assigned. A positive score is assigned when the reaction is greater to the CQ, and a zero is assigned if there is no clear difference. The magnitude of scores varies from 1 for a noticeable difference, to 2 for a strong difference, to 3 for a dramatic difference. Most assigned scores are 0 or 1, scores of 2 are far less common, and scores of 3 are unusual (Bell *et al.*, 1999). The examiner proceeds through the polygraph charts, independently assigning a score for each physiological parameter for each comparison of the responses to the RQ and the appropriate CQ. This is repeated for each RQ on the chart and for each chart. The scores are then summed to provide a total score for the test and the outcome is based on this total. If the total is –6 or lower, the outcome is deceptive; if the total is +6 or higher, the outcome is truthful; totals between –5 and +5 indicate an inconclusive outcome. These decision rules apply to tests that consist of three charts or five charts.

If the information obtained in the investigation indicates that the subject must answer all of the questions truthfully or all deceptively, the overall total for the test is used as the basis for the decision. For example, if the case information indicates that a single person robbed the Quick Mart, the subject is assumed to be deceptive or truthful to all of the questions and the total score is used for the decision. However, if the RQs address separate acts, more complex decision criteria are employed. If the total scores for the individual RQs are all in the same direction (all positive or all negative, ignoring totals of zero), then the overall total can be used as the outcome for all questions. However, if some question totals are positive and others negative, total scores of at least –3 or +3 for each RQ are required for a definite decision of deception or truthfulness, respectively (Podlesny and Truslow, 1993). For example, the suspect in the Quick Mart robbery might have played one of several roles, such as the gunman, the accomplice who took the money from the cash register, or the driver of the getaway car. Assume that the subject was the driver of the car and did not enter the store. When asked RQs about each of these possibilities, the subject would be truthful when denying being the gunman or taking the money (e.g., +4 and +5, respectively), but deceptive when denying robbing or being involved in the robbery (e.g., –3 and –6, respectively). The outcome of such a test would be evaluated separately for each of the three RQs, using cutoff scores of –3 and +3 for the totals on each of the three RQs.

Research has shown that there is no penalty or advantage to addressing multiple issues in a single question list (Barland *et al.*, 1989). However, when subjects may be truthful to one or more questions and deceptive to others, the accuracy of determining deception to any of the individual questions is substantially lower than determining if the subject was truthful overall on the test or was deceptive to at least one RQ (Barland *et al.*, 1989; Podlesny and Truslow, 1993; Raskin *et al.*, 1988).

The reliability of the Utah system of numerical evaluation was determined by having different raters independently interpret the same sets of polygraph charts. Correlations between total numerical scores assigned by independent raters in laboratory and field studies were typically around 0.90. (e.g., Honts, 1996; Kircher and Raskin, 1988; Podlesny and Raskin, 1978; Raskin and Hare, 1978; Raskin *et al.*, 1988). Numerical scoring by adequately trained and experienced interpreters produces extremely high reliability that compares favorably with any psychological test interpreted by humans.

Computer Interpretations

To provide more powerful, objective, and totally reliable polygraph chart interpretation and decision making, computer methods were developed at the University of Utah based on extensive analyses of features extracted from physiological recordings obtained from guilty and innocent subjects (Kircher and Raskin, 1981, 1988). Discriminant functions were developed to yield optimal separation of the groups based on linear combinations of the physiological data. The discriminant scores for individual subjects were entered into Bayes' Theorem to calculate the probability (ranging from 0.01 to 0.99) that the obtained physiological data indicated that the subject was truthful.

These methods were validated on data from confirmed polygraph examinations of criminal suspects (Raskin *et al.*, 1988). The computer diagnoses were somewhat more accurate than blind interpretations by skilled numerical evaluators, although the field study showed that the original examiners were slightly more accurate than the computer model. Apparently, the original examiners used the case information and their interactions with the subjects to adjust their numerical scoring to be more accurate. However, in terms of interpretations based solely on the polygraph charts, the computer outperformed the human interpreters. The results of these studies indicate that computer evaluations are extremely useful (Kircher and Raskin, 2002). Later in this chapter, we present a new study that evaluated several current methods for computer analysis of test outcomes.

UTAH DIRECTED-LIE TEST

The directed-lie question was proposed as a remedy for some of the problems inherent in the probable-lie CQs (Fuse, unpublished manuscript; Honts, 1994; Honts and Raskin, 1988; Horowitz et al., 1997). The PLT requires a trained and skilled examiner to obtain an accurate outcome. The results may be affected by the subject's interpretation and response to the probable-lie questions when they are introduced and discussed during the pretest interview.

Other problems with probable-lie CQs are related to the characteristics of examinees. Some examinees are very anxious about the subject matter of the probable-lie questions, making it difficult for the examiner to establish effective CQs. These questions may be personally intrusive and offensive to some subjects. For other subjects, they may encompass prior criminal behavior of a serious nature that poses a problem for the subject who may refuse to answer the questions. If a person is administered more than one test or tested on multiple occasions, it may become difficult to formulate new probable-lie questions that continue to be effective for the subject. Also, it may be difficult to explain the functions of probable-lie questions and their role in interpreting the outcome of the test to those who use the results of polygraph tests (investigators, lawyers, judges, and juries) and to laypersons. They may interpret strong physiological reactions to probable-lie questions as indicating that the subject is dishonest and guilty. For these reasons, the Directed-Lie Test (DLT) was developed (for a detailed description of the DLT, see Handler and Nelson, 2009; Raskin and Honts, 2002).

The results from the laboratory and the field seem to indicate that the DLT may be as accurate as the PLT and may have certain advantages (Kircher et al., 2010; Raskin and Honts, 2002). Directed-lie CQs are easily standardized, making it a more straightforward test to administer, it requires less manipulation of the subject and may create fewer problems for the subject, and it is more readily explained to laypersons, lawyers, judges, and juries.

OVERALL VALIDITY OF COMPARISON QUESTION TESTS

The validity of CQ polygraph tests has generated intense debate among scientists (Honts *et al.*, 2005; Iacono and Lykken, 2005). Although the majority of psychophysiologists have expressed generally positive attitudes concerning the usefulness of polygraph tests for assessment of credibility (Amato and Honts, 1994; Gallup Organization, 1984), the American Psychological Association expressed serious concerns about their scientific basis and some of their specific applications (Raskin, 1986b, p. 73). A detailed examination of the scientific literature is necessary to provide answers to this complex empirical question.

There has been a great deal of research, development, and experience with various techniques that employ physiological measures for assessing credibility concerning specific acts, events, or knowledge (Honts *et al.*, 2005). The first scientific laboratory study of the CQ technique was conducted at the University of Utah (Barland and Raskin, 1975a), although the technique had been in widespread use since it was introduced more than 65 years ago by Reid (1947).

The debate about the accuracy of CQTs for investigative and forensic purposes centers on two general sources of data from which the accuracy of such tests may be estimated. Data may be obtained either from laboratory simulations of criminal situations (mock-crime studies), or studies of actual cases that include testing of one or more suspects in a criminal investigation. Each type of study has advantages and disadvantages, and both types are needed to provide an overall picture of test accuracy.

Laboratory research has traditionally been an attractive alternative because the scientist can control the environment. Moreover, in credibility assessment studies, the scientist can know with certainty who is telling the truth and who is lying by randomly assigning subjects to conditions. Laboratory research on credibility assessment has typically made subjects deceivers by having them commit a mock crime (e.g., "steal" a watch from an office) and then instructing them to lie about it during a subsequent test. From a scientific viewpoint, random assignment to conditions is highly desirable because it controls for the influence of extraneous variables that might confound the results of the experiment (Shadish *et al.*, 2002).

The most accepted type of laboratory study realistically simulates a crime in which some subjects commit an overt transaction, such as a theft (Kircher *et al.*, 1988). While the guilty subjects enact a realistic crime, the innocent subjects are merely told about the nature of the crime and do not enact it. All subjects are motivated to produce a truthful outcome, usually by a cash bonus for passing the test. For example, one such study used prison inmates who were offered a bonus equal to one month's wages if they could produce a truthful outcome (Raskin and Hare, 1978).

The advantages of careful laboratory simulations include total control over the issues that are investigated and the types of tests that are used, consistency in test administration and interpretation, specification of the subject populations that are studied, control over the skill and training of the examiners, and absolute verification of the accuracy of test results. Carefully designed and conducted studies that closely approximate the methods and conditions characteristic of high-quality practice by polygraph professionals and that use subjects similar to the target population, such as convicted felons or a cross-section of the general community, provide the most generalizable results (Kircher *et al.*, 1988).

Laboratory research in general, and credibility assessment in particular, can be criticized for a lack of realism. This lack of realism may limit the ability of the scientist to apply the results of the laboratory to real-world settings. However, a study reported by Anderson *et al.* (1999) examined a broad range of laboratory-based psychological research. They concluded (Anderson *et al.*, 1999, p. 3): "Correspondence between lab- and field-based effect sizes of conceptually similar independent and dependent variables was considerable. In brief, the psychological laboratory has generally produced truths, rather than trivialities." Our position with regard to the high-quality studies of the CQT is similar; we believe that those studies produce important information about the validity of such tests and not trivial information as some of the critics have claimed (e.g., Iacono and Lykken, 2005). When surveyed, the majority of psychophysiologists and psychology and law researchers agreed (Honts *et al.*, 2002).

Accuracy of the PLT in the Laboratory

Honts (2004) reported that 11 high-quality published laboratory studies of the CQT indicate that the CQT is an accurate discriminator of truth-tellers and deceivers. Overall, the CQT correctly classified 90% of the subjects, and produced approximately equal numbers of false-positive and false-negative errors (for more detailed descriptions of laboratory studies, see Ad Hoc Committee on Polygraph Techniques, 2011; Raskin and Honts, 2002).

Accuracy of the PLT in the Field

The major disadvantage of laboratory simulations is the difficulty of completely simulating the real-life situation in which a person suspected of a crime is administered a polygraph test. To verify test accuracy under field conditions, it is necessary to use tests conducted on actual criminal suspects. However, field studies of criminal suspects have inherent problems. The major problem is obtaining verification of the suspect's actual guilt or innocence status, which can be very difficult in real cases. The best method uses confessions to verify the guilt and innocence of the examinees. Law enforcement cases that involve polygraph tests produce rates of confessions in the range of 30–80% (Office of Technology Assessment, 1983), but it is not known how these cases compare to those that did not produce confessions.

It is important that field studies select cases according to scientifically acceptable sampling procedures, using only cases in which properly trained polygraph examiners employed standard field methods for conducting the tests and interpreting their outcomes. It is our position that useful field studies of the psychophysiological credibility assessment tests should have all of the following characteristics:

• Subjects should be sampled from the actual population of subjects in which the researcher is interested. If the researcher wants to make inferences about tests conducted on criminal suspects, then criminal suspects should be the subjects who are studied.
• Subjects should be sampled by some random process. Cases must be accepted into the study without reference to either the accuracy of the original outcome or to the quality of the physiological recordings.
• The resulting physiological data must be evaluated by persons trained and experienced in the field scoring techniques about which inferential statements are to be made. Independent evaluations by persons who

have access to only the physiological data are useful for evaluating the information content of those data. However, the decisions rendered by the original examiners may provide a better estimate of the accuracy of polygraph techniques as they are actually employed in the field.
• The credibility of the subject must be determined by information that is independent of the specific test. Confessions substantiated by physical evidence presently are the best criteria available.

In 1983, the Office of Technology Assessment of the US Congress selected ten field studies that they felt had at least some degree of scientific merit. The overall accuracy of the polygraph decisions was 90% on criterion-guilty suspects and 80% on criterion-innocent suspects (Office of Technology Assessment, 1983). In spite of the inclusion of many studies with serious methodological problems, accuracy in field cases was higher than is claimed by some of the most vocal critics (Lykken, 1998).

A survey of the available field studies was performed by the Committee of Concerned Social Scientists (Honts and Peterson, 1997). They found four field studies that met the criteria for meaningful field studies of psychophysiological credibility assessment tests. Overall, the independent evaluations of the field studies produced results that are quite similar to the results of the high-quality laboratory studies. The average accuracy of field decisions for the CQT was 90.5%. However, in the field studies, nearly all of the errors made by the CQT were false-positive errors.

A recent field study by Ginton (2012) employed a novel approach that eliminated the need for external verification, i.e., confession or other evidence. He obtained 64 paired polygraph tests from the files of the Israel Police in which contradictory statements were provided by the two examinees in each pair. Independent analyses of the background material indicated that only one individual could have told the truth on the relevant questions, but which of the pair was unknown. Since the proportion of pairs with the same test outcome is inversely related to the accuracy of the test, an algebraic solution determined that the accuracy of CQT decisions was 94% on guilty suspects and 84% correct on innocent suspects. These results reinforce the findings of 90% overall accuracy of the field studies cited above. Significantly, Ginton's paradigm overcomes the objections of Iacono and Lykken (2005) and the National Research Council (2003) that the false-negative rate is underestimated and the confession criterion is not independent of the polygraph test result.

Although the high-quality field studies indicate a high accuracy rate for the CQT, these results were derived from independent evaluations of the physiological data. This is a desirable practice from a scientific viewpoint, because it eliminates possible contamination (e.g., knowledge of the case facts) and the overt behaviors of the subject during the examination that might have influenced the decisions of the original examiners. However, independent evaluators rarely testify in legal proceedings nor do they make decisions in most applied settings. It is usually the original examiner who makes the decision that affects how the investigation proceeds in an actual case and may provide court testimony. Thus, accuracy rates based on the decisions of independent evaluators may not be the figure of merit for legal proceedings and most applications. The Committee of Concerned Social Scientists summarized the data from the original examiners in the studies reported above and for two additional studies that are often cited by critics of the CQT (Raskin and Honts, 2002). The accuracy of the decisions made by the original examiners was 98% for innocent suspects and 97% for guilty suspects. These data suggest that the original examiners may be more accurate than the independent evaluators.

The National Research Council (2003) published an extensive review of polygraph testing. Their study was originally commissioned to assess the use of polygraphs in the context of government employment screening. Finding little research and useful data for such testing, the study committee changed its focus to an evaluation of the uses of polygraphs in specific issue testing. Although they raised many criticisms of polygraph testing, they found that seven studies of specific-incident polygraph tests in criminal investigation produced a median accuracy of 0.89 (National Research Council, 2003, Appendix H, p. 352). They qualified this result based on their view that there was a lack of independence between the polygraph test results and the criteria for ground truth used in the studies. In spite of this caveat, their report concluded (National Research Council, 2003, p. 197):

The available evidence indicates that in the context of specific-incident investigations and with inexperienced examinees untrained in countermeasures, polygraph tests as currently used have value in distinguishing truthful from deceptive individuals. However, they are far from perfect in that context, and important unanswered questions remain about polygraph accuracy in other important contexts. No alternative techniques are available that perform better ....

Following many concerns expressed by various experts about the methods and motives underlying the report by the National Research Council, the American Polygraph Association Ad Hoc Committee on Polygraph Techniques (2011) conducted a 4-year study of the scientific basis for polygraph techniques. They summarized results from 52 different experiments and surveys published in 37 different studies, including results from 289 scorers who provided a total of 12,665 scores for 2300 criterion deceptive examinations and 1983 criterion truthful exams. Fourteen different polygraph techniques were supported by multiple published studies that satisfied the qualitative and quantitative requirements for inclusion in the meta-analysis. The results for CQT specific-incident diagnostic techniques produced an average criterion accuracy of 92%.

The Polygraph Compared with Other Diagnostic Techniques

Crewson (2001) reported a meta-analysis that compared the accuracy and reliability of polygraph tests with standard tests commonly used for medical and psychological diagnoses. Following a computer-based search of the scientific literature, he reviewed 1158 articles and abstracts, and found 145 to be useful, resulting in data on 198 studies. Agreement between evaluators was evaluated with the κ statistic. For evaluators in the fields of polygraph, medicine, and psychology, the obtained κ coefficients were 0.77, 0.56, and 0.79, respectively. For field diagnostic assessments, the sensitivity of polygraph, medical, and psychological assessments were 0.92, 0.83, and 0.72, respectively. Specificity of polygraph, medical, and psychological diagnostic tests were 0.83, 0.88, and 0.67, respectively. The overall accuracy for polygraph tests (0.88) was comparable to medical diagnoses (0.86) and higher than psychological diagnoses (0.70). These results demonstrate that polygraph evidence is at least as reliable as many other types of accepted expert testimony (e.g., medical, psychiatric, and psychological opinions).

The foregoing evidence demonstrates that the results of high-quality scientific research from the laboratory and the field converge on the conclusion that properly conducted CQTs discriminate between truth-tellers and deceivers with an accuracy of approximately 90%. Moreover, original examiners, who are most likely to offer testimony, may produce even higher accuracy. There may be a tendency for the CQT to produce more false-positive than false-negative errors, but this trend in the current literature is not particularly strong. If there is a tendency for the polygraph to produce more false-positive than false-negative outcomes, then triers of fact should weight negative outcomes (passed polygraphs) more heavily than positive outcomes (failed polygraphs). To reduce the risk of false-positive errors, Krapohl (2005) suggested an approach that adjusts the decision criteria for evidentiary purposes (see below).

In response to critics of the polygraph, Honts and Schweinle (2009) studied the information gained with polygraph tests compared with credibility judgments made by professionals and laypersons in forensic and screening settings. In forensic settings, the polygraph provided substantial information gain across a large range of base rates of guilt for laboratory and field data. Even when 90% of the subjects were guilty, the polygraph results provided 27 times the information gain compared with the human judgments.

METHODS FOR DETERMINING TEST OUTCOMES

Methods for evaluating the results of a polygraph test have been developed for almost a century. The outcome of the original RIT was determined by the examiner visually inspecting the charts and forming an overall impression of the pattern of reactions (Raskin and Honts, 2002). There were no formal rules, and the examiner made a judgment based on the strength of reactions to the RQs and other unspecified information, such as the case facts and the subject's demeanor. This approach was subjective and depended on the skill and experience of the examiner. Aside from possibly verifying the accuracy of examiner decisions, there is an absence of scientific evaluation of this method.

The Reid Modified General Questions Test (MGQT; Reid and Inbau, 1977) introduced a global scoring method for evaluating test outcomes. The examiner inspected the polygraph charts and made a judgment about the relative strength of reactions to RQs and CQs. If the reactions appeared to be stronger to an RQ, the subject was deemed deceptive to that question. If the reaction to the CQ appeared to be stronger, the subject was deemed truthful to the RQ; lack of difference between the RQs and CQs was considered inconclusive. This method of comparing reactions to RQs and CQs represented an important advance over the RIT, but it remained a subjective process because of the lack of formal scoring rules.

Numerical Scoring

Seven-Point Scale

The first numerical scoring procedure was developed by Backster (Weaver, 1980, 1985). It used a complex set of rules for assigning scores on a seven-point scale that indicated the relative strength of reactions to the RQs and CQs. RQs were compared with the weaker of the surrounding CQs. By using a set of rules for assigning scores, this method represented a major advance, but the Backster procedures are highly complex and produced an unacceptable rate of false-positive errors (Raskin, 1986b).

The US Army Military Police School Polygraph Branch (1970) modified the Backster method, simplified the criteria and rules, and compared the first RQ in the question sequence to the stronger of the surrounding CQs. This represented a significant improvement over the Backster system (Weaver, 1985). However, it used up to 27 features of the physiological recordings for assigning scores, many of which had not been verified by scientific research and appeared to be contrary to psychophysiological knowledge.

The Utah scoring system modified the US Army Military Police School Polygraph Branch system. Based on extensive scientific studies by psychophysiologists at the University of Utah (Bell *et al.*, 1999), it increased the reliability and validity of the numerical scoring procedures by reducing the number of physiological features from 27 to ten, including the finger plethysmograph (for a direct comparison of the accuracy of the Utah and Department of Defense approaches, see Honts *et al.*, 2000).

The Utah numerical evaluation is a systematic approach that utilizes only the information obtained from the polygraph charts. All other sources of information, such as verbal and non-verbal behavior and case information, are formally excluded from the decision-making process. As compared with the Backster and US Army Military Police School Polygraph Branch/ Department of Defense Polygraph Institute (DoDPI) systems of the 1970s, the Utah method substantially reduced and refined the criteria for assessing the strength of reaction based on the principles of psychophysiology and extensive laboratory and field research. A detailed description of this scoring system is presented in Bell *et al.* (1999).

Subsequent research conducted at the University of Utah in 2004 (Kircher *et al.*, 2012) confirmed the need to substantially reduce the number of physiological features used by the DoDPI in scoring charts. This was incorporated into the DoDPI scoring procedures (Department of Defense Polygraph Institute, 2006). Following studies at the University of Utah (e.g., Kircher and Raskin, 1988), researchers at the DoDPI also confirmed that scoring up to five charts significantly increased the accuracy of decisions compared with scoring only the first three charts (Senter and Dollins, 2004; Senter *et al.*, 2004). Almost of all of the Utah scoring procedures have been adopted by the DoDPI. According to Handler and Nelson (2009): "[The Utah] technique provides some of the highest rates of criterion accuracy and inter-rater reliability of any polygraph examination protocol (Senter *et al.*, 2004; Krapohl, 2006) when applied in an event-specific testing situation."

Three-Point Scale

In an effort to obtain high reliability with the DoDPI scoring system, a three-point scoring system was developed in the 1990s (Krapohl, 1998). In this system, the evaluator makes a judgment as to which question, RQ or CQ, produced the stronger reaction. If the reaction to the RQ was stronger, –1 is assigned; if the CQ was stronger, +1 is assigned; if they appear to be essentially equal, 0 is assigned. The scores are summed, and total scores of –4 or lower are DI (Deception Indicated), scores of +4 or higher are NDI (No Deception Indicated), and scores of –3 to +3 are NO (No Opinion).

Krapohl compared the results obtained with the three-point scale to those obtained with the seven-point scale. Using the polygraph charts from a mock-crime study (Kircher and Raskin, 1988), the seven-point scores assigned by three experienced government evaluators and the two original Utah scorers were reduced to three-point scores by converting all non-zero scores to scores of +1 and –1. When the two resulting sets of scores were compared, the reliability and accuracy of the results were similar for the two scoring scales. This is not surprising since all scorers were experienced with the seven-point system and 90% of the individual assigned scores were between +1 and –1. However, the federal polygraph training program "advocates use of the seven-position scale. The seven-position scale has a tendency to reduce the number of 'No Opinion' decisions by allowing an examiner to assign greater values to each recording channel." (Department of Defense Polygraph Institute, 2006, p. 5)

SPOT SCORING

An additional decision rule used by many law enforcement and government agencies is the spot scoring rule (SSR) based on total scores for individual RQs (Capps and Ansley, 1992; Department of Defense Polygraph Institute, 2006). If the total score for any RQ is –3 or lower, the subject is deemed deceptive (DI) on the test, irrespective of the total for all questions. Total scores between 0 and –2 on any RQ are considered inconclusive (NO) unless the –6 threshold has already been reached for the total score. A truthful (NDI) result requires a positive value in each spot and a total of +6 or greater summed across all spots. Krapohl (1998) compared decisions made by two University of Utah and three federal evaluators who independently scored 100 laboratory subjects with or without the spot rule. He found that the spot rule increased the accuracy of decisions for guilty subjects from 90% to 95% and decreased the overall number of inconclusive results from 29% to 25%. However, the spot rule decreased the accuracy of decisions on innocent subjects from 97% to 85%. Thus, a slight increase in accuracy on guilty subjects with a slight overall decrease in inconclusives was offset by the large increase in false-positive errors. The Utah scoring does not use the spot rule.

EVIDENTIARY AND INVESTIGATIVE RULES

Krapohl (2005) proposed different rules for making decisions in investigative and evidentiary settings. He noted that the use of spot scoring may be effective in reducing false negatives in criminal investigation but may not be optimal for evidentiary purposes where false positives are costly. In two studies, experienced examiners independently scored large sets of confirmed examinations from criminal investigations (Krapohl, 2005; Krapohl and Cushman, 2006). They compared the results that used the spot scoring procedures described above (investigative rules) with what they termed evidentiary rules. If the total score is –6 or lower, the decision is DI; total scores of +4 or higher are NDI; if the total score is –5 to +3, then spot scoring is applied.

The overall accuracy of decisions was 86% for the investigative rule and 87.2% for the evidentiary rule, with inconclusive rates of 20% and 7%, respectively. The accuracy of investigative decisions was 95% for guilty suspects and 76% for innocent suspects, whereas the accuracy of evidentiary decisions was 90% for the guilty and 88% for the innocent. Thus, the evidentiary rule produced higher accuracy of decisions on innocent suspects and reduced the number of inconclusive outcomes for both groups of suspects. The accuracy for the evidentiary rule was more balanced for truthful and deceptive suspects, but the investigative rule produced fewer false-negative decisions (5% versus 10%) compared with fewer false-positive decisions for the evidentiary rule (12% versus 18%). The better performance of evidentiary rules on truthful suspects may be more appropriate for the courtroom where the costs of a false positive are high, whereas they may not be as appropriate for investigative settings where the cost of false-negative decisions may be high and the investigation provides opportunities to discover false-positive errors.

TWO-STAGE RULES

To reduce the problem with spot scoring, Senter and Dollins (2008a, b) evaluated a two-stage method for making decisions. They used seven-point numerical scores assigned to data from laboratory and field single-issue examinations. They compared three-chart total scores (3T) using the –6 and +6 decision rule, three-chart spot scores (3S), three-chart total scores followed by spot scores for inconclusive totals (3T3S), and spot scores followed by total scores for inconclusive spot results (3S3T). For laboratory examinations, both two-stage models reduced the number of inconclusive results and increased the total percentage of correct decisions relative to the 3T and 3S models; the latter produced the poorest results. For field examinations, both two-stage models reduced the number of inconclusive results and increased the total percentage of correct decisions relative to the 3T and 3S models, but two-stage models produced more errors than the 3T model. The authors concluded that the overall accuracy of the four models was similar, but the two-stage models had greater utility by rendering a higher percentage of decisions. They suggested that policy decisions regarding context of application and base rates of deception might dictate which model to apply.

Empirical Scoring System

In an effort to improve reliability, the empirical scoring system (ESS) was developed from the federal bigger-is-better scoring principle (Nelson *et al.*, 2008). This principle states that when a difference in the electrodermal reaction to an RQ and CQ does not meet the ratio required for a score of +1 or −1, "the response with the more significant amplitude will receive the value [1]. … Any visually perceptible amplitude difference between comparative responses is sufficient to award a value. Generally, if any type of measuring device is needed to discern which comparative amplitude response is greater, assign a zero to the analysis spot" (Department of Defense Polygraph Institute, 2006, p. 32). The ESS expanded this rule using a three-point scale for all physiological channels (Blalock *et al.*, 2009; Nelson *et al.*, 2008). In addition, the scores for the electrodermal channel were doubled to yield scores of −2, 0, or +2.

The ESS (Nelson *et al.*, 2011) uses the following procedures:

(1) Data are scored visually on the computer screen without printing the charts or making manual measurements.
(2) Reactions are scored until the end of the response if the onset of response is arguably attributable to the test stimuli, as determined by the overall quality and stability of the data and timeliness of the response onset.

(3) Responses are not scored if there is an apparent alternative cause, other than the test stimulus. Responses that begin before the onset of the stimulus and responses that begin more than several seconds after the answer are not scored.

(4) Electrodermal reaction is the vertical rise of amplitude from the lowest point following the stimulus onset until the end of the reaction.

(5) Cardiovascular reaction is the vertical increase from the lowest diastolic point following the stimulus onset until the end of the reaction.

(6) Respiratory reactions consist of reduction of respiration amplitude, slowing of respiration rate, and temporary increase of respiratory baseline for three cycles or more. Apnea, which is strongly correlated with the criterion of truth or deception and has been described as the ultimate form of respiratory suppression, is easily feigned, and should be scored only when it occurs at the RQs.

Nelson *et al.* (2008) evaluated the ESS with a sample of polygraph students in their eighth week of training who likely had been previously trained with the seven-point system. They employed "one primary scoring rule: the bigger-is-better principle in which any perceptible difference in magnitude between reactions to relevant and CQs is regarded as a scorable indicator of differential reaction" (Nelson *et al.*, 2008, p. 205).

The accuracy of seven polygraph students who employed the ESS was compared with the accuracy of ten practicing private, law enforcement, and federal polygraph examiners. The ESS student scorers performed as well as the practicing examiners (87.5% versus 86.5%). However, there are two major problems with the study. First, there is no way to know the extent to which the students' training with the seven-point system influenced the scores they assigned with the ESS, especially since the ESS has only a few explicit rules. Second, the ten practicing polygraph examiners were allowed to use a variety of scoring methods, some of which have little scientific basis and may be prone to substantial error. More recent studies (Nelson *et al.*, 2011) report that the ESS is as accurate as other scoring systems when performed by experienced examiners.

The rules for scoring using the "bigger-is-better" principle are somewhat vague when compared with other numerical scoring procedures. Over time, examiners not subject to a quality control requirement may develop idio-syncratic scoring (drift). As ESS has relatively few explicit rules, it may also be affected by subjective factors, such as expectations, case information, behavioral manifestations, and interactions with the subject These may not pose a major problem for government programs that mandate independent review of every examination, but they could produce lowered reliability of scoring by examiners who are not subject to such requirements or do not have ready access to independent review. Furthermore, the visual differ-ences observed on the computer screen are dependent on the sensitivity setting of the channel. Thus, assigned scores may be increased or decreased by changing the sensitivity of the displayed responses. Similar problems may occur when tracings are detrended. As ESS can be easily accomplished by automatic computer scoring (see below), it may be advisable to imple-ment that option in all computerized polygraph systems to provide a totally reliable method.

Computer Scoring

CPS Algorithm

Development of the first computerized polygraph system (CPS) and scor-ing algorithm began in 1978 at the University of Utah and became commer-cially available in 1991 (for a detailed history and description, see Kircher and Raskin, 2002). The examiner uses the CPS to conduct the test and record and store the physiological data. The data can then be analyzed automati-cally using the CPS algorithm. CPS measures skin conductance response amplitude, rise in relative blood pressure, and reduction in respiration line length (RLL) – the so-called Kircher features (Krapohl and McManus, 1999). It combines those measurements by means of a discriminant function into a single score that places the individual on a truthful–deceptive continuum. It then uses distributions of discriminant scores for known truthful and known deceptive individuals and Bayesian statistics to calculate the probability of deception for the test.

Numerous studies have demonstrated that the CPS algorithm provides highly accurate decisions that are at least as accurate as decisions rendered by expert examiners who used seven-point numerical scoring (Kircher and

Raskin, 2002). When the CPS algorithm was compared with PolyScore, AXCON, Chart Analysis, and Identifi algorithms (Dollins *et al.*, 2000), CPS produced the highest overall accuracy (91%) and was the only algorithm that did not produce a high number of false-positive errors (10% for CPS versus 21–27% for the other methods).

OSS-1

The OSS (Objective Scoring System)-1 was developed to improve the accuracy and agreement among scorers who use the seven-point numerical scoring method (Krapohl and McManus, 1999). They used data from three sets of confirmed, single-issue criminal cases. Using a method similar to calculations that are displayed in the CPS software, they converted the measurements of the three Kircher features to ratio values. They then divided the reactions to RQs by the reactions to the surrounding CQs (R5 compared with the stronger of C4 and C6) or adjacent CQs (R7 compared with C6 and R10 compared with C9). The range of ratios for each physiological measure were divided into seven equal portions of ratios for the entire dataset. Numerical scores on a seven-point scale were assigned to the values in each of the seven portions, with the smallest ratios assigned +3 (CQ strongest) and the largest –3 (RQ strongest). The scores for the electrodermal channel were doubled, and decisions were made with the same –6 and +6 cutoffs used by numerical scorers. The results indicated the OSS performed as well as experienced examiners who used the seven-point numerical system.

The accuracy of the OSS-1 was also evaluated on the mixed-issue MGQT. However, this was the old Reid format (Reid and Inbau, 1977) that has four RQs and only two CQs that are placed in positions that may minimize their effectiveness. The results of this study were poorer than for the earlier study that evaluated the OSS-1 with single-issue tests.

OSS-2

The OSS was subsequently revised to be applicable to more test formats. The OSS-2 compares each RQ to only the preceding CQ instead of allowing it to use the stronger surrounding CQs (Krapohl, 2002). When applied to the dataset from the original study (Krapohl and McManus, 1999), the results showed slightly higher accuracies for OSS-2. The authors concluded that the OSS-2 can be used with more versions of single-issue tests than the original OSS-1, which it replaced. A guide for performing the OSS-1 is found in Dutton (2000), which recommends decision cutoffs of +8 and –8. The OSS-2 has been incorporated as an option in most computerized polygraph systems.

OSS-3

Nelson *et al.* (2008) reported results using a major modification of OSS-2 known as OSS-3. This was designed to expand the capability to include scoring of multiple-issue and multiple-facet test formats with two to four RQs and three to five charts. As previous studies showed the electrodermal measures to be more diagnostic than relative blood pressure and respiration (e.g., Kircher *et al.*, 2005; Kircher and Raskin, 1978; Raskin *et al.*, 1988), they used component weightings of 0.50 for electrodermal, 0.33 for blood pressure, and 0.17 for respiration. In addition, they employed bootstrapping methods to derive estimates of the parameters of distributions of transformed scores. From these distributions, probabilities of truthfulness were computed for overall test outcomes and for each RQ in tests where the subject could have answered one or more RQs truthfully and one or more deceptively. They also incorporated two-stage rules with Bonferroni corrections to reduce false-positive errors.

Based on their results in applying OSS-3 to several datasets, Nelson *et al.* (2008, p. 208) concluded:

> OSS-3 is capable of meeting or exceeding the capability of previous OSS versions and many human scorers along several dimensions, including sensitivity to deception, specificity to truthfulness, reduced false-negative and false-positive results, and reduced inconclusive results for deceptive cases. The average of human scorers did not outperform OSS-3 on any dimension.

COMPARISON OF SCORING METHODS

To compare the various methods for determining test outcomes, we extracted amplitude of the electrodermal reaction, rise in cardiograph baseline, and RLL from polygraph examinations conducted in laboratory and field settings. The laboratory data consisted of single-issue probable-lie comparison tests and the field data consisted of multiple-issue Law Enforcement Pre-Employment Tests (LEPETs). Computer programs were developed to apply the rules of the various scoring methods to those common sets of measurements and to generate decisions. As none of the polygraph data in our analysis had been used to develop any of the scoring methods, the present study provides unbiased assessments of the relative effectiveness of the various scoring methods.

Procedures

Datasets

Decision outcomes were generated for each of two datasets. One dataset consisted of 84 male and female subjects in a previous mock-crime experiment conducted in our laboratory at the University of Utah using standard psychophysiological instrumentation and recording techniques (Bell *et al.*, 2008). Forty-two subjects were guilty of committing a mock theft of $20 from a secretary's purse and 42 subjects were innocent of the crime. All subjects were paid $30 for their participation and were promised an additional $50 bonus if they could pass the polygraph examination. Subjects were given a preliminary demonstration test with either positive or neutral feedback about the outcome of the demonstration test prior to the first presentation of the test questions. The demonstration test was followed by a single-issue PLT. The question series included neutral questions at positions 3, 6, and 9, probable-lie questions at positions 4, 7, and 10, and RQs at positions 5, 8, and 11. The set of questions was presented five times (charts) with a brief break between repetitions. Neutral questions and CQs were rotated over repeated presentations of the question sequence such that each RQ was preceded by each neutral and each CQ at least once.

The second dataset consisted of two series of questions for each of 58 individuals who applied for positions with a federal law enforcement agency. The polygraph data had been collected with Lafayette computerized polygraph systems. Each prospective employee had been given a counterintelligence LEPET followed several hours later by a suitability LEPET. The counterintelligence series covered espionage, sabotage, and terrorism or subversive activity. The suitability series covered undisclosed serious crimes, drug use, and falsifying information on the application form. Each series contained at least three or four repetitions of the test questions and the order of questions was varied over charts. Probable-lie questions and RQs were alternated in the sequence, although they were not always next to each other.

In the LEPET examinations, none of the examinees made any admissions concerning the RQs on the counterintelligence test and all examinees confessed that they had been deceptive to one or more of the RQs on the suitability test. We inferred that the subjects were truthful on the counterintelligence series because the base rate of deception on those issues is very low and subjects had little or no access to classified material or government equipment. In addition, each subject had confessed to at least one of the relevant issues on the suitability test. Confessions commonly are obtained when the polygraph examiner observes strong reactions to RQs and asks the subject about those reactions after the test. If the subject reacted when deceptive to RQs on the suitability series, then it is likely that the same individual would have reacted as strongly, if not more strongly, if he/she was deceptive to questions concerning espionage or sabotage. Deception would be expected to produce stronger reactions on the counterintelligence series because it was conducted first, the subject was less habituated, and the consequences of failing the counterintelligence series were more serious than those associated with failing the suitability issues.

Confessions provided commonly accepted confirmatory evidence of deception to one or more of the questions in the suitability series (see above). However, the particular questions to which the subject was deceptive were not documented in the data files provided to us. Since it was not possible to associate a deceptive polygraph outcome with a particular question to which the subject admitted guilt, the scoring method may have classified the subject as deceptive for the wrong reason (Barland *et al.*, 1989; Podlesny and Truslow, 1993; Raskin *et al.*, 1988). Nevertheless, if the subject was deceptive to any RQ on the suitability series, the agency would have reason to reject the person's application for employment. The scoring method would have utility and would serve its purpose, although the evidence for its diagnostic validity would be weaker than that obtained for the mock-crime experiment, where absolute knowledge of ground truth was available for every RQ and every subject.

Data Quantification

The laboratory and field data were stored in a common text format known as DACA ASCII (A. B. Dollins, personal communication, 31 August 2009). Each chart was stored in its own DACA ASCII file. The file contained continuous 60-Hz recordings of each recorded channel of physiological activity, and event marks to indicate the onset and offset of each test question and the moment the subject answered each question. We extracted features from the DACA ASCII recordings with a general-purpose computer program for psychophysiological research entitled CPSLAB, which was developed in our laboratory at the University of Utah over a period of 30 years. CPSLAB was programmed to extract the following three types of measurements from reactions to each RQ and each CQ on the test:

(1) *Peak amplitude of the electrodermal response.* An electrodermal response curve was defined by the 60-Hz samples for a 20-second segment that began at question onset. Within that interval, low points in the response curve were identified as changes from negative or zero slope to positive slope and high points in the response curve were identified as changes from positive slope to zero or negative slope. The difference between each low point and every succeeding high point was computed. Peak amplitude was defined as the greatest such difference.

(2) *Peak amplitude of the rise in the diastolic points of the cardiograph.* A 60-Hz diastolic response curve was defined by linear interpolation between adjacent diastolic points of the cardiograph from question onset for a period of 20 seconds. Within that interval, the same procedures used to measure peak amplitude of the electrodermal response were used to measure the peak amplitude of the rise in diastolic points of the cardiograph.

(3) *RLL.* Simple line length was the sum of absolute differences between adjacent 60-Hz samples of respiration starting at question onset for a period of ten seconds. Line length was measured separately for thoracic and abdominal respiration channels, and the two values were averaged. We also measured RLL for each respiration cycle and computed the cycle-weighted average line length for ten seconds following question onset (Matsuda and Ogawa, 2011). The latter approach was slightly less diagnostic of deceptive status than simple line length in both datasets and was abandoned in favor of simple line length.

Scoring Systems

The polygraph scoring methods for the present investigation included the CPS algorithm (Kircher and Raskin, 1988), OSS-2 (Krapohl, 2002), OSS-3 (Nelson *et al.*, 2008), and the ESS (Nelson *et al.*, 2008). We did not include OSS-1 because it had been replaced by OSS-2. Generally, CPS and OSS scoring systems use the features described above as measures of physiological arousal. As these features are tedious to obtain by hand, but are quickly and precisely measured by a computer, CPS and OSS analyses are typically automated. In contrast, the ESS was designed as a manual scoring alternative to traditional seven-point numerical scoring and does not require the use of a computer. To avoid measurements of RLL, ESS scores for respiration are based on visual assessments of reductions in respiration amplitude, slowing of respiration, and temporary increase in respiration baseline (Nelson *et al.*, 2011). In the present study, we used line length to compute ESS scores for respiration for two reasons. As all scoring systems were provided the same set of measurements, we could attribute differences in outcomes among the scoring systems to the efficiency with which they used those data to make accurate decisions, rather than their use of different physiological features. In addition, research indicates that RLL is more diagnostic of deception than are measures of decreases in respiration amplitude and rate and increases in respiration baseline, whether those measures are analyzed individually or in combination (Kircher and Raskin, 2002).

Data Transformations

The measurements of peak amplitude and line length obtained for CPS were transformed to z-scores within subjects. For the single-issue examinations, the mean z-score for RQ was compared with the mean z-score for CQ (Kircher and Raskin, 2002). For the multiple-issue examinations, CPS calculated the mean z-score for electrodermal, cardiograph, and respiration channels for each RQ individually; it then compared the mean for each RQ to the mean of all CQ combined.

The OSS and ESS decision models computed RQ/CQ ratios. Since the raw measurements of peak amplitude and line length (cumulative vertical excursion) were ratio scaled, there was no need to transform the data. Any transformation other than simple multiplication of the measurements by a positive constant would arbitrarily alter the ratios and could affect decision outcomes.

The ESS uses the bigger-is-better rule for manual scoring of polygraph charts. Polygraph interpreters assign a score of +1 or −1 if there is any "visually perceptible" difference between reactions to RQs and CQs. To automate the ESS for the present study, a perceptible difference was operationally defined as a difference between reactions to the RQ and CQ of at least 10% (Handler *et al.*, 2010). Consistent with the ESS, each of the −1, 0, and +1 scores for peak amplitude of the electrodermal response was multiplied by two to give twice as much weight to the electrodermal channel than the cardiograph or respiration channels.

Number of Charts

For all scoring methods, the first three charts were initially evaluated. If the test was inconclusive after three charts and additional charts were available, they were added to the first three charts in an attempt to resolve the inconclusive outcome. The test was considered inconclusive if it was not classified as truthful or deceptive based on all the available charts.

For the single-issue tests obtained in the laboratory, five charts of data were available for every subject. If the results were inconclusive after three charts, the outcome was based on all five charts. For the multiple-issue field tests, a fourth chart was available for 33 of 116 series (28%) and it was added to determine the outcome.

Single-Issue Decision Rules

For single-issue CQTs, all the scoring methods have established cutoffs for classification. For CPS, probabilities of truthfulness greater than or equal to 0.70 were classified as truthful, probabilities less than or equal to 0.30 were classified as deceptive, and probabilities between 0.30 and 0.70 were inconclusive. For OSS-2, the subject was classified as truthful if the total OSS score was greater than or equal to +8, deceptive if the total was less than or equal to −8, and inconclusive if the total was between the two cutoffs. OSS-3 computed the probability of truthfulness and reported the grand mean result for all RQs combined as significant response (SR), no significant response (NSR), or no decision (NO) (i.e., deceptive, truthful, and inconclusive, respectively).

The ESS cutoffs for single-issue tests were –4 and +2. If the grand total ESS score was less than or equal to –4, the subject was considered deceptive, a total score greater than or equal to +2 was considered truthful, and a score between the –4 and +2 cutoffs was inconclusive.

Two-Stage Rule for Multiple-Issue Tests

The CPS and OSS-2 were developed to provide decisions for single-issue examinations, whereas the OSS-3 and the ESS had established rules for making decisions in both single-issue and multiple-issue tests. To facilitate comparisons of the various scoring methods, we developed new, experimental rules to make decisions in multiple-issue tests for the CPS and OSS-2. For those scoring methods, the new rules followed the two-stage logic introduced by Senter and Dollins (2008).

For CPS, the two-stage rule used the probability of truthfulness for all RQs combined and the probability for each RQ. If the analysis of all RQs combined yielded a probability of truthfulness that exceeded or was equal to 0.70, the subject was classified as truthful. If the analysis of all RQs combined yielded a probability of truthfulness that was less than or equal to 0.30, the subjects was classified as deceptive. If the probability of truthfulness for all RQs combined was between 0.30 and 0.70, the result in the first stage was inconclusive. In the second stage, the probability of truthfulness was evaluated for each RQ individually. If the probability for any individual RQ was less than 0.30, the subject was classified as deceptive. Otherwise, the outcome was inconclusive.

For OSS-2, the measured reaction to an RQ question was divided by the reaction to the preceding CQ. The ratio was compared with published cutoffs and assigned an integer value that ranged from –6 to +6 for the electrodermal channel and from –3 to +3 for the cardiograph and respiration channels. The OSS scores were summed over channels and RQs to obtain a total score. If the total was +8 or greater, the subject was classified as truthful, if the total was less than or equal to –8, the subject was classified as deceptive, and if the total was between the ±8 cutoffs, the OSS scores for each RQ were examined individually. If the sum for any RQ was –4 or less, the subject was considered deceptive, otherwise the test was inconclusive.

For the OSS-3, decision outcomes were obtained from an Excel program entitled OSS-3 developed by Nelson. Measurements extracted from electrodermal, cardiograph, and thoracic and abdominal respiration recordings were copied into spreadsheets and processed automatically by the OSS-3 software. The OSS-3 Excel program indicated if the subject was deceptive to any one or more of the RQs or truthful to all RQs. If neither occurred, the result was inconclusive.

For the ESS, we used the cutoffs for multiple-issue examinations described by Nelson *et al.* (2011). If the subtotal ESS score for any RQ was –3 or less, then the subject was classified as deceptive; if the subtotals for all RQs were greater than or equal to +1, then the subject was classified as truthful. Any other outcome was considered inconclusive.

CQs

The CQs selected as the basis for comparison with the RQs varied across scoring methods. The CPS and OSS-3 used the mean response to all CQs (Kircher and Raskin, 2002; Nelson *et al.*, 2008); the OSS-2 used the preceding adjacent CQ. To determine whether the accuracy of decision outcomes for the ESS depended on the choice of the CQ, we obtained one set of decision outcomes using the stronger of surrounding CQs and another set of outcomes using the preceding CQs.

Results

Single-Issue Examinations

The decision outcomes for the 84 subjects in the single-issue laboratory experiment are presented in Table 3.3 for each of the scoring methods. For each method, the grand total for all RQs combined was compared with that method's standard cutoffs for single-issue tests. Table 3.3 presents the frequency of

TABLE 3.3 Decision Outcomes from Scoring Methods for Single-Issue Tests in a Laboratory Experiment ($n = 84$)

Scoring method[a]	CQ	Deceptive status	Correct	Wrong	Inconclusive	Correct decisions (%)	Mean % correct decisions	Detection efficiency
CPS	Mean	Deceptive	39	3	0	92.9	93.9	0.868[bc]
		Truthful	38	2	2	95.0		
OSS-2	Preceding	Deceptive	38	3	1	92.7	93.9	0.875[b]
		Truthful	40	2	0	95.2		
OSS-3	Mean	Deceptive	35	5	2	87.5	93.8	0.795[cd]
		Truthful	34	0	8	100.0		
ESS	Surrounding	Deceptive	25	14	3	64.1	82.1	0.693
		Truthful	42	0	0	100.0		
ESS	Preceding	Deceptive	39	3	0	92.9	92.8	0.850[bcd]
		Truthful	38	3	1	92.7		
Mean			36.7	3.5	1.7	91.3	91.3	0.816

[a] See text for abbreviations.
[bcd] Correlations with the same superscript do not differ from each other at $p < 0.01$ (two-tailed).

test outcomes separately for deceptive ($n = 42$) and truthful subjects ($n = 42$). The "Correct decisions (%)" column shows the percent correct decisions for each group, excluding inconclusive outcomes and the next column shows the mean percent correct decisions. The last column shows the correlation between deceptive status (coded –1 for deceptive subjects and +1 for truthful subjects) and decision outcome (coded –1 for deceptive, 0 for inconclusive, and +1 for truthful). The correlation provides a single summary index of diagnostic validity for a scoring system (Kircher *et al.*, 1988). Table 3.3 also indicates whether RQs were compared with the mean of all CQs, the stronger of surrounding CQs, or the preceding CQ.

Overall, 87.4% of the 84 cases were classified correctly, 8.3% were misclassified, and 4.0% were inconclusive. Correct decisions were higher on truthful subjects (90.9%) than deceptive subjects (83.9%). Excluding inconclusive outcomes, 91.3% of the decisions by all scoring methods combined were correct. Excluding inconclusives, use of the stronger surrounding CQs yielded more correct classifications of truthful subjects (100%) than deceptive subjects (64.1%). However, when the reactions to RQs were compared with the preceding CQs, there was little difference between truthful and deceptive subjects in the percentage of correct decisions or inconclusives. For single-issue tests, use of the surrounding CQs by ESS ($r = 0.69$) was less efficient than use of the preceding CQ by OSS-2 [$r = 0.88, t(81) = 4.46, p < 0.01$] or ESS-preceding [$r = 0.85, t(81) = 3.47, p < 0.01$]. There was little difference in mean accuracy of decisions among methods that used either the preceding CQ (93.3%) or the mean CQ (93.8%).

The OSS-2 achieved the highest mean accuracy and an optimal balance of false-positive and false-negative errors in these laboratory, single-issue tests. However, the mean accuracy achieved by CPS, OSS-2, OSS-3, and ESS with preceding CQ methods differed by less than 1.5%, and detection efficiency statistics for CPS, OSS-2, and ESS-preceding did not differ significantly from one another. OSS-2 had significantly higher detection efficiency than OSS-3 [$t(81) = 3.21, p < 0.01$] and ESS-surrounding [$t(81) = 4.46, p < 0.01$]. Area under the receiver operating characteristic (ROC) curve (AUC) (maximum 1.0) was computed as a summary measure of diagnostic accuracy for all scoring methods; it exceeded 0.95 for all scoring systems in Table 3.3.

Multiple-Issue Examinations

Table 3.4 presents the results for the various scoring methods applied to two LEPET examinations for each of 58 prospective employees of a federal law enforcement agency.

On average, 86.2% of the 116 LEPET series were classified correctly, 7.8% were misclassified, and 6.0% were inconclusive. Excluding inconclusive outcomes, 91.7% of the decisions were correct. On average, 90% of deceptive series (suitability) and 82.4% of truthful series (counterintelligence) were classified correctly.

As with the single-issue tests, the OSS-2 yielded the highest overall accuracy, low rates of inconclusive outcomes, and balanced rates of false-positive and false-negative errors. In the LEPET dataset, the OSS-2 significantly

TABLE 3.4 Decision Outcomes from Scoring Methods for Multiple-Issue Tests in a Pre-Employment Screening Study (n = 58)

Scoring method[a]	CQ	Deceptive status	Correct	Wrong	Inconclusive	Correct decisions (%)	Mean % correct decisions	Detection efficiency
CPS	Mean	Deceptive	44	8	6	84.6	91.4	0.828[b]
		Truthful	57	1	0	98.3		
OSS-2	Preceding	Deceptive	54	3	1	94.7	95.6	0.909
		Truthful	56	2	0	96.6		
OSS-3	Mean	Deceptive	55	2	1	96.5	92.6	0.837[bc]
		Truthful	47	6	5	88.7		
ESS	Surrounding	Deceptive	50	3	5	94.3	94.3	0.792[bcd]
		Truthful	49	3	6	94.2		
ESS	Preceding	Deceptive	58	0	0	100.0	81.9	0.705[bd]
		Truthful	30	17	11	63.8		
Mean			50.0	4.5	3.5	91.7	91.7	0.814

[a] See text for abbreviations.
[bcd] Correlations with the same superscript do not differ from each other at p < 0.01 (two-tailed).

TABLE 3.5 Mean (Standard Deviation) and Effect Size of Standardized Measurements for Single-Issue and Multiple-Issue Tests

		Single-issue tests (n = 84)			Multiple-issue tests (n = 58)		
Measurement	Deceptive status	RQ	CQ	Partial η^{2a}	RQ	CQ	Partial η^{2a}
Electrodermal	Deceptive	0.360 (0.236)	−0.360 (0.236)	0.579	0.295 (0.224)	−0.221 (0.168)	0.773
	Truthful	−0.199 (0.247)	0.199 (0.247)		−0.305 (0.248)	0.241 (0.200)	
Cardiograph	Deceptive	0.072 (0.273)	−0.072 (0.273)	0.195	0.142 (0.241)	−0.106 (0.180)	0.435
	Truthful	−0.200 (0.286)	0.200 (0.286)		−0.164 (0.269)	0.130 (0.212)	
Respiration	Deceptive	−0.181 (0.216)	0.181 (0.216)	0.217	−0.114 (0.183)	0.085 (0.137)	0.408
	Truthful	0.079 (0.282)	−0.079 (0.282)		0.140 (0.214)	−0.110 (0.168)	

^{a}Partial η^2 are reported for the Deceptive Status × Question Type interaction effect. All interaction effects were statistically significant, p < 0.05.

outperformed all other scoring methods. At the other extreme, ESS-preceding yielded 17 false-positive errors (29.3%) and 11 inconclusive outcomes (18.9%). The detection efficiency was significantly lower for ESS-preceding ($r = 0.705$) than for the OSS-2 [$r = 0.909$, $t(55) = 3.59$, $p < 0.01$] or the OSS-3 [$r = 0.837$, $t(55) = 2.82$, $p < 0.01$]. Use of the stronger surrounding CQs with the ESS was effective for both truthful and deceptive series, and yielded balanced error and inconclusive rates and highly accurate decisions for deceptive (94.3%) and truthful series (94.2%). Use of the preceding CQ was significantly more effective for the OSS-2 than the ESS. AUC estimates again exceeded 0.95 for all of the scoring methods, despite the high false-positive rate for the ESS-preceding.

Excluding inconclusive outcomes, the mean percent correct decisions across the single-issue and multiple-issue datasets were 94.8% for OSS-2, 93.2% for OSS-3, 92.7% for CPS, 87.3% for ESS-surrounding, and 87.3% for ESS-preceding.

The CPS algorithm was developed on laboratory, single-issue tests and cross-validated on single-issue criminal tests (Kircher and Raskin, 2002). This study represents the first time that CPS was used to make decisions on mixed-issue LEPET tests and a different discriminant function may be better suited for such tests. To evaluate this possibility, we developed a discriminant function for the LEPET data and tested it with a jackknife procedure (Lachenbruch and Mickey, 1968). The results showed that 99% of decisions were correct. However, the jackknife procedure is not a substitute for cross-validation with an independent set of data and these results should be viewed only as suggesting that such cross-validation may produce even better results than those obtained with the existing CPS algorithm used in this study.

Analysis of variance (ANOVA) was used to compare physiological reactions to RQs and CQs, and estimate effect sizes for electrodermal, cardiograph, and respiration measures. For each physiological measure, raw measurements were transformed to z-scores within subjects, and for each examination we computed a mean reaction to all available RQs and a mean reaction to all available CQs. Standardized measures of RLL were averaged for thoracic and abdominal channels to obtain a single mean line length for RQs and another mean line length for CQs for each examination.

ANOVAs were conducted separately with the mean RQ and mean CQ for each physiological measure and each test type (single-issue and multiple-issue). Each ANOVA had two factors: "Question Type" with two levels (RQ and CQ) and "Deceptive Status" with two levels (truthful and deceptive). Single-issue and multiple-issue examinations were analyzed separately because Deceptive Status was a between-group factor in the single-issue examinations and a within-subject factor in the multiple-issue examinations.

Means, standard deviations, and effect size (partial η^2) for the Deceptive Status × Question Type interaction are presented in Table 3.5. The means for RQs and CQs for the single-issue test have the same values but opposite signs because the original measurements had been transformed to z-scores and z-scores have a mean of zero. Negative z-scores are below the mean and positive z-scores are above the mean. Since each subject had a mean z-score of zero across question types, the main effect of Deceptive Status was precisely zero in each of these analyses.

In the single-issue tests, the electrodermal reactions of deceptive subjects to RQs were above the mean ($M = 0.36$) and their reactions to CQs were below the mean ($M = -0.36$). In contrast, truthful subjects reacted more strongly to CQs ($M = 0.20$) than to RQs ($M = -0.20$). As expected, deceptive subjects reacted more strongly to RQs, whereas truthful subjects reacted more strongly to CQs.

A partial $\eta^2 = 0.58$ was obtained for the electrodermal peak amplitude in the single-issue dataset. Partial η^2 is a measure of effect size that varies from 0 to 1 and indicates the proportion of variance in deceptive status that is explained by the physiological measure. Conceptually, it is a measure of the diagnostic validity of the measure for discriminating between truthfulness and deception. A partial $\eta^2 > 0.50$ is very large and rare in psychological research. The effects of the Deceptive Status × Question Type interaction were statistically significant for all of the physiological measures in Table 3.5.

Discussion

Scoring Systems

There was little difference in decision accuracy among the CPS, OSS-2, and OSS-3 scoring systems. However, a similar level of accuracy for the ESS depended on the choice of CQs for single-issue and multiple-issue tests. This generally high level of accuracy is not surprising since all scoring methods derived their decisions from a common set of physiological features; it appears that the features for the decision algorithms were well chosen. These findings support recommendations made in earlier reports (Kircher and Raskin, 1988, 2002).

The OSS-2 compared the RQ to the preceding CQ for both types of tests and it had the highest mean accuracy. The mean accuracy of decisions was 93.9% in the single-issue dataset and 95.6% in the multiple-issue dataset, with a nearly perfect balance of false-positive and false-negative errors. It is noteworthy that the OSS-2 achieved its highest decision accuracy on the multiple-issue dataset, even though it was not designed for use in multiple-issue examinations. By comparison, the OSS-3 produced decisions that were about 13% more accurate on truthful than deceptive subjects in the single-issue tests and about 8% more accurate on the deceptive than the truthful series in the multiple-issue tests. A scoring system with consistent performance across test protocols is preferable to a system with more false-positive errors for one protocol and more false-negative errors in another.

The AUC exceeded 0.95 across all scoring methods and settings, but it did not reflect important differences in error rates among the methods. High values for the AUC indicated that the scores used to classify cases as truthful or deceptive contained considerable diagnostic information, but the AUC was insensitive to suboptimal specification of decision cutoffs. For example, in the single-issue dataset, the AUC values for the ESS were 0.95 with the stronger surrounding CQs and 0.97 with the preceding CQ. However, 33.5% of deceptive subjects were incorrectly classified when the ESS used the stronger surrounding CQs, whereas only 7.1% were incorrectly classified when the ESS used the preceding CQ. These results indicate that for single-issue tests, if the stronger CQ was selected the ESS total contained considerable diagnostic information, but the cutoffs were wrong. The cut-offs should be shifted in the positive direction to reduce the risk of false-negative errors.

The correlation between decision outcomes and deceptive status was obtained as a summary measure of detection efficiency for each scoring method. Indices of detection efficiency were more reflective of the relationship between decision outcomes and deceptive status than the AUC. A Hotelling–Williams t-ratio (Bobko, 1995) was computed to test the difference between two correlations that shared a common variable (i.e., deceptive status). For each dataset, $\alpha = 0.01$ was used to reduce the risk of compounding Type 1 errors from the multiple comparisons. These tests were appropriate for the single-issue dataset because each subject provided a single polygraph examination. In the multiple-issue dataset, each subject provided two polygraph tests (one suitability series and one counterintelligence series). Since the Hotelling–Williams test may have been inappropriate for those potentially dependent observations, we conducted conservative tests with sample size and degrees of freedom based on the number of subjects ($n = 58$) rather than the number of series ($n = 116$).

For multiple-issue tests, the ESS performed better with the stronger surrounding CQ. Despite the potentially biasing effect of choosing the stronger CQ, the ESS was slightly more accurate on the deceptive than truthful series. Apparently, any bias introduced by selecting the stronger CQ was offset by the decision rule that classified the subject as deceptive if the subtotal for any RQ was less than or equal to –4. In contrast, use of the preceding CQ was relatively ineffective because the decision rule allowed four possible opportunities for the subject to fail the test and only one way for the subject to pass. This risk appears to have been offset by comparing the RQ to the stronger CQ.

The OSS-2 compared each RQ to the preceding CQ and its decisions were almost 97% correct on truthful LEPET series. In contrast to the ESS, the two-stage rule with the OSS-2 considered the subtotals for an individual RQ only when the total score failed to reach a ±8 cutoff. For the truthful series, only one result was inconclusive based on the total score and that individual was misclassified because one RQ subtotal was less than the –4 cutoff. Thus, the two-stage rule for the OSS-2 protected all but one of the truthful subjects from a second-stage decision rule that provided ample opportunity to fail the test. Although eight of the deceptive LEPET subjects were inconclusive based on the OSS-2 total score, seven of them failed the test in the second stage.

The OSS-2 algorithm produced the highest, most consistent, and balanced accuracies for deceptive and truthful subjects for single-issue and multiple-issue test protocols. Although the other three methods produced high accuracies for some combinations of test protocol and choice of CQ, they were substantially lower with other combinations. In the present study, the OSS-2 produced uniformly high accuracy without the need to vary the choice of CQ or computer algorithm for single- or multiple-issue test protocols.

Effect Size

The effect sizes for electrodermal, cardiograph, and respiration features in the single-issue dataset were consistent with prior laboratory research on the probable-lie technique (Raskin and Honts, 2002). In the field of psychology, effect sizes of the magnitude observed in the present study are unusual but are needed to achieve high levels of decision accuracy. The observed effect sizes also indicate the power of the three selected physiological components to distinguish between the truthful and deceptive groups. All scoring methods weighed the electrodermal measures more heavily than the cardiograph and respiration for good reason. The effect of deception was substantially greater on the amplitude of the electrodermal response than the rise in the cardiograph baseline or RLL.

A general-purpose computer program was used to extract the various physiological measurements for the present study. The program was not designed to implement certain criteria that may be included in software offered by computerized polygraph manufacturers for the express purpose of processing polygraph charts. For example, polygraph scoring rules may require that the onset of a physiological response begin within a limited number of seconds relative to question onset or the subject's verbal answer, and the quality and stability of the recordings must be considered (e.g., Nelson *et al.*, 2011). Considering the high levels of decision accuracy achieved with the measurements made by this program, it is doubtful that efforts to incorporate such rules would have had much effect on the decision outcomes. However, it is an open question if computer programs designed specifically to process polygraph charts would improve on these outcomes.

The estimates of effect size from the ANOVA were based on the mean reaction to all RQs combined. Theoretically, the reliability of means based on many observations is greater than the reliability of means based on fewer observations. Since we conducted ANOVA with the grand mean of RQs, the reliability of reactions to an individual RQ had little effect on the estimates of effect size. However, for multiple-issue tests, the reliability of measurement may play a more or less significant role in the outcome of the test depending on the scoring method. It plays a significant role in the ESS, which classifies the subject as deceptive if the total for any RQ is −4 or less. Thus, the subject passes or fails the test based on subtotals, each of which depends on only three or four repetitions of an RQ. In the present study, reliability was of less concern with the two-stage decision rules developed for the CPS and OSS-2, where reactions to an individual RQ were considered only if the outcome was inconclusive based on the total for all RQs.

The effect sizes for the physiological components were larger for the multiple-issue test than for the single-issue test and larger than any we have seen in all of our research on polygraph techniques. Although the field context is more compelling than a laboratory mock-crime experiment and may pro-duce larger effects, we expected the effect sizes in the multiple-issue dataset to be smaller than those in the single-issue dataset. Subjects made admissions to one or more RQs following the suitability series, but knowledge of the spe-cific issue(s) to which the subject admitted guilt was unavailable. To estimate effect sizes, we pooled reactions to all RQs on the test, some of which were probably answered truthfully and evoked relatively small reactions. Since we mixed reactions to questions answered deceptively with questions answered truthfully, we expected the differences between RQs and CQs for the decep-tive series to be attenuated, and that should have resulted in conservative estimates of effect size.

The unusually large effects obtained for the multiple-issue dataset were due in part to the use of a repeated-measures design. Typically, deceptive status is a between-groups factor, but in the multiple-issue dataset, it was a repeated measure with each subject truthful on one LEPET series and deceptive on the other. Error terms in repeated-measures designs usually are smaller than the error terms in between-group designs, and error is inversely related to estimates of effect size. For example, treating deceptive status as a between-groups factor in the multiple-issue dataset reduced the effect size for peak amplitude of the electrodermal response from 0.77 to 0.62. Nevertheless, an effect size of 0.62 for a single physiological measure is also uncharacteristically large for polygraph data.

Validity of Results

Iacono and Lykken (2005) raised the concept of criterion bias in a critique of field validity studies that use confessions to establish ground truth of deception. They argued that confessions commonly are obtained after a polygraph examiner scores the charts, decides the subject is deceptive, and interrogates. Therefore, the resulting sample of deceptive cases would be composed only of subjects who failed the test, were interrogated, and confessed. Thus, the analysis of the physiological data for that select sample of deceptive cases would erroneously indicate that the test is perfect or nearly perfect in identifying the guilty. In addition, guilty subjects who defeated the test were not interrogated, did not confess, and were not included in the sample of deceptive cases. Therefore, the criterion (guilt status) is not independent of the polygraph data and is contaminated.

Although the above reasoning has been contradicted logically (Honts *et al.*, 2005) and empirically (Honts, 1996; Krapohl *et al.*, 2002) for confession studies of the polygraph in criminal investigation, most of the counterarguments do not apply for the pre-employment screening tests. Criterion bias might be a plausible explanation for the exceptionally large effects obtained in the present multiple-issue dataset. Although estimating the validity of the LEPET from this dataset may be problematic, it provided a good opportunity to assess the relative effectiveness of the various scoring methods.

Criterion bias was not present in the single-issue dataset because subjects were randomly assigned to guilty and innocent treatment conditions before any polygraph data were collected. The observed accuracy rates for the CPS, OSS-2, and OSS-3 provided unbiased estimates of the validity of these automated scoring systems for single-issue tests.

The validity of the ESS when performed by human interpreters may be lower than indicated by the present study. Instead of the visual scoring of polygraph recordings practiced by field interpreters, the computer algorithm made precise measurements of the physiological responses and applied fixed cutoffs in exactly the same manner for every case. A scoring system that relies on human judgment introduces random error and possible biases into the decision process, which reduce test accuracy (Kircher and Raskin, 2002). Also, the accuracy rates reported here for the ESS may be higher than its field application because the computer-calculated line length (cumulative vertical excursion) was the measure of respiration suppression rather than human judgments based on visual estimates of reduced respiration amplitude and rate and temporary increases in respiration baseline. Existing research indicates that line length is more diagnostic than any of the ESS indicators of respiration suppression, even if those indicators are optimally combined to distinguish between truthful and deceptive individuals (Kircher and Raskin, 2002). A recent study with 32 senior federal polygraph interpreters revealed that computer measures of RLL outperformed every human interpreter's numerical evaluations of respiration by a significant margin (Kircher *et al.*, 2012).

The single-issue tests were conducted in a laboratory mock-crime experiment (Bell *et al.*, 2008). Questions may be raised about the generalizability of findings from laboratory experiments to field settings (National Research Council, 2003; Podlesny and Raskin, 1977; Pollina *et al.*, 2004). Pollina *et al.* (2004) found that the effects of deception were greater in the field than in a laboratory mock-crime experiment. These findings are consistent with the findings of a meta-analysis of mock-crime experiments that the more closely the laboratory procedures reproduced the field context, the larger the effects on physiological measures (Kircher *et al.*, 1988).

Pollina *et al.* (2004) also found that similar accuracy rates were obtained in the laboratory and field cases. However, they obtained significant differences in the effects of deception on electrodermal, cardiovascular, and respiration measures. Their findings do not agree with another study that compared physiological response profiles generated in laboratory and field settings (Kircher *et al.*, 1994; Raskin *et al.*, 1989). They observed no difference between laboratory and field settings in the diagnostic validity of any of the physiological measures. Moreover, they found no difference in the covariance structure of the physiological measures obtained in the two settings. Together, these findings suggest that statistical classifiers based on laboratory data in properly designed mock-crime experiments should work well on field data because the multivariate response profiles generated in the laboratory adequately reproduce the effects observed in the field. They also suggest that mock-crime experiments can provide valuable information about the efficacy of various field polygraph techniques. Members of the American Psychology-Law Society and the Society for Psychophysiological Research agree. The majority of survey respondents from both organizations said that decision and policy makers should give weight to the result of well-conducted laboratory studies (Honts *et al.*, 2002). However, because the two studies that compared polygraph data from laboratory and field settings produced different results, any decision model or recommendation based on laboratory data should be reevaluated with a representative sample of confirmed field cases (Podlesny and Raskin, 1977). This area needs more research.

The multiple-issue dataset were obtained from Lafayette computerized polygraph systems. We chose these data for our analyses because plots of mean electrodermal reactions to RQs and CQs suggested that the electrodermal signals had not been altered in any significant way by digital or hardware filters. Commercial computerized systems often include an option to filter the electrodermal data with a high-pass filter (automatic mode). High-pass filters eliminate baseline changes that commonly accompany electrodermal signals recorded with dry metal plates because these baseline changes can be dramatic compared with the phasic reactions to test questions. As the filter passes the relatively fast increases in the electrodermal reactions to test questions and removes slower changes characteristic of so-called plunging baselines, the filtered signal is flat and displays the phasic reactions more clearly. Many of the high-pass filters selectively attenuate the electrodermal responses to CQs because responses to CQs tend to rise more slowly to their peak than do responses to RQs, which are more abrupt (Honts, 1986; Raskin *et al.*, 1978). If human or computer measurements are taken from the high-pass filtered signal, the RQ/CQ ratios will be biased against the truthful individual. We recommend that polygraph examiners do not use the automatic mode that implements the high-pass filter. To prevent plunging baselines, polygraph examiners should use constant voltage circuits (Lykken and Venables, 1971) with direct recording (manual mode) and Ag/AgCl electrodes with isotonic electrode paste according to standards developed by the scientific community (Fowles *et al.*,1981; Handler *et al.*, 2010). A high-pass filter with a 10-second time constant can be used to stabilize the recording, as it has minimal effects on the amplitude and temporal characteristics of the phasic reactions to test questions. Even if the computer is capable of displaying high-pass filtered signals, the unfiltered data should always be stored on the computer. Human evaluations and computer measurements of electrodermal responses should always be made on the unfiltered data to avoid biasing the RQ/CQ ratio.

The National Center for Credibility Assessment (NCCA) recently convinced the four largest manufacturers of computerized polygraph systems in the United States and Canada to provide their polygraph data in a common data format, and the polygraph charts for both datasets used in this study had been stored in the common format developed for that purpose at the NCCA (A. B. Dollins, personal communication). NCCA is building a database of polygraph examinations, purged of personally identifying information, which could be made available to the scientific community for research. This development may be the single most important step in decades for research on polygraph techniques. Ideally, field cases in the database will be updated as information becomes available. For example, incontrovertible physical or genetic evidence and corroborated confessions or recantations could be used to confirm the veracity of a tested individual in a criminal case. Although these events are not common, with tens of thousands of polygraph tests conducted each year, a sizable number of confirmed cases might be accumulated in a short period of time. For pre-employment and periodic screening programs, polygraph results could be correlated with subsequent employee evaluations and disciplinary actions.

The National Research Council (2003) was critical of the polygraph for use in screening applications and criminal investigation because theory had not been developed to explain psychophysiological processes that underlie the reactions recorded by polygraph instruments. They concluded (National Research Council, 2003, pp. 2–3):

> Polygraph research has not developed and tested theories of the underlying factors that produce the observed responses. Factors other than truthfulness that affect the physiological responses being measured can vary substantially across settings in which polygraph tests are used. There is little knowledge about how much these factors influence the outcomes of polygraph tests in field settings ...
>
> ... *The lack of understanding* of the processes that underlie polygraph responses *makes it very difficult to generalize* from the results obtained in specific research settings or with particular subject populations to other settings or populations, or from laboratory research studies to real-world applications. [Emphasis added.]

There is little doubt that the field of credibility assessment would benefit from better theory. When that day comes, it will be necessary to evaluate predictions derived from the theory with empirical evidence, preferably from the field. Polygraph researchers can do much in the meantime to address the consequences of inadequate theory. In particular, researchers can assess the generalizability of results from different settings and populations. The availability of a large database of confirmed laboratory and field polygraph charts would provide opportunities to answer many of the following questions:

- Does the confession criterion for ground truth bias estimates of validity?
- Do physiological responses depend on context, motivation, or personal characteristics of the individual, such as age, sex, education level, or ethnicity?
- In criminal investigations, do physiological responses vary if the person is a suspect, witness, or victim?
- Do physiological responses vary with the type of crime?
- How are physiological responses affected by the person–situation interactions? For example, does the sex or ethnicity of the subject interact with the sex or ethnicity of the polygraph examiner?

- Do physiological responses vary for different test protocols? Are some polygraph test protocols more valid than others?
- Which characteristics of contexts, individuals, and person–situation interactions are associated with false-positive outcomes? Which characteristics predict false-negative outcomes?
- Do laboratory simulations reproduce the patterns and covariance structures of physiological responses observed in the field? Are some laboratory simulations better than others?

The database being developed at NCCA could be used to address concerns about generalizability and provide insights into the underlying basis for successful applications of polygraph techniques.

If the accuracy rates for the LEPET examinations in the present study are representative of all LEPET tests conducted for federal agencies, there may be little room for improvement. If they are not representative, an alternative test structure might prove beneficial for government screening programs. Currently, the counterintelligence series asks about espionage and sabotage, whereas the suitability series asks about undisclosed criminal activity, drug use, and falsification of information on the application form. If undisclosed criminal activity is introduced to the examinee in such a way that it includes illegal drug use, then both the counterintelligence and suitability tests could be considered binary-issue tests, each with two relevant issues. If the RQs on the counterintelligence series and suitability series are crossed, then reactions to different RQs could be compared and the use of probable-lie or directed-lie CQs could be avoided altogether. The so-called Relevant Comparison Test (RCT; see Hacker *et al.* in Chapter 5 of this volume) would include one series, for example, that paired espionage with illegal criminal activity. Another series would pair sabotage with falsification of information on the pre-employment form. The RCT would compare reactions to RQs that cover disparate issues within a series. Existing procedures for comparing reactions to CQs and RQs could be adapted to compare reactions to RQs within a series. If either RQ evokes a comparatively strong reaction, the subject would be considered deceptive to that relevant issue. If the reactions to RQs are similar, the subject would be considered truthful. Since both relevant issues on the test would have face-validity, each RQ would serve as a control for the other

RQ and the pretest phase of the test could be shortened or even automated (Honts and Amato, 2007).

Theoretically, the RCT can be defeated if the subject is deceptive to both RQs and reacts similarly to them. However, since the consequences associated with deception on the counterintelligence issues are greater than those associated with deception on the suitability issues and the base rate of deception on the counterintelligence issues is very low, the occasional individual who is deceptive to a counterintelligence question is likely to show a relatively strong reaction to that question even if the subject is deceptive to the suitability issue. It is far more likely that the subject will be truthful to the counterintelligence questions and deceptive to the suitability questions. In that case, reactions to the counterintelligence questions would provide an appropriate standard against which to judge the magnitude of responses to the suitability questions.

General state countermeasures are another potential problem for the RCT. In a traditional LEPET with CQs, a lack of difference between reactions to RQs and CQs would be considered an inconclusive outcome. For example, if a subject took a drug that attenuated reactions to all test questions, the test would be considered inconclusive. In an RCT, a lack of difference between reactions to the two RQs would be considered a truthful outcome. Although state countermeasures are a potential concern for the RCT, some comfort can be taken in the finding that there were very few inconclusive outcomes in the present study and research has demonstrated that drug countermeasures are not effective against the Concealed Information Test (CIT; see Honts in Chapter 4 of this volume).

APPLIED ISSUES

As the uses of polygraph techniques have grown in criminal investigation and evidence, there is increasing concern about factors that may adversely affect their accuracy and their uses in administrative and judicial proceedings (Honts *et al.*, 2005; Raskin, 1986b). Critics have pointed to potential problems of subjective factors and bias when polygraph examiners interpret charts and render decisions; use of physical and mental countermeasures, such as drugs, physical maneuvers, and mental states; personality characteristics of subjects, such as psychopathy; and the testing of victims (Iacono and Lykken, 2005). Some have raised questions about the value of tests conducted confidentially by defense counsel (Orne, 1975). This section discusses the scientific and practical aspects of some of these questions (for a detailed discussion of countermeasures, see Honts in Chapter 4 of this volume).

Decision Making

The foregoing analyses and resulting accuracies of computer methods for rendering decisions may lead to a solution of the ongoing controversy concerning the reliability and objectivity of decisions based on visual interpretation and scoring of polygraph charts by polygraph examiners. The extensive scientific literature indicates that trained examiners using validated scoring procedures can produce highly reliable and accurate results. However, examiner training, scoring procedures, and decision criteria vary widely as a function of training programs, quality control procedures, and policies of various federal, state, and local agencies. Court cases and the media are replete with disagreements among various polygraph experts and schools of thought. These disputes often raise legal and political questions about the value of polygraph testing and evidence, and minimize the utility of polygraph examinations.

Computerized interpretation of polygraph decisions provides a possible solution to many of these issues. At the University of Utah, we began such a quest almost 40 years ago, resulting in the development and application of the CPS algorithm in the 1980s. Since that time, numerous scoring methods have been developed, as described in this chapter. The results of the analyses described in this chapter appear to indicate that computer algorithms may produce decisions that are at least as accurate and sometimes more accurate than decisions rendered by skilled human interpreters. We suggest that decisions based on computer algorithms have the potential to replace the general practice of relying on human interpreters to render decisions by visual interpretation of polygraph recordings. Human decision making risks incorporating the effects of extra-polygraphic sources of information and bias, as well as lack of effective training and experience of the interpreter. Replacing the human interpreter with the best of the computer methods described herein has the potential to produce highly accurate decisions that are unaffected by the problems just described and to elevate the value of polygraph testing to a level commensurate with its demonstrated accuracy and utility.

Personality Factors

Mental status and personality are important considerations in deciding if a person is a suitable subject for a polygraph examination. The small amount of available evidence indicates that psychotic and other seriously disturbed individuals present higher risks of error (Abrams, 1977). Fortunately, these mental conditions are so extreme that most examiners should be able to identify them during the pretest interview. Other types of personality factors, such as psychopathy, may not be as apparent.

It is commonly believed that poorly socialized individuals and psychopaths can defeat polygraph tests because they are adept at lying and are deficient in moral development and social conscience (Waid and Orne, 1982). However, laboratory and field research has clearly demonstrated that poor socialization and psychopathy do not reduce the accuracy of CQTs. These studies have been conducted with college students and volunteers from the general community (Honts *et al.*, 1985), convicted felons and clinically diagnosed psychopaths (Patrick and Iacono, 1986; Raskin and Hare, 1978), and psychopathic criminal suspects who were given polygraph tests in actual investigations (Barland and Raskin, 1975b). Other investigators have produced similar results with CITs and CQTs (Office of Technology Assessment, 1983). The extensive scientific literature demonstrates that polygraph techniques are highly effective in detecting deception in poorly socialized and psychopathic individuals, but highly socialized individuals and even psychopaths may be subject to false-positive errors (Honts *et al.*, 1985; Patrick and Iacono, 1986).

Confidential Tests for Defense Attorneys

A major criticism of the validity of polygraph evidence offered by the defense in criminal cases is known as the "friendly polygrapher" hypothesis (Orne, 1975, p. 114). Orne proposed that a guilty criminal defendant or accused who takes a polygraph test is more likely to pass the test if it is confidential and requested by the defense attorney than if the subject is informed that adverse as well as favorable results will be disclosed to the prosecution. Orne's argument assumes that under the confidential or privileged situation, the guilty subject has little at stake and little to fear. Therefore, the guilty subject will be more confident, the examiner will be more supportive, and the results are more likely to be favorable. Orne based this hypothesis on the results of a weak laboratory study with college students who were administered card tests in an unrealistic setting (Gustafson and Orne, 1965).

The principles and procedures of CQ polygraph tests argue against the friendly polygrapher notion (Honts, 1997; Raskin, 1986a). First, the advisement of rights at the outset of the examination warns the subject that the results may be used as adverse evidence in court. In addition, the subject has a great deal at stake in the outcome. A deceptive result precludes the opportunity to use the polygraph to obtain a dismissal of the case or an acquittal at trial, as well as increased legal costs and a fear of disruption of the subject's relationship with the defense attorney. To pass a CQT, the subject must show larger reactions to the CQs and the friendly polygrapher hypothesis offers no explanation of how reduced concern can result in larger reactions to the CQs than to the RQs. One study (Timm, 1982) showed no effects of increased confidence in beating the CIT test, even when subjects were given a drug (placebo) that they were told would help them to beat the test and a number test that indicated that their lie was not detected.

Beyond the logical failings of the friendly polygrapher notion, none of the available data support Orne's supposition. Laboratory studies where there is little at stake routinely produce detection rates of in excess of 90%. If Orne's hypothesis was correct, one would expect laboratory studies of the CQT to produce relatively more false-negative than false-positive errors. This is clearly not supported by the data. Honts (1997) reviewed 20 laboratory studies of the CQT with a total of 567 guilty subjects and 490 innocent subjects. The false-negative rate was 12% and the false-positive rate was 16%. This outcome is opposite to the prediction generated by the friendly examiner hypothesis. Notably, six of the 20 laboratory studies examined by Honts reported no errors with guilty subjects, despite a lack of fear of any negative sanctions associated with failing the test.

There are two published sets of data from tests of criminal suspects that also contradict the friendly examiner hypothesis. Raskin (1986a) presented complete data from 12 years of his confidential CQT examinations for defense attorneys and non-confidential tests for law enforcement, courts, and stipulated situations. He reported that 58% of suspects who were informed that the results would be provided to the prosecution passed their tests, but only 34% of those who took confidential defense tests were able to pass. In addition, the numerical scores were significantly more negative (in the deceptive direction) for confidential tests compared with the non-confidential tests. Honts (1997) presented a similar set of data from 14 years of his confidential and non-confidential examinations. He reported that 44% of the confidential tests were passed, while 70% of the non-confidential tests were passed. The foregoing analysis and data clearly demonstrate that the friendly examiner hypothesis fails on all counts. It is illogical, unsupported by laboratory studies, and is contradicted by data from actual field cases.

Testing Victims

Suspects and defendants are not the only subjects of polygraph examinations. In some jurisdictions for some types of cases (e.g., suspicious robberies, questionable sexual assaults), the complaining witness may be asked to take a polygraph examination to demonstrate the veracity of the allegations. As there is trauma associated with such events, actual victims may be more likely than other suspects to show reactions to the RQs when they answer truthfully. The problem is compounded by the anger and indignation experienced by many victims who are asked to prove that they really were assaulted.

In a field study of CQ polygraph examinations conducted by a law enforcement agency (Horvath, 1977), all but one of the false-positive errors occurred on victims of sexual or physical assault or robbery (G. H. Barland, personal communication, 18 September 1982). Owing to these problems, the American Psychological Association raised concerns about administering polygraph tests to victims of crimes (Mervis, 1986). Such applications should be approached with great caution and only when there is a strong basis for suspicion. The alleged perpetrator is usually a more suitable and appropriate subject for a polygraph test.

Government Use of Polygraphs

The US Government is the most frequent user of polygraph tests for criminal investigation, counterintelligence, foreign intelligence, law enforcement and national security screening, and exculpation. Numerous federal agencies use the polygraph to investigate criminal acts and vet employees, including the Federal Bureau of Investigation, Bureau of Alcohol, Tobacco, Firearms, and Explosives, Secret Service, Drug Enforcement Agency, all of the Armed Services, Department of Energy, Central Intelligence Agency, National Security Agency, Defense Intelligence Agency, and the National Reconnaissance Office. The NCCA of the US Department of Defense conducts and funds a substantial amount of scientific research on the polygraph, sets standards, and trains all federal polygraph examiners.

In Fiscal Year 2011, the Department of Defense conducted 43,434 polygraph examinations, not including the National Security Agency and other classified programs. Of these examinations, 41,057 were conducted as a condition of access to highly sensitive positions requiring classification clearance, 1537 were for criminal investigation, and 840 were counterintelligence tests (Office of the Under Secretary of Defense for Intelligence, 2011). Clearly, the Department of Defense places heavy reliance on the ability of the polygraph to detect hostile attempts to penetrate our national security system. The official position of the NCCA is that polygraphs are 90% accurate when properly administered by a competent examiner. However, there remain serious problems with regard to high rates of false-positive errors when base rates of deception are very low (Raskin, 1984, 1986a) and the lack of adequate research on the accuracy of screening examinations (National Research Council, 2003).

SUMMARY AND CONCLUSIONS

CQT polygraph techniques are complex and controversial methods that are extensively employed in investigation and administrative and evidentiary proceedings. The voluminous scientific literature indicates that they can be highly accurate when properly employed in appropriate circumstances, but they are also subject to abuse and misinterpretation. There are also many myths concerning their accuracy and effectiveness, and the ways in which they are employed. This chapter has described procedures for administering the CQT, the various methods for determining test outcomes, the scientific evidence concerning its validity, a detailed analysis and discussion of computer algorithms for determining test outcomes, and various issues surrounding the applications of such tests. Careful consideration of these features, combined with thorough analysis of each particular case in which they have been or might be applied, should provide a guide to making judicious decisions about when and how the CQT should be used.

Acknowledgments

A great deal of the research described in this chapter was conducted with the assistance and collaboration of Charles R. Honts, Steven W. Horowitz, and John A. Podlesny, whose help is gratefully acknowledged. The LEPET data used in this analysis were provided by Andrew B. Dollins, and used with permission, as part of DIA contract HHM402-11-P-0174 with the National Center for Credibility Assessment.

REFERENCES

Abrams, S., 1977. A Polygraph Handbook for Attorneys. Lexington Books, Lanham, MA.

Ad Hoc Committee on Polygraph Techniques, 2011. Meta-analytic survey of criterion accuracy of validated polygraph techniques. Polygraph 40, 193–305.

Amato, S.L., Honts, C.R., 1994. What do psychophysiologists think about polygraph tests? A survey of the membership of SPR. Psychophysiology 31, S22.

Anderson, C.A., Lindsay, J.J., Bushman, B.J., 1999. Research in the psychological laboratory: truth or triviality? Current Directions in Psychological Science 8, 3–9.

Barland, G.H., Raskin, D.C., 1975a. An evaluation of field techniques in detection of deception. Psychophysiology 12, 321–330.

Barland, G.H., Raskin, D.C., 1975b. Psychopathy and detection of deception in criminal suspects. Psychophysiology 12, 224.

Barland, G.H., Honts, C.R., Barger, S.D., 1989. Studies of the Accuracy of Security Screening Polygraph Examinations. Department of Defense Polygraph Institute, Fort McClellan. AL. Available from https://antipolygraph.org/documents/barl and-honts-barger-1989.pdf.

Bell, B.G., Kircher, J.C., Bernhardt, P.C., 2008. New measures improve the accuracy of the directed-lie test when detecting deception using a mock crime. Physiology and Behavior 94, 331–340.

Bell, B.G., Raskin, D.C., Honts, C.R., Kircher, J.C., 1999. The Utah numerical scoring system. Polygraph 28, 1–9.

Blalock, B., Cushman, B., Nelson, R., 2009. A replication and validation study on an empirically based manual scoring system. Polygraph 38, 281–288.

Bobko, P., 1995. Correlation and Regression: Principles and Applications for Industrial/Organizational Psychology and Management. McGraw-Hill, New York.

Bradley, M.T., Janisse, M.P., 1981. Accuracy demonstrations, threat, and the detection of deception: cardiovascular, electrodermal, and pupillary measures. Psychophysiology 18, 307–315.

Capps, M.H., Ansley, N., 1992. Analysis of federal polygraph charts by spot and chart total. Polygraph 21, 110–131.

Crewson, P.E., 2001. A comparative analysis of polygraph with other screening and diagnostic tools. Polygraph 32, 57–85.

Department of Defense Polygraph Institute, 2006. Test Data Analysis: DoDPI Numerical Evaluation Scoring System. Department of Defense Polygraph Institute, Fort McClellan, AL.

Dollins, A.B., Krapohl, D.J., Dutton, D.W., 2000. Computer algorithm comparison. Polygraph 29, 237–247.

Dutton, D.W., 2000. Guide for performing the objective scoring system. Polygraph 29, 177–184.

Elaad, E., Kleiner, M., 1986. The stimulation test in polygraph field examinations: a case study. Journal of Police Science and Administration 14, 328–333.

Fowles, D.C., Christie, M.J., Edelberg, R., Grings, W.W., Lykken, D.T., Venables, P.H., 1981. Publication recommendations for electrodermal measurements. Psychophysiology 18, 232–239.

Gallup Organization, 1984. Survey of the members of the Society for Psychophysiological Research concerning their opinions of polygraph test interpretations. Polygraph 12, 153–165.

Ginton, A., 2012. A non-standard method for estimating accuracy of lie detection techniques demonstrated on a self-validating set of field polygraph examinations. Psychology, Crime & Law, DOI: 10.1080/1068316X.2012.656118.

Gustafson, L.A., Orne, M.T., 1965. Effects of perceived role and role success on the detection of deception. Journal of Applied Psychology 49, 412–117.

Handler, M., Nelson, R., 2009. Utah approach to comparison question polygraph testing. Polygraph 38, 15–33.

Handler, M., Nelson, R., Krapohl, D., Honts, C.R., 2010. An EDA primer for polygraph examiners. Polygraph 39, 68–108.

Honts, C.R., 1986. Countermeasures and the physiological detection of deception: a psychophysiological analysis. Dissertation Abstracts International 47, 1761B.

Honts, C.R., 1994. The psychophysiological detection of deception. Current Directions in Psychological Science 3, 77–82.

Honts, C.R., 1996. Criterion development and validity of the control question test in field application. The Journal of General Psychology 123, 309–324.

Honts, C.R., 1997. Is it time to reject the friendly polygraph examiner hypothesis? Paper presented at the *Annual Meeting of the American Psychological Society*, Washington, DC.

Honts, C.R., 2004. The psychophysiological detection of deception. In: Granhag, P., Strömwall, L. (Eds.), Detection of Deception in Forensic Contexts. Cambridge University Press, Cambridge, pp. 103–123.

Honts, C.R., Amato, S., 2007. Automation of a screening polygraph test increases accuracy. Psychology, Crime and Law 13, 187–199.

Honts, C.R., Peterson, C.F., 1997. Brief of the Committee of Concerned Social Scientists as Amicus Curiae. United States v. Scheffer. Supreme Court of the United States.

Honts, C.R., Raskin, D.C., 1988. A field study of the validity of the directed lie control question. Journal of Police Science and Administration 16, 56–61.

Honts, C.R., Schweinle, 2009. Information gain of psychophysiological detection of deception in forensic and screening settings. Applied Psychophysiology and Biofeedback 34, 161–172.

Honts, C.R., Amato, S., Gordon, A., 2000. Validity of Outside-Issue Questions in the Control Question Test: Final Report on Grant no. N00014-98-1-0725. Submitted to the Office of Naval Research and the Department of Defense Polygraph Institute. DTIC# ADA376666. Applied Cognition Research Institute, Boise State University, Boise, ID.

Honts, C.R., Raskin, D.C., Kircher, J.C., 1985. Effects of socialization on the physiological detection of deception. Journal of Research in Personality 19, 373–385.

Honts, C.R., Raskin, D.C., Kircher, J.C., 1992. Effectiveness of control questions answered "Yes": dispelling a polygraph myth. Forensic Reports 5, 265–272.

Honts, C.R., Raskin, D.C., Kircher, J.C., 2005. The scientific status of research on polygraph techniques: the case for polygraph tests. In: Faigman, D.L., Kaye, D., Saks, M.J., Saunders, J. (Eds.), Modern Scientific Evidence: The Law and Science of Expert Testimony. West Publishing, St Paul, MN, pp. 571–605.

Honts, C.R., Thurber, S., Cvencek, D., Alloway, W., 2002. General acceptance of the polygraph by the scientific community: two surveys of professional attitudes. Paper presented at the American Psychology-Law Society Biennial Meeting, Austin, TX 7–10 March.

Horowitz, S.W., Kircher, J.C., Honts, C.R., Raskin, D.C., 1997. The role of CQs in physiological detection of deception. Psychophysiology 34, 108–115.

Horvath, F.S., 1977. The effect of selected variables on interpretation of polygraph records. Journal of Applied Psychology, 62,127–136.

Iacono, W.G., Lykken, D.T., 2005. The scientific status of research on polygraph techniques: the case against polygraph tests. In: Faigman, D.L., Kaye, D., Saks, M.J., Saunders, J. (Eds.), Modern Scientific Evidence: The Law and Science of Expert Testimony. West Publishing, St Paul, MN, pp. 605–655.

Kircher, J.C., Raskin, D.C., 1981. Computerized decision-making in the detection of deception. Psychophysiology 18, 204–205.

Kircher, J.C., Raskin, D.C., 1988. Human versus computerized evaluations of polygraph data in a laboratory setting. Journal of Applied Psychology 73, 291–302.

Kircher, J.C., Raskin, D.C., 2002. Computer methods for the psychophysiological detection of deception. In: Kleiner, M. (Ed.), Handbook of Polygraph Testing. Academic Press, London, pp. 287–326.

Kircher, J.C., Horowitz, S.W., Raskin, D.C., 1988. Meta-analysis of mock crime studies of the control question polygraph technique. Law and Human Behavior 12, 79–90 [Reprinted in Polygraph, 18, 1989, 1–14.].

Kircher, J.C., Kristjansson, S., Gardner, M.K., Webb, A.K., 2012. Human and computer decision making in the psychophysiological detection of deception. Polygraph 41, 77–126.

Kircher, J.C., Packard, T., Bell, B.G., Bernhardt, P.C., 2010. Effects of prior demonstrations of polygraph accuracy on outcomes of probable-lie and directed-lie polygraph tests. Polygraph 39, 22–67.

Kircher, J.C., Raskin, D.C., Honts, C.R., Horowitz, S.W., 1994. Generalizability of statistical classifiers for the detection of deception. Psychophysiology 31, S73 (abstract).

Krapohl, D.J., 1998. A comparison of 3- and 7-position scoring scales with laboratory data. Polygraph 27, 210–218.

Krapohl, D.J., 2002. Short report: update for the objective scoring system. Polygraph 31, 298–302.

Krapohl, D.J., 2005. Polygraph decision rules for evidentiary and paired testing (Marin Protocol) applications. Polygraph 34, 184–192.

Krapohl, D.J., 2006. Validated polygraph techniques. Polygraph 35, 149–155.

Krapohl, D., Cushman, B., 2006. Comparison of evidentiary and investigative decision rules: a replication. Polygraph 35, 55–63.

Krapohl, D., McManus, B., 1999. An objective method for manually scoring polygraph data. Polygraph 28, 209–222.

Krapohl, D., Shull, K.W., Ryan, A.A., 2002. Does the confession criterion in case selection inflate polygraph accuracy estimates? Forensic Science Communications 4 (3). Available from http://www.fbi.gov/about-us/lab/forensic-science-communications/fsc/july2002/krapohl.htm.

Lachenbruch, P.A., Mickey, M.R., 1968. Estimation of error rates in discriminant analysis. Technometrics 10, 1–11.

Lykken, D.T., 1998. A Tremor in the Blood: Uses and Abuses of the Lie Detector. Plenum, New York.

Matsuda, I., Ogawa, T., 2011. Improved method for calculating the respiratory line length in the concealed information test. International Journal of Psychophysiology 81, 65–71.

Mervis, J., 1986. Council takes stand on AIDS, polygraph; creates science post. American Psychological Association Monitor 11 March.

National Research Council, 2003. The Polygraph and Lie Detection. National Academies Press, Washington, DC.

Nelson, R., Krapohl, D., Handler, M., 2008. Brute force comparison: a Monte Carlo study of the objective scoring system version 3 (OSS-3) and human polygraph scorers. Polygraph 37, 185–215.

Nelson, R., Handler, M., Shaw, P., Gougler, M., Blalock, B., Russell, C., Cushman, B., Oelrich, M., 2011. Using the empirical scoring system. Polygraph 40, 67–78.

Offe, H., Offe, S., 2007. The comparison question test: does it work and if so how? Law and Human Behavior 31, 291–303.

Office of Technology Assessment, 1983. Scientific Validity of Polygraph Testing: A Research Review and Evaluation. US Government Printing Office, Washington, DC.

Office of the Under Secretary of Defense for Intelligence, 2011. Department of Defense Polygraph Program Process and Compliance Study Report. US Government Printing Office, Washington, DC.

Orne, M.T., 1975. Implications of laboratory research for the detection of deception. In: Ansley, N. (Ed.), Legal Admissibility of the Polygraph. Charles C. Thomas, Springfield, IL, pp. 94–119.

Patrick, C.J., Iacono, W.G., 1986. The validity of lie detection with criminal psychopaths. Psychophysiology 23, 452–453.

Podlesny, J.A., Raskin, D.C., 1977. Physiological measures and the detection of deception. Psychological Bulletin 84, 782–799.

Podlesny, J.A., Raskin, D.C., 1978. Effectiveness of techniques and physiological measures in the detection of deception. Psychophysiology 15, 344–358.

Podlesny, J.A., Truslow, C.M., 1993. Validity of an expanded-issue (modified general question) polygraph technique in a simulated distributed-crime-roles context. Journal of Applied Psychology 78, 788–797.

Pollina, D.A., Dollins, A.B., Senter, S.M., Krapohl, D.J., Ryan, A.H., 2004. Comparison of polygraph data obtained from individuals involved in mock crimes and actual criminal investigations. Journal of Applied Psychology 89, 1099–1105.

Raskin, D.C., 1979. Orienting and defensive reflexes in the detection of deception. In: Kimmel, H.D., van Olst, B.H., Orlebeke, J.F. (Eds.), The Orienting Reflex in Humans. Erlbaum, Hillsdale, NJ, pp. 587–605.

Raskin, D.C., 1984. Statement on polygraphs for counterintelligence purposes in the Department of Defense. Hearing before United States Senate Committee on Armed Services. US Government Printing Office, Washington, DC 66–81.

Raskin, D.C., 1986a. Statement on Polygraph Protection Act of 1985 (S. 1815). In: Hearing before United States Senate Committee on Labor and Human Resources. US Government Printing Office, Washington, DC, pp. 56–87.

Raskin, D.C., 1986b. The polygraph in 1986: scientific, professional, and legal issues surrounding applications and acceptance of polygraph evidence. Utah Law Review 1986 (1), 29–74.

Raskin, D.C., Hare, R.D., 1978. Psychopathy and detection of deception in a prison population. Psychophysiology 15, 121–136.

Raskin, D.C., Honts, C.R., 2002. The comparison question test. In: Kleiner, M. (Ed.), Handbook of Polygraph Testing. Academic Press, London, pp. 1–48.

Raskin, D.C., Barland, G.H., Podlesny, J.A., 1978. Validity and Reliability of Detection of Deception. Final Report to the National Institute of Law Enforcement and Criminal Justice (Contract 75-NI-99–0001). US Government Printing Office, Washington, DC.

Raskin, D.C., Kircher, J.C., Honts, C.R., Horowitz, S.W., 1988. A Study of the Validity of Polygraph Examinations in Criminal Investigation. Final Report to the National Institute of Justice (Grant Number 85-IJ-CX-0400). Department of Psychology, University of Utah, Salt Lake City, UT.

Raskin, D.C., Kircher, J.C., Horowitz, S.W., Honts, C.R., 1989. Recent laboratory and field research on polygraph techniques. In: Yuille, J.C. (Ed.), Credibility Assessment. Kluwer, Dordrecht, pp. 1–24.

Reid, J.E., 1947. A revised questioning technique in lie detection tests. Journal of Criminal Law, Criminology and Police Science 37, 542–547.

Reid, J.E., Inbau, F.B., 1977. Truth and Deception: The Polygraph ("Lie Detector") Technique. Williams & Wilkins, Baltimore, MD.

Senter, S.M., Dollins, A.B., 2004. Comparison of question series and decision rules: a replication. Polygraph 33, 223–233.

Senter, S.M., Dollins, A.B., 2008a. Optimal decision rules for evaluating psychophysiological detection of deception data: an exploration. Polygraph 37, 112–124.

Senter, S.M., Dollins, A.B., 2008b. Exploration of a two-stage approach. Polygraph 37, 149–164.

Senter, S.M., Dollins, A.B., Krapohl, D.J., 2004. A comparison of polygraph data evaluation conventions used at the University of Utah and the Department of Defense Polygraph Institute. Polygraph 33, 214–222.

Shadish, W.R., Cook, T.D., Campbell, D.T., 2002. Experimental and Quasi-experimental Designs for Generalized Causal Inference. Houghton Mifflin, Boston, MA.

Stern, R.M., Ray, W.J., Davis, C.M., 1980. Psychophysiological Recording. Oxford University Press, New York.

Swinford, J., 1999. Manually scoring polygraph charts utilizing the seven-position numerical analysis scale at the Department of Defense Polygraph Institute. Polygraph 28, 10–27.

Thompson, R.F., 2000. The Brain: A Neuroscience Primer, third ed. Worth, New York.

Timm, H.W., 1982. Effect of altered outcome expectancies stemming from placebo and feedback treatments on the validity of the guilty knowledge technique. Journal of Applied Psychology 67, 391–400.

US Army Military Police School Polygraph Branch, 1970. Chart Interpretation. US Army Military Police School, Fort Gordon, GA.

Waid, W.M., Orne, M.T., 1982. The physiological detection of deception. American Scientist 70, 402–409.

Weaver, R.S., 1980. The numerical evaluation of polygraph charts: evolution and comparison of three major systems. Polygraph 9, 94–108.

Weaver, R.S., 1985. Effects of differing numerical chart evaluation systems on polygraph examination results. Polygraph 14, 34–42.

CHAPTER

4

Countermeasures and Credibility Assessment

Charles R. Honts

Department of Psychology, Boise State University

OUTLINE

Introduction 133
Polygraph 134
Requirements for a Successful Polygraph Countermeasure 135

Spontaneous Countermeasures 137

GS Countermeasures 139

Information Countermeasures 140

SP Countermeasures 143
SP Countermeasures and the CQT 143
SP Countermeasures and the CIT 144
Misinformation and the CIT 146

Pharmacological Amnesia: A New Countermeasure Threat? 147

Possible Solutions to the Problems of Countermeasures 148
Instrumental Detection of Countermeasures 148
Statistical Detection of Countermeasures 149

Current Anti-Countermeasure Training 149

A Theoretical Description of the Mechanism of Effective Countermeasures 151

The Future of Scientific Research on Countermeasures? 154

References 155

INTRODUCTION

In all assessments where the subject of the assessment can benefit from the outcome, there must be a concern by the assessor that the assessed will cheat in some way to alter the outcome of the assessment to his/her benefit. As a general example, in education a great deal of effort and expense is devoted to counter cheating on written assignments. iParadigms LLC (www.iparadigms.com) is an Oakland, California company that develops and markets software (Turnitin) to detect plagiarism in college students' papers. iParadigms LLC also markets a product for students (Writecheck) that helps them check their work for plagiarism. iParadigms LLC's current annual revenue is reported as $16 million (http://www.insideview.com/directory/iparadigms-llc). However, there are scientific studies that show Turnitin to be ineffective. Fiedler and Kaner (2010) report a study where they submitted as student papers the unaltered text of 24 publications of original education research to Turnitin and MyDropBox (a Turnitin competitor). Turnitin reported low similarity codes for 21 of the 24 previously published papers and failed to flag any of the papers as fully plagiarized. MyDropBox (now SafeAssign by Blackboard; http://www.mydropbox.com) classified 18 of the 24 as low similarity, but indicated that two of the submissions were fully plagiarized. Fiedler and Kaner also reported that despite the very modest objective performance of the plagiarism detection program, their survey of deans in the United States indicated that 87% of the responding deans had positive impressions of the effectiveness of these programs. Some commentators have suggested that companies such as iParadigms LLC are profiteering by supplying software to both sides of the plagiarism issue (Schneier, 2011). As the final part of this example, I conducted a Google search (15 October 2013) of the phrase "beat Turnitin" that returned 14,900 hits, of which 736 were videos purporting to show ways to beat the Turnitin plagiarism software. By all indications, the contest between plagiarizers and plagiarism detection is an accelerating arms race.

Situations that involve formal credibility assessment present a prime example of the classic problem illustrated with the plagiarism example. This volume illustrates that for a variety of important, and often life-critical needs, people must assess the credibility of others. The innate inability to detect deception in other humans is likely the product of a coevolutionary process where deceivers evolve new deception skills while the receivers evolve new deception detection skills. Given what is at stake, it is not surprising that people have attempted to develop a variety of strategies and techniques to alter the outcomes of technology-based credibility assessment. In the present chapter, I address the existing empirical literature on efforts to thwart technology-based credibility assessment procedures and I conclude by attempting to put the subject into a theoretical context. The polygraph is considered as the prototypical example because it has the widest application and the largest scientific literature on countermeasures; however, as the other credibility assessment techniques move into application it is likely that countermeasures will be developed to each. This is already an evolving issue with the central nervous system (CNS) approaches (see Johnson in Chapter 6 of this volume).

Polygraph

In the polygraph profession and the associated scientific literature, things that subjects might do to defeat or distort a polygraph examination are known as countermeasures. The topic of polygraph countermeasures was addressed in a number of reviews (Barland, unpublished manuscript; Gudjonsson, 1983; Honts, 1987; Honts and Amato, 2002; Krapohl, 2009; Lykken, 1998; Office of Technology Assessment, 1983), but relatively little research was published on the topic. In recent years, it appears that all US Government funding and research on the topic of countermeasures has been conducted in the classified environment and is thus not available for public discussion, evaluation, or use (National Research Council, 2003).

In my 1987 review (Honts, 1987), I divided countermeasures into two large families: *general state* (GS) countermeasures and *specific point* (SP) countermeasures. That division still seems to have organizational value and is followed in the subsequent sections. GS countermeasures are intended to alter the general physiological and/or psychological state of the subject for the entire period of the examination and are not focused on any specific portion of the polygraph examination. The most commonly noted type of GS countermeasure is the use of drugs. SP countermeasures are intended to alter the psychological and/or physiological state of the subject at specific points during the examination. The purpose of SP countermeasures is either to produce a physiological response that would normally not occur, or would be small, or to inhibit a physiological response that would be large without the intervention of the countermeasure.

Requirements for a Successful Polygraph Countermeasure

The requirements for a successful countermeasure vary with the polygraph technique being employed. With the most commonly used test in forensic practice, the Comparison (Control) Question Test (CQT; see Raskin and Kircher in Chapter 3 of this volume), a countermeasure user faces a formidable problem. To provide a conclusive result, the CQT requires differential responses between two types of critical stimuli: relevant questions (RQs) and comparison questions (CQs). RQs are direct accusatory questions that address the matter under investigation and are expected to evoke relatively large reactions from guilty subjects. CQs are designed to evoke relatively strong physiological responses from innocent subjects. They are designed to be either assumed lies (probable-lie comparison tests) or known lies (directed-lie comparison tests). To be successful, a guilty countermeasure user must produce larger responses to the CQs than to the RQs. This must be done in the face of RQs to which the subject is lying. Moreover, the countermeasures must be implemented in a manner that is not observable to the polygraph examiner, either by visual inspection of the subject (often by live video and/or recording) or from an analysis of the physiological data.

With the Concealed Information Test (CIT), the potential countermeasure user has more options than with the CQTs. In a CIT, key items are created from case information. Key items are supposed to be memorable pieces of information from the crime that are known only to investigators and to the perpetrator of the crime. Key items are randomly sequenced with at least five foil items that are not actual details of the crime. The most common way of scoring a CIT uses the system first described by Lykken (1959). In the Lykken scoring system, only the amplitude of electrodermal response is scored. The first item in a series is never scored and the remaining items are rank-ordered from largest to smallest. The largest item is assigned a score of 2, the second largest item a score of 1, and all the remaining items a score of 0. All values for the keys are then summed. If the sum is greater than or equal to the number of keys plus 1, the subject is reported to be knowledgeable of the crime.

To be successful against a CIT, a countermeasure user must change his/her reactivity so that on most of the question series at least two foils produce larger electrodermal responses than do the key items. Theoretically, countermeasures that affect the GS of the subject could be effective against the CIT. Moreover, any countermeasure that inhibits all responding to CIT items could be effective. Similarly, any countermeasure that produces maximal responding to all items might also be effective. However, such extreme GS manipulations might cause an examiner to be suspicious, simply because of the dramatic or unusual nature of the subject's general response patterns.

A potentially more successful approach to countermeasures against a CIT might be to attempt to dramatically increase responding to two of the foil items of each series. If the responses to one or two of the foils could be augmented to the point of a larger response than the key item, then the subject would beat the test.

A third approach to countermeasures against the CIT would be to attempt to interfere with the actual episodic memory for the crime. One approach to this type of countermeasure would be to attempt to replace details of the original memory with the same misinformation techniques that are used to create false memories (Loftus and Hoffman, 1989). Moreover, new research suggests that there may be pharmacological interventions that might be used to erase specific episodic memories (Adler, 2012).

A third examination technique still in some use within the polygraph profession is the Relevant–Irrelevant Test (RIT). The RIT asks a series of RQs interspersed with irrelevant (neutral) questions. Since there are no studies in the published scientific literature demonstrating the validity of the RIT as used in the field, even under ideal conditions (e.g., Horvath, 1988; Horowitz *et al.*, 1997; also see the study by Barland *et al.*, 1989), it does not make much sense to consider countermeasures used against the RIT. How do you go about beating an invalid test? Other than in the section on spontaneous countermeasures, the RIT does not receive additional mention in this chapter.

SPONTANEOUS COUNTERMEASURES

Spontaneous countermeasures are attempts to influence exam outcomes that are employed without apparent forethought or planning by the subject. Although there are anecdotal reports of spontaneous countermeasure use in the field (e.g., Barland, 2009; London and Krapohl, 1999; Raskin, 1990), to my knowledge there are no systematic field studies of spontaneous countermeasure use. However, this topic has been examined in laboratory settings. Honts *et al.* (1988) found that although 65% of their guilty subjects reported the use of spontaneous countermeasures, such countermeasures were routinely ineffective. The Honts *et al.* (1988) subjects reported using a variety of countermeasures that ranged from vague mental efforts to "control their physiology" to the application of SP countermeasures, such as pressing their toes to the floor on specific questions. Honts *et al.* (1988) reported that none of the deceptive subjects who used spontaneous countermeasures produced a truthful outcome nor were inconclusive rates increased. None of their innocent participants attempted to use countermeasures during their examinations.

Honts *et al.* (2001) collected spontaneous countermeasure data from a large study of the effects of outside issues on the CQT. In a sample of 192 subjects (96 innocent) they found that 82.3% of their guilty subjects and 42.7% of their innocent subjects attempted one or more spontaneous countermeasures. Their statistical analyses replicated the earlier findings by failing to reveal any significant effects of spontaneous countermeasures with guilty subjects. However, the spontaneous use of countermeasures by innocent subjects significantly moved their numerical scores in the negative (deceptive) direction.

Otter-Henderson *et al.* (2002) replicated the Honts *et al.* (1988, 2001) analysis using an RIT in the context of a mock-screening study. With guilty subjects, they found similar results to the earlier studies; 77.5% of the guilty subjects attempted one or more spontaneous countermeasures. Statistical analyses revealed no effects for the use of spontaneous countermeasures by deceptive subjects. However, Otter-Henderson *et al.* (2002) also found that 30% of their innocent subjects used one or more spontaneous countermeasures in an effort to help them pass the test. Their statistical analyses failed to reveal any effects of spontaneous countermeasure use.

Kircher *et al.* (2006) reported a laboratory study of the effect of audio versus audiovisual presentation of the questions in an RIT screening situation. All subjects falsified two of eight items on an employment form and were then tested about their falsification of information on the employment form. After the testing was completed, subjects were interviewed about countermeasure use and were then given a computer-based questionnaire about countermeasure use. All of the subjects reported the spontaneous use of countermeasures during both the interview and the computer-based survey. The use of spontaneous countermeasures had no impact on test outcomes. Interestingly, subjects were more willing to endorse countermeasure items on the computer-based questionnaire than they were during the interview. This finding has implications for future research on spontaneous countermeasures, suggesting that participants might be more forthcoming in computer-based questionnaires.

Honts and Reavy (2009) compared the validity of the probable-lie and the directed-lie variants of the CQT. In their debriefing, they questioned participants about spontaneous countermeasure use. With the traditional probable-lie CQTs, 83.9% of the guilty and 16.4% of the innocent subjects reported spontaneous countermeasure use. With the directed-lie variant of the CQT, 71.4% of the guilty and 21.3% of the innocent subjects reported spontaneous countermeasure use. The differences in frequency of spontaneous countermeasure attempts between the probable-lie and the directed-lie subjects were not statistically significant. Analyses failed to find any significant effects of spontaneous countermeasures nor were there interactions of spontaneous countermeasure use with CQ type.

In summary, five laboratory studies examined the effects of spontaneous countermeasures and produced generally consistent findings. Spontaneous countermeasure attempts by subjects attempting deception are common. However, for guilty subjects they produced no effects on outcomes or inconclusive rates. Over the decade of the 1990s, the incidence of spontaneous countermeasure use by innocent subjects sharply increased, but in the most recent assessment the rate of innocent spontaneous countermeasure use was low. Consistently, the use of countermeasures by innocent subjects increased the likelihood that they would be found deceptive. Despite widespread public information about countermeasures and commentary in the popular literature indicating that polygraph tests could be easily beaten by spontaneous countermeasure users (e.g., Lykken, 1998), there simply is no scientific evidence to support that contention.

GS COUNTERMEASURES

A number of GS countermeasures can be imagined. The most commonly mentioned countermeasure in this category is the use of drugs. Presumably autonomic nervous system inhibitors would reduce a subject's physiological reactivity to test items. Moreover, large doses or powerful drugs might block all phasic autonomic physiological reactivity. However, either case should at worst result in an inconclusive outcome with a CQT, since the CQT requires stronger reactions to the CQs to produce a truthful-appearing outcome. The possible effects of drugs against the CIT are not as clear. The evaluation of the CIT does not require differential reactivity between keys and foils in the same way that the CQT does for RQs and CQs. Presumably, a lack of response to any of the test items would result in a conclusion of no knowledge. However, it seems unlikely that a field polygraph examiner would be willing to render an opinion on a subject who was completely non-responsive during an examination. Moreover, a dose of drugs sufficient to block all autonomic physiological reactivity would seem likely to produce behavioral changes that could be obvious to the examiner.

Research on drug countermeasures does not indicate that they are a serious threat to either the CIT or the CQT. Several commonly available prescription drugs were studied. Waid et al. (1981) reported that the tranquilizer meprobamate was effective in reducing the accuracy of a CIT with knowledgeable subjects. However, that study has questionable external validity. The subjects of the study were college students who over-learned a word list on which they were subsequently tested. No explicit motivation was associated with the outcome of the test. In 1983, in a statement before the National Advisory Panel to the Office of Technology Assessment, Orne reported that an attempt to replicate this effect with the CQT failed to produce effects (Office of Technology Assessment, 1983).

Iacono et al. (1984) reported a constructive replication of the Waid et al. (1981) study in which they tested the effects of Valium and Ritalin on the CIT. Iacono et al. (1984) used a more realistic paradigm than did Waid et al. (1981). In the Iacono et al. (1984) study, participants watched a videotape of a burglary that was recorded in a first-person-off-the-shoulder mode. Subjects were asked to imagine that they were committing the burglary as they watched the film and a small monetary reward was offered for passing the CIT. Iacono *et al.* (1984) failed to replicate the tranquilizer effects reported by Waid *et al.* (1981). Similarly, Iacono *et al.* (1984) found no effects of the energizer Ritalin on the CIT. Iacono *et al.* (1992) reported a subsequent drug countermeasure study of the CIT in which diazepam, meprobamate, and propranolol were all found to be ineffective as countermeasures to the CIT.

A study conducted at the University of Texas Health Science Center by Gatchel *et al.* (unpublished manuscript) examined the effects of propranolol on the CQT using a mock-crime study where the subjects were tested by two professional polygraph examiners. The only significant effect of propranolol was to improve the accuracy rate with Innocent subjects who took the drug.

There have been two studies of the effects of alcohol on the CQT. Bradley and Ainsworth (1984) found no effects of alcohol intoxication at the time of the test (when alcohol was used as a countermeasure). However, they reported that alcohol intoxication during the commission of the mock crime reduced the accuracy for guilty subjects. O'Toole *et al.* (1994) failed to replicate the effects of intoxication at the time of the crime effects reported by Bradley and Ainsworth (1984). O'Toole *et al.* (1994) also reported no countermeasure effect of alcohol intoxication at the time of the examination on either the CIT or the CQT.

Other GS countermeasures have been suggested in the literature, including exercising to exhaustion, hypnosis, and mental efforts to relax, rationalize, or disassociate throughout the examination. However, the existing literature suggests that none of these GS countermeasures are effective against either the CIT or the CQT.

INFORMATION COUNTERMEASURES

With the growth of the Internet, the availability of information about how the polygraph works and about countermeasures to the polygraph has grown rapidly. Google searches in June 2013 found the following hit rates for these exact phrases: "polygraph" (4,590,000), "polygraph countermeasure" (3820), and "beat the polygraph" (72,100). Given the volume of information available on the Internet about the polygraph and polygraph countermeasures, concern about the effects of that information seem to be justified.

In a study that predated the Internet, Rovner *et al.* (Rovner *et al.*, 1979; Rovner, 1986) examined the effects of information and practice on the CQT in a laboratory study that served as Rovner's dissertation. They used a 2 × 3 factorial design in which half of the subjects enacted a mock crime and half did not. One-third of the subjects (Standard) received no other treatment. One-third (Information) of the subjects were given a "beat the polygraph" document that contained accurate and complete information about the nature of the CQT. The document informed subjects about the nature of RQs and CQs, and informed subjects about the scoring of the CQT. It was made clear to subjects that in order to pass the test, they would have to produce larger responses to the CQs than to the RQs. Subjects were also given an extensive list of maneuvers they might attempt to create or enhance their responses to the CQs. The final third of the subjects (Information Plus Practice) received the "beat the polygraph" information and were then given the chance to practice their chosen countermeasures during a two-chart mock polygraph test conducted by a confederate of the researchers.

One result of the Rovner *et al.* study was very clear – information had no effect on the accuracy of the CQT with either innocent or guilty subjects. There was identical accuracy for CQTs with both innocent and guilty subjects who had or had not been exposed to the information manipulation. Information plus practice increased both the false-negative and the false-positive rates. However, statistical analyses of the numerical scores revealed no significant effects with guilty subjects across the three conditions, but did indicate that numerical scores for innocent subjects in the Information Plus Practice condition were lower than for the other two conditions. Unfortunately, the effects of the Information Plus Practice condition are difficult to interpret because they are confounded. Subjects in the Information Plus Practice condition were given two polygraph tests where they could practice their countermeasures while attached to an instrument. Then they were immediately given their actual polygraph examination. Thus, the first question repetition of the actual polygraph examination was the third repetition of the questions for the Information Plus Practice subjects. The fact that actual testing immediately followed the practice manipulation raises the possibility that habituation was the active agent rather than practice. Until additional research is conducted to separate the effects of countermeasure practice from those of habituation, the nature of the Information Plus Practice effect in the Rovner *et al.* study will remain ambiguous.

Honts and Alloway (2007) directly examined whether or not providing subjects with accurate information from the Internet would affect the validity of the Test for Espionage and Sabotage (a directed lie variant of the CQT). They divided 40 participants into four equal groups: guilty, guilty-informed, innocent, and innocent-informed. During a first appointment, participants either did or did not commit a mock crime of theft. Some were then provided with a book (Maschke and Scalabrini, 2000) that contained detailed information on the CQT, including possible countermeasures. Masche and Scalabrini (2000) claim that the suggestions in their book will help truthful subjects to pass the CQT, which they believe has an unacceptably high false-positive rate. Honts and Alloway (2007) told their informed participants that if they read and followed the suggestions in the book, they would have a much better chance of obtaining the bonus that was offered for producing a truthful outcome on their upcoming polygraph examination. After one week with the book, all participants were administered a CQT. Following the polygraph examination, participants responded to a questionnaire that asked them about their behavior and perceptions during their examination. Honts and Alloway (2007) found no significant effects of providing information on the validity of the CQT. However, in direct contradiction to Masche and Scalabrini's (2000) prediction, reported use of countermeasures was associated with a lower probability of truthfulness for both deceptive and truthful participants.

Concerns that readily available information will enable guilty individuals to produce false-negative errors seem unfounded. Moreover, the results actually indicate that the use of countermeasures described on the Internet was associated with a lower probability of obtaining a truthful test result, which was exactly the opposite outcome predicted by the countermeasure proponents.

SP COUNTERMEASURES

Research strongly suggests that spontaneous and information countermeasures do not pose serious problems for polygraph validity. However, training in SP countermeasures might offer a potential for effectiveness. Anything that can either inhibit or enhance responding differentially could pose a problem for both the CIT and the CQT.

SP Countermeasures and the CQT

Dawson (1980) conducted an early mock-crime study of the effects of mental imagery as a countermeasure. He found that method actors who used mental imagery as a countermeasure were ineffective in altering CQT polygraph outcomes. However, one possible criticism of the Dawson (1980) study is that his subjects were not informed about the nature of the CQT nor were they informed about how it was scored. Thus, they may not have applied their mental imagery countermeasure in an effective manner.

Honts and his colleagues have reported a systematic series of mock-crime laboratory studies that examined the effects of countermeasure training on the CQT. In all of these studies, subjects who enacted a mock crime were given person-to-person training in the use of one or more countermeasures. Countermeasure subjects were fully informed about the nature of the test they were going to be given and about how it would be scored. Then they were specifically instructed how and when to employ their countermeasures. Subjects were then coached in using the countermeasure unobtrusively during a mock presentation of a question list similar to the questions they would be given in their actual examination. However, unlike the subjects in the Rovner (1986) study, subjects in the Honts studies were never attached to an instrument during their training. Honts *et al.* (1985) reported two studies of the effects of the physical countermeasures of biting the tongue and/or pressing the toes to the floor during the CQs. Although they produced minimal findings in their first experiment, there were significant effects in their second experiment where 47% of the countermeasure-trained subjects produced false-negative outcomes. In a constructive replication of the second Honts *et al.* (1985) experiment that used a stronger motivational context, Honts *et al.*

(1987) reported a 70% false-negative rate following training to press the toes and bite the tongue during the CQs.

The next study in the Honts countermeasure series (Honts et al., 1994) attempted to determine the underlying nature of the countermeasure effects. There were four countermeasure conditions in Honts et al. (1994). They were interested in determining the relative contribution of psychological and physiological reflex factors to the effectiveness of countermeasures. Three of the countermeasure conditions replicated physical countermeasure conditions from previous studies. Subjects were instructed to either bite their tongue, press their toes to the floor, or do both simultaneously during the CQs. Subjects in the fourth countermeasure condition received the same information but were instructed to pick a number larger than 200 and to silently count backwards by sevens during the CQs. Honts et al. (1994) reported that the mental countermeasure produced a significant effect, but its effect was not as strong as the effects associated with the physical countermeasures. These results suggest that both psychological and physiological reflex factors contributed to the effectiveness of the countermeasures examined by Honts and his colleagues.

SP Countermeasures and the CIT

In an early study, Kubis (1962) reported no effects for the use of modified yoga (disassociation) on the CIT. However, more recent studies have found significant effects of training in countermeasures. Elaad and Ben-Shakhar (1991) examined the effects of mental dissociation on the CIT by having their subjects count sheep throughout the polygraph examination. They reported a reduction in the differentiation between key and foil items, but the effect was small. This is not surprising since the manipulation represented a less than optimal strategy for a countermeasure user. Had subjects been instructed to count only on the foil items, their effects might have been much larger.

Honts et al. (1996) examined possible effects on the CIT by applying the same techniques and training used by Honts et al. (1994) against the CQT. Countermeasure subjects in Honts et al. (1996) were instructed to use their countermeasure on two foil items of the test. They reported that the physical and mental countermeasures significantly reduced correct detection rates to 10% and 40%, respectively.

Honts and Kircher (1995) reported additional analyses of the Honts *et al.* (1996) data by examining the countermeasure detection methods described by Lykken (1960) in a countermeasure study of the CIT. Lykken's subjects were informed about the nature of the CIT and were told that to beat the CIT they would have to produce responses to the foil items. They were attached to an instrument and were allowed to practice making voluntary physiological responses. Lykken described a scoring system to detect countermeasures that involved creating a distribution of ranks, and reported that the scoring system was highly effective and the countermeasures highly ineffective against the CIT. Ben-Shakhar and Furedy (1990, p. 74) made the following statement about the Lykken (1960) scoring system, "… the GKT [CIT] can be made immune to such manipulations by adopting sophisticated scoring techniques." Honts and Kircher (1995) demonstrated that not only did the Lykken (1960) scoring system fail to detect the countermeasures employed in the Honts *et al.* (1996) study, but it also did a very poor job of detecting the non-countermeasure using knowledgeable subjects. Further examination of the Lykken manuscript suggests why his distribution analysis gave the illusion of validity; it appears that few of the subjects in Lykken (1960) actually used a countermeasure in an effort to beat the test.

Ben-Shakhar and Dolev (1996) reported a study of the effects of a mental countermeasure on the CIT. They informed their countermeasure subjects about the nature of the CIT and told them that to pass the test they would have to produce responses to the foil items. Countermeasure subjects were told to recall an emotional situation from the past during some of the foil items. Some countermeasure subjects were given a practice test and feedback on their ability to generate physiological responses by using the countermeasure. Ben-Shakhar and Dolev (1996) reported that both countermeasure conditions were effective in reducing detection and that the addition of practice did not increase the effectiveness of the countermeasure. However, the effect sizes for countermeasures in this study were much smaller than those reported by Honts *et al.* (1996).

Misinformation and the CIT

Another possible problem for knowledge-based tests is the influence of misinformation on memory. The presentation of misinformation concerning an event has been shown to influence eyewitness' recollection of crime-relevant details in numerous investigations (see the review by Loftus, 2003). Amato-Henderson *et al.* (1996) examined the effects of misinformation on guilty suspects' CIT performance. Prior to being administered a CIT, guilty suspects were provided with misinformation concerning details of their crime. Half of the CIT series (three items) represented items where suspects had not received misinformation; the remaining three items incorporated crime-relevant details where post-event misinformation was given. The CIT items associated with the misinformation contained the key (the correct crime-relevant information) and five foils, one of which represented the misinformation provided to the suspects following the crime commission. To determine the effects of misinformation on CIT performance, skin resistance amplitude data were scored using the procedures described by Lykken (1959). Regardless of the success of the misinformation manipulation (i.e., whether or not the guilty suspects demonstrated the misinformation effect on a multiple choice memory test), a majority (54.2%) of guilty suspects were incorrectly classified as truthful using Lykken's scoring procedures. Amato-Henderson *et al.* (1996) reported that the mere *introduction* of misinformation rather than the *effects* of misinformation led to lowered Lykken scores, hence a higher rate of false-negative errors on the CIT. The pattern of physiological responses in Amato-Henderson *et al.* (1996) indicated that when the misinformation was effective in changing the subjects, verbal reports of memory, the actual item from the event appeared to have been overwritten by the misinformation.

A rather rich empirical basis exists examining the influence of memory-related factors on the CIT. For example, Waid *et al.* (1981) reported a relationship between memory for CIT items and frequency of detection, with better memory for test items associated with a higher probability of detection. Bradley and Rettinger (1992) investigated whether innocent suspects with crime-relevant information could be found innocent on the CIT. Their findings indicated that although the innocent (but knowledgeable) suspects had CIT scores less indicative of guilt when compared with a guilty suspect group, 50% were misclassified as guilty. Given the findings from the Amato-Henderson *et al.* (1996) investigation into the effects of misinformation on the CIT, memory-related problems and possible countermeasure efforts need further empirical attention, especially within other testing formats. One can hypothesize, however, that memory-related countermeasures would have a much greater impact on knowledge-based tests, such as the CIT, than other test formats.

PHARMACOLOGICAL AMNESIA: A NEW COUNTERMEASURE THREAT?

While the Amato-Henderson *et al.* (1996) data show that episodic memory for details and the validity of the CIT can be negatively affected by deliberate post-event misinformation, a rapidly emerging area in memory research concerns mechanisms and methods for altering or even erasing memories during the reconsolidation process (Adler, 2012). It is now clear that every time a memory is recalled, it becomes vulnerable to alteration. It appears that after each recall, a memory goes through a process of reconsolidation and during that reconsolidation the memory can be altered though various forms of overt interference (e.g., misinformation, guided imagery, altered photographs). Through similar processes, complete false memories can be created (Loftus, 2003). A new line of research suggests that the administration of certain drugs during the reconsolidation process can cause the recently recalled memory to be effectively erased. Much of this research has been done with animal models, but recent research shows that it has clinically meaningful effects in the treatment of post-traumatic stress disorder and drug addiction (Milton and Everitt, 2012). It is easy to imagine that similar techniques could provide a nearly perfect countermeasure to the CIT. A guilty suspect facing a likely CIT would obtain one of the consolidation disrupting drugs (e.g., commonly prescribed drugs like propranolol), attempt to recall as much as possible about the crime, and then take the drug. The drug would disrupt the reconsolidation of the memory of the crime, significantly degrading it or even erasing it. The guilty suspect then could take a CIT and produce no indication of criminal knowledge and potentially be cleared. Such a countermeasure would be devastating for all CITs, even those based on CNS measures. Moreover, the use of such a countermeasure would be undetectable by the polygraph examiner, although it might be suggested by drug testing.

The possible effects of pharmacological amnesia are clearly in need of research (e.g., would this countermeasure work for CQTs?).

POSSIBLE SOLUTIONS TO THE PROBLEMS OF COUNTERMEASURES

There seem to be three possible approaches to solving the problems of countermeasures against detection of deception tests. One approach would be to use counter-countermeasures. That is, the examiner would engage in strategies designed to prevent the subject from ever using countermeasures. If you are concerned that the subject is going to press his/her toes to the floor, the subject's feet could be elevated. If you are concerned that the subject is going to bite his/her tongue, then you could require that the mouth be held open during the examination. However, it seems likely that as soon as a counter-countermeasure is employed another countermeasure could be developed. The list of preventive measures necessary to thwart all possible countermeasures could and would grow quickly to the absurd. Moreover, it is not clear that there are effective counter-countermeasures that could be used against mental countermeasures.

The second possible approach to the problem is to develop countermeasure detectors. Research has consistently shown that polygraph examiners are very poor at detecting the use of trained countermeasures, either from observing the subject during the examination or from an examination of the resulting data (Honts and Hodes, 1983; Honts *et al.*, 1985, 1987, 1994, 2001). Typical of this research was the study by Honts *et al.* (2001). In that study, three US federal polygraph instructors scored the charts and made decisions about countermeasure use. They also rated their confidence in how likely it was that countermeasures were used. The federal instructors' decisions about countermeasure use were unreliable and the average validity coefficient was –0.01. Perhaps the most disturbing aspect of these data was the finding that when countermeasures were said to be present, 48% of those accused of using countermeasures were actually innocent subjects.

Instrumental Detection of Countermeasures

Most polygraph instruments offer the option of movement sensors and those sensors seem effective at detecting movement. Unfortunately, I know of no published scientific data exploring the efficacy of those devices in detecting the types of countermeasures that have been shown to be effective. The important issues for these sensors is discriminating between movement associated with countermeasures and naturally occurring movements displayed by innocent subjects. As demonstrated in the Honts *et al.* (2001) countermeasure detection study, many of the behaviors that examiners associate with countermeasures are natural behaviors generated by the innocent. In addition, movement sensors are most unlikely to be able to detect mental countermeasures. Finally, instrumental countermeasure detection methods are likely to encounter the same coevolution problem that makes counter-countermeasures an unproductive strategy. If a knowledgeable opponent knows that movement sensors will detect pressing the toes against the floor, then he/she could choose to tense a muscle that would not be detected or could resort to a mental countermeasure. The cycle could be endless.

Statistical Detection of Countermeasures

A potentially more promising strategy was reported by Honts *et al.* (1994). They used statistical analyses of the physiological data to determine if the responses produced by innocent subjects could be discriminated from the physiological responses produced by guilty countermeasure subjects. They reported some success. This increased the detection rate with countermeasure subjects to 78% – a rate comparable to the 75% detection rate of guilty control subjects in that study. However, Honts *et al.* (1994) noted that their subject sample size was small. This made it likely that their discriminant analysis overfit their data and overestimated the accuracy rates. The authors called for additional research on this promising approach to the countermeasure problem, but to date no further research has been published. The US Government's apparent decision to classify all research on countermeasures is probably responsible for the lack of known progress on this issue (National Research Council, 2003).

CURRENT ANTI-COUNTERMEASURE TRAINING

Despite the general lack of published findings supporting the notions that countermeasures can be detected, or effective countermeasure use is occurring in the field, or informational countermeasures can impact the validity of polygraph tests, the US Government and others now offer advanced training on how to detect and counter polygraph countermeasures (Department of Defense, 2010; Menges, 2005; National Center for Credibility Assessment, http://www.ncca.mil/ce_program.htm). Moreover, at least one expert is offering testimony opposing the admission of polygraphs in American courts purportedly based on his own observations and upon unpublished US Government research (Barland, 2009). Barland testified that the US Government has case files from confession-confirmed deceptive polygraphs that document the use of the Williams (2013) countermeasure material. Barland claimed that based on those case studies, he has identified respiratory signatures that uniquely identify individuals who used the Williams materials to learn countermeasures. Barland also claimed that the Williams respiratory signatures never occur naturally and are thus unique to countermeasure attempts by persons trained with the Williams (2013) material.

Honts and Crawford (2010) tested Barland's new countermeasure detection claims in a randomly selected sample of 92 polygraph examinations from a mock-crime experiment of variations of the CQT (Honts and Reavy, 2009). Approximately half of the 250 participants were guilty of a mock crime of theft. All were given CQTs using the US Government methods and field polygraph equipment. Following their polygraph examinations and after they were paid for their participation, subjects were debriefed concerning any countermeasures they may have used during the examination. Approximately 80% of the guilty reported the use of countermeasures and approximately 20% of the innocent reported countermeasure use. For both the guilty and the innocent, manipulation of respiration was the most commonly reported countermeasure. Countermeasure use was unrelated to accuracy. Although some subjects report obtaining countermeasure information from the Internet, none reported having seen the Williams (2013) material.

Honts and Crawford (2010) reviewed the respiratory recordings of the 92 randomly chosen participants from Honts and Reavy (2009) and recorded the frequency of occurrence of the five patterns illustrated and recommended in *How to Sting the Polygraph* (Williams, 1996). In their Innocent sample, they observed 88 spontaneous occurrences of the Williams patterns, but their Guilty sample showed only 59 spontaneous occurrences of the alleged countermeasure signatures. Occurrence of the alleged countermeasure patterns was not associated with reported countermeasure use. They also calculated how many individuals displayed at lease one occurrence of each Williams pattern. For innocent subjects, the highest occurrence was for Pattern 1, with 51% displaying that pattern at least once. For innocent subjects, the lowest occurrence was for Pattern 3, which was never observed. For guilty participants the most common pattern was also Pattern 1, with 49% displaying the pattern at least once. As with innocent participants, no occurrence of Pattern 3 was observed.

Barland's (2009) assertions that the Williams respiratory patterns are unique signatures associated with his countermeasure training and that they never occur spontaneously are clearly falsified by these data for every pattern except Pattern 3. Additional research will be needed to see if Pattern 3 does sometimes occur without countermeasure training. Pattern 1 was displayed by more than half of the innocent participants. If Barland's testimony about current Government practice were followed, more than half of the Innocent participants in the Honts and Reavy (2009) study would have been incorrectly classified as countermeasure users and considered deceptive on their polygraph test. If Barland's (2009) claims about the US Federal Government research and training on countermeasure detection is being widely used in the field, then innocent suspects may be put at substantial risk of false-positive errors. That risk is substantially exacerbated by what appears to be current US Government policy to interrogate suspects with inconclusive outcomes (Honts, 2013).

A THEORETICAL DESCRIPTION OF THE MECHANISM OF EFFECTIVE COUNTERMEASURES

Vrij *et al.* (e.g., Vrij, 2008; Vrij *et al.*, 2011) have noted that one of the primary theoretical differences between liars and truth-tellers is that liars experience more cognitive demand (sometimes called cognitive load) than do truth-tellers. Compared with the truth-teller, more of a liar's finite cognitive resources are used when being examined about the situation in question. Vrij *et al.* (2012) attribute this increased demand to a number of factors that may be involved. Formulating the lie may be cognitively difficult. Normally, liars are less likely than truth-tellers to take their credibility for granted, and are thus more likely to monitor and attempt to control their appearance so that they appear truthful; because liars do not take their credibility for granted, liars may monitor the interviewer's reactions more carefully in order to assess their success in lying. Liars may focus on the task of reminding themselves to act and role-play as truthful. Liars must suppress the truth while they are lying, since speaking the truth often happens automatically; producing a lie is more intentional and deliberate, and thus requires mental effort. Since liars' resources are already depleted by the process of lying, Vrij *et al.* advocate using interview procedures that increase cognitive demand, with the expectation that increased cognitive demand will increase the differences between truth-tellers and liars, and increase detections (for a related approach, see Hartwig *et al.* in Chapter 1 of this volume). Their predictions have met with some success (Vrij *et al.*, 2012).

If one thinks about psychophysiological detection of deception (PDD) in a manner similar to Vrij *et al.*, a relatively simple theoretical framework can be suggested. Cognitive load is associated with increased psychophysiological responding. In a CQT, for liars the RQs have a large cognitive load for many of the reasons described by Vrij *et al.* During the RQs, the liar must suppress the truthful response and produce a deceptive response; liars must also contain and control their memories of the act under investigation. The liar will be focused on his/her physiological responses to the RQ because of the immediate threat they pose, and the liar is likely to be highly focused on the polygraph examiner to search for clues about the success of his/her lies. For the liar, the CQs are likely to engender much less cognitive load as they clearly are of less immediate threat. For the truth-teller, a denial to the RQs is the automatic response; nothing needs to be suppressed. The truth-teller has no memory of the act under investigation to contain or control. However, the truth-teller must suppress an automatic response to the CQs and will have memories to contain and control for those questions. It seems likely that during the CQs the truth-teller will be self-monitoring his/her physiological responses and looking for feedback clues from the polygraph examiner.

The CIT has an even simpler theoretical explanation within this framework. If the CIT has been properly formulated and the liar has memory for the items chosen, then the key items should provoke a high level of cognitive demand for the same reasons as the RQs in a CQT. For the liar, the foils should be similar and generate very low cognitive demand. For the truth-teller, the key and foils should be highly similar and generate no differential in cognitive demand. This theoretical analysis suggests that the physiological responses in CQTs and CITs should be similar since they are both produced by increases in cognitive demand. At lease one finding in the PDD literature suggests that this may be the case. Honts *et al.* (1996) applied a discriminant analysis model developed on the CQT to the analysis of a CIT. In setting up the analysis, they treated the key item as a single RQ and the four associated keys (the first item in each series was not analyzed) as CQs. They developed a discriminant analysis model based on their data, and also applied the Kircher and Raskin (1988) model that was developed and validated with CQT data. The resultant models were quite similar and produced statistically indistinguishable results. Honts *et al.* (1996) noted that the results suggest that similar processes underlie the differential reactivity in both the CQT and the CIT.

The same theory may offer a simple explanation concerning the underlying processes in the demonstrated countermeasure successes in the PDD literature. One of the curious findings from the PDD countermeasure literature is that Honts *et al.* (Honts, 1986; Honts *et al.*,1994) failed to find any significant physiological differences among the four countermeasure groups. In that study, countermeasure subjects were trained to use SP countermeasures during the CQs of a CQT. Some of the subjects self-induced pain, some tensed muscles, some self-induced pain and tensed muscles, and some engaged in a countermeasure of mental arithmetic. If the physiological effects observed in the charts were simply the product of mechanical processes associated with the various activities, then one would expect differences in the multivariate analyses of the raw physiological measures, but none were reported. However, if a single underlying process was responsible for the observed physiological responses, then no differences would be expected.

I propose that cognitive demand is likely the process underlying the successful demonstrations of countermeasures in the PDD literature. Consider the task assigned to the countermeasure subjects in the Honts studies. They were instructed in CQT methods, and were trained to recognize RQs and

CQs. That monitoring process increased cognitive demand. Their instructions indicated that when a CQ was recognized, they were to execute a given countermeasure task. Recognition and task initiation increased cognitive demand. They were told to stop the countermeasure task to answer, answer with a lie as instructed, and then re-engage in the countermeasure task. All these processes increased cognitive demand. Subjects were specifically instructed to self-monitor while performing the countermeasure so that their countermeasure was unobservable, thus increasing cognitive demand. It also seems very likely that while performing countermeasures, the subjects increased their monitoring of the polygraph examiner to look for cues that their countermeasures had been discovered.

THE FUTURE OF SCIENTIFIC RESEARCH ON COUNTERMEASURES?

Current prospects for scientific advancements in the area of countermeasure research are not great in the United States. Research on polygraph countermeasures is resource-intensive and expensive to conduct. Such research generally is beyond the resources of academic researchers unless they receive external support. Research funding for detection of deception research in the United States is centered at the National Center for Credibility Assessment. It appears that the US Government has a policy that all countermeasure research will be classified (National Research Council, 2003). As a result, very little government-funded research on countermeasures has been conducted in an open environment in the United States since the beginning of the 1990s.

Countermeasure research conducted and contained in the classified environment is of no benefit to the scientific community nor the polygraph profession at large. This deplorable situation stifles scientific advancement and limits progress in the profession. Unfortunately, the prospects for any change in US Government policy on this matter are minimal. One federal polygraph examiner even suggested that the US Congress pass a law prohibiting the publication of research on polygraph countermeasures (Menges, 2005). Until a more enlightened attitude is evidenced by the US Government, it is likely that little progress will be made in this area by US scientists. Researchers in other countries are strongly encouraged to continue their work in this important line of research and publish their findings in the open literature.

REFERENCES

Adler, J., 2012. Erasing painful memories. Scientific American 306 (5), 56–61.

Amato-Henderson, S.L., Honts, C.R., Plaud, J.J., 1996. Effects of misinformation on the Concealed Knowledge Test. Psychophysiology 33, S18 (abstract).

Barland, G.H., 2009. Laura Lee vs. Mahendra Gupta, M.D and Linton Hospital, d/b/a Linton Medical Center. Sworn Deposition. Case No. 15-06-C-00057, Civil No. 06-C-57. State of North Dakota in District Court, County of Emmons, South Central Judicial District.

Barland, G.H., Honts, C.R., Barger, S.D., 1989. Studies of the Accuracy of Security Screening Polygraph Examinations. Department of Defense Polygraph Institute, Fort McClellan, AL.

Ben-Shakhar, G., Dolev, K., 1996. Psychophysiological detection through the guilty knowledge test: effects of mental countermeasures. Journal of Applied Psychology 81, 273–281.

Ben-Shakhar, G., Furedy, J.J., 1990. Theories and Applications in the Detection of Deception: A Psychophysiological and International Perspective. Springer, New York.

Bradley, M.T., Ainsworth, D., 1984. Alcohol and the psychophysiological detection of deception. Psychophysiology 21, 63–71.

Bradley, M.T., Rettinger, J., 1992. Awareness of crime-relevant information and the guilty knowledge test. Journal of Applied Psychology 77, 55–59.

Dawson, M.E., 1980. Physiological detection of deception: measurement of responses to questions and answers during countermeasure maneuvers. Psychophysiology 17, 8–17.

Department of Defense, 2010. Instruction: Polygraph and Credibility Assessment (PCA) Procedures (No. 5210.91). Available from http://www.dtic.mil/whs/directives/corres/pdf/521091p.pdf.

Elaad, E., Ben-Shakhar, G., 1991. Effects of mental countermeasures on psychophysiological detection in the guilty knowledge test. International Journal of Psychophysiology 11, 99–108.

Fiedler, R.L., Kaner, C., 2010. Plagiarism-detection services: how well do they actually perform? IEEE Technology and Society Magazine 29 (4), 37–43.

Gudjonsson, G.H., 1983. Lie detection: techniques and countermeasures. In: Lloyd-Bostock, S.M.A., Clifford, B.R. (Eds.), Evaluating Witness Evidence. Wiley, New York, pp. 137–155.

Honts, C.R., 1986. Countermeasures and the physiological detection of deception: a psychophysiological analysis. Dissertation Abstracts International 47, 1761B.

Honts, C.R., 1987. Interpreting research on countermeasures and the physiological detection of deception. Journal of Police Science and Administration 15, 204–209.

Honts, C.R., 2013. Current FBI polygraph/interrogation practices put the actually innocent at risk of false confession. Paper presented at the American Psychology-Law Society Meeting, Portland, OR, 7–9 March.

Honts, C.R., Alloway, W., 2007. Information does not affect the validity of a comparison question test. Legal and Criminological Psychology 12, 311–312.

Honts, C.R., Amato, S., 2002. Countermeasures. In: Kleiner, M. (Ed.), Handbook of Polygraph Testing. Academic Press, London, pp. 251–264.

Honts, C.R., Crawford, M., 2010. Polygraph countermeasures cannot be detected from respiratory signatures: Government policy puts the innocent at risk. Paper presented at the American Psychology-Law Society Meeting, Vancouver. 17–20 March.

Honts, C.R., Hodes, R.L., 1983. The detection of physical countermeasures. Polygraph 12, 7–17.

Honts, C.R., Kircher, J.C., 1995. Legends of the concealed knowledge test: Lykken's distributional scoring system fails to detect countermeasures. Psychophysiology 32, S41 (abstract).

Honts, C.R., Reavy, R., 2009. Effects of comparison question type and between test stimulation on the validity of comparison question test. Final Progress Report on Contract No. W911Nf-07-1-0670. Submitted to the Defense Academy of Credibility Assessment. Boise State University, Boise, ID.

Honts, C.R., Amato, S., Gordon, A.K., 2001. Effects of spontaneous countermeasures used against the comparison question test. Polygraph 30, 1–9.

Honts, C.R., Hodes, R.L., Raskin, D.C., 1985. Effects of physical countermeasures on the physiological detection of deception. Journal of Applied Psychology 70, 177–187.

Honts, C.R., Raskin, D.C., Kircher, J.C., 1987. Effects of physical countermeasures and their electromyographic detection during polygraph tests for deception. Journal of Psychophysiology 1, 241–247.

Honts, C.R., Raskin, D.C., Kircher, J.C., 1994. Mental and physical countermeasures reduce the accuracy of polygraph tests. Journal of Applied Psychology 79, 252–259.

Honts, C.R., Raskin, D.C., Kircher, J.C., Hodes, R.L., 1988. Effects of spontaneous countermeasures on the physiological detection of deception. Journal of Police Science and Administration 16, 91–94.

Honts, C.R., Devitt, M.K., Winbush, M., Kircher, J.C., 1996. Mental and physical countermeasures reduce the accuracy of the concealed knowledge test. Psychophysiology 33, 84–92.

Horowitz, S.W., Kircher, J.C., Honts, C.R., Raskin, D.C., 1997. The role of comparison questions in physiological detection of deception. Psychophysiology 34, 108–115.

Horvath, F., 1988. The utility of control questions and the effects of two control question types in field polygraph techniques. Journal of Police Science and Administration 16, 198–209.

Iacono, W.G., Boisvenu, G.A., Fleming, J.A., 1984. Effects of diazepam and methylphenidate on the electrodermal detection of guilty knowledge. Journal of Applied Psychology 69, 289–299.

Iacono, W.G., Cerri, A.M., Patrick, C.J., Fleming, J.A.E., 1992. Use of antianxiety drugs as countermeasures in the detection of guilty knowledge. Journal of Applied Psychology 77, 60–64.

Kubis, J.F., 1962. Studies in lie detection: computer feasibility considerations, Technical Report 62-205, US Air Force Systems Command (Contract No. AF 30(602)-2770, Project No. 5534). Fordham University, New York.

Kircher, J.C., Raskin, D.C., 1988. Human versus computerized evaluations of polygraph data in a laboratory setting. Journal of Applied Psychology 73, 291–302.

Kircher, J.C., Woltz, D.J., Bell, B.G., Bernhardt, P.C., 2006. Effects of audiovisual presentations of test question during relevant–irrelevant polygraph examinations and new measures. Polygraph 35, 25–54.

Krapohl, D.H., 2009. A taxonomy of polygraph countermeasures. Polygraph 38, 89–105.

Loftus, E.F., 2003. Our changeable memories: legal and practical implications. Nature Reviews Neuroscience 4, 231–234.

Loftus, E.F., Hoffman, H.G., 1989. Misinformation and memory: the creation of new memories. Journal of Experimental Psychology: General 118, 100–104.

London, P.S., Krapohl, D.J., 1999. A case study in PDD countermeasures. Polygraph 28, 143–148.

Lykken, D.T., 1959. The GSR in the detection of guilt. Journal of Applied Psychology 43, 385–388.

Lykken, D.T., 1960. The validity of the guilty knowledge technique: the effects of faking. Journal of Applied Psychology 44, 258–262.

Lykken, D.T., 1998. A Tremor in the Blood: Uses and Abuses of the Lie Detector. Plenum, New York.

Maschke, G.W., Scalabrini, G.J., 2000. The lie behind the lie detector. Available from https://antipolygraph.org/lie-behind-the-lie-detector.pdf.

Menges, P., 2005. Polygraph countermeasures: where we were, where we are. Available from https://antipolygraph.org/documents/menges-countermeasures-rome-2005.

Milton, A.L., Everitt, B.J., 2012. The persistence of maladaptive memory: addiction, drug memories and anti-relapse treatments. Neuroscience and Biobehavioral Reviews 36, 1119–1139.

National Research Council, 2003. The Polygraph and Lie Detection. National Academies Press, Washington, DC.

Office of Technology Assessment, 1983. Scientific validity of polygraph testing: a research review and evaluation. Technical Memorandum OTA-TM-H-15. US Congress, Washington, DC.

O'Toole, D., Yuille, J.C., Patrick, C.J., Iacono, W.G., 1994. Alcohol and the physiological detection of deception: arousal and memory influences. Psychophysiology 31, 253–263.

Otter-Henderson, K., Honts, C.R., Amato, S.L., 2002. Spontaneous countermeasures during polygraph examinations: an apparent exercise in futility. Polygraph 31, 9–14.

Raskin, D.C., 1990. Hofmann, hypnosis, and the polygraph. Utah Bar Journal 3 (9), 7–10.

Rovner, L.I., 1986. The accuracy of physiological detection of deception for subjects with prior knowledge. Polygraph 15, 1–39.

Rovner, L.I., Raskin, D.C., Kircher, J.C., 1979. Effects of information and practice on detection of deception. Psychophysiology 16, 197–198 (abstract).

Schneier, B., 2011. The effectiveness of plagiarism detection software. Available from http://www.schneier.com/blog/archives/2011/09/the_effectivene_2.html.

Vrij, A., 2008. Detecting Lies and Deceit: Pitfalls and Opportunities, second ed. Wiley, Chichester.

Vrij, A., Leal, S., Mann, S., Fisher, R., 2012. Imposing cognitive load to elicit cues to deceit: inducing the reverse order technique naturally. Psychology, Crime and Law 18, 579–594.

Waid, W.M., Orne, E.C., Orne, M.T., 1981. Selective memory for social information, alertness and physiological arousal in the detection of deception. Journal of Applied Psychology 66, 224–232.

Waid, W.T., Orne, E.C., Cook, M.R., Orne, M.T., 1981. Meprobamate reduces accuracy of physiological detection of deception. Science 212, 71–73.

Williams, D., 1996. How to Sting the Polygraph. Sting Publications, Chickasha, OK. Available from http://api.ning.com/files/Vh7by9YJkBbrznNb-rDkgcVLMmPJJ7JxTWyb-jGzwiHY-4vuHmHBtjAhHWx9*6V6PzkFYs9BJERf2eTdRGcd82-oK4fVS34-Q/Howto StingthePolygraphWilliamsDoug.pdf.

Williams, D., 2013. Learn how to always pass your polygraph test!. Available from http://www.polygraph.com.

Detecting Deception Using Ocular Metrics During Reading

Douglas J. Hacker, B. Brian Kuhlman, John C. Kircher,
Anne E. Cook, Dan J. Woltz

Educational Psychology Department, University of Utah

OUTLINE

Introduction	161	*Why Reading Behaviors can be Used to Detect Deception*	180
Physiological and Psychological Bases of Pupil Dilation	**164**	**How Ocular Metrics During Reading can be Used to Detect Deception**	**183**
Light Reflex	165		
Startle Response	165	**Laboratory Experiment 1**	**188**
Fatigue	166	*Method*	188
Pain	166	Design	188
Emotional Arousal	167	Materials	189
Cognitive Load	168	Apparatus	189
Eye Blinks	170	Measures	189
		Procedure	190
Evoked Pupillary Responses During Deception	**172**	*Results*	191
		Response Time	191
Using Reading Behaviors to Detect Deception	**174**	Pupil Dilation	192
Eye Movements in the Study of Reading	174	Reading Measures	192
Examinations of Eye Movements to Infer Cognitive States and Information Processing	177	Discriminant Analyses	192
		Discussion	193

Credibility Assessment
http://dx.doi.org/10.1016/B978-0-12-394433-7.00005-1

Laboratory Experiment 2   **195**
  Method   *196*
    Design   196
    Apparatus   197
    Materials   197
    Measures   197
  Results   *197*
    Manipulation Check   197
    Response Time   198
    Pupil Dilation   198
    Reading Measures   198
    Discriminant Analyses   198
  Discussion   *199*

Field Study 1   **199**
  Method   *200*
    Participants   200
    Apparatus   200

    Materials   200
    Measures   200
    Procedure   201
  Results   *202*
  Discussion   *202*

Field Study 2   **203**
  Method   *204*
    Examinees   204
    Apparatus   204
    Materials   205
    Measures   205
    Procedure   205
  Results   *206*
  Discussion   *206*

Conclusion   **207**

References   **210**

INTRODUCTION

Six people, two females and four males, were shown five pictures one at a time. The pictures were of a baby, a mother and baby, a nude male, a nude female, and a landscape scene. Before each picture presentation, each person had his/her pupils photographed on 16-mm infrared film 20 times over a 10-second period. Their pupils were photographed again 20 times over a 10-second period when the picture was presented. The images of the pupils were projected on a screen so that measurements of the pupil size before and during each picture presentation could be hand measured, averaged, and then compared. In this study, Hess and Polt (1960) were testing a hypothesis originally suggested by Charles Darwin that pupil dilation was related to fear and other emotions (Andreassi, 2000). Hess and Polt speculated that pupillary changes were mediated by the sympathetic nervous system (SNS) and could be used as "both a quantitative and a qualitative measure of greater or less interest value and pleasure value of visual stimuli" (Hess and Polt, 1960, p. 350).

Confirming predictions, Hess and Polt found nearly 25% increases in pupil area when participants viewed pictures judged to be of interest to them and an 8% constriction in pupil area when they viewed a picture judged uninteresting. Moreover, there was a pronounced sex effect: female participants experienced dilated pupils when viewing pictures judged to be interesting to women (i.e., the pictures of the baby, mother and baby, and nude male), whereas male participants experienced dilated pupils when viewing pictures judged to be interesting to males (i.e., the nude female). Hess and Polt concluded, "The responses to the pictures of the partially nude man and woman are what logically would be expected. Men are more interested in partially nude women, while women are more interested in partially nude men" (Hess and Polt, 1960, p. 132).

This was not the first time pupillary changes were viewed as indicators of emotional arousal. Nearly 20 years earlier, Berrien and Huntington (1943) examined participants' pupils in an attempt to detect deception. In contrast to truthful participants, they found that deceptive participants exhibited slow dilations of the pupil followed by rapid constrictions. They interpreted these findings as "indicative of the emotion usually accompanying deceit" (Berrien and Huntington, 1943, p. 449). Unfortunately, this pattern was found in only 50% of their cases. Rather than finding an emotion-based test for deception that relied exclusively on pupillometry, their final conclusion was that changes in pupil size were no more indicative of deceit than other known physiological responses.

Hess and Polt's (1960) work, however, caught the imagination of numerous researchers and set off a flurry of research activity that examined the effect of visual stimuli on pupil dilation as moderated by a person's attitude. All sorts of commercial products, television advertisements, sexual content, and political affiliations were rated for pleasantness or unpleasantness on the basis of whether pupils dilated or contracted, respectively (Goldwater, 1972; Loewenfeld, 1999). By the late 1960s and early 1970s, the promise of this research waned quickly after more controlled investigations began to make clear that the methodology used by most researchers was seriously flawed. Investigators failed to control for ambient lighting, color of stimuli, or distance to stimuli, all of which affect pupil dilation (Goldwater, 1972; Loewenfeld, 1999). In addition, numerous studies that examined pupil constriction indicated that "emotional stimuli and all other sensory and psychologic stimuli do not constrict the pupil" (Loewenfeld, 1999, p. 667). This is not to say that emotion has no influence on pupil dilation – as will be discussed later, emotional arousal is associated with pupil dilation – but the eventual conclusion was that there was no reliable association between pupil constriction and interest.

Subsequent to their work with emotion stimuli, Hess and Polt (1964) reported that cognitive effort was associated with pupil dilation. Citing work by Bumke (1911), who observed that pupil dilation occurred under conditions of mental and physical effort, attention, and affect, Hess and Polt (1964) hypothesized that changes in pupil size could be correlated with mental activity. To test this hypothesis, they conducted an experiment that used techniques that were similar to their earlier work, but in this case, five participants were presented with multiplication problems of varying difficulty; the easiest was 7×8 and the most difficult 16×23. Although the relation was not perfect, increasing difficulty of the multiplication problem was associated with an increase in pupil diameter. When shown a problem, participants' pupils gradually increased in diameter, peaked immediately before an answer was given, and then returned to the initial level. Hess and Polt concluded that "pupil response will prove to be a valuable tool in the study of problem-solving and other mental processes" (Hess and Polt, 1964, p. 1192). Unlike their assertions regarding the effects of interest on pupil dilation, which gained little if any additional empirical support, their discovery of an association between mental effort and pupil dilation initiated a plethora of experiments corroborating these findings.

Research following Hess and Polt's work demonstrated that pupil dilation was associated with increased difficulty on a wide variety of cognitive tasks, including transformation of digit strings (Kahneman and Beatty, 1966), mental arithmetic (Ahern and Beatty, 1979; Bradshaw, 1968; Schaefer et al., 1968), sentence processing (Just and Carpenter, 1993; Schluroff, 1982), letter processing (Beatty and Wagoner, 1978), reaction time (Bradshaw, 1970), recall tasks (Elshtain and Schaefer, 1968), psychological judgments (Kahneman and Beatty, 1967), and lexical translation (Hyönä et al., 1995). The use of pupil dilation as a psychophysiological index of cognitive effort has become commonplace in cognitive science.

In the context of our work, we have proposed that oculomotor measurements obtained during reading can be used to detect deception. This idea was introduced in a study by Baker et al. (1992). They used traditional psychophysiological techniques for recording eye movements with surface electrodes attached to the face. Although they had limited success in detecting deception in their investigation, they paved the way for research with modern eye-trackers that provide continuous measures of gaze position as well as pupil size. However, research in this area is still in a nascent state and many questions remain. To be able to anticipate the conditions under which the techniques are effective, we need a deeper understanding of the psychophysiological processes that underlie the observed effects on oculomotor measures.

In this chapter, we will present the current scientific evidence on pupillometry and eye movements during reading. We first provide an overview of the physiological and psychological bases of pupil dilation, after which we turn our attention to how pupillometry has been used as a psychophysiological index of cognitive effort and emotional arousal. We will include in this section a discussion of eye blinks. Pupil dilation and eye blinks have provided insights into the time course of cognitive activity starting from early stimulus onset, moving to sustained exposure to stimulus, and ending with activity subsequent to stimulus removal (Siegle *et al.*, 2008; Steinhauer and Hakerem, 1992). We then narrow our focus to studies that have examined evoked pupillary responses during deception. Once a foundation regarding pupillometry is completed, we provide an overview of the research that has examined eye movements to study reading behaviors. With the background in pupillometry and reading established, we next discuss our rationale for why and how pupil responses and eye movements during reading can be combined to detect deception. We end the chapter with a discussion of two laboratory studies and two field studies we have conducted to examine our thesis.

PHYSIOLOGICAL AND PSYCHOLOGICAL BASES OF PUPIL DILATION

In structure, the pupil is simple: a hole in the center of the iris muscle through which light passes to the retina. In function, the opening and closing of the pupil by the iris is complex. The dilations and constrictions of the iris are under the control of the autonomic nervous system (ANS), and therefore, are largely unconscious. Both subsystems of the ANS – the parasympathetic nervous system (PNS) and the SNS – play a role in iris dilations and contractions. Pupils can begin to dilate within 200 ms and can reach a maximum of 8 or 9 mm (Andreassi, 2000). Constrictions are also rapid, occurring in about the same amount of time, and can reduce the size of the pupil to about 1.5 mm. The operation of the irises in the two eyes is consensual in that when one iris constricts or dilates, the other iris simultaneously follows suit. The most common function of the iris is to adjust the amount of light that enters the eye. Constrictions reduce the amount of light that enters the eye and dilations increase the light. However, dilations and constrictions occur under other circumstances, such as emotional arousal, cognitive load, or adjusting the eye to better focus on near objects.

There are two sets of muscles that control the iris: radial fibers, called the dilator pupillae, are controlled by the SNS, and circular fibers, called the sphincter pupillae, are controlled by the PNS. Actions originating from the two branches of the ANS often have opposite effects. Activation of the SNS leads to quick mobilizing actions, such as the "flight-or-fight" response, and activation of the PNS leads to dampening or slowing actions, such as the "rest-and-digest" response (Andreassi, 2000). Signals from the SNS, which originate in the hypothalamus, relax the dilator pupillae. Signals from the PNS, which originate from a group of cells in the midbrain called the Edinger–Westphal nucleus, constrict the sphincter pupillae. Although the SNS and PNS tend to operate independently, there are times when the two act cooperatively. For example, during times of stress, the SNS becomes activated, but the PNS can subsequently react to bring the iris back to equilibrium. Thus, pupil dilation can occur in two ways: inhibition of the PNS can relax the sphincter pupillae, and activation of the SNS can relax the dilator pupillae.

Pupillary changes have a variety of causes: light reflex, startle reflex, fatigue, pain, emotional arousal, and cognitive load. Each of these causes will be described followed by a brief discussion of eye blinks.

Light Reflex

As mentioned earlier, a major function of the iris is to control the amount of light that enters the eye. The dilations and contractions that control light entering into the eye occur continually and can be very slight, as when the light intensity on a computer monitor increases or decreases, or when an individual's visual focus shifts from reading a book to an object several feet away. However, when exposure to excessive light occurs, the iris can contract within 200 ms to prevent damage to the retina.

Startle Response

As early as the 1870s, pupils were observed to dilate in response to being startled (Andreassi, 2000). Often referred to as the startle response, the iris quickly dilates when a person is exposed to strong, rapid noises or unexpected physical contact. The dilation occurs in as little as 200 ms and can persist even if the startled person is exposed to a bright light, which under normal conditions should constrict the iris. This would indicate that the startle reaction initiated by the SNS can temporarily override the light reflex that usually occurs automatically.

Fatigue

Hess (1972) noted that fatigue had a measurable impact on pupil dilation, with greater fatigue associated with decreases in dilation. Geacintov and Peavler (1974) used pupil constriction as a measure of fatigue in telephone workers across an entire work day (presumably an 8-hour day). Pupil measurements showed that the participants' pupils decreased an average of 0.32 mm between morning and evening measurements. Although small, this was a significant decrease from morning to evening, which, when paired with participants' subjective reports of fatigue, indicated that pupillary constriction is correlated with fatigue.

Over a more restricted time frame, Kahneman et al. (Kahneman and Beatty, 1967; Kahneman and Peavler, 1969) observed baseline changes in pupil diameter during experimental tasks that took participants 30–40 minutes to complete. The mean pupil diameter was 4.11 mm at the beginning of the experiment and 3.92 mm at the end of the experiment. However, even with the changes in baseline, there were no consistent changes in the proportion of change that occurred while participants were engaged in cognitive activities. That is, there was pupil constriction with time on task; however, the proportion of pupil dilation as compared with baseline under cognitive load did not change over the course of the experiment.

Pain

Work by Ellermeier and Westphal (1995) demonstrated that pupil dilation was associated with increases in pain. Chapman et al. (1999) followed up on this finding in an experiment in which they delivered a painful electric shock to a fingertip of volunteer participants to observe the effects on the pupil diameter response (PDR). A PDR was noted at approximately 330 ms post-stimulus and peaked at approximately 1250 ms. The magnitude of the pupil response varied directly with increasing intensity of the noxious electrical stimulation and showed no habituation over multiple trials. The changes in the magnitude of pupil dilation ranged from 0.10–0.45 mm at the lowest intensity of the electrical stimulation to 0.45–0.85 mm at the highest intensity.

These researchers hypothesized "that the PDR reflects central processing of a threatening event. This processing is probably not specific to pain as a sensory modality, but it may be specific to potentially threatening stimuli" (Chapman *et al.*, 1999, p. 50). As sensations of pain are known to excite the hypothalamus, the pupil dilations that occur as a consequence of noxious stimuli likely reflect activity of the SNS (Hess and Polt, 1960).

Emotional Arousal

Hess and Polt (1960) had hypothesized that pupil dilation was mediated by signals from the SNS originating in the hypothalamus – the portion of the brain, in part, responsible for emotional and behavioral arousal. This connection to the hypothalamus as the origin of pupil dilation has also been supported by studies of pain and stress, both having strong connections to emotional arousal, and both being associated with activity in the hypothalamus. Although Hess and Polt's conclusion that the pupil constricts in response to negative stimuli is no longer tenable, findings of dilation in response to positive and negative stimuli have received considerable support.

To re-evaluate the relationship between emotional arousal and pupil responses, and to assess the contributions of the SNS and PNS to pupil dilation, Bradley *et al.* (2008) recorded pupil response, skin conductance, and heart rate from participants exposed to pleasant, unpleasant, and neutral pictures. Skin conductance has been shown to vary with skin moisture produced by sweating, and sweating is controlled by the SNS. Therefore, if a strong association exists between pupil dilation and skin conductance, the SNS is the more likely cause for pupil dilation when the individual is emotionally aroused. In contrast, heart rate deceleration is mediated primarily by the PNS. Therefore, if an association exists between pupil dilation and heart rate deceleration, the PNS would be the more likely cause of the pupil dilation that accompanies affective states.

Participants showed increased pupillary responses when viewing pleasant or unpleasant pictures as compared with neutral pictures. This same response was reported by Partala *et al.* (2000) when their participants listened to affectively pleasing sounds compared with neutral sounds. Bradley *et al.* also found that pupillary changes covaried with skin conductance but not heart rate, supporting the notion that the pupil dilation that occurs when viewing emotional pictures reflects SNS activity rather than PNS activity. This evidence, along with other studies on the impact of emotion on pupil dilation, supports the conclusion that pupil dilation is associated with emotionally engaging stimuli regardless of valence (Bradley *et al.*, 2008).

Some caution must be taken when attempting to generalize these findings to other sources of emotional arousal. The neural basis of pupil dilations may differ for viewing pleasant, unpleasant, or neutral pictures, or listening to pleasing sounds and reading emotionally engaging text. The interplay of cognitive and affective processes during reading may cause increases in sympathetic activity, decreases in parasympathetic activity, or some combination of the two.

Vo *et al.* (2008) and Bayer *et al.* (2011) found that when single emotionally charged words are used as stimuli in low or high demanding cognitive tasks, pupil dilation is actually dampened rather than heightened. Bayer *et al.* proposed that because of the highly symbolic nature of reading words, there may be less activation of the SNS during reading than when viewing pictures or hearing sounds, which may provide more direct access to emotions. However, these researchers cautioned that additional research is needed to investigate the effects of more extensive written text rather than single words. They acknowledged that extended texts can have "their impact on autonomic functions, which they undoubtedly can, as everybody knows from love letters or messages that are not as friendly" (Bayer *et al.*, 2011, p. 1560).

Cognitive Load

As previously discussed, Hess and Polt (1964) showed that pupil dilation was a function of mental activity. Since that seminal research, numerous studies have shown that task-evoked pupillary responses (TEPRs) can be used as an analytic tool to measure processing load and cognitive resource capacity that is sensitive to within-task, between-task, and between-individual variations (Kahneman, 1973). TEPRs provide a reliable psychophysiological index of the momentary processing load during performance of a wide variety of cog-nitive activities: visual imagery of concrete versus abstract concepts (Paivio and Simpson, 1966), recall and transformation of digit strings (Kahneman and Beatty, 1966), mental multiplication (Ahern and Beatty, 1979; Hess and Polt, 1964), verbal learning (Kahneman and Peavler, 1969), paired associates learn-ing (Colman and Paivio, 1970), pitch discrimination (Kahneman and Beatty, 1967), signal detection (Beatty, 1982), letter processing (Beatty and Wagoner, 1978), and lexical translation (Hyönä et al., 1995).

All of these studies point to a clear finding that when a person is engaged in most types of cognitive processing, pupil dilations occur as a direct func-tion of the intensity of the mental effort. Once the load on cognitive process-ing drops, the pupil constricts. Excessive demands on processing, however, can eliminate or even reverse the relation between mental workload and pupil size. Granholm et al. (1996) showed using a digit-span task that TEPRs increased when presented with five to nine digits, but decreased when pre-sented with 13 digits. The decrease may have occurred because cognitive resources of the participants had been exceeded or because the task became too difficult and participants simply refused to engage in it any longer.

More germane to our proposed use of reading behaviors to detect deception is whether TEPR occur during language processing. In an early experiment to measure TEPR, Ahern and Beatty (1981) used Baddeley's Grammatical Rea-soning Task, in which sentences such as "A follows B" followed by an exem-plar "BA" were read to participants. The sentences differed in grammatical complexity and participants had to respond either true or false to each. The magnitude of pupil changes differed significantly as a function of sentence complexity, with greater complexity associated with greater dilation.

In a related experiment, Beatty and Schluroff (1980; as reported in Beatty, 1982) examined the effects of syntactic and semantic organization on TEPRs and performance in the encoding and reproduction of six-word sentences that were presented orally to participants. The sentences were of three types: normal construction, syntactically scrambled, and semantically scrambled. Their results showed greater TEPRs for the scrambled sentences from the very onset of the sentence presentation. Greater syntactic and semantic organization of the sentences reduced the TEPRs, indicating that cognitive demands were reduced when processing normal text.

Just and Carpenter (1993) used sentences that were more characteristic of text that is normally encountered during reading. The sentence structure varied on the basis of being object-relative (e.g., "The reporter that the senator attacked admitted the error publicly after the hearing.") or subject-relative (e.g., "The reporter that attacked the senator admitted the error publicly after the hearing."). Based on prior research, the structure of subject-relative sentences makes them more easily read and comprehended. Results indicated that when readers encountered more demanding sentence structures, they showed significant increases in pupil diameter, indicating that processing demands increase when sentence comprehension becomes more difficult. In addition to increases in pupil diameter, readers had longer gaze durations during the processing of demanding sentence structures. Just and Carpenter (1993) concluded that the cognitive resources necessary for comprehension vary with the complexity of the text and the increased demands on resources from reading more complex text can be ameliorated by allocating more time to comprehension.

This allocation policy may bring about a tradeoff relation between speed and accuracy of comprehension. Some readers in Just and Carpenter's (1993) studies attempted to maintain or increase reading speed when they encountered difficult text, but they did so at the cost of failing to comprehend. However, other readers slowed down when they encountered difficult text and devoted greater cognitive resources to comprehension. Therefore, when text is difficult to comprehend, "the comprehension process can maintain its speed and sacrifice accuracy or sacrifice its speed and maintain its accuracy" (Just and Carpenter, 1993, p. 334). What allocation strategy a reader will use likely depends on the goal of the reader. If the goal is comprehension, then speed will be sacrificed to maintain comprehension. If the goal is simply to complete a reading task, then comprehension will be sacrificed to maintain speed.

Eye Blinks

At a basic physiological level, eye blinks serve to remoisten the cornea. Each eye blink takes about 120 ms. Tecce (1992) has shown that on average adults need to blink about 2–4 times per minute to serve that function, but because a person blinks about 15–20 times per minute, blinks likely serve a variety of functions. For example, blinks may serve as a short restorative process for cognitive processing or as a way to facilitate the processing of information by modulating the size of incoming visual information streams. Blink rates have also been associated with nervousness, stress, fatigue, and mood states. Pleasant moods are associated with decreased blink rates, whereas unpleasant moods are associated with increased blink rates (Tecce, 1992). More germane to our purposes, Andreassi (1973) and Bauer et al. (1985) have shown that blinks are responsive to cognitive demands: blinks are inhibited under high cognitive demands and increase when demands are low.

The use of eye blinks as a psychophysiological index of cognitive activity has received considerable attention in the past few years and, more recently, blinks in conjunction with pupil dilation have provided a more complete picture of information processing. At first glance, the use of eye blinks along with pupil dilation would appear to preclude their concomitant use as psychophysiological indices of cognitive activity: eye blinks are measured when the eye is closed and pupil dilations are measured only when the eye is opened. A common practice for researchers interested in pupil dilation as a measure of cognitive load is to remove eye blinks from the data and interpolate pupil diameter measures during the times blinks occur. As blinking reduces the amount of light entering the eye, momentarily putting the iris into darkness, the pupil should dilate with blinks. Then, upon opening the eye lid, the retina is immersed in light, which should result in a constriction. Therefore, blinking can potentially interfere with pupillometric measures of dilation associated with cognitive load (Fukuda et al., 2005).

Some researchers have argued that because both eye blinks and PNS-mediated pupil constrictions originate in the Edinger–Westphal nucleus located in the medial frontal cortex, there is a neurological reason to believe that the two measures may be highly correlated. However, pupil and blink data appear to relate to different aspects of information processing. Using a digit-sort task and a typical Stroop task, Siegle et al. (2008) focused on the concomitant use of pupil dilation and blinks as complementary measures of information processing. On both tasks, blink activity was prominent just prior to peak cognitive load, was inhibited as pupil dilation increased to a maximum during performance, and was again prominent following peak cognitive load. Thus, blinks provided salient markers for the beginning and end of information processing, whereas pupil dilation varied with cognitive load. Siegle *et al.* concluded that "Reporting on blinks and pupil dilation in the same manuscript can provide convergent validity for explanations involving the time course of cognitive load, from preparation, onset of load, peak processing, and the offset of or recovery from cognitive load" (Siegle *et al.*, 2008, p. 686).

EVOKED PUPILLARY RESPONSES DURING DECEPTION

For nearly 70 years, deception researchers have been interested in the use of pupillary response to differentiate deceptive from truthful people. One of the earlier experiments was conducted by Berrien and Huntington (1943) who attempted to use pupillary changes to measure emotional disturbances believed to be associated with lying. As pupillary changes were linked to tension and emotional excitement, these two researchers hypothesized that if these affective reactions accompanied a person's deceit, they would be able to use pupillary responses as a valid indicator of his/her attempted deceit.

Along with blood pressure, Berrien and Huntington measured pupillary responses using an innovative but dubious methodology. They positioned a short-focus telescope in proximity to the participants' pupils so that the cross-hairs in the field of the telescope were brought tangent to the pupils. When the pupils dilated, the telescope was moved to the right or left by the researcher and the movement was transmitted to a recording pen attached to the telescope. Forty college students were asked to participate in a mock crime. Students assigned to a guilty condition were told to steal a dime, report back to the laboratory, and to lie to all questions connecting them to the crime. Students assigned to an innocent condition did not engage in the crime and simply waited outside the laboratory before they saw the researcher.

The results showed little correspondence between pupillary responses and vascular pressure changes; however, Berrien and Huntington did find: (1) some guilty participants exhibited a slow dilation followed by a rapid constriction in response to questions concerning their guilt, and (2) a sudden change in the stability of the pupil was found more often in the guilty participants. Unfortunately, Berrien and Huntington's findings showed that for about 50% of the participants, the dilation followed by constriction effect "was no more characteristic of the guilty than the innocent" (Berrien and Huntington, 1943, p. 445).

Subsequent researchers assumed that TEPRs were reactions to the unpleasant task of lying or the negative threatening consequences of being caught in a lie (Dionisio *et al.*, 2001). For example, Heilveil (1976) examined pupil dilation when participants were truthful or deceptive to personal questions that were designed to increase emotional reactions but reduce the amount of cognitive effort necessary to answer. Bradley and Janisse (1981) used the threat of physical pain (i.e., an electric shock), and Dumoff (1978; as reported in Bradley and Janisse, 1981) used psychological pain (i.e., a threat to the participant's ego) to elicit pupillary responses when being deceptive. The results of these experiments generally did show significant associations between pupil dilation and deception.

More recently, however, deception researchers have turned their attention to the hypothesis that being deceptive is more cognitively demanding than being truthful (Johnson *et al.*, 2005; Lubow and Fein, 1996; Seymour *et al.*, 2000; Vendemia *et al.*, 2005; Vrij, 2008; Vrij *et al.*, 2007, 2009; Walczyk *et al.*, 2003, 2009). As increased pupillary responses are associated with increased cognitive demands or increases in information processing (see above, e.g., Ahern and Beatty, 1979; Beatty and Wagoner, 1978; Hess and Polt, 1964; Just and Carpenter, 1993; Kahneman 1973; Kahneman and Beatty, 1966), the cognitive workload hypothesis holds that TEPR will be evident during deception and can be used as a psychophysiological index of deception.

In contrast to requiring simple "Yes" or "No" responses, Dionisio *et al.* (2001) used a high-load recall task in which participants were provided with paragraph-length stories and asked to confabulate either deceptive or truthful answers about information in the stories. In addition, participants were instructed to "try to make their lies as believable as possible" (Dionisio *et al.*, 2001, p. 207). The researchers hypothesized that placing a higher cognitive load on participants for deceptive responses than for truthful responses would lead to greater differences in pupil dilations between deceptive and truthful people. Their results supported their cognition-based theory of deception: for 92% of the participants, deceptive responses produced larger TEPRs than truthful responding. Dionisio *et al.* (2001) did entertain the possibility that emotional arousal may contribute to the pupil effects; however, they designed their research to reduce emotionality as a factor by (1) putting low-level emotional demands on the participants, (2) asking emotionally neutral questions, and (3) associating no risk or cost with being caught in a lie. Although there is likely little chance to produce a purely cognitive test of deception, especially in "real-life" contexts in which dire consequences could result from being deceptive, combining tasks that are both cognitively demanding and emotionally arousing may produce greater differentiation between truthful and deceptive people.

USING READING BEHAVIORS TO DETECT DECEPTION

Before we discuss how reading behaviors can be used to detect deception, we first describe how eye movements have been used to study reading. We discuss the various types of eye movements that occur during reading and how they are measured. With this foundation on eye movements established, we then describe how eye movements during reading have been used to investigate the cognitive processes involved in reading. We end this section with a rationale for why reading behaviors might be used to detect deception.

Eye Movements in the Study of Reading

Since the 1970s, a great deal of research has been conducted that examines the eye-movement behaviors of people as they read text. Various eye-tracking systems designed to measure eye movements provide detailed "microscopic" levels of analyses of where the eyes move while people are engaged in reading tasks. Far from the techniques pioneered by Hess and Polt (1960) in which the eye was photographed and pictures of pupil dilation were measured with rulers, new techniques make use of closed-circuit silicon matrix cameras that employ low-intensity infrared light to illuminate the eye and capture real-time eye movements and changes in pupil size (Andreassi, 2000).

The microscopic analyses derived from these new techniques have yielded great insights into the lexical, linguistic, and cognitive processes and states activated during reading, and have significantly added to current theories of language processing (for a review, see Rayner, 1998; Rayner *et al.*, 2012).

There are two underlying assumptions fundamental to the analysis and interpretation of eye-tracking data obtained during reading: the immediacy and eye–mind assumptions (Just and Carpenter, 1987). The immediacy assumption holds that as a word is encountered in a text, the reader immediately interprets the meaning of the word. Rather than waiting until after a group of words have been read (e.g., words in a clause) and generating an interpretation of the words only after they have all been read, a reader interprets the meaning of each word as it is encountered. The reader may engage in additional processing that includes all the words subsequent to reading them (e.g., a sentence wrap up process), but as each word is read, its semantic attributes are activated immediately.

The eye–mind assumption holds that a reader's eyes remain fixated on a word as long as that word is being actively processed (Just and Carpenter, 1987). A word may be further processed after the eyes no longer are fixated on it, but as the eyes fixate on a word, the assumption is that the word is currently being processed. When considering the practical implications of the eye–mind assumption, fixations approaching 1000 ms would indicate that the reader may be having difficulty understanding the word or disambiguating multiple meanings of the word, or the reader may be giving greater relevance to the word. As fixation durations are influenced by attentional span, maintaining attention and remaining fixated on a word for longer than 1000 ms would indicate that the reader's attention likely has drifted to other thoughts and the meaning of the word is no longer being processed. Fixations shorter than 50 ms would indicate possible subliminal processing of the word.

During normal reading of English, with the predominant left-to-right movement of the eyes, reading proceeds through a pattern that includes eyes first fixating on a collection of characters or spaces followed by rapid movements, called saccades, to the following collection of characters or spaces. Eye fixations last about 200–250 ms and, depending on the size of the font, approximately seven to nine characters or spaces can be kept in foveal view, with about three characters or spaces in parafoveal view to the right or left of a fixation (Rayner, 1998). Saccades are used to bring new regions of text into foveal view and average two to eight letters in length. Saccades are brief, lasting approximately 20–50 ms but average about 30 ms (Rayner, 1978). Fixations account for about 90% of the time during reading and saccades account for about 10% (Andreassi, 2000). Visual stimuli go undetected during a saccade, a phenomenon known as saccadic suppression, and some evidence suggests that general information processing may be suppressed as well during a saccade (Irwin *et al.*, 1995). However, because saccades are so rapid, "black outs" on information processing may go unnoticed (Irwin *et al.*, 1995).

Most words are fixated; however, many words are skipped. Content words are fixated about 85% of the time and function words about 35% of the time, although this varies with word length, with words of about eight letters or longer almost always being fixated (Daneman and Carpenter, 1983). In general, with the increase in word length, the probability of fixating a word increases. Also, as the conceptual difficulty of a text increases, the number and duration of fixations increase, saccade length decreases, and the frequency of regressions (i.e., backward saccades) increases. Words that are semantically related to previously encountered words are fixated for shorter periods than if the previously encountered words were not semantically related (Morris, 1994). Re-reading text results in fixations that are shorter in duration, with the decrease in time being more salient for low-frequency words (Rayner *et al.*, 1995). Fixation time for a pronoun varies as a function of how easy the link to its antecedent is made (Ehrlich and Rayner, 1983). Words that require the reader to make an inference are fixated for less time than when an inference is not required (O'Brien *et al.*, 1988). When an incorrect interpretation of a syntactically ambiguous phrase is made, fixation times on the disambiguating word increase and readers typically regress to re-read the ambiguous content (Frazier and Rayner, 1982).

Regressions (i.e., right-to-left eye movements in English) tend to be only a few letters long and only about 10–15% of saccades are regressions. Many regressions occur to correct for overly long saccades to the right, although longer regressions (i.e., more than ten letters/spaces) occur because the reader may not have understood the text and returns his/her gaze to the point in the text where the comprehension failure is believed to have occurred. Regressions often occur on return sweeps from the end of one line to the beginning of the next. In these cases, readers miss the first words of a line and need to correct to the left. Once the first word is brought into foveal view, the first fixation on that word tends to be longer than other fixations and the last fixation on a line of text tends to be shorter.

There are numerous eye-movement measures that can be taken during reading. Saccade latency is the amount of time a reader takes to plan and execute an eye movement. Fixation duration is the amount of time the eyes are fixated on a particular point in a text. First fixation duration is the amount of time a reader first fixates on a word regardless of whether it is the only fixation on a word or the first of multiple fixations on a word. Gaze duration is the total amount of time of all fixations made on a word prior to a saccade to another word. Regression latency is the amount of time a reader takes to plan and execute a backwards movement of the eyes. First pass is the initial reading time of a region of text consisting of all forward fixations. Go-past time is the amount of time for a first pass through a region of text, plus any additional time spent on regressions in that region or previous regions before the reader goes beyond that region. Fixation frequency is the number of fixations in a region of text. Second-pass duration is the amount of time re-reading a region of text. Total time is the sum of all times spent reading and re-reading a region of text. In general, there are problems directly mapping reading processes (e.g., lexical access, integration) onto any one of these measures of eye movements because the measures contain overlapping information; therefore, researchers typically adopt a more convergent measurement approach wherein they report several oculomotor measures of information processing for a region of text (Rayner, 1998).

Examinations of Eye Movements to Infer Cognitive States and Information Processing

Research over the past 30 years has convincingly supported the claim that eye-movement measures taken during reading can be used to infer the moment-to-moment cognitive processes and states of the reader (e.g., Just and Carpenter, 1980; McConkie *et al.*, 1979; Rayner, 1978, 1998; Rayner and Duffy, 1986; Rayner and Liversedge, 2011; Rayner *et al.*, 1989). Moreover, the recording of eye movements during reading provides important information about readers' strategic processing of text in response to specific goals for reading (Hyönä and Nurminen, 2006; Kaakinen and Hyönä, 2010).

Questions remain, however, concerning the nature of the moment-to-moment cognitive processing and mental states that are indexed by eye movements. Do eye movements index simple visual processing of textual stimuli or do they index deeper states of cognitive and linguistic processing? One group of researchers has pursued investigations of eye movements under conditions that have relied primarily on the presentation of single words to participants. These researchers propose that preceding any language processing of text during reading, there is a stage of visual processing and that this stage of visual processing reflects, in part, cognitive strategies or heuristics that are designed to optimize the perception of visual material during language processing (e.g., Vitu, 2011).

This oculomotor view can be contrasted with a linguistic/cognitive view that is supported by researchers whose investigations are predominantly spurred by questions regarding eye movements specific to more complex reading that entails reading of multiple words and most often complete sentences (e.g., Just and Carpenter, 1993; Rayner and Liversedge, 2009). Proponents of this view propose that eye movements reflect processing efforts involved in readers' construction of a mental representation of text. These efforts would include the retrieval of word meanings, the ongoing processing of syntactic and semantic information derived from the text, and the interpretation of textual information in light of world knowledge.

Considering the focus of the present chapter, the most desirable conclusion to draw would be that the latter group has the preferred outlook on eye movements during reading, and the former group has only peripheral interest in more complex reading and therefore only peripheral application to our concerns. However, eye-movement behaviors at local levels of text (e.g., simple word characteristics) can have significant effects on eye movements when processing larger chunks of text during complex reading, and the theoretical and empirical lines that separate the two views are not as clear as one would hope.

Consider, for example, the effects that visual perception of word characteristics can have on eye movements. Word length, frequency, and predictability exert strong influences on eye movements. Word length can determine whether a word is fixated, where within the word it is fixated, how many times it is fixated, and whether regressions are required to fully process the word. For example, words of one or two characters are skipped on average about 76% of the time, but this drops to 42% of the time for four characters and to about 5% of the time for nine or ten character words (Rayner and McConkie, 1976; Vitu *et al.*, 2001). Word length also exerts strong effects on where fixations occur within a word. The preferred viewing position for short words (e.g., four or five letters) is somewhere right of center, but for longer words (e.g., eight letters) tends to be at the center of the word (Vitu *et al.*, 2001). Relatedly, where a fixation lands on a word (i.e., landing site) depends on where the prior fixation has occurred (i.e., the launch site). If the landing site on a word occurs toward the beginning of a longer word, the chances that the word is refixated greatly increase (Nuthmann *et al.*, 2005). High-frequency words in our lexicon are typically skipped during reading, or if fixated, the fixation on the word will be short in duration. In contrast, low-frequency words are typically fixated for longer periods. Finally, words with high predictability in a text are typically skipped during reading or, if fixated, fixated for short periods of time.

Rayner and Liversedge (2011) have acknowledged the importance of the oculomotor view of reading and believe that "visual/oculomotor processes have strong effects" (Rayner and Liversedge, 2011, p. 753) on reading. However, their belief is that these effects usually occur rapidly after a word has been first fixated. The importance of a word being lexically identified is obvious, because only after a word has been identified can syntactic and semantic information be extracted and incorporated into the ongoing construction of a meaningful text. Therefore, syntactic and semantic processing depend on and follow lexical processing (Rayner and Liversedge, 2011). Early reading measures (e.g., first and single fixations) likely reflect to a large extent initial lexical processing, and later reading measures (e.g., regressions, go-past times, total time) likely reflect semantic and discourse processing. Higher-order cognitive processes involving discourse processing, such as plausibility, syntactic disambiguation, clause construction, anaphoric resolution, and inferential processing are likely to occur later in the visual processing of text and have strong influences on eye movements and pupil size.

A useful distinction made by Rayner and Liversedge (2011) concerns the cognitive processing necessary to decide *where* to move the eyes versus *when* to move the eyes. They propose that the "where" decision is driven by low-level visual processing, such as word length, frequency, and predictability, and the "when" decision is largely driven by linguistic/cognitive processing. The "where" decision is made rapidly and on the basis of whether a word has been recognized. The "when" decision is driven by the reader's recognition that a meaningful mental representation of text has been constructed and interpretations of that meaning have been reconciled with world knowledge. To adequately explain eye movements and variance in pupil size during reading, issues of when and where are needed to fully explain the cognitive processes responsible for visual processing of text and the cognitive processing responsible for higher-order comprehension processing. However, Rayner and Liversedge maintain that the "battle over what influences eye movements appears to be largely resolved in favor of the view that whilst visual characteristics of text do affect where and when we fixate during reading, it is the case that cognitive and linguistic processing also have a very significant, if not predominant, influence" (Rayner and Liversedge, 2011, p. 763).

Why Reading Behaviors can be Used to Detect Deception

Under most circumstances, the purpose of reading is to construct a meaningful mental representation of a text that is consistent, coherent, and integrated into the reader's background knowledge. The extent to which consistency, coherence, and integration are achieved will determine the quality and extent of the reader's comprehension of a text. Constructing a mental representation of a text, like most human endeavors, is goal oriented (Carver and Scheier, 1998) and the goals a reader has will alter how a text is read. For example, reading for pleasure versus reading to edit will alter the reader's online comprehension processes of a text (Kaakinen, and Hyönä, 2010; van den Broek *et al.*, 2001), and consequently result in varying mental representations of the text. Under normal reading conditions, people focus their goals on semantic levels of text representation, but goals for reading could very well be focused on other levels of text representation (e.g., a copy editor searching for spelling or grammatical errors). In most cases, goals for reading are explicit, such as reading a text for the specific purpose of finding the key idea contained within it. However, some goals can be implicit, as in the case of the reader who, when trying to find the key idea in a text, discovers a misspelled word. Although finding misspelled words was not an explicit goal, discovering the misspelling may come as an automatic consequence of reading for meaning (Hacker, 1997).

Most goals are hierarchical in nature (Conway, 2005): higher-level goals are often translated into lower-level goals (i.e., goals that serve to accomplish the higher-level goal). For instance, a reader with the higher-level goal to comprehend a text will read with the intent of developing a mental representation of that text. As the reader monitors and controls the generation of the text representation (i.e., self-regulating comprehension; Hacker, 2004), he/she may encounter some unknown words. In this case, the reader needs to develop a lower-level goal, the purpose of which is to find the meaning of the unknown words. This lower-level goal may be focused on developing strategies such as checking a dictionary or asking someone more knowledgeable.

Often, goals change as a task progresses (Carver and Scheier, 1998; Conway, 2005; Rijlaarsdam and van den Bergh, 1996). In the case of reading, as a mental representation of the text develops, the goals for reading may change. The text being read modifies the reader's knowledge and that new knowledge may result in a change in goals. For instance, gradually getting more and more engrossed in reading a novel may intensify the reader's attention during reading. Also, goals can be replaced by other goals. A reader may realize that a goal cannot be satisfied, in which case the goal may be dropped in favor of others. The generation and changing of goals is an active within-person cognitive endeavor, with the reader assuming greater or lesser engagement depending on such things as (1) task variables, for instance the kind of text, the topic of the text, or text difficulty, (2) person variables, such as motivation, level of knowledge, or reading ability, and (3) strategy variables, which would include how the text should be read to achieve the goals (Flavell, 1979).

An individual's goals for reading influence the selection of a set of standards of evaluation (SoE) (Baker, 1984, 1985; Baker and Zimlin, 1989; Hacker, 1994, 1997) or standards of coherence (van den Broek *et al.*, 2011). SoE or standards of coherence are implicit or explicit criteria that drive the automatic and strategic processing of text at each level of text representation. Low-level representations of text relate to meaning and syntax, whereas higher semantic levels involve inferential processing, such as referential, causal, spatial, temporal, or logical deductive and inductive reasoning (Graesser *et al.*, 1994). Although SoE and standards of coherence are similar concepts, we have adopted the former concept because standards can be used either implicitly or explicitly to guide reading at all levels of text representation and are not relegated to only textual coherence.

To illustrate how SoE operate, consider the example given above. A reader with the higher-level goal to comprehend a text could have implicit standards that guide reading for comprehension, explicit standards specifically designed to read to create coherence from one sentence to the next, or both. If the outcome of applying a standard indicates that comprehension has failed, the reader will need to make an assessment of why comprehension has failed and develop lower-level goals to reinstate comprehension. If the assessment indicates that the comprehension failure is due to unknown words, the reader will then establish a SoE at the lexical level and examine individual words for their meaning. If the assessment is due to referential ambiguity, the reader will then need to establish a SoE at a syntactic level to resolve the ambiguity. Thus, SoE serve as strategies the reader employs to achieve specific goal-oriented reading behaviors.

Research has shown that a reader's goals for reading and the implicit or explicit SoE that the reader selects affect the kinds of reading in which the reader engages (Baker, 1984, 1985; Baker and Zimlin, 1989; Beal, 1990; Beal *et al.*, 1990; Hacker, 1997, 2004; Kaakinen and Hyönä, 2010; van den Broek *et al.*, 2011). For instance, Hyönä *et al.* (2002) and Hyönä and Nurminen (2006) identified two key behaviors in competent adult readers: (1) the speed at which a sentence is read for the first time, and (2) lookback frequency. Both of these reading behaviors have been reported in verbal protocols by competent readers as being strategically employed for specific purposes during reading (e.g., slowing reading on difficult words or checking whether critical information can be recalled) (Pressley and Afflerbach, 1995). Although some reading behaviors may be the result of highly automatized cognitive or physiological processing (i.e., recall the "where" decision to move the eyes), there are clearly identifiable reading behaviors that are employed by readers as conscious strategies to achieve specific goals (i.e., recall the "when" decision to move the eyes).

As a person's goals for reading and the implicit or explicit SoE that are used affect the kinds of reading in which a reader engages, we hypothesized that specific goals for reading and the SoE used to achieve those goals would be identifiable by specific reading behaviors. Focusing our attention on detecting deception, our research question was: "Would the goal to conceal the truth during reading lead to uniquely identifiable reading behaviors?" We proposed that a person who reads with the goal to conceal the truth will adopt SoE to achieve that goal. The goals and SoE of a deceptive individual will result in reading behaviors that differ from those of a truthful person whose goals do not include deception. That is, a deceptive person's reading will differ from that of a truthful person. Although the differences may be subtle, with modern eye-tracking technology, they should be discernible.

HOW OCULAR METRICS DURING READING CAN BE USED TO DETECT DECEPTION

To understand how reading behaviors and ocular metrics can be used to detect deception, we must first establish the context for reading. Three variables define the context: (1) *task variables* (e.g., the content of the texts to be read and the level of reading difficulty), (2) *person variables* (e.g., participants' goals, reading ability, motivation, and emotionality), and (3) *strategy variables* (i.e., the SoE the participants use either implicitly or explicitly during reading to achieve goals).

The first context that we arranged involved a laboratory experiment in which we administered our oculomotor deception test. In this experiment, some participants had committed a mock theft of $20 from a secretary's purse, other participants downloaded personal information from an unattended personal computer, and the remaining participants were innocent of both crimes. All participants were instructed to deny having been involved in either crime. They were told to respond as quickly and accurately as possible or they would fail the test, and they were motivated by a cash reward to appear innocent of both crimes.

The Relevant Comparison Test (RCT) was administered to each participant. The RCT contained a series of True/False statements. One set of relevant statements addressed the theft of the $20, e.g., "I did not take the $20 from the secretary's purse." Another set of relevant statements addressed the theft of the personal information, and the remaining statements were neutral, e.g., "The sky is blue on sunny days." Statements about the crime the participant had committed were labeled R1 and statements about the crime the participant did not commit were labeled R2. The statements were presented one at a time and the order was mixed. The RCT was so named because diagnoses of truth and deception are based on comparisons of oculomotor responses to R1 and R2 test statements. Our hypothesis was that the goals and SoE used for reading vary for people who attempt to conceal their guilt and people who are innocent, and that the varying goals and SoE are made evident in their reading behaviors and pupil responses. Table 5.1 shows the proposed reading goals and SoE that participants would use to respond to the statements. There likely would be variability in how the goals and standards are used due to individual differences in reading ability. For instance, for some readers the goals and standards could be implicit in nature and for other readers explicit, or they could be performed serially or in parallel. Examining the effects of reading fluency on how the goals and standards are managed are important lines for future research. In addition, because emotionality contributes to pupil dilation, the levels of emotionality associated with each type of statement need to be considered.

"Goal$_1$: appear innocent" applies to both deceptive and truthful individuals, but the goal has greater importance for the former and consequently greater impact on their reading. The remaining goals and SoE also apply to both deceptive and truthful individuals, but for truthful individuals, the SoE for both crimes are the same and follow those described for R2 statements. Also, because truthful individuals have nothing to conceal, the emotional arousal for all types of statements is lower than for deceptive people.

TABLE 5.1   Goals, SoE, and Emotionality of Participants that Contributed to Their Reading Behaviors

Goals	SoE	Cognitive demand	Emotion
$Goal_1$: appear innocent		More attention devoted to maintaining this goal in guilty participants	Greater arousal in guilty participants
$Goal_{2.1}$: read accurately			
$Goal_{2.2}$: read quickly			
$Goal_3$: identify statement type	SoE_1: read for comprehension		
	SoE_2: read to identify each statement type from its unique characteristics		
$Goal_4$: employ SoE for each statement type	Neutral SoE_1: read to undo negation		Low arousal
	R2 SoE_1: read to identify key word(s)		Higher arousal
	R2 SoE_2: read to evaluate key word(s)		
	R2 SoE_3: read to undo negation	Increased demand	
	R1 SoE_1: read to identify key word(s)		Higher arousal
	R1 SoE_2: read to evaluate key word(s)		
	R1 SoE_3: read to undo negation	Increased demand	
	R1 SoE_4: read to evaluate response to appear innocent (reverse response)	More resources invested by guilty participants to reverse a truthful answer	Highest arousal for guilty participants
$Goal_5$: respond to statement			

R1 refers to statements relevant to the crime committed, R2 refers to statements relevant to the crime not committed.

Both "$Goal_{2.1}$: read accurately" and "$Goal_{2.2}$: read quickly" develop in direct response to the instructions given: at the outset of the protocol, participants were told, "To appear innocent, you should respond as quickly and as accurately as you possibly can." Based on the work of Just and Carpenter (1993), when faced with reading for speed or reading for comprehension, readers must develop an allocation strategy to meet the multiple demands. Readers in the present context must be accurate in their reading to avoid answering incorrectly; therefore, "$Goal_{2.1}$: read accurately" would take precedence over "$Goal_{2.2}$: read quickly." However, they must also read quickly, and even though this goal may be secondary to the first, attempting to satisfy the two goals is demanding of cognitive resources. These two goals are salient for both truthful and deceptive individuals, but they are more salient for deceptive individuals whose accurate and quick responding is critical to conceal their guilt. Therefore, the cognitive demands from combining these two goals is greater for deceptive than truthful individuals.

Although participants were not directly exposed to the three statement types prior to responding to them, "$Goal_3$: identify statement type" likely forms online shortly into the protocol after several exposures to the statements. How quickly this goal and the corresponding SoE develop also depends on individual differences in reading ability. To satisfy this reading goal, an implicit SoE "SoE_1: read for comprehension" and an explicit standard "SoE_2: read to identify each statement type from its unique characteristics" must be used with all statements. For fluent readers, the implicit SoE has low demand on cognitive effort, but the explicit standard at least initially places additional demands on cognitive effort.

"$Goal_4$: employ SoE for each statement type" requires that once a statement is identified as belonging to one of the three types, different SoE are used to respond to it. Answering the neutral statements places fewer demands on cognitive resources than answering the other two statement types because only general world knowledge needs to be accessed. In addition, there is low emotional arousal to neutral statements in comparison to the other two statement types. An additional SoE is needed to undo negations before a correct response can be given. Undoing negations requires additional cognitive resources (MacDonald and Just, 1989), but this requirement for additional resources is present while reading all negations across statement type.

Statements referring to the crime the individual did not commit (i.e., R2 statements) require two SoE and a third for the negations. In our experiment, reading involved identifying key words that dealt with either "cash" or "credit card" to determine the relevance of the statement. After participants judged that a statement was not relevant to them, they choose either a true or false response, whichever made them appear innocent. Although participants did not commit the crime referred to in the R2 statements, the presence of threat in the statement potentially increases emotional arousal in comparison to neutral statements.

For deceptive participants, R1 statements require three SoE and a fourth for the negations. As with the R2 statements, reading involved identifying key words that dealt with either "cash" or "credit card" to determine the relevance of the statement. Once relevance was established, the statement was evaluated for a true or false response. As these statements were incriminating, the participant had to develop the correct answer and then reverse the answer to maintain the deception. For example, the statement, "I took the $20 from the secretary's purse," for a guilty person was True, but that answer had to be reversed to conceal the truth. Finally, because the R1 statements dealt with the crime the participant did commit, the presence of threat was highest for these statements, bringing emotional arousal to its highest level in comparison to the other two statement types.

In sum, the differences in reading behaviors between deceptive and truthful participants lie in (1) the goals for reading, (2) the SoE used to read the statements, (3) the cognitive demands associated with maintaining and executing the goals, and (4) the emotional arousal elicited by the statements. For innocent participants, there is no deception, thereby reducing cognitive and emotional demands on reading to meet "Goal$_1$: appear innocent." Also, the standard, "R1 SoE$_4$: read to evaluate response to appear innocent (reverse response)" is not required and participants have only to respond truthfully to all statements. This makes the SoE identical for reading R1 and R2 statements, and reading behaviors should be similar across the two statement types. Compared with guilty participants, the innocent participants will have lower levels of cognitive load and emotional arousal for R1 and R2 statements, and innocent participants will show lower levels of dilation for neutral statements and higher but similar levels of pupil dilation for R1 and R2 statements.

For participants guilty of either of the two crimes, the goals for reading are the same, but the differences in the SoE among the three statement types place differing demands on cognitive effort. The number of standards increase from neutral statements to R2 statements and from R2 statements to R1 statements, and as the number of standards increases, the cognitive effort required to apply the standards also increases. In addition, there is an increase in emotional arousal from neutral statements to R2 statements and from R2 to R1 statements. The combined increases in cognitive effort and emotional arousal will produce increases in pupil dilation, with the largest increases occurring for the statements relevant to the crime committed.

We had hypothesized that the differing goals and SoE between deceptive and truthful participants and between participants who had committed one of the two crimes would be identifiable by unique reading behaviors. As this context for reading that we contrived is unlike other reading contexts that have been investigated, specific predictions concerning how reading behaviors would differ were difficult to make, and competing predictions were justified in some cases. We had a strong theoretical rationale for differences in pupil responses, but the theory did not predict the exact nature of differences in reading patterns. We left it up to empirical research to determine if or how reading patterns would distinguish among the groups. In two laboratory experiments, we tested our hypotheses regarding pupil size and differences in reading behaviors (Cook *et al.*, 2012; Osher, 2006; Webb, 2008; Webb *et al.*, 2006, 2009). In the first experiment, along with changes in pupil dilation, we measured response time and response errors. We also recorded several measures of reading behavior that can occur within a single response: fixation frequency (number of fixations), initial reading time (first-pass duration), and subsequent re-reading (second-pass duration). The second experiment was designed to replicate the results from the first experiment and investigate the role of other variables that could influence the accuracy of an oculomotor test for deception that was based on a combination of behavioral and oculomotor measures.

LABORATORY EXPERIMENT 1

Method

Design

Twenty-four males and 16 females were randomly assigned to either an innocent condition ($n = 20$), "Cash" condition ($n = 10$), or "Card" condition ($n = 10$) in a $3 \times (3 \times 3)$ mixed design. They ranged in age from 18 to 36 years [mean (*M*) = 22.35 years, standard deviation (SD) = 4.3], were predominantly Caucasian (82.5%), single (77.5%), and students at the University of Utah (92.5%). The between-subjects variable was guilt, and the two within-subjects factors were statement type (neutral, cash, and card) and repetition (three repetitions of test statements).

Materials

There were 48 test statements (16 neutral, 16 cash crime, and 16 card crime), which were repeated three times in different orders. Each statement type required an equal number of true and false responses, and each group of true and false statements was subdivided into equal numbers of statements with and without negation.

Apparatus

Participants' eye movements were monitored using an Applied Sciences Laboratory (ASL) Model 501 head-mounted eye-tracker. Participants had freedom of head movement while wearing the eye-tracker. Eye movement and pupil diameter were recorded at 60 Hz (i.e., 60 times per second) from the participant's right eye.

Measures

Each statement was surrounded by a region-of-interest (ROI) that was 32 mm in height, started with the first character, and ended with the period at the end of the statement. The dependent measures were: pupil diameter, response time, response accuracy, number of fixations, first-pass duration, and second-pass duration. Number of fixations, first-pass duration, and second-pass duration were recorded when participants had fixated within the ROI for each statement.

PUPIL DIAMETER

Reading onset was defined as the first sample of the first of four consecutive fixations in the ROI. The difference in pupil diameter between the first sample and each subsequent sample for a period of four seconds provided an evoked pupil response curve and represented changes in pupil response over time from stimulus onset. Area under the evoked pupil response curve was computed to obtain a single measure of the magnitude of the pupil response (Kircher and Raskin, 1988).

MEASURES OF READING BEHAVIORS

Number of fixations was the number of times a participant fixated in the ROI. First-pass duration was the sum of durations of all fixations in the ROI until the participant moved somewhere outside the ROI. Second-pass duration was the sum of durations for all fixations that the participant made while re-reading the statement after having fixated outside the ROI. To adjust for differences in length as a function of statement type, number of fixations was converted to number of fixations per character, and response time and first- and second-pass reading times were converted to milliseconds per character (Rayner, 1998).

Procedure

Each participant reported alone to a room on campus, read and signed the consent form, and read the instructions from a computer screen. No researcher was present at the initial study location. After reading the instructions, the participant was given the option to discontinue the study. Participants who decided to continue were randomly assigned to one of three conditions. Guilty condition participants were informed that they had no more than 30 minutes to complete their assigned crime. Participants in the "Cash" crime were instructed to steal $20 from a secretary's purse; participants in the "Card" crime were instructed to steal credit card information from a student's computer. Innocent participants were given general descriptions of the crimes but did not enact them. To ensure that guilty and innocent participants arrived at the lab at approximately the same time, innocent participants were told to report to the lab after waiting 20–35 minutes.

To motivate participants to pass the test, guilty and innocent participants were promised a $30 bonus in addition to their $30 in pay ($60 total) if they appeared truthful to all of the statements on the test. Prior to their arrival at the lab, all participants were also given the following instruction:

> [Y]ou must not make the examiner suspicious at any point during the test. The test is based on the idea that a person who committed a crime will have a difficult time

answering quickly and honestly to questions about the crime. You could make the examiner suspicious if it takes you a long time to answer the questions or if you make lots of mistakes. To appear innocent, you should respond as quickly and as accurately as you possibly can.

In the laboratory, each participant was seated in front of the computer monitor. The ASL eye-tracker was attached and calibrated. The participant was informed that statements would be presented individually on the computer screen and each statement required a true or false response. Each statement was presented on a single line in the center of the computer monitor beginning near the left edge of the screen. To answer true or false, the participant used a mouse to click one of two radio buttons that appeared on the right side of the screen adjacent to the statement. When the participant answered, the statement was replaced by the next statement in the preprogrammed sequence. The 48 statements were repeated in three blocks in pseudo-random order separated by an unrelated filler-task that took 5–10 minutes to complete. After completion of the test, the participant was informed if he/she passed the test, was debriefed, paid, and released.

Results

Repeated measures analysis of variance (RMANOVA) was used to analyze the data. As our main interest in the analyses concerned the two-way interaction between statement type × guilt and the three-way interaction involving statement type × guilt × time, only these significant interactions are reported.

Response Time

There was a significant interaction between statement type and guilt. Participants who were guilty of stealing the cash took less time to respond per character on the cash statements than on the neutral or card statements, and participants who were guilty of stealing the credit card information took less time to respond on the card statements than on either the cash or neutral statements. Innocent participants' response times did not differ as a function of statement type.

Pupil Dilation

Changes in pupil size for four seconds following statement onset were analyzed using a RMANOVA. Innocent participants showed significantly greater pupil dilation in response to crime-relevant statements than neutral statements, and their pupil dilations in response to cash and card statements were similar. Guilty participants showed larger dilations while reading statements concerning the crime they committed: cash-crime participants showed larger dilations to cash statements and card-crime participants showed larger dilations to card statements. Additional tests indicated that innocent participants reacted more strongly to crime-related statements than to neutral statements.

Reading Measures

For number of fixations per character, there was an interaction between statement type and guilt. Participants guilty of taking the cash made fewer fixations when reading statements about the cash than when reading about the credit card; participants guilty of taking the credit card information made fewer fixations on statements about the credit card than the cash. For innocent participants, the number of fixations varied little across statement types.

Analysis of first- and second-pass durations also showed interactions between statement type and guilt. For guilty participants, first-pass reading times were shorter for crime statements than for neutral statements. In addition, participants guilty of the cash crime spent less time re-reading statements about the cash, whereas participants guilty of the credit card crime spent less time re-reading statements about the credit card. For innocent subjects, first-pass durations did not differ across statement type.

Discriminant Analyses

Discriminant analyses were conducted to assess the degree to which pupil response, number of fixations, first-pass duration, and second-pass duration could be used to differentiate among the three treatment conditions. For each outcome measure, responses to neutral, cash, and card statements were used to derive three new variables. The primary outcome variable was the difference between responses to cash and card statements. We expected this difference to differentiate between the two guilty groups. Another variable was the mean response to neutral statements, which provided a general measure of arousal or vigilance. The last variable was the difference between the combined mean response to cash (R1) and card (R2) statements and the response to neutral statements (i.e., [R1 + R2]/2 − N). Guilty participants were expected to show greater differences between crime-related and neutral statements than innocent participants.

Stepwise discriminant analysis was used to select subsets of the available oculomotor measures for discriminant functions that classified cases into cash, card, and innocent groups (Kircher and Raskin, 1988). The analysis produced two significant discriminant functions. The first discriminant function used the difference in pupil response between crime-related and neutral statements as well as number of fixations on neutral statements to discriminate between participants in guilty and innocent groups ($R^2 = 0.49$, $p < 0.01$). The second discriminant function used the difference in pupil response to cash and card statements and the difference in second-pass re-reading of cash and card statements to discriminate between the two guilty groups ($R^2 = 0.41$, $p < 0.01$). The discriminant functions correctly classified nine of ten (90%) cash-crime participants, eight of ten (80%) card-crime participants, and 17 of 20 (85%) innocent participants. Combined, the selected oculomotor measures yielded 85% correct classifications.

Discussion

We had hypothesized that differences between deceptive and truthful participants lie in (1) the goals for reading, (2) the SoE used to read the statements, (3) the cognitive demands associated with maintaining and executing the goals, and (4) the emotional arousal elicited by the statements, and that these differences would be reflected in pupil dilation and reading behaviors. Consistent with these predictions, differences between guilty and innocent participants in pupil dilation and reading behaviors were diagnostic of group membership and contributed to decisions that were correct for over 80% of the participants.

As innocent participants were not deceptive, "Goal$_1$: appear innocent" played a less salient role in reading than for guilty participants, but the other five goals remained. In addition, because the innocent participants were free from guilt, emotional arousal would be lower as compared with guilty participants. As there was only one SoE for neutral items with low arousal, pupil dilation would be at a minimum for these statements. Card and cash statements had a greater number of SoE than for neutral statements, but for innocent participants, the number of SoE were the same for both crimes; therefore, these two types of statements would elicit higher but comparable levels of cognitive load than neutral statements, resulting in comparable increases in pupil dilation as compared with neutral statements. The analysis of the pupil data confirmed these predictions: pupil dilation was lowest for neutral statements and higher but similar for cash and card statements. Although the innocent participants did not commit either of the crimes, statements pertaining to the crimes may have been perceived as threats because if they appeared deceptive on those statements, they would not receive the $30 bonus.

For participants guilty of either of the two crimes, the goals for reading were the same, but the number of SoE differed for the three statement types and the effort required to process the statements varied as a function of the number of SoE. The SoE increased from neutral statements to R2 statements and from R2 statements to R1 statements, and there were corresponding increases in cognitive load. In addition, there was an increase in emotional arousal from neutral statements to R2 statements and from R2 to R1 statements. The combined increases in cognitive effort and emotional arousal resulted in increased pupil dilation for statements reflective of guilt. The analysis of the pupil data again confirmed these predictions: for both crime groups, pupil dilation was lowest for neutral statements, higher for statements about the crime not committed, and highest for the statements about the crime committed. The increase in pupil dilation for the crime not committed may have resulted because participants, although not guilty of the crime, may have perceived the statements as threatening.

Although we expected that reading behaviors would differ given the goals for reading and the differing SoE for each condition in the experiment, we were uncertain about how they would differ. Our results showed that participants guilty of a crime had fewer fixations, read faster, and did less re-reading on the statements relevant to the crime they had committed in comparison to statements concerning the other crime and neutral statements. In contrast, innocent participants made about as many fixations, and spent about as much time reading and re-reading all three types of statement. These findings in conjunction with the pupil data can be interpreted in terms of the goals and SoE participants had for reading.

At the outset of the experiment, participants were given two goals for reading: "$Goal_{2.1}$: read accurately" and "$Goal_{2.2}$: read quickly." These two goals in tandem placed a heavy load on cognitive processing. Guilty participants appear to have met the increased demands as evidenced by faster response times, faster reading times, less re-reading, and high accuracy when responding to R1 statements, but meeting these increased demands came at a cost of greater cognitive effort as evidenced by increased pupil dilation. In addition, because there were no discernible repetition effects, participants continued to put forth the cognitive effort across the three repetitions to manage reading speed and accuracy. Pursuit of "$Goal_3$: identify statement type" and its associated "SoE_2: read to identify each statement type from its unique characteristics" appear to have been initiated early in the reading of each statement, and as soon as unique characteristics were identified, the participants engaged in fast and accurate reading. Once participants identified the unique characteristics, "$Goal_4$: employ SoE for each statement type" and the associated SoE were engaged to provide answers that concealed their guilt.

LABORATORY EXPERIMENT 2

In addition to assessing the reliability of results from the first experiment, in Experiment 2, we sought to investigate the role of other variables that could influence the accuracy of an oculomotor test for detecting deception. In the first experiment, we attempted to motivate all participants to pass the test with monetary rewards. As motivation to deceive may affect the diagnostic validity of measures of deception (Kircher *et al.*, 1988), in Experiment 2, we manipulated motivation by varying the monetary rewards participants could earn if they passed the test. Second, in Experiment 1, the complexity of statement structure varied from simple to complex. Consequently, participants may have responded more easily to some statements than others regardless of guilt status. This may have increased unwanted variability and diminished our ability to distinguish among the groups. To better understand the impact of linguistic processing demands, we manipulated sentence complexity by presenting a mixed set of simple and complex statements to half our participants, and only simple statements to the other half. Third, because the use of eye blinks as a psychophysiological index of cognitive activity has received considerable attention in the literature and, more recently, blinks in conjunction with pupil dilation have provided a more complete picture of information processing (Andreassi, 1973; Bauer *et al.*, 1985; Siegle *et al.*, 2008; Stern *et al.*, 1984), we introduced eye blinks to provide convergent validity concerning the cognitive load participants experienced in response to the three types of statements. Fourth, the three repetitions of the statements we used in Experiment 1 may have been insufficient to observe habituation effects. In Experiment 2, we increased the number of repetitions of statements from three to five.

The context for reading remained essentially the same in Experiment 2: we used a mock crime and had participants respond true or false to the three statement types (i.e., neutral statements, statements related to a crime committed, and statements related to another crime), an equal number of negation and non-negation statements were constructed for each statement type, we instructed participants to respond quickly and accurately to the statements, and our participants were drawn from the same population. In Experiment 1, there was an innocent group and two guilty groups. In Experiment 2, there was an innocent group and only one group of guilty participants. The guilty participants in Experiment 2 stole $20, although all participants were led to believe that there was another guilty group that stole an exam. Therefore, the goals and SoE shown in Table 5.1 are applicable to the present experiment. In this case, R1 refers to statements about the theft of the $20 and R2 refers to statements about the theft of the exam, which no one committed.

Method

Design
Participants were either innocent or guilty of stealing $20 from a secretary's purse. To retain a non-neutral comparison condition for our statements, participants were led to believe that another crime (i.e., stealing an exam from

a professor's office) had been committed. Fifty-six females and 56 males were randomly assigned to one of eight cells in a $2 \times 2 \times 2 \times 2 \times (3 \times 5)$ mixed design. The between-subjects variables were guilt (guilty versus innocent), motivation ($30 versus $1), statement difficulty (mix of simple and complex statements versus simple statements only), and sex (male versus female). The two within-subject factors were statement type (neutral, cash, and exam) and repetition (five repetitions of each statement). Participants ranged in age from 18 to 67 years, were predominantly Caucasian, and students at the University of Utah.

Apparatus

An Arrington ViewPoint eye-tracker was used to record eye movements and pupil diameter from the right eye at 30 Hz. Test statements were presented in a single line in the center of a 19-inch computer monitor.

Materials

Participants responded to 48 statements on five occasions. Sixteen statements pertained to the theft of the $20, 16 pertained to the theft of the exam, and 16 were neutral. The numbers of correct true and false statements and statements with and without negation were crossed and balanced within statement types. Half of the participants received a mixed set of statements that contained both simple and complex statements, and half received only simple statements. Complex statements included a relative clause, e.g., "The twenty dollars that was in the office is not in my possession."

Measures

Experiment 2 included all of the outcome measures in Experiment 1 and added two measures of blink rate: blink rate was the number of blinks per second for each statement, and next statement blink rate was the number of blinks per second for the statement that followed.

Results

Manipulation Check

The monetary bonus was rated as more important to participants promised $30 for a truthful outcome than to participants promised only $1 for a truthful outcome Participants' self-reports were consistent with our intention to manipulate levels of motivation to pass the test.

Response Time

Guilty participants responded more quickly when they lied to statements concerning the theft of the $20 than when they answered truthfully to neutral statements or statements about the theft of the exam. Innocent participants generally responded more quickly than guilty participants, and differences among statement types were smaller for innocent than guilty participants.

Pupil Dilation

For guilty participants, pupil dilation was significantly greater to cash statements than to exam statements. For innocent participants, pupil dilation was slightly but significantly greater for exam statements than for cash statements.

Reading Measures

Guilty participants made fewer fixations while reading statements about the crime they committed than statements about the other crime or neutral content. For innocent participants, there was little difference in numbers of fixations for the three statement types. For number of fixations, the incentive manipulation had a greater effect on innocent participants than guilty participants: the innocent participants in the high motivation condition made fewer fixations than innocent participants in the low motivation condition. In addition, mixed statements (i.e., simple and complex statements) were fixated more often than simple statements.

The effects of guilt and statement type on first- and second-pass duration were similar to those obtained in Experiment 1. In addition, blink rates were lower for guilty participants when they read statements about the crime they had committed than for other statements. Blink rates for innocent participants did not vary over statement types.

Discriminant Analyses

Stepwise linear discriminant analysis was performed with 12 measures that were significantly correlated with group membership. Four variables were selected for the discriminant function. They included the difference between first-pass duration for cash and exam statements, the difference between pupil responses to cash and exam statements, the difference between second-pass durations for crime and neutral statements, and the difference between next statement blink rates for crime and neutral statements. The function correctly classified 46 of the 56 guilty participants (82.2%) and 50 of the 56 innocent participants (89.3%). When the four variables selected in Experiment 1 were used to classify the cases in Experiment 2, accuracy dropped by about 5% to 78.6% for guilty participants and 82.1% for innocent participants (80.4% overall).

Discussion

The patterns of results from Experiment 2 replicated and extended those of Experiment 1. As compared with statements answered truthfully, while reading statements answered deceptively, guilty participants showed larger increases in pupil diameter, made fewer fixations, spent less time reading and re-reading statements, and suppressed eye blinks.

High-motivated innocent participants made fewer fixations than low-motivated innocent participants. Conversely, there was no difference between high- and low-motivated guilty groups in number of fixations. This suggests that guilty participants may be intrinsically motivated to avoid detection, whereas innocent participants invested more effort to earn a large reward than a small one.

FIELD STUDY 1

This field study was conducted at an office of the US Government. A federal employee served as the recruiter and proctor for the study. The study was designed to test for violations of two employment rules that prohibited employees from (1) bringing a cell phone into a Sensitive Compartmented Information Facility (SCIF), and (2) unreported unofficial foreign travel (UFT). Of the two, the former was the more common violation.

Although the present study was conducted in the field and involved "real-life" violations rather than a mock crime, the context for reading differed little from the contexts that we had established in the laboratory: participants responded either "True" or "False" to three statement types (i.e., neutral statements, statements related to the cell phone, and statements related to the UFT), an equal number of negation and non-negation statements were constructed for each statement type, participants were instructed to respond quickly and accurately to the statements, and, although our participants differed from the population drawn on for our laboratory studies, they were typically college educated and fluent readers. Therefore, the goals and SoE shown in Table 5.1 are applicable to this study as well. In this case R1 refers to statements about bringing a cell phone into a SCIF and R2 refers to statements about UFT.

Method

Participants

A total of 94 federal employees participated. Of these, 31 were male and 63 female, and the number of years employed at this organization ranged from about one month to 35 years ($M = 5.4$ years, SD = 6.8). Although education requirements vary by position at this government organization, the typical employee is college educated.

Apparatus

Participants' eye movements were monitored using a monocular head-mounted Arrington eye-tracker. Eye movement and pupil size were recorded from the participant's right eye at 30 Hz.

Materials

Forty-eight statements were repeated five times in separate trial blocks. The statements were divided into three types: 24 statements addressed neutral topics (general world knowledge), 12 addressed the cell phone violation, and 12 addressed the UFT. Each statement type required an equal number of true and false responses, and each group of true and false statements was subdivided into equal numbers of statements with and without negation.

Measures

The same outcome measures that were used in Experiment 2 were used in the present study.

Procedure

Participants were recruited via word of mouth. During recruitment, prospective participants were given a brief description of the study, screened for inclusion criteria (i.e., over 18 years old, proficient in English, and able to read without corrective lenses), informed about the participation reward (i.e., one hour paid time off plus normal pay during their participation in the study), and given an appointment.

Upon arriving at the testing room, each participant was given informed consent. Participants then were seated in front of the computer monitor and asked to wear a headphone set, which was used to deliver the instructions that were read aloud by a computerized text-to-speech generated voice. Delivery of the instructions lasted approximately five minutes. During this time, the proctor left the room.

The instructions informed participants that the oculomotor test was designed to test for violations of the two employment rules (i.e., bringing a cell phone into a SCIF and unreported UFT). Participants were told that if they had committed either security violation they had to lie and respond as though they were innocent or withdraw from the study. Participants who had not committed a security violation were instructed to be truthful on the test. The instructions also informed participants that they were to answer the statements quickly and accurately, and they would receive an additional hour of release time if they were able to pass the test.

After five minutes, the proctor returned to the testing room, attached and calibrated the eye-tracker, and started the test. The 48 test statements were presented in different orders five times separated by a brief unrelated test of general knowledge.

After completion of the test, the eye-tracker was removed, and the participants were given a paper-and-pencil post-test questionnaire that asked them to report the truth regarding their violations of the cell phone use or UFT. Therefore, knowledge of the participants' actual guilt or innocence of the two violations was obtained by self-identification as being innocent ($n = 43$) or guilty of the cell-phone violation ($n = 51$). The participants were assured that their answers on the questionnaire would not be reported to anyone within that government organization. They were given a self-addressed stamped envelope to mail the questionnaire to a researcher at the University of Utah.

Results

To classify participants into guilty and innocent groups, we first aggregated each of the dependent variables (i.e., response time and accuracy, pupil dilation, responses, reading behaviors, and blink rate prior to and following the participant's response) by statement type for each participant across all trial blocks. Then, for each of these aggregates, (1) statements about the security violations were contrasted with neutral statements, and (2) cell phone statements were contrasted with UFT statements. These contrast measures were used in a series of RMANOVAs and a final discriminant function analysis.

Statement type by guilt interactions were significant for mean pupil diameter, area under the curve for pupil size, blink rate following the participant's answer to a test statement, and re-reading. The statement type by guilt effect sizes ranged from 8% (blink rate) to 21% of the variance (mean pupil diameter).

Similar to the laboratory studies, we conducted a stepwise linear discriminant function analysis to classify innocent and guilty participants. The function correctly classified 36 of the 43 innocent participants (83.7%) and correctly classified 37 of the 51 guilty participants (72.5%). Overall, the discriminant function analysis accurately classified 77.7% of participants.

Discussion

Results from our first field study largely replicated the main findings from our two laboratory studies. Again, as compared with statements answered truthfully, while reading statements answered deceptively, guilty participants showed greater increases in pupil diameter, spent less time re-reading statements, and increased blink rate following the participant's response. Participants pursued reading goals to increase their reading speed and comprehension accuracy. Once the goal to identify statements types was achieved, they could pursue the next goal, which was to evaluate each statement and respond so as to appear innocent. The increased cognitive demands required to meet the reading goals and associated SoE for the statements that implicated them in a violation of cell phone rules coupled with potential increases in emotional arousal resulted in increases in pupil dilation.

Although the accuracy of classification of guilty and innocent participants was less in the field study (77.7%) than in our laboratory studies (85% and 85.7%), it still was moderately effective at discriminating between the groups. When we established an inconclusive region, which is common in polygraph tests (see Raskin and Kircher in Chapter 3 of this volume), nine of 94 outcomes were inconclusive (9.6%), and mean accuracy for the remaining 85 participants was 82.5%.

The difference in accuracy between the laboratory and field settings may have been due to the salience of the infractions for the participants. As compared with the mock theft of $20 from a secretary's purse, carrying a cell phone into a SCIF was an actual violation of the rules, but it was not uncommon, and cognitive engagement and emotional arousal may have been lower in the field than in the laboratory experiments. In addition, results from Experiment 2 suggest that higher levels of motivation produce larger effects on oculomotor measures. Although the participants in the field study were offered an additional hour of release time to pass the test, this incentive may have been insufficient to achieve the accuracy rates observed in the laboratory experiments.

FIELD STUDY 2

The second field study was conducted at the Latin American Polygraph Institute (LPI) in Bogota, Colombia. LPI provides pre-employment credibility assessment services to a number of industries. Participants were job applicants referred to LPI by their potential employer. This study was actually a collection of several smaller studies involving job applicants for widely varying professions that were combined into a single analysis. Our protocol in this study involved real-life violations of two criteria that are important to employers: personal history of drug use and falsification of academic background information on job applications.

The context for reading in the present study was similar to the first field study, and the goals and SoE shown in Table 5.1 are still applicable. R1 in this case referred to statements about personal history of drug use, and R2 referred to falsification of academic background information.

Method

Examinees

The examinees were job applicants whose prospective employers agreed to allow LPI to run our protocol in addition to the pre-employment polygraph examination. Job applicants for a wide variety of professions were combined into this one analysis. In all, 341 applicants were initially recruited for this study. However, our attrition rate was high: 72 applicants yielded unusable eye-tracking data and were removed from the analysis. Ground truth was unavailable for 165 of the tested individuals. The remaining sample consisted of 104 applicants (61 male, 43 female). Of these, 15 were applying for jobs in aviation, 48 for work as security guards, four for automotive work, 22 for jobs in credibility assessment, and eight for jobs in shoe manufacturing industries. Most of the applicants were young adults. Highest level of education varied from primary school ($n = 3$), secondary school ($n = 48$), security guard training certificate ($n = 8$), technician training certificate ($n = 25$), professional degree ($n = 14$), and technologist degree ($n = 6$). Follow-up background checks on the applicants confirmed that all of them in this sample were truthful regarding their educational background. Drug testing or personal admissions from the applicants during interviews following our testing indicated that 30 were guilty of a drug-use violation within 30 days of testing and 74 were innocent of this violation.

Apparatus

Eye movements were monitored with a monocular head-mounted Arrington eye-tracker at 30 Hz.

Materials

Forty-eight statements were repeated five times in separate trial blocks. The statements were divided into three types: 24 statements addressed neutral topics about general world knowledge, 12 addressed personal history of drug use, and 12 addressed falsification of academic background information. Each statement type required an equal number of true and false responses, and each group of true and false statements was subdivided into equal numbers of statements with and without negation.

All of the statements were written in English and then translated into Spanish, the native language of our applicants. As a quality control measure, the Spanish statements were then translated back into English by a different person, compared with the original English statements, and then revised in the Spanish versions. This process was iterated until the researchers were satisfied with the translation of the 48 items.

Measures

The same outcome measures that were used in Experiment 2 were used in the present study.

Procedure

When the applicants arrived for testing, they were asked to sign a consent form. The applicant then was seated in front of the computer monitor and asked to wear headphones, which were used to deliver the instructions that were read in Spanish by a computerized text-to-speech generated voice. During this time, the proctor left the testing room. The instructions informed the applicants about the nature of the test, which was to test for the individual's own drug use and not drug use by family members or other related drug activities (e.g., drug possession or drug dealing), and to test for falsification of academic background information given on a questionnaire. The instructions also informed applicants that they were to answer the statements as quickly and accurately as possible to avoid appearing guilty.

After about five minutes, the proctor returned to the testing room, attached and calibrated the Arrington eye-tracker, and started the test. The applicants then read another set of test instructions on the computer screen. They were informed that test statements would be presented individually on the computer screen and they should press one of two keys on the keyboard to indicate whether each statement was true or false. Each statement was presented on a single line in the center of the computer monitor beginning at the left edge of the screen. The selected answer was displayed on screen briefly and then the next statement in the preprogrammed sequence appeared. The 48 statements were repeated in five blocks that were separated by a brief unrelated test of general knowledge.

After completion of the testing, the eye-tracker was removed and the applicant was given an appointment to appear for drug testing. LPI handled the administration of the drug testing and the investigation of participants' academic background.

Results

As with the first field study, the results of greatest interest to us involved the statement type by guilt interactions. In contrast to our earlier studies, this interaction was not significant for any of our measures. Also, in contrast to our earlier studies, approximately 24% of the neutral, drug, and academic background questions were answered incorrectly. In our other studies, the error rates varied from 3% to 11%. Since none of the oculomotor measures discriminated between truthful and deceptive individuals, discriminant analysis was not conducted as it was in our earlier studies.

Discussion

In our initial discussion about using reading behaviors to detect deception, we described three types of variables that need to be examined to establish a context for reading: task variables, person variables, and strategy variables. The task variables (i.e., reading and responding to the three statement types) and strategy variables (i.e., the SoE) remained relatively consistent across all of the studies reported here. However, the person variables in the present study may have varied from the others.

First, there was a great deal of attrition in this study. Of the 341 people who were initially engaged to participate, only 104 remained. There were two primary reasons for this high attrition rate: unusable eye-tracking data and an inability to obtain ground truth. The end result was that we may have ended up with a sample that was unrepresentative of the target population.

The second way in which the person variables in the present study may have varied from the others, and likely the more critical of the two, involved reading ability. Some examinees were applying for jobs in aviation or as polygraph examiners and had higher levels of education in comparison to other applicants who were applying for jobs as security guards, automotive jobs, or shoe manufacturers. Although we did not test for reading ability, the various levels of education likely were correlated with reading ability. The higher error rates in responses to the statements that we obtained in this study suggest that reading ability may have been low. In a test of deception that relies heavily on reading, it stands to reason that reading ability will affect the results. Whether poorer readers can adequately apply the SoE to their reading or whether they develop completely different standards to cope with the task are questions that loom large for us. For example, whether a lack of reading fluency would allow "$Goal_{2.1}$: read accurately" and "$Goal_{2.2}$: read quickly" to be carried out without invoking some allocation strategy that gave preference to one or the other is a concern. Moreover, whether the SoE for each statement type could be applied without overloading cognitive resources is an additional concern.

The results of this study suggest that adequate reading ability is a prerequisite for this method to detect deception. Ways in which the effects of poor reading ability can be ameliorated need to be investigated in future research. We have initiated research that provides statements orally along with a visual presentation. Although results are preliminary, they are promising, which suggests that when given assistance in reading, the multiple demands posed by poor reading skills may be more manageable.

CONCLUSION

Although pupillary response has been used before to detect deception, pupillary response in conjunction with eye movements and blinks during reading is an innovative approach to detecting deception. The laboratory and field studies summarized here have provided mixed support for this approach.

As the oculomotor measures in the second of our two field studies failed to discriminate between truthful and deceptive examinees, additional research is needed to develop a better understanding of the psychophysiology and psychology that underlie the effects on oculomotor and behavior responses. We have speculated that the weaker results in the second field study may have been due to the low reading abilities of the examinees. Certainly, less fluent readers may have difficulty dealing with the various goals for reading and the multiple SoE demanded from the reading task. Poorer readers, in response to high reading demands, may adopt different SoE to cope with the demands. Applying standards in serial rather than parallel is one way to reduce demands; however, in a serial approach, if there is a breakdown at one point, subsequent reading may stop or be altered. Some of our readers in the second field study may have encountered a breakdown in reading and simply gave up. This would account for the higher error rates reported in that study in comparison to the other studies.

We have relied on research that has shown that being deceptive is more cognitively demanding and emotionally arousing than being truthful. We also have relied on research that has shown that a person's goals for reading and the implicit or explicit SoE that are used to achieve those goals affect the manner in which a text is read and the kinds of reading in which a reader engages. We then contextualized these findings in a reading task that asked people to respond either "True" or "False" to three types of statements: neutral statements, statements related to a crime that guilty participants had committed, and statements related to a crime that had not been committed. Reading of the statements was further manipulated by asking participants to respond quickly and accurately to the statements, otherwise delays in their reading could possibly reveal their deception.

To respond to the reading task, participants established a goal hierarchy for their reading with different SoE, or strategies for reading, associated with the goals. Innocent participants were not deceptive, and based on their fast response times and high accuracy rates, they complied with instructions to read quickly and accurately. Their accurate responses suggest that they employed the standards for reading that we had proposed: reading for comprehension, identifying the three statement types, undoing negations, and identifying and evaluating key words. However, because they had committed no crime, the SoE used for the two crime-related statement types did not differ. This resulted in reading behaviors and pupil dilations that differed little across the two crime-related statements types. There was a slight increase in pupil dilation for the crime-related statements over the neutral statements, but this increase may have been due to having more SoE to use for the crime statements requiring greater cognitive resources, higher emotional arousal elicited by a perceived threat in these statements, or both.

Guilty participants established the same goal hierarchy and SoE as the innocent participants. However, the goal to "appear innocent" was more salient for them, and they had to employ one additional SoE: "read to evaluate the response to appear innocent (reverse response)." As deception requires cognitive effort, we had anticipated that participants would expend greater cognitive effort when being deceptive, but our instruction to respond quickly and accurately likely added to this cognitive load. They complied with instructions to respond quickly and accurately but did so only *when they were deceptive*; they read statements answered deceptively more rapidly than statements answered truthfully, as evidenced by fewer fixations, faster first- and second-pass durations, faster response times, and suppressed blink rates when reading crime-related statements. The efficiency with which they read the incriminating statements while managing the greatest number of SoE resulted in the highest levels of cognitive load as indicated by the greatest increases in pupil dilation. The combination of highly efficient reading with high cognitive effort produced a number of diagnostic indicators of deception. The additional element of high emotional arousal for these statements may have contributed to the diagnostic value of pupil changes.

Our theory proposes that the differences in reading behaviors between deceptive and truthful people lie in (1) the goals for reading, (2) the SoE used to read the statements, (3) the cognitive demands associated with maintaining and executing the goals, and (4) the emotional arousal elicited by the statements. A research agenda that sets out to systematically manipulate one or more of these components may lead to an increased ability to discriminate between deceptive and truthful people. For instance, our theory would predict that discrimination between deceptive and truthful people would be enhanced by manipulations that would: (1) generate different goals for reading for deceptive people than for truthful people, (2) increase the number of SoE for deceptive people so that there are greater cognitive demands on reading when lying, (3) alternatively, decrease the number of SoE for truthful people to lower their cognitive demands when reading, and (4) make the content of test items more emotionally arousing for deceptive people than for truthful people. In addition to testing these predictions, more research is needed to assess the effects of individual differences in reading fluency and determine if countermeasures can be used to defeat oculomotor tests for deception.

References

Ahern, S.K., Beatty, J., 1979. Pupillary responses during information processing vary with Scholastic Aptitude Test scores. Science 205, 1289–1292.

Ahern, S.K., Beatty, J., 1981. Physiological evidence that demand for processing capacity varies with intelligence. In: Friedman, M., Dos, J.P., O'Connor, N. (Eds.), Intelligence and Learning. Plenum Press, New York, pp. 121–128.

Andreassi, J.L., 1973. Alpha and problem solving: a demonstration. Perceptual and Motor Skills 36, 905–906.

Andreassi, J.L., 2000. Psychophysiology: Human Behavior and Physiological Response, fourth ed. Erlbaum, Mahwah, NJ.

Baker, L., 1984. Children's effective use of multiple standards for evaluating their comprehension. Journal of Educational Psychology 76, 588–597.

Baker, L., 1985. How do we know when we don't understand? Standards for evaluating text comprehension. In: Forrest-Pressley, D.L., MacKinnon, G.E., Waller, T.G. (Eds.), Metacognition, Cognition, and Human Performance. Academic Press, New York, pp. 155–205.

Baker, L., Zimlin, L., 1989. Instructional effects on children's use of two levels of standards for evaluating their comprehension. Journal of Educational Psychology 81, 340–346.

Baker, L., Goldstein, R., Stern, J.A., 1992. Saccadic eye movements in deception. Report DoDPI92-R-003. Department of Defense Polygraph Institute, Fort McClellan, AL.

Bauer, L.O., Strock, B.D., Goldstein, R., Stern, J.A., Walrath, L.C., 1985. Auditory discrimination and the eyeblink. Psychophysiology 22, 629–635.

Bayer, M., Sommer, W., Schacht, A., 2011. Emotional words impact the mind but not the body: evidence from pupillary responses. Psychophysiology 48, 1533–1561.

Beal, C.R., Bonitaitubus, G.J., Garrod, A.C., 1990. Fostering children's revision skills through training in comprehension monitoring. Journal of Educational Psychology 82, 275–280.

Beatty, J., 1982. Task-evoked pupillary responses, processing load, and the structure of processing resources. Psychological Bulletin 91, 276–292.

Beatty, J., Schluroff, M., 1980. Pupillometric signs of brain activation reflect both syntactic and semantic factors in language processing. Paper presented at the Meeting of the Society of Psychophysiological Research, Vancouver. October.

Beatty, J., Wagoner, B.L., 1978. Pupillometric signs of brain activation vary with level of cognitive processing. Science 199, 1216–1218.

Berrien, F.K., Huntington, G.H., 1943. An exploratory study of papillary responses during deception. Journal of Experimental Psychology 32, 443–449.

Bradley, M.T., Janisse, M.P., 1981. Accuracy demonstrations, threat, and the detection of deception: cardiovascular, electrodermal, and pupillary measures. Psychophysiology 18, 307–315.

Bradley, M.T., Micolli, L., Escrig, M.A., Lang, P.J., 2008. The pupil as a measure of emotional arousal and autonomic activation. Psychophysiology 45, 602–607.

Bradshaw, J.L., 1968. Pupil size and problem solving. Quarterly Journal of Experimental Psychology 20, 116–122.

Bradshaw, J.L., 1970. Pupil size and drug state in a reaction time task. Psychonomic Science 18, 112–113.

Bumke, O., 1911. Die Pupillen Störungen, Die Geistes, und Nervenkrankheiten. Fischer, Jena.

Carver, C.S., 1998. Scheier, M.F. On the Self-regulation of Behavior. Cambridge University Press, New York.

Chapman, C.R., Oka, S., Bradshaw, D.H., Jacobson, R.C., Donaldson, G.W., 1999. Phasic pupil dilation response to noxious stimulation in normal volunteers: relationship to brain evoked potentials and pain report. Psychophysiology 36, 44–52.

Colman, F., Paivio, A., 1970. Pupillary dilation and mediation processes during paired-association learning. Canadian Journal of Psychology 24, 261–270.

Conway, M.A., 2005. Memory and the self. Journal of Memory and Language 53, 594–628.

Cook, A.E., Hacker, D.J., Webb, A.K., Osher, D., Kristjansson, S., Woltz, D.J., Kircher, J.C., 2012. Lyin' eyes: ocular-motor measures of reading reveal deception. Journal of Experimental Psychology: Applied 18, 301–313.

Daneman, M., Carpenter, P.A., 1983. Individual differences in integrating information between and within sentences. Journal of Experimental Psychology: Learning, Memory, and Cognition 9, 561–584.

Dionisio, D.P., Granholm, E., Hillix, W.A., Perrine, W.F., 2001. Differentiation of deception using pupillary responses as an index of cognitive processing. Psychophysiology 38, 205–211.

Dumoff, M.G., 1978. Discriminating emotion and mental effort with autonomic measures: pupil size and heart rate as differential measures of cognition and anxiety. Doctoral Dissertation. University of Manitoba.

Ehrlich, K., Rayner, K., 1983. Contextual effects on word perception and eye movements during reading. Journal of Verbal Learning and Verbal Behaviors 20, 641–655.

Ellermeier, W., Westphal, W., 1995. Gender differences in pain ratings and pupil reactions to painful pressure stimuli. Pain 61, 435–439.

Elshtain, E.L., Schaefer Jr., T., 1968. Effects of storage load and word frequency on pupillary responses during short-term memory. Psychonomic Science 12, 143–144.

Flavell, J.H., 1979. Metacognition and cognitive monitoring: a new area of cognitive developmental inquiry. American Psychologist 34, 906–911.

Frazier, L., Rayner, K., 1982. Making and correcting errors during sentence comprehension: eye movements in the analysis of structurally ambiguous sentences. Cognitive Psychology 14, 178–210.

Fukuda, K., Stern, J.A., Brown, T.B., Russo, M.B., 2005. Cognition, blinks, eye-movements, and pupillary movements during performance of a running memory task. Aviation, Space, and Environmental Medicine 76 (7 Suppl.), C75–C85.

Geacintov, T., Peavler, W., 1974. Pupillography in industrial fatigue assessment. Journal of Applied Psychology 59, 213–216.

Goldwater, B.C., 1972. Psychological significance of pupillary movements. Psychological Bulletin 77, 340–355.

Graesser, A.C., Singer, M., Trabasso, T., 1994. Constructing inferences during narrative text comprehension. Psychological Review 101, 371–395.

Granholm, E., Asarnow, R.F., Sarkin, A.J., Dykes, K.L., 1996. Pupillary responses index cognitive resource limitations. Psychophysiology 33, 457–461.

Hacker, D.J., 1994. Comprehension monitoring as a writing process. In: Butterfield, E.C. (Ed.), Children's Writing: Toward a Process Theory of the Development of Skilled Writing. JAI Press, Greenwich, CT, pp. 143–172.

Hacker, D.J., 1997. Comprehension monitoring of written discourse across early-to-middle adolescence. Reading and Writing: An Interdisciplinary Journal 9, 207–240.

Hacker, D.J., 2004. Self-regulated comprehension during normal reading. In: Ruddell, R.B., Unrau, N. (Eds.), Theoretical Models and Processes of Reading, fifth ed. International Reading Association, Newark, DE, pp. 775–779.

Heilveil, I., 1976. Deception and pupil size. Journal of Clinical Psychology 32, 675–676.

Hess, E.H., 1972. Puppillometrics. In: Greenfield, N.S., Sterbach, R.A. (Eds.), Handbook of Psychophysiology. Holt, Rinehart & Winston, New York, pp. 491–531.

Hess, E.H., Polt, J.M., 1960. Pupil size as related to interest value of visual stimuli. Science 132, 349–350.

Hess, E.H., Polt, J.M., 1964. Pupil size in relation to mental activity during simple problem-solving. Science 143, 1190–1192.

Hyönä, J., Nurminen, A.M., 2006. Do adult readers know how they read? Evidence from eye movement patterns and verbal reports. British Journal of Psychology 97, 31–50.

Hyönä, J., Lorch Jr., R.F., Kaakinen, J.K., 2002. Individual differences in reading to sum-marize expository text: evidence from eye fixation patterns. Journal of Educational Psychology 94, 44–55.

Hyönä, J., Tommola, J., Alaja, A.M., 1995. Pupil dilation as a measure of processing load in simultaneous interpretation and other language tasks. The Quarterly Journal of Experimental Psychology 48A, 598–612.

Irwin, D.E., Carlson-Radvansky, L.A., Andrews, R.V., 1995. Information processing during saccadic movements. Acta Psychologica 90, 261–273.

Johnson Jr., R., Barnhardt, J., Zhu, J., 2005. Differential effects of practice on the exec-utive processes used for truthful and deceptive responses: an event-related brain potential study. Cognitive Brain Research 24, 386–404.

Just, M.A., Carpenter, P.A., 1980. A theory of reading: from eye fixations to comprehen-sion. Psychological Review 87, 329–354.

Just, M.A., Carpenter, P.A., 1987. The Psychology of Reading and Language Compre-hension. Allyn & Bacon, Boston, MA.

Just, M.A., Carpenter, P.A., 1993. The intensity of dimension of thought: pupillometric indices of sentence processing. Canadian Journal of Experimental Psychology 47, 310–339.

Kaakinen, J.K., Hyönä, J., 2010. Task effects on eye movements during reading. Journal of Experimental Psychology: Learning, Memory, and Cognition 36, 1561–1566.

Kahneman, D., 1973. Attention and Effort. Prentice-Hall, Englewood Cliffs, NJ.

Kahneman, D., Beatty, J., 1966. Pupil diameter and load on memory. Science 154, 1583–1585.

Kahneman, D., Peavler, W.S., 1969. Incentive effects and pupillary changes in associa-tion learning. Journal of Experimental Psychology 79, 312–318.

Kircher, J.C., Raskin, D.C., 1988. Human versus computerized evaluations of polygraph data in a laboratory setting. Journal of Applied Psychology 73, 291–302.

Kircher, J.C., Horowitz, S.W., Raskin, D.C., 1988. Meta-analysis of mock crime stud-ies of the control question polygraph technique. Law and Human Behavior 12, 79–90.

Loewenfeld, I.E., 1999. The Pupil: Anatomy, Physiology, and Clinical Applications. Iowa State University Press, Ames, IA.

Lubow, R.E., Fein, O., 1996. Pupillary size in response to a visual guilty knowledge test: new technique for the detection of deception. Journal of Experimental Psychology: Applied 2, 164–177.

MacDonald, M.C., Just, M.A., 1989. Changes in activation levels with negation. Journal of Experimental Psychology: Learning, Memory, and Cognition 15, 633–642.

McConkie, G.W., Hogaboam, T.W., Wolverton, G.S., Zola, D.W., Lucas, P.A., 1979. Toward the use of eye movements in the study of language processing. Discourse Processes 2, 157–177.

Morris, R.K., 1994. Lexical and message-level sentence context effects on fixation times in reading. Journal of Experimental Psychology: Learning, Memory, and Cognition 20, 92–103.

Nuthmann, A., Engbert, R., Kliegl, R., 2005. Mislocated fixations during reading and the inverted optimal viewing position effect. Vision Research 45, 2201–2217.

O'Brien, E.J., Shank, D.M., Myers, J.L., Rayner, K., 1988. Elaborative inferences during reading: do they occur on-line? Journal of Experimental Psychology: Learning, Memory, and Cognition 14, 410–420.

Osher, D.B., 2006. Multimethod assessment of deception: oculomotor movement, pupil size, and response time measures. Doctoral Dissertation. University of Utah.

Paivio, A., Simpson, H.M., 1966. The effect of words abstractness and pleasantness on pupil size during an imaginary task. Psychonomic Science 5, 55–56.

Partala, T., Jokiniemi, M., Surakka, V., 2000. Pupillary responses to emotionally provocative stimuli. In: Proceedings of the 2000 Symposium on Eye Tracking Research and Applications. ACM Press, New York, pp. 123–129.

Pressley, M., Afflerbach, P., 1995. Verbal Protocols of Reading: The Nature of Constructively Responsive Reading. Lawrence Erlbaum Associates, Hillsdale, NJ.

Rayner, K., 1978. Eye movements in reading and information processing. Psychological Bulletin 85, 618–660.

Rayner, K., 1998. Eye movements in reading and information processing: 20 years of research. Psychological Bulletin 124, 372–422.

Rayner, K., Duffy, S.A., 1986. Lexical complexity and fixation times in reading: effects of word frequency, verb complexity, and lexical ambiguity. Memory and Cognition 14, 191–201.

Rayner, K., Liversedge, S.P., 2011. Linguistic and cognitive influences on eye movements during reading. In: Liversedge, S.P., Iain, I.D., Everling, S. (Eds.), The Oxford Handbook of Eye Movements. Oxford University Press, New York, pp. 751–766.

Rayner, K., McConkie, G.W., 1976. What guides a reader's eye movements. Vision Research 16, 829–837.

Rayner, K., Raney, G.E., Pollatsek, A., 1995. Eye movements and discourse processing. In: Lorch, R.F., O'Brien, E.J. (Eds.), Sources of Coherence in Reading. Erlbaum, Hillsdale, NJ, pp. 9–36.

Rayner, K., Pollatsek, A., Ashby, J., Clifton Jr., D., 2012. The Psychology of Reading, second ed. Psychology Press, New York.

Rayner, K., Sereno, S.C., Morris, R.K., Schumauder, A.R., Clifton, C., 1989. Eye movements and on-line language comprehension processes. Language and Cognition Processes 4, 21–49.

Rijlaarsdam, G., van den Bergh, H., 1996. The dynamics of composing: an agenda for research into an interactive compensatory model of writing: many questions, some answers. In: Levy, C.M., Randsdell, S. (Eds.), The Science of Writing:

Theories, Methods, Individual Differences, and Applications. Erlbaum, Mahwah, NJ, pp. 107–125.

Schaefer Jr., T., Ferguson, J.B., Klein, J.A., Rawson, E.B., 1968. Pupillary responses during mental activities. Psychonomic Science 14, 137–138.

Schluroff, M., 1982. Pupil responses to grammatical complexity of sentences. Brain and Language 17, 133–145.

Seymour, T.L., Seifert, C.M., Shafto, M.G., Mosmann, A.L., 2000. Using response time measures to assess "guilty knowledge". Journal of Applied Psychology 85, 30–37.

Siegle, G.J., Ichikawa, N., Steinhauer, S., 2008. Blink before you think: blinks occur prior to and following cognitive load indexed by pupillary responses. Psychophysiology 45, 679–687.

Steinhauer, S.R., Hakerem, G., 1992. The pupillary response in cognitive psychophysiology and schizophrenia. In: Friedman, D., Bruder, G. (Eds.), Psychophysiology and Experimental Psychopathology: A Tribute to Samuel Sutton (Annals of the New York Academy of Sciences 658). New York Academy of Sciences, New York, pp. 182–204.

Stern, J.A., Walrath, L.C., Goldstein, R., 1984. The endogenous eyeblink. Psychophysiology 21, 22–33.

Tecce, J.J., 1992. Psychology, Physiology and Experimental Psychology. McGraw-Hill, New York 375–377.

van den Broek, P., Lorch Jr., R.F., Linderholm, T., Gustafson, M., 2001. The effect of readers' goals on inference generation and memory for texts. Memory & Cognition 29, 1081–1087.

van den Broek, P., Bohn-Gettler, C.M., Kendeou, P., Carlson, S., White, M.J., 2011. When a reader meets a text: the role of standards of coherence in reading comprehension. In: McCrudden, M.T., Magliano, J.P., Schraw, G.J. (Eds.), Text Relevance and Learning from Text. Information Age, Charlotte, NC, pp. 123–139.

Vendemia, J.M.C., Buzan, R.F., Green, E.P., 2005. Practice effects, workload, and reaction time in deception. American Journal of Psychology 118, 413–429.

Vitu, F., 2011. On the role of visual and oculomotor processes in reading. In: Liversedge, S.P., Iain, I.D., Everling, S. (Eds.), The Oxford Handbook of Eye Movements. Oxford University Press, New York, pp. 731–749.

Vitu, F., McConkie, G.W., Kerr, P., O'Regan, J.K., 2001. Fixation location effects on fixation durations during reading: an inverted optimal viewing position effect. Vision Research 41, 3513–3533.

Vo, M.L.H., Jacobs, A.M., Kuchinke, L., Hofmann, M., Conrad, M., Schacht, A., Hutzler, F., 2008. The coupling of emotion and cognition in the eye: introducing the pupil old/new effect. Psychophysiology 45, 130–140.

Vrij, A., 2008. Detecting Lies and Deceit: Pitfalls and Opportunities, second ed. Wiley, Chichester.

Vrij, A., Mann, S., Kristen, S., Fisher, R.P., 2007. Cues to deception and ability to detect lies as a function of police interview styles. Law and Human Behavior 31, 599–518.

Vrij, A., Leal, S., Granhag, P.A., Mann, S., Fisher, R.P., Hillman, J., Sperry, K., 2009. Outsmarting the liars: the benefit of asking unanticipated questions. Law and Human Behavior 33, 159–166.

Walczyk, J.J., Mahoney, K.T., Doverspike, D., Griffith-Ross, D.A., 2009. Cognitive lie detection: response time and consistency of answers as cues to deception. Journal of Business and Psychology 24, 33–49.

Walczyk, J.J., Roper, K.S., Seemann, E., Humphrey, A.M., 2003. Cognitive mechanisms underlying lying to questions: response time as a cue to deception. Applied Cognitive Psychology 17, 755–774.

Webb, A.K., 2008. Effects of motivation and item difficulty on oculomotor and behavioral measures of deception. Doctoral Dissertation. University of Utah.

Webb, A.K., Hacker, D.J., Osher, D., Cook, A.E., Woltz, D.J., Kristjansson, S., Kircher, J.C., 2009. Eye movements and pupil size reveal deception in computer administered questionnaires. In: Schmorrow, D.D., Estabrooke, I.V., Grootjen, M. (Eds.), Foundations of Augmented Cognition. Neuroergonomics and Operational Neuroscience. Springer, Berlin, pp. 553–562.

Webb, A.K., Kristjansson, S.D., Osher, D., Cook, A.E., Kircher, J.C., Hacker, D.J., Woltz, D.J., 2006. Multimethod assessment of deception on personnel tests: reading, writing, and response time measures. Journal of Credibility Assessment and Witness Psychology 7, 164–168.

CHAPTER

6

The Neural Basis of Deception and Credibility Assessment: A Cognitive Neuroscience Perspective

Ray Johnson Jr., Ph.D.

Department of Psychology, Queens College/City University of New York

OUTLINE

Introduction	219	Neurocognitive Studies of Deception	238
The Neurocognitive Approach	220	*Instructed Lies, Tactical Monitoring,*	
		and the GKT	239
Functional Neuroimaging Techniques	222	ERP Results	242
Electrophysiological Techniques	223	Hemodynamic Results	246
Hemodynamic Techniques	226	Hemodynamic Results in GKT	
		Experiments	249
Methods for Assessing Causal		*Intention-based Lies and Strategic*	
Relations between Brain Activity		*Monitoring*	251
and Cognition	228	ERP Results	251
Early CNS studies	229	Hemodynamic Results	255
		ERP Indices of Guilty Knowledge	
Toward a Cognitive Description of		*and Concealed Information*	259
Deception	231	*Deceptions about Attitudes, Beliefs,*	
Working Memory	232	*and Personal Evaluations*	261
Long Term Memory	234	*Post-Retrieval Processing as a Model*	
Executive Processes and		*for Real-World Deceptions*	266
Cognitive Control	237		

Deception Effects on Cognitive Workload 270
Effect of Practice on Deceptive-Related
    Processing   271
Causal Results from Loss-of-Function
    Studies   277

Forensic Applications   **280**
ERP Results   281

Hemodynamic Results   282
Future Directions   **284**
Conclusions   **288**
References   **289**

INTRODUCTION

For several decades, investigators have been searching for ways to detect deception and assess credibility by employing both behavioral and biological methods. The polygraph, with its ability to measure autonomic nervous system responses reflecting anxiety, has been and remains the primary biologically-based technique for detecting deception. Over the past decade researchers have begun investigating the neurocognitive basis of deception with the goal of understanding how deception-related processing is instantiated in the brain and how central nervous system (CNS) measures might be used as an adjunct and/or possible replacement for the polygraph. The importance of this research cannot be overstated given that all internal and external manifestations of deceptive behavior described in this book, from the initial idea through every facet of planning and execution, depends entirely on CNS function. Therefore, all credibility assessment measures, whether behavioral, cognitive, or emotional, have correlates in measures of CNS activity. Nevertheless, our understanding of how deception maps onto particular cognitive processes and brain networks remains rudimentary and far from complete. As will be argued here, increasing our understanding of the neurocognitive processes underlying deception promises to enhance both the utility of current methods and the development of new scientifically-based methods of deception detection and credibility assessment.

Determining which cognitive processes are used during a behavior as complex and multi-faceted as deception has been hampered by a variety of factors. There are many ways one can be deceptive, which vary considerably in nature and complexity (see Vrij, 2008 for an extensive treatment of all types of deceptions). These variations in turn interact with the characteristics of the person perpetrating the deception to determine which particular cognitive and emotional sequelae are associated with each type of deception. Consequently, the cognitive operations involved will be affected not only by factors such as the importance and circumstances surrounding the deception but also by the personality and personal habits of the deceiver, e.g., how often they lie. A further complicating factor is the lack of a single, widely accepted definition of deception (see Vrij, 2008), which limits the ability to design controlled empirical studies aimed at identifying the cognitive processes and neural mechanisms involved. The definition used here, which captures many of the essential features, is that deception occurs when an individual intentionally offers an expression of an internal representation that differs from the actual nature of that representation in order to gain some reward. The inclusion of a reward component introduces another layer of complexity to the processing involved, requiring additional cognitive and non-cognitive processes, such as those related to any emotions engendered by the deception. Thus, creating an overarching understanding of all the various processes involved across the full spectrum of types of deception will require considerable research effort.

The aim of this chapter is to provide an introduction to how cognitive neuro-scientists study the neurocognitive basis of a complex function like deception and describe what this approach has revealed about how deception is instanti-ated in the brain. Despite the fact that this area of research began only a little over a decade ago, with only a few dozen reports published to date, it has pro-duced important insights into the cognitive and neural basis of some aspects of deception. An overview of the neurocognitive approach is followed by a brief primer on the basic principles underlying the new functional brain imag-ing techniques that are the foundation of the cognitive neuroscientist's arma-mentarium and the source of these new research findings. A brief summary of the initial psychophysiological research is followed by a review of the extant literature on the cognitive and neural basis of deception, as well as the efforts to develop these findings into new brain-based methods of credibility assess-ment. Finally, some suggestions for future research and conclusions are offered.

THE NEUROCOGNITIVE APPROACH

Cognitive neuroscience, a multi-disciplinary field that emerged in the mid-1990s, has the goal of understanding how brain function gives rise to mental activity in humans. Thus, researchers focus on characterizing both the brain networks responsible for different cognitive functions and the specific cogni-tive processes performed in each node within these networks. A general aim is the creation of a functional anatomy of cognitive processing through the unification of psychology and neurobiology. A core feature of this new field is its inter-disciplinary approach, which combines the knowledge, methods, and theoretical constructs from four different disciplines: experimental psychology, neuropsychology, neurobiology, and computational neuroscience.

Experimental psychology provides an empirical foundation for the creation of information-processing models of cognitive functions, as well as identifying their constituent processes. These models generally assume that cognitive functions can be modeled as a series of unique operations or processing stages performed between stimulus and response. Another fundamental tenet of this approach is that mental operations take time and thus can be revealed by experimental manipulations that affect the duration of these processes. Reaction time (RT) measures are a vital tool for revealing differences in the timing of mental processes. Findings from these studies have demonstrated repeatedly that, whereas any given cognitive function may be characterized by a unique combination of processes, these constituent processes are typically general-purpose and thus are called upon whenever they can aide processing, e.g., long term memory retrieval. Hence, for any cognitive function, e.g., deception, it is theoretically possible to specify a unique set of cognitive processes even though the specific processes involved will also participate in many other cognitive functions.

Experimental psychologists of the 1960–1980s lacked the technology necessary to map cognitive processes onto underlying brain structures. This was the province of neuropsychologists who studied the effects of brain damage on human cognitive function. These loss-of-function studies provide important information on which brain areas are necessary for normal functioning in a particular cognitive domain. Although seemingly different, experimental psychology and neuropsychology studies each provide a systems-level analysis, albeit by studying intact and damaged brains, respectively. The information on brain function provided by these two disciplines is synergistic on another level because, whereas data derived from studies of intact systems necessarily are correlational, data derived from patient populations provide a vital source of causal data about brain-behavior relations. By contrast, neurobiologists have a long history of studying brain function at the cellular level, in both intact and damaged systems, which provides an entirely different perspective on how cognitive functions occur in the brain. Finally, computational neuroscience, the most recently created discipline, arose from efforts by computer scientists to model brain functions, both at the systems and neural levels, with computer programs.

Given that research in these four disciplines was conducted largely independently in the past, a major advantage of cognitive neuroscience arises from its merging of the theories and empirical results from each discipline to create a richer and more multi-faceted understanding of brain-behavior relations. Perhaps most important, this multi-disciplinary approach encourages researchers to integrate their results with those from other methods when creating new models of cognitive and brain function. Overall, cognitive neuroscientists attempt to answer a hierarchal series of questions including: 1) How are higher mental functions represented in different neuronal networks and neural systems? 2) How are these functions partitioned into separate components? and 3) What computations are performed by each component? By answering these questions, information about the underlying brain activity and functions can be combined with behavioral models to create more sophisticated neurocognitive models of mental functions. Thus, the aim of the studies reviewed below is to provide a detailed spatiotemporal functional anatomy of the cognitive and brain processes used when a person is deceptive.

FUNCTIONAL NEUROIMAGING TECHNIQUES

A major impetus for the advent of cognitive neuroscience was a series of technological advances that included the development of powerful new scanners that permit researchers to study brain activity when humans perform higher-cognitive functions. The revolutionary impact of these technologies, which has been compared to the development of the microscope and the telescope, permits researchers to observe the activity of normal and abnormal human brains as information is processed in a wide variety of tasks. These functional neuroimaging techniques include measures of brain electrical activity (event-related potentials or ERPs, magnetoencephalography or MEG) and hemodynamic, i.e., blood flow, measures (positron emission tomography or PET, functional magnetic resonance imagery or fMRI, near infrared spectroscopy or NIRS). Given that all insights into the neural basis of deception have come from the use of these techniques, a brief introduction to each is provided before reviewing the results obtained from the available neurocognitive studies.

Electrophysiological Techniques

Although the ERP technique has been widely used since the 1960s, recent technological advances have dramatically altered its ability to reveal the spatiotemporal characteristics of the brain activity underlying cognitive functions. From the 1960s through the 1980s, the price of amplifiers restricted most investigators to recording from a relatively small number of midline scalp recording sites, i.e., most frequently over parietal (Pz), central (Cz), and frontal (Fz) brain areas. The *zeitgeist* was that specific patterns of ERP activity could not be linked to specific underlying brain structures and, as in the case of experimental psychologists, no attempt was made to do so. Instead, ERP studies were designed to find correlates of various psychological processes such as attention and surprise. The 1990s brought large reductions in the price of amplifiers, making it possible to record from much larger arrays of scalp electrodes, and studies with 32, 64, and even 128 scalp electrodes became common. Recording ERPs from larger electrode arrays vastly increased spatial resolution and allowed researchers to improve the quantification of task-related changes in the scalp distribution of ERP components, which are linked to changes in underlying brain activity. Just as new hemodynamic techniques (see below) owed their genesis to the development of mathematical algorithms for image construction, Scherg (1990; Scherg and Picton, 1991) introduced his brain electrical source analysis (BESA) program, which provides backward and forward methods for calculating the locations of the brain sources of scalp-recorded ERP activity. The resulting enhanced ability to link scalp-recorded ERP activity to underlying brain structures engendered a seismic shift in the way most researchers use ERPs. For example, BESA provides a powerful method for integrating ERP and hemodynamic results, permitting researchers to combine the superior temporal resolution of ERPs with the superior spatial resolution of hemodynamic techniques to enhance our understanding of the spatiotemporal characteristics of the neural processes underlying cognitive functions.

Whereas behavioral measures, such as RT and accuracy, can provide much useful information, it is difficult in practice to use them to parse the identity and/or duration of the multiple processing stages that occur between stimulus and response. By contrast, the ERP technique offers an ideal method for studying the neurocognitive basis of deception because it provides a continuous measure of brain activity elicited by the covert sensory and cognitive processes that occur between stimulus and response. ERP waveforms extracted from the electroencephalogram (EEG) provide a direct measure of neural activity by virtue of the fact that they arise from extracellular excitatory and inhibitory post-synaptic potentials. The ERP consists of a series of potentials, called peaks or components, that each possess specific spatiotemporal characteristics and whose presence is determined by the particular processing elicited by external and internal events (see Picton *et al.*, 1995, 2000 for reviews). Given its multi-component nature, the ERP provides a method for tracking the passage of information through the CNS and its millisecond resolution provides unmatched information about the timing of neural activity. In addition to providing latency and duration information, the amplitude, scalp distribution, and response to experimental variables for each ERP component provide information about the extent of neural activity, pattern of neural source activity, and sensory and cognitive processes that occur, respectively. Moreover, ERP experiments always employ event-related designs in which different stimulus categories occur randomly within a block of trials. This contrasts with experiments employing blocked designs in which, for example, different stimulus categories are presented in different trial blocks. Block design experiments can produce experimental comparisons that are confounded by extraneous variables and strategy differences. Finally, because the ERP technique is entirely non-invasive and relatively inexpensive, information processing activities can be studied as often as desired in virtually anyone across the entire life span.

The ability of the ERP technique to provide detailed information on the onset and duration of brain activity representing many different cognitive processes means that it can provide unique insights into the differential processing that occurs for truthful and deceptive responding. To augment its high temporal resolution, ERP averages can be synchronized to different events in a trial in order to both reveal the brain activity and cognitive processes associated with each event and/or eliminate or reduce the inevitable effects of variability in the timing of various processes (see Johnson *et al.*, 2011 for a discussion and examples of this point). For example, ERP averages are typically synchronized to the occurrence of stimulus onset, which best reveals brain activity that occurs early in the processing sequence, such as perceptual processes and any cognitive processes that tend to be more closely coupled to stimulus presentation, e.g., onset of memory search. By contrast, long- or variable-duration processes, which are typically more closely coupled to the end of the processing sequence, are best revealed in response-synchronized averages. Examples of processes in this category include those related to memory retrieval, post-retrieval processing, and identification of intention-based responses. Hence, by calculating and quantifying both stimulus- and response-synchronized ERP averages, it is possible to build a comprehensive and detailed picture of the serial and parallel processing that occurs between stimulus and response and how this is affected during deception.

Despite providing imprecise information about the anatomical locations of the neural generators responsible for scalp-recorded ERP components, the scalp distribution of each component can provide a rich source of information about when different brain networks are activated by different cognitive processes. This is due to the fact that the pattern of electrical gradients recorded from the scalp at any given time is determined by the location(s) and orientation(s) of the activated neurons, which are in turn determined by the specific sensory and cognitive processes elicited by the stimulus and task information. Hence, changes in scalp distribution indicate that the pattern of brain activation differs across conditions (see Johnson, 1993 for a discussion on this point). Further, with sufficient numbers of electrodes, i.e., 32 or more, the spatiotemporal characteristics of an ERP component can be sharpened considerably with current source density (CSD) analysis, which computationally filters out the contributions of more distant cortical and subcortical generators to scalp-recorded activity at each location (cf., Picton *et al.*, 1995). By representing the second spatial derivative of scalp potential fields, CSD maps reveal the locations of local cortical sources and sinks of radial current, with spatial resolution increasing with the number of scalp-recording sites. Therefore, even with modest numbers of recording sites, e.g., 32, it is possible to localize cortically-generated activity to a particular brain lobe and even to anatomically relevant subregions within that lobe.

More precise information on the locations of ERP generators can be obtained with Scherg's (1990) BESA technique. Using back-calculation algorithms, BESA finds the best fit between the observed pattern of scalp-recorded ERP activity and a set of neural generators located in the brain (see Miltner *et al.*, 1994 for a simulation study). Alternatively, precise anatomical data on the locations of activated brain areas, e.g., obtained from fMRI scans, can be seeded into BESA to determine which aspects of the scalp-recorded ERP activity are associated with specific fMRI-localized brain activations. This forward calculation approach avoids the pitfalls and assumptions of back-calculation approaches and can provide otherwise unavailable temporal information, i.e., timing and duration, about fMRI brain activations (see Johnson *et al.*, 2008a).

Magnetoencephalography (MEG) and ERPs are closely-related techniques because MEG detects the weak magnetic fields co-generated by brain electrical activity. Hence, MEG provides a magnetic counterpart of both EEG and ERPs. The sensors used to detect the brain's magnetic fields have also decreased greatly in size and expense over the past 10–15 years, so very large recording arrays have become possible, e.g., up to 256 channels, for improved spatial resolution. The physics are such that MEG contains more information for accurately locating the neural sources of magnetic fields than is available from electrical fields, although the same physics means that only axially-oriented neural generators in the sulci, i.e., the "valleys" in brain surface, can be localized. MEG equipment still remains relatively expensive to buy and maintain and thus the ERP technique will likely remain the more widely-used method for detecting brain electrical activity.

In sum, ERPs provide a useful tool for studying the neurocognitive basis of deception, particularly when the full range of ERP analysis techniques is used to characterize the spatiotemporal information about the neural events underlying specific cognitive processes.

Hemodynamic Techniques

Unlike ERPs, hemodynamic imaging techniques provide an indirect measure of brain activity because they capture the increases and decreases in blood flow that occur when brain areas are activated and deactivated during task performance. The first widely used hemodynamic technique was PET, which uses radioactive tracers to reveal changes in blood flow via changes in the amount of radio-labeled water that diffuses out of capillaries. As it is mildly invasive, PET has been largely supplanted by the newer fMRI technique. For fMRI scans, participants are placed in a strong magnetic field and changes in task-related blood flow are quantified by detecting differences in the ratio of oxygenated and de-oxygenated blood via their different magnetic properties. This is referred to as the blood oxygen level dependent, or BOLD, method. FMRI is non-invasive and has the added benefit of providing detailed anatomical scans to go with functional blood flow scans.

Hemodynamic techniques are characterized by excellent spatial resolution, with fMRI being considerably better than PET, but very poor temporal resolution relative to the speed of cognitive processes. This poor temporal resolution arises from the fact that the circulatory system's sluggish response to the need for additional blood flow does not peak until 8–10 seconds after brain activity increases, i.e., the hemodynamic response. Hemodynamic techniques also have a poor signal-to-noise ratio because task-related alterations in blood flow typically only change blood flow by about 3% from resting levels. Consequently, as with ERPs, there is the need to average fMRI data over time or trials to increase the signal-to-noise ratio. To mitigate the problems created by the slow hemodynamic response and small signal size, most fMRI studies use blocked experimental designs in which all, or nearly all, trials within a block are of the same type. To reveal the brain activity associated with a particular cognitive process or stimulus type, comparisons are made across different blocked conditions. Some newer fMRI studies use more powerful event-related designs that permit averaging over randomly occurring events for within-block comparisons. Finally, the strength of the magnetic field used in fMRI, measured in Tesla (T), can be increased to further enhance spatial resolution.

The success of the fMRI technique has led researchers to find new ways to use the information available in the magnetic resonance signal. One such method, diffusion tensor imaging (DTI), reveals the connectivity between activated brain areas by mapping the movement of water molecules in the white matter pathways that connect different brain areas. Given that brain networks underlie every cognitive function, DTI can show how different activated areas are connected and function as a whole. Although the DTI technique has yet to be used in deception studies, in the future it may provide useful information on how network connections differ during truthful and deceptive responding.

The newest hemodynamic technique, NIRS, is a non-invasive and lower-cost technique that takes advantage of the fact that the scalp, skull, and brain are essentially transparent to near-infrared light (see Gratton and Fabiani, 2001 for a review). NIRS reveals areas of cortical activation by detecting the differential absorption properties of oxygenated and de-oxygenated blood. Unlike fMRI, NIRS permits continuous monitoring of changes in cerebral blood flow and, with available wireless instrumentation, has the advantage that it can be used to study freely-moving participants. However, the NIRS technique is also limited and it cannot duplicate fMRI's whole-brain views because it only permits scanning of cortical tissue. Despite the fact that it is still in the early stages of development, the first research using the NIRS technique to study deception has already appeared (see below).

In summary, whereas all three hemodynamic techniques, i.e., PET, fMRI, and NIRS provide excellent information about the locations of activated brain areas during task performance, only electrophysiological techniques, i.e., ERPs and MEG provide the vital timing information required to create detailed information-processing models. Hence, a thorough understanding of how deception-related processing is instantiated in the brain is likely to be obtained only by combining the results from hemodynamic and electrophysiological techniques.

METHODS FOR ASSESSING CAUSAL RELATIONS BETWEEN BRAIN ACTIVITY AND COGNITION

One feature common to both ERP and hemodynamic techniques is the correlational nature of the information they provide about task-related changes in brain activity. The fact that specific patterns of ERP and/or hemodynamic activity may be regularly associated with particular cognitive functions does not mean that they are necessary for the production of that cognitive function.

While such information is very useful, it is also vital to have causal information about brain-behavior relations. Neuropsychological approaches can fill this role by studying brain-damaged individuals whose ability to be deceptive is compromised. Alternatively, cognitive function in normal controls can be studied with transcranial magnetic stimulation (TMS), which has the ability to alter cortical function directly in a non-invasive and reversible manner. Initially developed in the 1980s and refined in the early 1990s, TMS uses brief pulses of a strong magnetic field to disrupt the electrical activity in specific brain locations at specific times, thereby creating what has been referred to as a temporary "lesion" (see Walsh and Cowey, 2000, for a review). The brain area stimulated by the TMS pulse, and the depth of stimulation, depends on several factors, including coil shape and pulse characteristics. Nevertheless, it is possible to temporarily disrupt processing in specific brain areas with a high degree of spatial and temporal resolution, thereby providing important causal information about the role of a brain area in a particular cognitive function.

EARLY CNS STUDIES

Two general approaches have been employed to study deception and credibility assessment; those seeking to detect the presence of guilty knowledge in a person's memory and those seeking to uncover the brain-behavior relations underlying deception. The former approach was spurred by Lykken's (1959) development of the guilty knowledge test (GKT), which came out of his belief that deceptive behavior would not be associated with a detectable "specific lie response." Hence, rather than focus on deception-related processing, the GKT or concealed information test (CIT) was designed to determine if a deceptive person possessed specific critical information that an innocent person would not possess. Lykken's approach has been widely used in the intervening years by researchers attempting to develop brain-based GKT and CIT methods. Although GKT/CIT procedures require deceptive responses because the deceptive person must respond that he/she does not know the relevant information, they are neither designed to nor capable of revealing information about the cognitive processes used to perpetrate the deception.

Prior to the advent of the neurocognitive approach, researchers attempted to use the properties of a cognitive component of the ERP to detect the presence of guilty knowledge. Farwell and Donchin (1991) pioneered the use of ERPs in this context with their seminal study using a modified version of Lykken's GKT. The underlying idea was that the presence of concealed information could be revealed via a specific pattern of ERP activity, without the need for overt responses. Their procedure was based on the fact that the amplitude of the late positive component (LPC; aka P300, P3b) of the ERP is inversely related to the perceived category probabilities of stimuli, which are detected automatically by the brain (see Johnson, 1986, 1988 for reviews). The method of choice for capturing information about how stimuli are categorized, referred to as the "Oddball" paradigm, typically involves presenting two or three categories of stimuli. In their Oddball GKT, Farwell and Donchin (1991) presented relevant guilty knowledge items (Probes) randomly and infrequently. The series also contained two categories of control stimuli. One of these consisted of unrelated Target stimuli, presented with the same frequency as Probe items, which participants were required to detect. The other category was for Irrelevant stimuli, which were presented much more frequently and did not require detection. The idea was that, if an individual possesses the relevant guilty knowledge, then the infrequently occurring Probe stimuli will automatically elicit a large LPC like that elicited by the infrequent Target stimuli. By contrast, if the individual has no knowledge of the Probe items, then they will be treated like Irrelevant stimuli and elicit only a small LPC. Using the pattern of LPC amplitudes elicited in their individual participants, Farwell and Donchin (1991) reported that they could correctly classify 87.5% of their participant's deceptive responses. Since that initial study, a number of other investigators have used this approach to detect when persons either attempt to conceal particular memories or feign amnesia. For the results of these studies, the reader is directed to a review by Rosenfeld (2011).

Despite the appeal of this simple, straightforward GKT method, it is critically flawed due to its complete dependence on a single ERP component, i.e., the LPC, to make Truthful-Deceptive (T-D) classifications regarding the presence of concealed information. As demonstrated by Rosenfeld and colleagues (Rosenfeld et al., 2004), this dependence on the LPC makes the method highly susceptible to simple countermeasures. Another fundamental problem arises from the fact that Oddball stimuli do not appear to be capable of eliciting a measurable LPC in all individuals. This problem was elucidated in studies by Mertens and Allen (2008; Allen and Mertens, 2009) who demonstrated that the magnitude of the difficulty of reliably quantifying the LPC in some individuals is high enough that any LPC-based GKT is likely to fail to provide conclusive T-D classifications in an unacceptably high percentage of the population.

Such discouraging results are not surprising and should be expected for any credibility assessment procedure based on a single physiological variable. Indeed, it is hard to imagine that the polygraph ever would have gained widespread use if it depended on a single measure of autonomic nervous system (ANS) activity. The solution to this problem lies in the development of credibility assessment tools that incorporate multiple, simultaneously, and sequentially obtained behavioral and/or brain-based measures that capture different aspects of deception-related processing. In this way, the loss of any one/few measures in any individual would not lead to a failed assessment. As argued below, achieving this goal should be possible with neurocognitive approaches that take full advantage of the complexity of the cognitive and brain processes that underlie deception.

TOWARD A COGNITIVE DESCRIPTION OF DECEPTION

The genesis of the neurocognitive approach to studying deception arguably occurred during a Central Intelligence Agency workshop in August, 1996. This workshop was intended to be a forum for discussing the cognitive and neural basis of deception and deception detection and how these might be studied with the newly developed functional neuroimaging methods. Given that one cannot successfully formulate a lie or deception without first identifying the truthful response, one idea put forth was that deception likely involves the use of additional cognitive processes superimposed on those normally used when one is truthful. Although the nature of these additional processes was left unspecified, it is reasonable to suggest that all processing relevant to formulating and producing a deceptive response is under conscious control. Such processes, referred to as controlled processes, are flexible, require continuous attention, and demand access to limited resources. There are a number of possible candidate processes that might be used to perpetrate a deception, including working memory and long-term memory. Since that workshop, another set of cognitive processes, known collectively as executive or cognitive control processes, has become a topic of intense study. By virtue of the fact that executive processes are used to implement cognitive control over all thought and behavior, these processes can also be expected to play a central role in deception. To facilitate understanding of the neurocognitive results reviewed below, a brief introduction to these three categories of cognitive processes is provided here.

Working Memory

Baddeley and colleagues conducted a series of experiments during the 1970s and 1980s that resulted in the replacement of the prevailing concept of short term memory with a new working memory system (see Baddeley, 2012 for a recent review). Unlike the previous single-store view of short term memory, working memory is seen as being more central to cognition. Baddeley conceptualized working memory as the seat of consciousness and the cognitive "work space" where information from the senses can be combined with information from long term memory during decision making. Baddeley and colleagues demonstrated empirically that working memory can be divided into a number of major components, including an articulatory loop for storing and maintaining verbal material, a visuo-spatial sketchpad for storing and maintaining non-verbal material, and a central executive that exerts control over both systems. The central executive is also responsible for maintaining and manipulating information, decision making, and selecting goal-directed behaviors. An extensive series of functional neuroimaging studies has now linked the various subsystems of working memory to specific brain circuits (e.g., Owen *et al.*, 1998; Smith and Jonides, 1998, 1999; Curtis and D'Esposito, 2003) and distinct patterns of ERP activity (see Johnson, 1995 and Ruchkin *et al.*, 2003 for reviews). Although a variety of brain areas are activated during working memory operations, the most relevant here is the fact that the central executive is located in dorsolateral prefrontal cortex (DLPFC) (see Figure 6.1). More recently, an enhanced understanding of how different executive

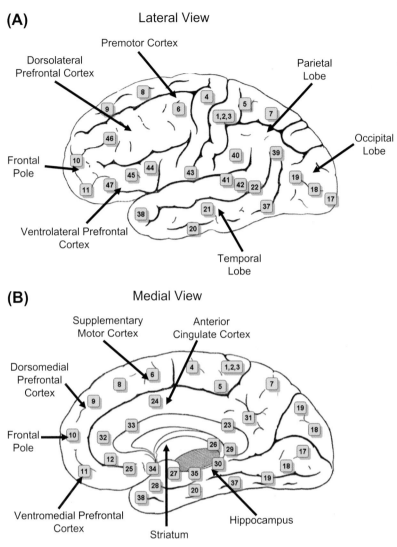

FIGURE 6.1   A. Lateral view of the brain showing the different anatomical regions described in the text. The numbers are those assigned by Brodmann in the 19th century based on his anatomical studies of the cerebral cortex and represent differences in the cellular composition in different cortical areas. More recently, hemodynamic studies have found that the brain areas activated in cognitive studies appear to correspond roughly to these areas. Hence, many hemodynamic papers report the locations of activated brain areas in terms of Brodmann's areas. B. Medial view of the brain.

processes interact with the various working memory systems has produced a shift toward identifying the essential control processes that enable working memory to work (Nee *et al.*, 2013).

Given its vital role in cognition and consciousness, the central executive component of working memory represents an important candidate for inclusion in processing models of deception. However, it is important to note that the combined storage capacity of the central executive and the verbal subsystem is severely limited and believed to be roughly what one can say in two seconds. Even with Baddeley's addition of an "episodic buffer" to provide additional storage and serve as an interface between working memory and long term memory (Baddeley, 2000), the capacity of this buffer is still too small to store large amounts of information or to hold it for more than some minutes. Thus, contrary to popular notions about short and long term memory, the distinction between these two stores is based on their respective storage limits, i.e., very brief and indefinite, and not on the basis of whether particular information is generally retrievable after days or weeks. Consequently, although working memory processes are necessarily involved in formulating and executing deceptions, most deceptions will be about the past and thus about information stored in long term memory.

Long Term Memory

Results from a large number of neurocognitive studies over the past three decades have dramatically altered our understanding of how long term memory is processed and stored in the brain. One important finding, which bears on nearly all deception and credibility assessment research, is that long term memory is *not* a movie-like representation of a person's past. On the contrary, long term memory has been shown to be quite fallible and subject to insertion of memories for events that never happened (see Schacter and Loftus, 2013 for a discussion of memory and the law). In a manner analogous to the demise of single-store models of short term memory, long term memory is widely recognized as consisting of a collection of separate but interacting neural systems that process and store different types of information, operate in different ways, and reside in different brain areas.

Long term memory has been divided into two broad categories, explicit and implicit (e.g., Cohen and Squire, 1980; Squire, 1992). Explicit memories are the most relevant to deception studies because they are the consciously accessible, verbalizable memories that would be the source of all deceptions about one's past or knowledge. Tulving (1983) divided explicit memories into two categories: episodic and semantic. Episodic memory is where personal memories are processed and stored and includes not only information about our experiences but also the specific spatiotemporal information about the context in which those experiences occurred. By contrast, semantic memory is a fact-based store for general knowledge that has no associated contextual information. Given that many episodic memories for everyday events are rapidly lost, or at least are not readily retrievable, the episodic system has been subdivided to include a separate store for autobiographical memories, which are the important events that constitute one's history. Finally, personal semantic information, such as names of parents, siblings, friends, and teachers, and present and past addresses, is another category of declarative memory, although whether this information is best characterized as a type of episodic or semantic memory remains the subject of debate (see Renoult *et al.*, 2012 for a recent review).

At present, it is generally agreed that there is a high degree of overlap in the brain circuits for episodic and autobiographical memory (e.g., Cabeza *et al.*, 2004; Burianova and Grady, 2007). Hemodynamic studies have consistently shown that retrieval of both episodic and autobiographical memories activate many of the same brain areas (e.g., Cabeza *et al.*, 2004; Burianova and Grady, 2007; see Gilboa, 2004 and Cabeza and St. Jacques, 2007 for reviews). Further, even the differences emphasized in some accounts, e.g., that autobiographical memory is much more self-relevant and has stronger links to perceptual and emotional processes (e.g., Gilboa, 2004), can be characterized as being more quantitative than qualitative. In accord with this view, there is considerable evidence that autobiographical retrieval typically produces greater activation than episodic retrieval in a number of cortical visual areas (Conway *et al.*, 2001, 2003; Gilboa *et al.*, 2004; Cabeza and St. Jacques, 2007; Johnson *et al.*, 2011), which could provide a method for detecting deceptions about falsified autobiographical events. Similarly, retrieval of personal semantic memories produces the same pattern of recollection-related ERP activity as episodic and autobiographical retrieval (Johnson *et al.*, 2002a, b) and activates many of the same brain areas as retrieval of episodic or autobiographical memories, rather than those areas activated by retrieval of non-personal, factual knowledge

(Maguire and Mummery, 1999; Levine *et al.*, 2004; Svoboda *et al.*, 2006). Given these overall similarities, for the purposes of the present paper, both episodic and autobiographical memories will be treated as belonging to one category, with quantitative differences in the amount of retrieval-related activity.

Another aspect of memory function highly relevant to understanding deceptions about items in long term memory is that events are not encoded or stored in their entirety. Rather, what and how much is remembered from any given episode is determined by which aspects of the event were attended and, most important, how that information was processed. That is, deep, meaningful processing that makes reference to previously-formed memories produces new memories that are stronger and contain greater detail than those for events processed with less contact with previously-stored memories. Thus, the nature of the initial encoding processes is vital because it determines both what can be remembered and the amount of associated detail that can be remembered. This explains why different eyewitnesses to the same event can have such different memories of the event; what each remembers is related to which aspects of the event were attended, the perceived novelty of the event, and the type of processing they engaged. Put another way, it is widely accepted that episodic memories are stored records of the processing that occurred at the time the event was experienced, e.g., perceptions, feelings, and thoughts, rather than an accurate record of what actually occurred. This is evidenced by the fact that the sensory and cognitive processing engendered during memory retrieval has been shown to recapitulate the processing that occurred at the time the memory was encoded (e.g., Rugg *et al.*, 2008).

Studies of false memories, i.e., memories for events that one might think occurred but did not actually occur, have found that they generate a pattern of brain activity that is nearly identical to that generated for true memories. One of the main differences, however, is that because they did not occur in the real world, false memories are associated with reduced levels of activation in brain areas where sensory information is processed (e.g., Cabeza *et al.*, 2001). Relevant to situations involving deception, results such as these indicate that, even if one were to carefully memorize a fabricated story to cover real events, memories for the fabricated story would not contain the appropriate sensory information. Therefore, this principle of encoding-retrieval similarity for episodic memories could be used to validate reported memories for experienced events. This exemplifies how taking advantage of new information about the neural basis of episodic memory can potentiate the development of more sophisticated methods for detecting whether the memories being offered during an interrogation are truthful accounts or are merely confabulations.

Finally, in studying the nature of deception-related processing or attempting to detect guilty knowledge, most neurocognitive studies have episodic, autobiographical, or personal semantic memories as the object of the lie or concealed information. In this context, it is important to note that the success of all long term memory-based deceptions depends entirely on the proper identification and retrieval of the truthful memory so that an appropriate alternative, deceptive response can be formulated.

Executive Processes and Cognitive Control

Over the past ten years, neurocognitive studies have greatly increased our understanding of the nature and function of executive processes, both how they implement cognitive control in a wide variety of tasks and how they are instantiated in the brain (for reviews see Ridderinkhof *et al.*, 2004; Braver and Barch, 2006; Koechlin and Summerfield, 2007; Badre, 2008). Executive processes is a collective term used to describe a variety of cognitive functions that work separately and in concert to control and coordinate the selection and execution of all goal-directed actions. Consequently, these processes, most of which are controlled and resource demanding, are believed to underlie the ability to interact successfully with the environment in all situations. For example, it is generally thought that executive processes help control actions by providing the means to monitor and resolve response conflicts whenever interference arises from competing information streams or when there is competition between alternative responses, e.g., between making the prepotent truthful response and making a deceptive response. Executive processes are responsible for such functions as inhibiting unwanted responses and detecting and inhibiting erroneous responses, e.g., truthful responses during deceptions. Other executive processes are used in dual-task situations when a person must coordinate and flexibly allocate the use of his/her cognitive resources between tasks and in situations when he/she must switch between the performance of two different tasks, e.g., switching between making truthful and deceptive responses. In addition, other executive processes are required to adjudicate between competing response tendencies and others are needed to inhibit competing and/or undesired responses.

It is evident, therefore, that these and other cognitive control processes will play a vital role in the ability to create and execute every deception and that deceptive responses require greater use of these control processes than truthful responses.

NEUROCOGNITIVE STUDIES OF DECEPTION

To date, only a few dozen neurocognitive studies of deception have appeared in the peer-reviewed literature. They have already produced a number of important insights into how deception-related processing is instantiated in the brain. The goals of this research are varied, with some studies designed to establish neurocognitive models of the processes used during different types of deception and others designed to create improved methods for detecting guilty knowledge and malingering. Nevertheless, the ultimate goal of even basic research studies is the creation of a scientifically-based armamentarium of deception detection and credibility assessment tools.

Most of the basic neurocognitive studies of deception have used the experimental approach developed by Furedy and colleagues (Furedy *et al.*, 1988; Ben-Shakhar and Furedy, 1990) following Lykken's (1959) early work. Furedy and colleagues attacked the question of how information about the cognitive processes used to perpetrate deception could be revealed experimentally. They argued that, even in the absence of a unique lie response, deception-related processing can be studied if it is properly isolated from other concurrent processing. Thus, they proposed the differentiation-of-deception paradigm in which deception-related processing is isolated by comparing results from two conditions that differ only in whether there are truthful or deceptive responses. Although developed by Furedy *et al.* (1988) specifically to investigate the ANS correlates of deception, this paradigm has been successfully used by cognitive neuroscientists to study the brain processes underlying deception.

The extant neurocognitive studies of deception have attempted to model two general types of deception. The first and simplest type of deception can be thought of as well-rehearsed lies. These lies involve simply making "opposite" responses, e.g., responding "no" for "yes," and can be characterized as instructed lies in experimental settings. A second, more sophisticated type of deception involving spontaneous, intention-based lies depends on processing conducted in real time to identify intentional, goal-directed deceptive responses. Validating and refining these models necessitates determining which cognitive processes are required by each, as well as the extent to which these processes are shared across deceptions.

The following review is structured around a series of cognitive studies conducted over the past decade using the ERP (Johnson *et al.*, 2003, 2004, 2005, 2008a) and fMRI (Ganis *et al.*, 2003, 2009) techniques. It is important to remember that, due to their different strengths and weaknesses, ERP experiments emphasize the temporal characteristics of the cognitive processes involved whereas fMRI experiments emphasize the locations of activated brain areas. Although both cognitive ERP and fMRI studies have employed the differentiation-of-deception approach, so far few attempts have been made to integrate the complementary results from these two functional neuroimaging techniques. Thus, although the results from both these techniques are largely presented separately, the presence of similar and/or overlapping findings is noted whenever possible within the constraints imposed by differences in methods and paradigms.

Instructed Lies, Tactical Monitoring, and the GKT

Our approach to creating a conceptual framework for studying the neurocognitive basis of deception began by categorizing the general types of processes that might be used to perpetrate a deception (Johnson *et al.*, 2003, 2004). We argued that deception-related processing could be temporally divided into two broad categories: (1) the initial cognitive/emotional processes used to formulate the rationale, intent, and strategies relevant to the deception, and (2) those used to select and execute the deceptive response. When we began our studies about 15 years ago, the latter category seemed to provide the more tractable problem to research. We also reasoned that, although the processes required to formulate a successful deception vary across individuals and circumstances, the need to consciously select and execute a response that is incompatible with the truth is a necessary component of all deceptions.

As noted above, a variety of executive processes work together to implement cognitive control and an important subset of these consist of the processes used for response monitoring and inhibition. Research has shown that at least some monitoring processes occur continuously and automatically, i.e., do not require processing resources, and they appear to be part of a neural circuit designed to prevent humans from making erroneous responses. Hemodynamic studies over the past decade have revealed considerable detail about the neural basis of this circuit and led to the conclusion that the anterior cingulate cortex (ACC) plays a central role in response monitoring and error detection. When erroneous responses occur, they are detected by the ACC, which sends a signal to DLPFC to upregulate the amount of attention devoted to task performance. The resulting increased attention leads to a reduction in errors on subsequent trials and produces a phenomenon known as post-error slowing because responses are slowed on trials following errors (e.g., Gratton et al., 1992; MacDonald et al., 2000). This ACC-DLPFC circuit functions on a moment-to-moment basis and should also actively work to prevent deceptive responses, which by definition are erroneous responses. Because these particular monitoring processes function in the interval between a stimulus and subsequent response and are focused on short-term trends, Johnson et al. (2003) labeled them tactical monitoring processes.

Findings from a variety of tasks have demonstrated that ACC activity also increases whenever stimuli create conflicting response tendencies and/or uncertainty about the identity of the best response (e.g., Carter et al., 1998; Barch et al., 2000; Botvinick et al., 2001), and even when there is residual uncertainty about having just made the correct response (Johnson et al., 2004). In addition, control processes associated with inhibiting unwanted responses also activate ACC, as well as right ventrolateral prefrontal cortex (VLPFC) (e.g., Mostofsky and Simmonds, 2008; Goghari and MacDonald, 2009). The specific ACC areas involved in response inhibition are different from those used during error detection and correction (e.g., Gavaran *et al.*, 2002), which led Swick and colleagues (Turken and Swick, 1999; Swick and Jovanovic, 2002) to suggest that the ACC is a multi-functional brain area, with control and monitoring functions performed in different regions (see also Ridderinkhof *et al.*, 2004). It is important to note that the ACC is part of the limbic system, which is evolutionarily older and morphologically different than the cerebral cortex. At least some of the executive processes performed in the ACC do not appear to be subject to conscious manipulation, which suggests that they would not be susceptible to conscious countermeasures designed to foil credibility assessment tests.

Response monitoring demands invariably increase whenever competing response tendencies arise, such as when the pre-potent truthful response competes with a deceptive response for execution. Consequently, to ensure the success of any deception, additional control processes must be brought online in order to, for example, adjudicate between different possible responses and inhibit any unintended responses. Unlike tactical monitoring processes, however, these additional control processes require attention and resources from the limited available pool. Therefore, even the simplest deceptive responses would be distinguishable from truthful responses because of the greater workload and cognitive effort required.

Prior to cognitive studies of deception, all investigations into the nature of cognitive control used perceptually-based response conflicts. This was done, for example, by imbuing stimuli with multiple features, with each associated with a different, conflicting response. This raised the question of the relevance of previous results on cognitive control processes to deception because almost all deceptions are conceptually-based, due to their being based on retrieved memories. Hence, although the hemodynamic results cited above are directly applicable to understanding perceptually-based deceptions about the present, e.g., lies in various games or saying the light was green when it was red, it was not known if the same monitoring, adjudicating, and inhibitory processes would be used during conceptually-based deceptions about the past. Whereas perceptually-based conflicts are experienced in essentially the same way across individuals, conceptually-based conflicts are specific to each individual and depend entirely on whether particular items are stored in his or her memory. Hence, there was a need to determine whether there is a single, general-purpose processor for all response conflicts, regardless of the source of conflicting information, or separate specific-purpose processors for perceptually- and conceptually-based conflicts.

In summary, by virtue of their central role in controlling and coordinating the selection and execution of willed actions, executive processes such as those used to implement tactical response monitoring and inhibit pre-potent truthful responses were expected to play a central role in every deception. The importance of these processes is highlighted by the fact that their failure could result in the inadvertent execution of truthful responses, heightening the risk of being caught in a lie. We also suggested that the majority of cognitive processing occurring at the time of highly-practiced deceptions would be devoted primarily to management of the response conflict associated with executing a deceptive response (Johnson *et al.*, 2003, 2004). Nevertheless, even if these control processes comprise only a small fraction of the overall processing at the time the deception is perpetrated, their successful execution is essential to avoid compromising all preceding deception-related processing.

ERP Results

To study the possible role of tactical monitoring processes in deception, we used a standard episodic memory recognition task performed under truthful and deceptive instructions. Participants were presented with a list of previously memorized words randomly intermixed with an equal number of non-memorized words, and their task was to categorize each word as either known ("old") or unknown ("new") and press one of two buttons as quickly as possible. In the Truthful condition, participants correctly identified the old and new words. In the Instructed Lie condition, participants were told to hide what they knew and respond incorrectly by pressing the button opposite of the correct choice (press the "new" button for "old" words and vice versa). Note that because old and new words were stored in episodic and semantic memory, respectively, deceptive responses about these words were equivalent to "self" and "other" lies.

It is important to note that a fundamental problem with all Instructed Lie conditions in which an "opposite" response is called for is that the validity of the results depends entirely on the participant's compliance with the instructions. That is, simply by reversing the stimulus-response assignments surreptitiously, participants can counter the conflicting response tendencies inherent in Instructed Lies. Participants have an incentive to use this countermeasure because, as noted, the additional control processes and effort required for deceptive responding in this condition increases overall task workload. If this countermeasure were implemented, then RTs for both truthful and deceptive responses would not be expected to differ. To prevent implementation of this simple countermeasure, we randomly inserted "catch" trials consisting of equal numbers of the words "OLD" and "NEW" into the stimulus series on 20% of the trials. Participants were instructed to respond using the same stimulus-response assignments as required for truthful responses whenever these catch stimuli appeared, and that failure to do so would expose their use of this countermeasure. Moreover, this procedure makes any attempted use of this strategy immediately evident because the response conflict effects, e.g., slowed RTs and/or altered ERP activity, are shifted from the Instructed Lies to the catch trials. To maintain the differentiation-of-deception approach, catch trials were also included in the Truthful condition.

The presence of the catch trials in our Instructed Lie condition also accentuated the natural task-switch aspect of all real-world deceptions (Johnson et al., 2003). That is, on every lie trial, responses associated with truthful and deceptive tasks must be selected in rapid succession according to the rules and stimulus-response mappings for each, i.e., the truthful response must be identified before a deceptive response can be selected, in addition to activating inhibitory processes to prevent execution of the truthful response. Research has demonstrated that successful switching from one task to another requires a different set of executive processes (e.g., Monsell, 2003), which adds to the overall differences between truthful and deceptive responses.

Consistent with the idea that all deceptions require additional executive processes, even simple, highly-practiced Instructed Lies produced a complex pattern of altered behavioral and ERP activity compared to that for Truthful responses. Behaviorally, RTs for Instructed Lies were significantly slower and more variable than RTs for Truthful responses, regardless of whether they were about items that were (self) or were not (other) previously experienced. Slowed RT is a standard indicator of increased task difficulty and this finding has since been replicated in other ERP studies of Instructed Lies (Wu *et al.*, 2009; Hu *et al.*, 2011).

In accord with our hypothesis that executing deceptive responses requires greater cognitive control and tactical monitoring processes, Instructed Lies about both self- and other-related memories elicited a significantly larger medial frontal negativity (MFN), an ERP component that peaks about 70 ms after a response (Johnson *et al.*, 2000b, 2004, 2005). The MFN is elicited when there are conflicting response tendencies and/or ambiguities about how stimuli should be categorized (e.g., Gehring and Knight, 2000; Ridderinkhof *et al.*, 2004). These investigators and others have produced considerable support for the idea that MFN amplitude indexes the overall level of conflict associated with executed responses. Consistent with the hemodynamic results reviewed above on the role of the ACC in conflict monitoring and management, multiple laboratories have found evidence that the neural generators of the MFN are located in or near the ACC (Ullsperger and von Cramon, 2001; Gehring and Willoughby, 2002; Johnson *et al.*, 2004). Consistent with the workload increases brought on by this additional processing, Instructed Lies also elicited smaller LPCs compared to Truthful responses (Johnson *et al.*, 2003), which is a well-established indicator of increased workload (see below).

Whereas the MFN component appears in response-synchronized ERP averages, other researchers have reported that this ACC activity can be revealed in the central-frontal N2 component in stimulus-synchronized ERPs (e.g., Bartholow *et al.*, 2005; see Folstein and Van Petten, 2008 for a review). For example, Hu *et al.* (2011) found increased N2 amplitudes for Instructed Lies about personal semantic memories (name, birth date, hometown) and, at least for these stimuli, with greater N2 amplitude increases for self- rather than for other-referential lies.

Another ERP difference between truthful and deceptive responses was found over the centromedial frontal cortex *prior* to the execution of deceptive responses. Whereas Truthful responses elicited a brief pre-response-positivity (PRP), Instructed Lies were characterized by an overlapping negative potential that significantly reduced PRP amplitude (Johnson *et al.*, 2004). Given that this effect was present during the last 200 ms before the Instructed Lie RTs, we interpreted it as reflecting the need to select a deceptive response following selection of the truthful response. This interpretation was bolstered by findings from recent studies of the Simon Task, in which the pre-potent, stimulus-based response must be inhibited and replaced with an intention-based response (Vallesi *et al.*, 2005). The selection of these intention-based alternate responses are believed to be controlled by a neural circuit consisting of the DLPFC, supplementary motor area (SMA), and ACC (e.g., Jahanshahi and Frith, 1998; Lau *et al.*, 2004). In this circuit, SMA is believed to play the central role in linking cognition, i.e., intent, to the control and production of volitional actions (see Haggard, 2008 and Nachev *et al.*, 2008 for reviews).

One ERP index of motor cortical activity is the pre-movement potential, a negative potential that steadily increases in amplitude in the interval preceding a voluntary response (e.g., Kornhuber and Deecke, 1965). Recently, Vallesi *et al.* (2005) demonstrated that pre-movement potential amplitudes increased, i.e., became more negative, when participants had to override a pre-potent response in favor of executing the opposite response. Given the timing and polarity of the pre-response amplitude reductions for our Instructed Lies, it is reasonable to posit that these changes were due to temporally overlapping pre-movement potentials. The fact that these results were obtained in the context of a differentiation-of deception experimental design suggests that the pre-response processing underlying both of these patterns of ERP activity was specific to the selection and/or execution of deceptive responses.

To address the question of whether perceptually- and conceptually-based response conflicts are processed similarly, a second aim of our initial studies was to directly compare their effects on behavioral and ERP measures (Johnson *et al.*, 2003, 2004). In two perceptual conditions, participants made truthful responses or Instructed Lies upon seeing random presentations of the words "LEFT" and "RIGHT." Comparing results from these perceptual conditions with the results from memory conditions revealed that the effects of response conflict on behavioral measures (RT, SD of RT) and ERP activity (MFN, LPC,

PRP) for perceptually- and conceptually-based conflicts were indistinguishable from one another (Johnson *et al.*, 2003, 2004). In addition, tactical monitoring processes appeared to function in a manner that was independent of other perceptually- and conceptually-related cognitive processes used to perform these tasks. For example, the same increases in RT and MFN amplitude and the same decreases in LPC and PRP amplitude were found regardless of 1) whether the word stimuli were highly repeated or all different, 2) whether participants denied having particular memories or falsely claimed to have particular memories, or 3) whether the probability of making incompatible responses was 80% or 100%. Finally, it is important to note that all of these behavioral and ERP differences were about the same magnitude for both self- and other-based lies and thus were unrelated to whether the lies were or were not self-referential. Taken together, we concluded that the executive processes used to detect and resolve response conflicts operate independently of many or all other cognitive operations. The insensitivity of tactical monitoring processes to these other cognitive variables may be due to the fact that they appear to be performed in the evolutionarily older ACC.

Based on this overall pattern of results, we concluded that a single cognitively encapsulated, general-purpose processor is responsible for detecting and possibly adjudicating response conflicts, regardless of the source of the conflicting response information (Johnson *et al.*, 2003, 2004). This is a positive result for credibility assessment because it indicates that tests should work equally well for deceptions about the past or present and self or other. Further, to detect practiced deceptions, credibility assessment tools will likely need to rely more on detecting excessive use of executive processes and less on detecting the types of deception-related processing that could be done in advance of when the deceptive responses are actually produced.

Hemodynamic Results

Ganis and colleagues (2003) created a cognitive model of different types of deceptions and sought to determine whether they rely on the same or different mixtures of cognitive processes. They proposed a taxonomy in which deceptions could be classified on two orthogonal dimensions according to whether they 1) were based on memorized or spontaneously-generated information, and 2) did or did not fit a coherent narrative. To test their conceptual framework, they employed two lie conditions designed to be at the extremes of both of these dimensions (Spontaneous Isolated vs. Memorized Scenario). Their Spontaneous Lies were about episodic memories and thus had many of the same elements as our Instructed Lies. Ganis *et al.* (2003) predicted that 1) both types of lies would create greater response conflict and thereby increase the demands on response monitoring processes compared to truthful responses, and 2) that Scenario Lies would place greater demands on working memory processes compared to that required for Isolated Lies. Further, they hypothesized that Spontaneous Lies would be based on a mixture of episodic and semantic memories and that memories for real experiences would be associated with greater perceptual detail than memories for fabricated experiences.

To generate the necessary scenario-based stimuli, Ganis *et al.* (2003) interviewed their participants a week prior to the experimental session to obtain detailed information about their actual experiences, e.g., a memorable work experience, and then collaboratively generated an alternative, internally-consistent scenario that described the best "vacation they ever took." Participants were asked to rehearse and memorize the vacation scenario in the interim so they could answer questions about it when they were in the fMRI scanner. The fMRI results revealed that, compared to Truthful responses, Spontaneous Lies elicited additional activity in a number of brain areas, including the ACC, those involved in episodic memory retrieval, e.g., left and right anterior prefrontal cortex, parahippocampal gyrus, right precuneus, and other areas, e.g., left motor cortex. Thus, even for their simple Spontaneous Lies about personal experiences, Ganis *et al.* (2003) found increased activity in brain areas known to be a part of the networks underlying monitoring and adjudicating response conflict and episodic memory retrieval.

The basic results from both our and Ganis *et al.*'s model-based approaches to studying deception have been replicated in many subsequent studies of Instructed Lies, most of which were done using the same old-new episodic recognition paradigm as we used. For example, numerous studies have shown that RTs for Instructed Lies are slower than those for Truthful responses (Abe *et al.*, 2006, 2007, 2008; Fullam *et al.*, 2009; Ganis *et al.*, 2009; Nunez *et al.*, 2005; Spence *et al.*, 2001, 2004), although this is not a universal result (Ganis *et al.*, 2003; Bhatt *et al.*, 2009; Sip *et al.*, 2010). Moreover, slowed RTs have been found for Instructed Lies about other types of memory stimuli, including autobiographical (e.g., Nunez *et al.*, 2005), personal semantic (e.g., Abe *et al.*, 2007), pictures (e.g., Ito *et al.*, 2011), and daily activities (Spence *et al.*, 2001; Fullam *et al.*, 2009). Similarly, Instructed Lies generally elicit greater ACC blood flow than Truthful responses (Nunez *et al.*, 2005; Abe *et al.*, 2006; Bhatt *et al.*, 2009; Ganis *et al.*, 2009; Ito *et al.*, 2011, 2012; Lee *et al.*, 2009), although this too is far from a universal result (Spence *et al.*, 2001; Abe *et al.*, 2008; Fullam *et al.*, 2009). Across studies, many additional brain areas were activated, including DLPFC areas associated with working memory (Spence *et al.*, 2001; Ganis *et al.*, 2003; Nunez *et al.*, 2005; Abe *et al.*, 2006, 2008; Bhatt *et al.*, 2009; Lee *et al.*, 2009; Ito *et al.*, 2011, 2012) and episodic memory retrieval (Nunez *et al.*, 2005; Abe *et al.*, 2008; Bhatt *et al.*, 2009; Fullam *et al.*, 2009; Ganis *et al.*, 2009), as well as VLPFC and other areas believed to be involved in inhibiting unwanted responses (Spence *et al.*, 2001; Nunez *et al.*, 2005; Abe *et al.*, 2006; Ganis *et al.*, 2009; Fullam *et al.*, 2009; Ito *et al.*, 2011, 2012; Lee *et al.*, 2009). Readers wanting additional details about these studies are directed to a number of excellent reviews of the hemodynamic literature (Spence *et al.*, 2004; Spence and Kaylor-Hughes, 2008; Abe, 2009, 2011; Christ *et al.*, 2009).

The Instructed Lie studies reviewed thus far, from both ERP and hemodynamic techniques, show clear overlap in their results. For example, in addition to the RT results, the ACC findings found in hemodynamic studies fit well with our MFN results. Moreover, a small subset of these fMRI studies also reported finding activation in premotor (PM) or SMA areas (Spence *et al.*, 2001; Ganis *et al.*, 2003; Abe *et al.*, 2008; Ito *et al.*, 2011, 2012), which could be related to our finding of altered PRP activity. However, the failure of a number of fMRI studies to find either increased RTs or increased ACC and/or PM-SMA activity may indicate the surreptitious use of countermeasures by their participants. That is, the failure of some fMRI studies to find increased RTs and/or increased blood flow in the ACC may have been due to their including data from participants who invoked the countermeasure of reversing the stimulus-response assignments. Given the blocked designs used in these experiments, coupled with their lack of catch trials, the possibility that their results were confounded in this way cannot be ruled out.

Taken together, the results of these ERP and hemodynamic experiments demonstrate that, despite the apparent simplicity of Instructed Lies, brain activity for deceptive responses is nevertheless significantly altered compared to that for truthful responses, which appears to be due at least partly to the increased use of executive processes. These truthful-deceptive differences have been obtained across a variety of paradigms involving different types of memory stimuli and different mixtures of cognitive processes, suggesting that an essential aspect of deception is captured in these Instructed Lie paradigms.

Hemodynamic Results in GKT Experiments

Researchers using hemodynamic measures have also studied Instructed Lies about events in the present or very recent past. These studies have been done in the context of GKT/CIT scenarios and they used essentially the same experimental design as that used in the ERP GKT studies mentioned above. Typically, participants were required to make Instructed Lies about their knowledge regarding possession of specific information (playing cards, bank notes, a specific number). Using a somewhat more realistic scenario, Mohamed and colleagues (2006) had a limited number of participants (N = 6) fire a gun inside the hospital before undergoing a GKT about the episode in the scanner. The presence of guilty knowledge in all these fMRI studies was revealed by comparing the brain activity elicited by probe, target, and irrelevant stimulus categories. In contrast to the studies of Instructed Lies reviewed above, which only infrequently found activation of DLPFC areas associated with working memory function, most GKT studies report DLPFC activation (Langleben *et al.*, 2002, 2005; Kozel *et al.*, 2005, 2009a; Phan *et al.*, 2005; Gamer *et al.*, 2007; Hakun *et al.*, 2008; Monteleone *et al.*, 2009; Nose *et al.*, 2009). Overall, these fMRI GKT studies are also characterized by more consistent activations in brain areas associated with executive processes. For example, the majority of GKT studies found increased ACC activity (Langleben *et al.*, 2002, 2005; Kozel *et al.*, 2005, 2009a, 2009b; Mohamed *et al.*, 2006; Gamer *et al.*, 2007; Hakun *et al.*, 2008; Monteleone *et al.*, 2009; Nose *et al.*, 2009), and all reported increased VLPFC activation (Langleben *et al.*, 2002, 2005; Phan *et al.*, 2005; Mohamed *et al.*, 2006; Gamer *et al.*, 2007, 2012; Hakun *et al.*, 2008; Kozel *et al.*, 2005, 2009a, 2009b; Monteleone *et al.*, 2009; Nose *et al.*, 2009), consistent with the idea that probe stimuli engendered greater use of inhibitory processing. Moreover, as in some Instructed Lie studies reviewed above, a subset of these fMRI GKT investigations also found increased activations in PM-SMA areas (Langleben *et al.*, 2002, 2005; Kozel *et al.*, 2005, 2009a, 2009b; Gamer *et al.*, 2007, 2012).

In an effort to link their fMRI results more closely with one of the key components of the polygraph, a number of these investigators also recorded skin conductance responses (SCR) in the same participants (Kozel *et al.*, 2005; Mohamed *et al.*, 2006; Gamer *et al.*, 2007, 2012). The studies by Gamer and colleagues (Gamer *et al.*, 2007, 2012), for example, revealed that increases in SCR activity were positively correlated with increased blood flow for lies in both right VLPFC and SMA. Finally, in the first use of the NIRS imaging technique in a GKT study, Tian *et al.* (2009) reported increased activation broadly over prefrontal areas when participants lied about having stolen a ring or watch. Although the spatial resolution in this early study is far less than is standard for fMRI studies, the NIRS technique may yet prove its usefulness in uncovering the brain mechanisms underlying deception.

As currently formulated, GKT/CIT studies are optimized to reveal the presence of concealed information and do not provide information on the neurocognitive processes used to make deceptive responses. In all these GKT/CIT experiments, participants acquired the guilty knowledge shortly before being placed in the scanner. Nevertheless, despite the brief intervals between acquisition and test, the interval is likely too long for the information to have been maintained in working memory. Thus, these procedures most likely test the contents of episodic memory, which is what would occur in real-world situations. Finally, it should be noted that the pattern of blood flow changes associated with Instructed Lies about specific guilty knowledge or concealed information is similar to that seen in differentiation-of-deception ERP and fMRI studies using stimuli pertaining to past events. One interesting difference is the fact that as a group, the variability in the patterns of hemodynamic activity across these GKT studies is much less than that in the fMRI studies of Instructed Lies reviewed above. This higher degree of consistency across fMRI GKT studies is probably due to the much higher degree of similarity in both their experimental designs and the stimuli being lied about than is typical in fMRI or ERP differentiation-of-deception studies. Nevertheless, there do appear to be some interesting differences in the activated brain networks in these two paradigms, as well as in the balance of activity within different brain areas in these networks. The most striking of these differences is the apparently greater contribution of working memory processes in the fMRI GKT/CIT scenarios. Future studies should attempt to disambiguate the neurocognitive differences between the GKT and differentiation-of-deception paradigms.

Intention-based Lies and Strategic Monitoring

Although Instructed Lies provide a useful model of some deceptions, many others are more complex and involve related or interacting parts such as would occur in a coherent narrative or story. The added complexity of these deceptions suggests that, to be successful, additional cognitive and executive processes must be recruited to ensure that all selected responses remain consistent. Reasoning that the duration of tactical monitoring processes is too limited to perform this function, we posited that longer-term, "strategic" monitoring processes would be required to ensure that selected responses have the required consistency to conform to an individual's goals, as well as with past and future responses (Johnson *et al.*, 2003, 2004). Hence, a major distinction between tactical and strategic monitoring processes is their duration, with the former operating during brief, stimulus-response intervals and the later over extended intervals and potentially large numbers of responses. We also posited that strategic monitoring processes would be consciously controllable to permit response contingencies to be updated in real time as required. Moreover, we suggested that these response monitoring processes must be hierarchically organized, with strategic processes providing the context in which tactical processes must operate (Johnson *et al.*, 2008a). In this way, strategic monitoring processes ultimately determine which stimuli will or will not generate response conflict. Put another way, the conceptual nature of complex, strategic deceptions means that goals and strategies determine when deceptive responses need to be made, thereby determining at the tactical level which stimuli will or will not generate response conflict.

ERP Results

Continuing our processing approach, we hypothesized that goal-directed and/or narrative-based deceptions would differ from Instructed Lies in two important ways: the addition of 1) strategic monitoring processes to make responses conform to one another, and 2) processes related to selecting intention-based responses. At the time we formulated the concept of strategic monitoring, it had not appeared in the literature and it was unclear how such processes would work or if they would be associated with a specific pattern of ERP activity. To create a scenario requiring strategic monitoring, we asked participants to make goal-directed truthful and deceptive responses about self and other items within a single block of trails. Participants were instructed to hide the truth about their memories by generating random responses with the caveat that they needed to meet the goal of making roughly equal numbers of truthful and deceptive responses in each of the four response categories over the block of trials, i.e., self-truthful, self-deceptive, other-truthful, and other-deceptive (Johnson *et al.*, 2003, 2004). As in the Instructed Lie condition, catch stimuli, i.e., "OLD" and "NEW," were again randomly presented on 20% of the trials.

Although we recognized that different processes would be required to make Self-generated and Instructed Lie responses, we did not fully appreciate the magnitude of the differences at the time of our early experiments. In the interim, researchers have studied the neural basis of stimulus- and intention-based responses and have shown that they are best understood as being at opposite ends of a response continuum (cf., Waszak *et al.*, 2005; Herwig *et al.*, 2007). In this scheme, Instructed Lies fall into the category of responses whose selection is highly constrained by external factors, i.e., press opposite, and thus fall on the stimulus-based/experimenter-instructed end of the continuum. By contrast, selection of self-generated, goal-directed responses are relatively unconstrained and thus lie on the opposite, intention-based end of the continuum (cf., Waszak *et al.*, 2005; Herwig *et al.*, 2007). In a series of studies, Waszak and colleagues used ERPs to investigate the neural basis of both types of responses and found that, compared to stimulus-based responses, intention-based responses elicited pre-movement potentials that were significantly more negative and began earlier prior to the response. Their results fit well with research showing PM-SMA involvement in transforming intentions into volitional actions (e.g., Lau *et al.*, 2004; Haggard, 2008; Nachev *et al.*, 2008) and they concluded that these two different modes of action selection can be distinguished on the basis of their underlying neural activity (Waszak *et al.*, 2005).

Maintaining the differentiation-of-deception type of approach, we compared the behavioral and ERP results for Self-generated Lies with those for Instructed Lies in order to better reveal the differences between these two types of lies (Johnson *et al.*, 2003, 2004). This comparison revealed that, as expected, processing for Self-generated Lies was qualitatively and quantitatively different from that for Instructed Lies. Behaviorally, RTs for Self-generated Lies were quantitatively different from RTs for Instructed Lies because they were significantly slower. This finding has been at least partly replicated by others who compared RTs obtained under similar experimental conditions with those for their truthful responses (Vendemia *et al.*, 2005; Wu *et al.*, 2009). Qualitatively, RTs for Self-generated Lies were different because, unlike the relatively normal, bell-shaped RT distributions seen for Instructed Lies and Truthful responses, RT distributions for self-generated truthful and deceptive responses, about both self and other memories, were prolonged and more rectangular. This difference in RT variability is consistent with the presence of different underlying selection processes for intention- and stimulus-based responses (cf., Waszak *et al.*, 2005; Herwig *et al.*, 2007).

Large differences between the ERPs elicited by Self-generated and Instructed Lies were also obtained. For example, MFN activity elicited by Self-generated Lies was considerably larger than that elicited by Instructed Lies. Moreover, in accord with the goal-directed nature of both truthful and deceptive responses made within this condition, MFN amplitude increases were the same for all responses. Further, the differential nature and time course of strategic and tactical monitoring processes was evidenced by our finding that the MFNs elicited by Self-generated Lies were due to a different pattern of neural source activity in the ACC than that for MFNs elicited by Instructed Lies (Johnson *et al.*, 2004). This result also confirms findings indicating the involvement of the ACC in multiple executive processes (Turken and Swick, 1999; Swick and Jovanovic, 2002). In addition, the MFNs elicited in both conditions were temporally overlapping indicating that strategic monitoring processes continued after the response, in parallel with tactical monitoring processes, with no evidence of differential latencies despite the large differences in task difficulty. These findings suggest that, to the extent that these different monitoring processes are invoked to varying degrees in different deception paradigms, the resulting differential mixtures of generator activity could explain the high degree of variability in the coordinates of the ACC activations reported in different fMRI studies. Finally, our hypothesis that strategic monitoring processes would require increased use of controlled processing resources, thereby increasing workload, was supported by the finding that LPC amplitudes for Self-generated Lies were reduced significantly compared to those elicited by Instructed Lies (see below).

In our formulation, strategic monitoring processes should begin earlier relative to the response than tactical monitoring processes in order to guide selection of intention-based responses. Consistent with this prediction, the ERP activity elicited in the 300-400 ms interval prior to Self-generated Lies was unlike that elicited by either Instructed Lies or Truthful responses. Specifically, compared to the brief, small amplitude reductions overlapping the PRP component for Instructed Lies relative to Truthful responses, the magnitude of the pre-response negativity for Self-generated Lies began much earlier and was large enough to essentially eliminate the PRP component. As for the MFN, the same pre-response activity was elicited by self-generated truthful and deceptive responses about both self and other memories, as would be expected when selected responses for all categories must conform to the same goal.

At the time, we interpreted the large alterations in amplitude and duration of the pre-response activity over medial frontal brain areas as being due solely to the use of strategic monitoring processes (Johnson et al., 2004). However, based on the recent research on stimulus- and intention-based responses referred to above, it seems more likely that the pre-response negativity in our studies represents a combination of two distinct, temporally overlapping processes, one reflecting strategic monitoring and one reflecting the processing required to make intention-based responses. Indeed, the spatio-temporal characteristics of the ERP waveforms elicited at central scalp by our self-generated responses are remarkably similar to those reported by Waszak et al. (2005) for intention-based responses. Moreover, the differential amounts of pre-response negativity elicited by our Self-generated and Instructed Lies bear a striking resemblance to the differential amplitudes of the pre-movement potentials reported by Waszak et al. (2005) for their stimulus- and intention-based responses.

To better understand the nature of the altered pre-response activity elicited by our Self-generated Lies, we conducted an experiment to determine if our pre-response negativity is due to processing related strategic monitoring, selection of intention-based responses, or a combination of both (Johnson, unpublished data). To do this, we created a condition that was intermediate between the tactically-monitored, stimulus-based responses in our

Instructed Lie condition and the strategically-monitored, intention-based responses in our Self-generated Lie condition. To mimic the Self-generated Lie paradigm, the intermediate condition required participants to monitor the number of two categories of stimuli in two different streams of randomly occurring events. However, while the strategic monitoring demands of this task remained the same, only stimulus-based responses were required. This distinction resulted from the fact that the identity of the correct response on each trial was indicated by the category counts once they were updated based on the category of the current stimulus. The results revealed that all four event categories in the intermediate condition were characterized by pre-response negativities of about the same pre-response duration, but with only one-half of the amplitude, as those in our Self-generated Lie condition. Thus, these data support the interpretation that both strategic monitoring and intention-based response selection processes are simultaneously active in the pre-response interval for goal-directed Self-generated Lies, whether truthful or deceptive. In this context, it is worth noting that there is little if any need to either engage strategic monitoring processes or make intention-based responses when selecting truthful responses in credibility assessment situations. Consequently, the presence of these pre-response negativities would be an indication of deceptive responding.

Intention-based Lies about the present were also studied in a face-to-face game scenario. Carrion *et al.* (2010) recorded ERPs while their participants lied or told the truth, both with and without deceptive intent, according to their goals as they played the game. The circumstances of the game were roughly equivalent to those in an interrogation when responses are adapted continuously based on the other person's responses. Although the investigators only reported results for the medial frontal N450 component, they did find that, similar to our results, self-generated truthful and deceptive responses both elicited an enhanced N450 component compared to those elicited by Instructed Lies.

Hemodynamic Results

Overall, relatively few fMRI researchers have studied self-generated deceptions with differentiation-of-deception designs. One notable exception was

Ganis *et al.*'s (2003) study mentioned above that compared fMRI activity for highly-memorized Instructed Lies to that for Spontaneous Lies about events in a coherent story. Their findings showed that Spontaneous Lies generated more activation in a variety of brain areas, including the ACC, right anterior prefrontal cortex, and precuneus, with the latter two areas being typically associated with retrieval of episodic and autobiographical memories. Ganis and colleagues (2003) also found increased activation in left and right motor areas for Self-generated Lies. As with our results, Ganis *et al.* found significantly different patterns of brain activity for Instructed and Self-generated Lies, although which aspects of their increased activation might relate to strategic monitoring or intention-based response selection remains unclear.

In an attempt to increase the emotional salience of the stimuli being lied about, Spence *et al.* (2008) collected information from participants who were acquaintances of the experimenters about "embarrassing incidents" in their lives. They used instructions similar to ours and required participants to make self-generated random truthful and deceptive responses, again with the goal of making equal numbers of each. Rather than using a differentiation-of-deception approach, their truthful-deceptive comparisons came from the same random condition, which eliminated the possibility of seeing brain activity related to either strategic monitoring or intention-based response selection processes. Hence, the only significant differences in truthful-deceptive fMRI activations that Spence *et al.* (2008) found were in bilateral VLPFC.

Intention-based response selection is also an important cognitive process when individuals attempt to fake a memory impairment for gain by hiding what they know in a forensic investigation, i.e., malingering. Investigations of the neurocognitive differences between truthful and malingering responders have generally used old-new recognition tests coupled with instructions to make self-generated random responses on each trial. As in the case of fMRI GKT research, malingering studies have also tended to produce highly consistent results and replicate the results of other deception paradigms, including the GKT. For example, all studies to date have found that simulated malingering was associated with increased activity in both DLPFC and VLPFC areas (Lee *et al.*, 2002, 2005; Browndyke *et al.*, 2008; Liang *et al.*, 2012), and two of these studies also reported increased activation in

PM-SMA areas (Lee *et al.*, 2005; Liang *et al.*, 2012). Despite switching to the auditory modality and eliminating the requirement for long-term memory retrieval, McPherson *et al.* (2012) also found increased activation bilaterally in DLPFC and VLPFC regions in their study of malingering. Their results strengthen the argument that the areas of common activation are not due to the memory retrieval aspect of most malingering paradigms and are more likely related to deception-related processes. It is interesting to note that, for reasons that remain unclear, the more applied malingering and GKT fMRI research produced more consistent activations of brain areas associated with working memory and response selection processing than is the case in more basic studies of deception.

Intention-based responses about present events have also been a central component in two recent fMRI studies. Using an approach similar to Carrion *et al.*'s (2010), Sip *et al.* (2010) used a face-to-face interactive game scenario in which participants decided whether to make truthful or deceptive responses based on the current state of play while in the fMRI scanner. Although eschewing the differentiation-of-deception approach, paradigms like this do capture the interactive aspect of many deceptions in which individuals must strategically monitor an opponent's responses in order to shape the choice of their own goal-directed truthful and deceptive responses. Sip *et al.* (2010) showed that false claims, i.e., deceptive responses, were associated with increased hemodynamic activity in prefrontal and parietal cortex, but truthful claims were associated with increased blood flow in frontopolar cortex. Presumably due to the absence of an independent truthful condition, no increased activity was evident in ACC or DLPFC. However, Sip *et al.* (2010) did report finding increased blood flow in PM-SMA areas, which might be related to our finding of increased pre-response activity for strategically monitored intention-based responses.

A study reported by Greene and Paxton (2009) used a novel approach to revealing the processing associated with intention-based deceptions. They used fMRI to scan participants while they performed in different conditions in which they did or did not have the opportunity to lie to the experimenters about their performance. In the different conditions, participants either reported their predictions about the outcome of coin flips in advance of the flip or after the flip via self-report. In an interesting twist, there were no instructions to lie nor any inducements provided to do so. Rather, the decision to lie was an entirely personal choice that individuals could make in order to increase their monetary gain in the experiment. Indeed, not all participants chose to lie and, unlike the within-subject designs used in all other deception experiments, participants were categorized as being Honest or Dishonest based on their performance (percentage of trials in which they lied).

In accord with other deception studies, Greene and Paxton (2009) found that, compared to the "truthful" condition i.e., tell the experimenter your prediction in advance, dishonest participants in the self-report condition showed increased hemodynamic activity in the ACC, anterior prefrontal cortex, right DLPFC, and bilateral VLPFC. In addition, the magnitudes of these hemodynamic activations were positively correlated with their frequency of lying. By contrast, no differences were seen in the patterns or magnitudes of brain activation across conditions for the honest group, presumably due to the fact that all responses in both conditions were truthful. However, participants in the dishonest group, who needed to select intention-based responses in the self-report condition, also generated SMA activation. Consistent with our Self-generated Lie results, Greene and Pazton (2009) also found no differentiation between the patterns of activation associated with intermixed truthful and deceptive responses for dishonest participants in the self-report condition. To maximize their gains while not giving themselves away, deceptive participants had to avoid misreporting their predictions on every self-report trial and thus presumably used strategies to determine when to lie and when to tell the truth. Their finding of greater prefrontal activity was replicated in a recent NIRS study that used a paradigm modeled on theirs (Ding *et al.*, 2013). In sum, although atypical of most deception paradigms, Greene and Paxton (2009) created one of the more ecologically valid paradigms with which to study naturally occurring lies.

A surprising aspect of the ERP and fMRI studies with Self-generated Lies reviewed here is the general absence of the expected working memory activity. With the exception of Greene and Paxton (2009) and malingering studies, none of these other ERP or fMRI studies showed the expected DLPFC activity associated with working memory processing. Potential explanations include the possibility that the networks used during strategic monitoring have their own stores or that the working memory loads imposed by these tasks were below the threshold to be detected by these imaging techniques. There is some support for the latter possibility in that the loads imposed in the Johnson *et al.* (2003, 2004) and Ganis *et al.* (2003) experiments, in particular, are much less than those typically used in studies of working memory. For example, when compared directly, blood flow increases during episodic retrieval were much less than when participants held four words in working memory (Cabeza *et al.*, 2002). However, the results of Green and Paxton (2009) and malingering studies raise the possibility that the contribution of working memory processes to deception increases along with the realism of the scenario used to elicit the deceptions.

ERP Indices of Guilty Knowledge and Concealed Information

Based on the studies reviewed above, Lykken's (1959) GKT procedure can provide a useful, albeit narrow, window on the presence of limited, highly constrained amounts of concealed information. However, there could be other situations in which it would be useful to have methods that can directly reveal information about the contents of an individual's memory, as well as being able to distinguish real memories from practiced fabrications or false memories. In this context, researchers have demonstrated that the ERP can provide direct, reliable, neurocognitive measures of the presence of specific memories. Fortunately, because stimuli have obligatory access to long term memory, any appropriate cue will elicit retrieval of episodic and/or semantic memories. Indeed, this obligatory retrieval is the fundamental reason why the Farwell and Donchin (1991) GKT procedure works and produces the LPC probability effects that are used to determine if the person has knowledge of the information of interest. Using ERPs in a neurocognitive framework, however, affords the ability to detect directly from which memory system(s) the memories are retrieved, which episodic retrieval processes were used, whether episodic retrievals represent real memories or confabulations, and the timing of memory retrieval. Finally, new research (described below) suggests that it may be possible to determine whether retrieved memories are being manipulated following retrieval as part of a deception.

A substantial body of research, extending back to the early 1980s, has revealed a series of ERP components, each with its own spatiotemporal characteristics, whose activity correlates with different episodic retrieval-related processes. These components are revealed when ERPs elicited by items not stored in episodic memory ("new") are subtracted from ERPs elicited by items in episodic memory ("old"). The resulting old-new difference ERPs reveal a series of components that have distinct spatiotemporal characteristics and are known collectively as the old/new or episodic memory (EM) effect (see Johnson, 1995; Friedman and Johnson, 2000; Rugg and Curran, 2007 for reviews). For example, the vague feeling that something has been experienced before, such as when a face in a crowd seems familiar, elicits ERP activity that is maximal at frontal-central scalp between 300 and 500 ms after stimulus onset (mid-frontal EM effect). If, however, the same cue also produces recollection, e.g., one recognizes a face as a particular acquaintance, an ERP component that is maximal at left parietal scalp between 500 and 800 ms (parietal EM effect) is elicited. These two patterns of brain activity have been shown to reflect the familiarity and recollection processes, respectively, associated with episodic retrieval (cf., Mandler, 1980). Further, these patterns of ERP activity are only elicited when a cue makes contact with an episodic memory and not when a person wrongly classifies a new item as being old (false alarms) (cf., Johnson et al., 1998). The overall pattern of episodic retrieval-related ERP activity is richer and more complex than can be covered here, so the interested reader is encouraged to consult the reviews cited above for additional details.

At this point, a number of studies have confirmed that the spatiotemporal characteristics of the recollection-related parietal EM effect are unaffected by whether a person truthfully or deceptively categorizes a stimulus as being known or unknown. Further, this result was obtained regardless of whether participants made Instructed (Tardif et al., 2000; Johnson et al., 2000, 2003, 2005) or Self-generated Lies (Johnson et al., 2003, 2005) about simple episodic memories. Other studies have extended these basic findings to include Instructed and Self-generated Lies about specific autobiographical memories (Johnson et al., 2002b) and Instructed Lies about personal semantic memories (names of family members, friends, schools attended, etc.) (Johnson et al., 2002a). Equally important for any index of guilty knowledge, these studies also replicated previous results showing that ERP correlates of episodic retrieval are elicited only by previously experienced events. Thus, episodes falsely claimed to have been experienced, i.e., confabulations and other-related lies, could be differentiated from true memories based on their failure to elicit episodic recollection-related ERP activity. Further, while the cues in recognition tests necessarily must duplicate the original items exactly, i.e., referred to as "copy cues," this is not feasible for testing autobiographical memory. However, having successfully elicited a parietal EM effect during cued recall of episodic memories previously (Johnson *et al.*, 1998a), we created 1-5 word stimuli designed to cue recall of specific autobiographical memories gathered during an interview a week prior to the experiment (Johnson *et al.*, 2002b, 2008). Despite the fact that participants had never previously experienced the specific cues that were used, a parietal EM effect with the same characteristics as those elicited during episodic recognition was elicited, albeit later in time in accord with the greater difficulty of recall compared to recognition (cf., Johnson *et al.*, 1998b). As would be expected based on the idea that retrieved memories are recapitulations of encoded events, recall of autobiographical memories was characterized by large amplitude ERP activity over primary and secondary visual cortex (Johnson *et al.*, 2008a). Thus, ERPs can provide a useful method for probing whether individuals have personal episodic or semantic (general knowledge) memories for particular people, places, or events in credibility assessment settings.

Deceptions about Attitudes, Beliefs, and Personal Evaluations

In the differentiation-of-deception research reviewed thus far, participants could identify the deceptive response simply by retrieving the appropriate item from episodic or semantic memory stores. Further, all these deceptions were essentially close collaborations between experimenters and participants because the information being lied about was known to both parties, a fact that was also known to both parties. In many situations, however, there may be little or no ground truth about, for instance, what an individual knows or thinks. Hence, studying the processing underlying deceptive responses in situations when the veridicality of an individual's answers cannot be verified independently may help bridge the gap between laboratory studies and real-world deceptions.

In an attempt to study more realistic, intention-based deceptions, we used a set of stimuli about attitudes, beliefs, and preferences, which frequently engender deceptive responses in everyday life (Johnson *et al.*, 2008a). These highly self-referential cognitive constructs are distinct from most other mental processes because they embody evaluative judgments that are based on internal scales reflecting the individual's values, which are only known to themselves. Such value judgments play an essential role in everyday behavior because they provide the basis for deciding which behaviors and activities to engage in and which to avoid, as well as which people, places, things, and ideas are viewed positively or negatively. Given the extent to which individual behavior is based on attitudes, beliefs, and preferences, it is reasonable to posit that the values associated with each will be viewed as being more important and/or more central to their self concept, even in comparison to specific episodic or autobiographical memories. Further, studying deceptive responses about attitudes introduces the possibility of characterizing how valence, a central but previously ignored component of most deceptions, affects deception-related processing.

Each of these different types of personal evaluative judgments, which will be referred to collectively as attitudes, have characteristics that make them qualitatively different from the memory-derived stimuli used in the deception studies reviewed above. For example, although the valence assigned to each attitude object is based on autobiographical and/or episodic memories for specific life events, stored attitude representations are believed to represent schematic versions of these events that lack any specific contextual information associated with the original events. The resulting abstraction is viewed as a relatively stable memory representation, or "tag," containing information related to the valence and/or the type of response associated with the particular attitude object, e.g., approach or avoid.

When confronted with a choice, stored attitude representations can engender two types of real-time evaluations, reflexive and reflective, which are not always congruent. That is, whereas reflexive evaluations are rapid, automatic, and based on unconscious processing, reflective evaluations are slower and arrived at via controlled, resource-demanding processing (e.g., Lieberman, 2003, 2007). This latter category is most relevant here because it allows individuals to incorporate information about current goals and situational exigencies to modify the contents of their stored attitude representations in order to permit selection of new and/or alternative responses. Hence, the kinds of evaluative processing engendered by reflective attitude evaluations are likely to be the same or similar to the processing that occurs when a deceptive individual evaluates, for example, signs of belief or disbelief in the person they are trying to deceive. In this way, the reflective processing of attitude stimuli can be seen as a model for the kinds of real-time evaluative processing that occurs in real-world deceptions.

To determine the extent to which valenced, evaluation-based deceptions are similar to the emotionally neutral memory- and perception-based deceptions studied previously, we asked participants to make Truthful responses and Instructed Lies about their attitudes regarding a wide variety of concepts (Johnson *et al.*, 2008a). The concepts, which varied in complexity and concreteness, included social, political, religious, and moral issues (interracial marriage, god, censorship, birth control, abortion, patriotism), famous individuals (Hillary Clinton, Yasser Arafat, Rudolph Giuliani, Bin Laden), and personal preferences (music, foods). Individually-tailored stimulus sets were created based on ratings obtained one week prior to the experimental session. Although these ratings were meant to provide ground truth about each individual's true evaluations, people often exaggerate or misrepresent the nature of their attitudes and beliefs when asked. The effect of valence on deception was studied by including equal numbers of highly-rated positive and negative items in every stimulus set.

Maintaining a differentiation-of-deception approach, we compared Truthful responses and Instructed Lies about the same attitude items in different conditions, with 20% catch trials in each ("AGREE" and "DISAGREE"). In accord with our previous results, the behavioral data revealed that RTs for Instructed Lies about attitudes were less accurate and significantly slower than those for Truthful responses (Johnson *et al.*, 2008a). Moreover, consistent with the idea that attitudes are perceived as being more important to individuals than other memories, the RT cost (deceptive RT minus truthful RT) for attitudes was considerably greater compared to Instructed Lies about any other types of specific memories previously studied. In fact, the 200 ms RT cost for Instructed Lies about attitudes represents a two-fold increase over the 100 ms RT cost for equivalent Lies about autobiographical memories in the same participants (Johnson *et al.*, unpublished results) and an almost four-fold increase over the 58 ms RT cost for Instructed Lies about episodic memories (Johnson *et al.*, 2003). In addition, the RT distributions for attitude responses, whether truthful or deceptive, were more rectangular than the typical positively-skewed distributions and closely resembled those for the self-generated responses in our earlier studies.

This increased behavioral cost of making Instructed Lies about attitudes, coupled with the greater RT variability, was associated with ERP activity that was both quantitatively and qualitatively different from what we found for Instructed Lies about other perceptual and conceptual stimuli (Johnson *et al.*, 2008a). For example, MFN amplitudes were much larger than in previous studies and twice as large as those for Instructed Lies about episodic memories. In keeping with the inverse MFN-LPC relation found previously, these larger MFNs were associated with much smaller LPCs, which resembled those for our Self-generated Lies about episodic memories (Johnson *et al.*, 2003, 2005). Moreover, unlike all our previous studies of Instructed Lies, reflective attitude evaluations elicited pre-response negativities comparable to those for Self-generated Lies about episodic (Johnson *et al.*, 2004, 2005), autobiographical (Johnson *et al.*, 2002a), or personal semantic memories (Johnson *et al.*, 2002b). Thus, overall, the altered behavioral and ERP activity elicited by Instructed Lies about attitudes closely resembled the behavioral and ERP changes that were elicited by our more complex and goal-directed Self-generated Lies. Nevertheless, the enhanced ERP effects for deceptions about attitude concepts relative to other stimuli is unlikely to be due to their highly self-relevant nature because no similar increases were evident for Instructed Lies about autobiographical events or personal factual information. Consequently, we suggested that self-referential evaluations ending in an overt response automatically engender strategic monitoring processes to ensure that, over time, evaluations are consistent with one another and with one's self image when interacting with others (Johnson *et al.*, 2008a).

Support for this interpretation came from the fact that even truthful attitude evaluations elicited more pre-response negativity than previously seen for Instructed Lies about specific autobiographical events (Johnson *et al.*, unpublished data). In our view, strategic monitoring processes are engendered, albeit to a variable extent, whenever situations require one's responses to fit into a coherent whole, such as occurs when one conveys highly self-referential personal information or a narrative.

Another novel finding in this study was the presence of pre- and post-response valence effects on the ERP that differed between Truthful responses and Instructed Lies. Prior to Truthful responses, positively-valenced concepts were characterized by larger negativities than negatively-valenced concepts over medial central-frontal scalp, a difference that was significantly magnified when participants made Instructed Lies. However, whereas these valence effects appeared only in the pre-response interval for Truthful responses, they persisted even after the response for Instructed Lies. That is, larger MFNs were elicited when participants responded that they disagreed with concepts with which they agreed, compared to responses indicating that they agreed with concepts with which they actually disagreed. This pattern of MFN results suggests that participants experienced greater conflict from denying the goodness of concepts they view positively than from denying the badness of items they view negatively. We suggested that these reactions might represent a kind of denial-of-self reaction for lies about concepts viewed positively and an instance of compliance for lies about negative concepts, i.e., when people alter their responses to reduce potential interpersonal conflict in social settings (Johnson *et al.*, 2008a). While it is easy to imagine that compliance reactions could also have occurred for Truthful responses, there was no evidence of this being the case due to the absence of any similar post-response valence-related MFN activity. Given that even basic Instructed Lies about attitudes produced valence effects on ERP activity, additional effects of valence on deception-related processing can be expected, particularly in scenarios in which the stakes are higher.

ERP activity in our attitude paradigm was also elicited over a prolonged interval preceding the response over three brain areas where fMRI researchers have frequently reported finding activations for Instructed

Lies (Johnson *et al.*, 2011). For example, attitude evaluations elicited different patterns of ERP activity over left and right VLPFC, which as noted above, are probably the most frequently activated areas in fMRI studies of deception and guilty knowledge. Similarly prolonged potentials were seen over medial prefrontal cortex (mPFC) in roughly the same region where greater activation was found by Ganis *et al.* (2003) for lies fitting a coherent memorized story.

In a follow-up study, we had participants make truthful and instructed lies about whether particular trait adjectives were self-descriptive (Johnson *et al.*, 2008b). For example, participants were required to make "ME" or "NOT ME" evaluative judgments when presented with words like "Trustworthy," "Polite," and "Loyal." Overall, both the behavioral and ERP results for these personal evaluations were very similar to those in our attitude study, with the possible exception that some truthful-deceptive differences were larger for trait evaluations.

In an effort to combine the superior temporal information inherent in ERPs with the superior spatial information provided by fMRI, we used the Talairach coordinates for three brain areas activated in a fMRI study of evaluative judgments similar to ours (Zysset *et al.*, 2002). However, because Zysset *et al.* only studied truthful responses, we also averaged the locations of the ACC activations from Spence *et al.*'s (2001) and Ganis *et al.*'s (2003) studies of Instructed Lies. The resulting four dipole locations were seeded into BESA, resulting in an excellent fit between predicted and obtained scalp-recorded ERP activity (see Johnson *et al.*, 2008b for additional details), suggesting that the ERP activity elicited by Instructed Lies about these attitude evaluations could have arisen from the brain areas activated in the Zysset *et al.* (2002) study of evaluative judgments. Such results demonstrate the value of combining ERP and fMRI results to provide a more detailed understanding of how deception-related processing maps onto brain activity in both the temporal and spatial domains.

Post-Retrieval Processing as a Model for Real-World Deceptions

The results from our attitude and trait studies support the idea advanced above that the reflective processing engaged when generating attitude evaluations provides a useful model for studying the kind of processing expected to occur during interactive, goal-directed deceptions. Given that the purpose of spontaneous reflective attitude evaluations is to modify the contents of retrieved memories to conform to current plans and goals, by definition this processing occurs in the interval between memory retrieval and the response. Unlike the situation for attitude evaluations, reflective evaluations should not be a normal part of the processing required to identify truthful responses about past or present events. According to this view, the processing of truthful and deceptive responses can be seen as analogous to the differential processing required in memory retrieval and evaluative judgment tasks. That is, the goal in memory retrieval tasks, and for truthful responses in general, is simply to determine whether a particular cue makes contact with memory/is the truth. Consequently, the absence of any need for post-retrieval processing means that all truthful responses should be characterized by the presence of a brief retrieval-response interval. By contrast, reflective deceptions, like attitude evaluations, require manipulation of the contents of retrieved memories in a more-or-less prolonged post-retrieval evaluation process to generate appropriate intention-based deceptive responses (Johnson *et al.*, 2011). Thus, truthful responses and reflective deceptive responses are best characterized as memory and working-with-memory tasks, respectively (Johnson *et al.*, 2011; cf., Moscovitch, 1992). In retrospect, the prolonged RTs and highly variable RT distributions associated with our Self-generated Lie conditions reviewed above are exactly what would be expected if participants engaged post-retrieval processing to decide whether making a truthful or deceptive response on any given trial would best meet their goals. Hence, it is reasonable to posit that the presence of extended retrieval-response intervals will be a defining characteristic of reflective deceptions.

At present, only the ERP technique has the requisite temporal resolution to detect variations in the duration of post-retrieval processing. To assess the presence of such processing, we compared the duration of retrieval-response intervals obtained during attitude evaluations and cued recall of autobiographical memories (Johnson *et al.*, 2011). Although RTs in both these tasks were long and highly variable, the timing of the LPC, which normally occurs within about 100 ms of the response, was substantially different across conditions. That is, attitude evaluations were characterized by a LPC that appeared relatively soon after stimulus onset and, on average, about 350 ms prior to the response. More important, these LPCs appeared 300-400 ms earlier than those for autobiographical retrievals, despite the fact that RTs for attitude evaluations were even slower than those for autobiographical retrievals. In addition, the early LPC for attitude evaluations was followed by a second, late LPC (cf., Johnson and Donchin, 1985), which occurred at the same time relative to the response as the single LPCs elicited by autobiographical retrievals. We showed that, whereas the early LPC was associated with retrieval of the attitude representation, the late LPC was elicited after completion of the attitude evaluation resulting in an agree or disagree categorization (Johnson et al., 2010). This meant that the usual differential contributions of memory retrieval and category-related processing to overall LPC amplitude, which typically occur at the same time, were temporally separated for attitude items. That is, unlike all previous LPC paradigms in which the retrieval indicated category membership of the stimulus, the attitude stimuli could only be categorized as "agree" or "disagree" at the completion of the post-retrieval evaluation process. By contrast, a single LPC peak was elicited by both You and Not You autobiographical cues just prior to the response. This dual-LPC pattern of ERP activity for attitude evaluations was replicated in a second condition in which participants had to make a semantic evaluation about the same attitude concepts. For the semantic evaluations, participants had to decide whether each attitude item was best characterized as being "active" or "inactive" (Johnson et al., 2011). These impersonal semantic evaluations showed the same pattern of prolonged post-retrieval processing and associated changes in ERP activity as obtained for the personal attitude evaluations. Taken together, the results for both personal and impersonal evaluations of the same attitude stimuli indicate that more-or-less prolonged post-retrieval processing is a hallmark of all reflective evaluations, whether truthful or deceptive.

To better link the altered pattern ERP activity elicited by attitude evaluations to post-retrieval processing, we analyzed brain-behavior relations as a function of evaluation difficulty. One recent cognitive model of attitude evaluations suggests that, during the evaluation process, the contents of retrieved memories can be modified repeatedly in an iterative manner until a response is selected. In this way, the number of cycles through the iterative loop, and therefore the duration of post-retrieval processing, increases along with the complexity of the evaluative processing required to reach an appropriate decision (e.g., Cunningham and Zelazo, 2007). To test the tenets of this model, we divided the trials from our attitude and autobiographical conditions into fast and slow categories with a median-split analysis on RT (Johnson *et al.*, 2010). As expected, retrieval of autobiographical memories was character- ized by the usual, uniformly brief retrieval-response intervals, regardless of retrieval difficulty. By contrast and in accord with the model's predictions, rapid evaluations were characterized by short retrieval-response intervals and slow evaluations by longer retrieval-response intervals. As would be expected, the ERP activity elicited during the retrieval-response interval was focused over DLPFC, similar to where retrieved memories were previously shown to be maintained in working memory (Johnson *et al.*, 1998b). These findings were subsequently replicated and extended in an experiment in which the difficulty of conceptually-based relational judgments was manip- ulated over multiple levels on an a priori basis (Henkell *et al.*, 2010). Finally, it is interesting to note that many of the spatial aspects of these ERP results are consistent with the findings of increased DLPFC activity in a variety of fMRI studies of deception and guilty knowledge (Spence *et al.*, 2001; Ganis *et al.*, 2003; Nunez *et al.*, 2005; Abe *et al.*, 2006, 2008; Hakun *et al.*, 2008; Bhatt *et al.*, 2009; Ito *et al.*, 2011, 2012).

In summary, the unique way in which evaluative judgments are processed appears to capture aspects of the cognitive processing likely to be an impor- tant component of many real-world deceptions. First, unlike the emotionally- neutral stimuli used thus far in deception studies, personal evaluations require valence judgments and thus engender emotional processing. Second, the frequent need to inhibit the reflexive response associated with an attitude item, while processing and selecting a reflective, intention-based response, is a requirement of most or all real-world deceptions. Third, the differential dura- tion of the retrieval-response intervals for truthful and deceptive responses suggests that indicators of post-retrieval processing might be developed into tools for deception detection and credibility assessment. Taken together, the requirement to make overt, valenced evaluations of oneself in attitude and trait evaluations appears to provide a useful model for future studies of more realistic deception scenarios.

Deception Effects on Cognitive Workload

In addition to the studies reviewed thus far, other researchers have noted that, compared to truthful responses, deceptive responses require additional processing, including greater use of executive processes (see Vrij, 2008 for a review). This conceptualization has been supported by the results of a majority of the studies reviewed above, which found longer and less accurate RTs for deceptive responses, a hallmark finding in all paradigms that engender conflicting response tendencies (e.g., MacLeod, 1991). Consistent with the RT results, we found that the amplitude of the LPC component of the ERP decreased significantly for both Instructed and Self-generated Lies in direct proportion to the concomitant increases in the amplitude of the MFN. As noted above, MFN amplitude provides an index of the extent to which executive processes are engendered to monitor and resolve conflicting response tendencies (Johnson *et al.*, 2003, 2004, 2005). Moreover, we showed that the magnitude of these workload effects increased along with the importance of the stimuli that elicited deceptive responses. This was particularly evident when participants made Instructed Lies about their strongly held attitudes and beliefs, as well as their personal trait evaluations (Johnson *et al.*, 2008a, 2008b).

A second factor affecting workload arises from the extra processing stemming from the fact that, for a deception to be successful, the truthful response must be identified before an alternative deceptive can be selected. Consequently, we suggested that deceptive responding can be thought of as being equivalent to any dual-task situation, with the deception task being performed in addition to the primary task of identifying truthful responses (Johnson *et al.*, 2003). It has been known since the 1970s that, in dual-task situations, LPC amplitudes for primary task stimuli decrease directly with the amount of processing resources directed to a concurrent secondary task (see Johnson, 1986, 1988 for reviews). In accord with the results of those studies, we and others have found that Instructed Lies elicit smaller LPCs than Truthful responses about a variety of stimuli, including self- and other-related memories (Johnson *et al.*, 2003, 2005; Hu *et al.*, 2011) and attitude evaluations (Johnson *et al.*, 2008a; Tu *et al.*, 2009). It is also notable that these LPC amplitude reductions for conceptually-based deceptive responses were of the same magnitude as those for perceptually-based conflicts (e.g., Magliero *et al.*, 1984; Doucet and Stelmack, 1999; Johnson *et al.*, 2003). As would be expected, the slower and more variable RTs associated with deceptions involving strategic monitoring and Self-generated Lies engender greater reductions in LPC amplitude, even when compared to Instructed Lies. Moreover, consistent with the requirement to make intention-based, goal-directed responses on every trial, the LPC amplitude reductions for self-generated responses were the same, regardless of whether a truthful or deceptive response was selected (Johnson *et al.*, 2003, 2005, 2008). Finally, it is important to note that all these findings of reduced LPC amplitudes were obtained in response-synchronized averages, which eliminates the possibility that they were artifactually created as a result of differences in response timing across trials and/or conditions.

Taken together, these LPC results provide CNS-based confirmation of the behavioral measures indicating that being deceptive increases workload dynamically in relation to the complexity and importance of the deception. In this context, it should be remembered that, even though workload increases naturally with increasing task complexity, processing of the truthful response remains the sole task in the absence of a decision to respond deceptively. Hence, using an ERP-based differentiation-of-deception approach during credibility assessment should make deception-related increases in workload readily apparent. However, given the lack of any counterpart of these workload-related LPC changes in hemodynamic measures, it appears that only ERPs can be used to create a brain-based index of increased workload during deception.

Effect of Practice on Deceptive-Related Processing

It is reasonable to posit that, conditions permitting, individuals will rehearse and/or practice their deceptive responses many times prior to the actual act. Thus, the ultimate usefulness of brain-based methods for deception detection and credibility assessment will likely depend on the extent to which they produce results that are stable across multiple tests and/or sessions. A basic question, therefore, concerns the degree to which practice can diminish or eliminate one of the central aspects of deceptive responses, which is their dependence on the increased use of executive processes. Despite the importance of this question, remarkably little effort has been devoted to assessing the stability and reliability of deception-related alterations in behavioral or neurocognitive activity. At this time, all investigations of practice effects have used behavioral or ERP measures, with no extant fMRI studies.

Given our demonstration that the conflicts inherent in conceptually-based deceptions are fundamentally the same as those involved in perceptually-based response conflicts (Johnson *et al.*, 2003, 2004), the extensive body of research on the latter type of conflict may provide useful insights into the effects of practice on deceptive responding. Perceptual studies have consistently found that conflict-related RT increases typically persist after thousands of trials and/or weeks of practice (see MacLeod, 1991 for a review). It is important to note that practice decreases RT in these tasks for the same reasons it decreases RT in virtually all tasks, through generalized effects that increase the efficiency of task performance. However, this increased efficiency has been shown to be restricted to the processing of task information, and practice does not appear to lead to greater efficiency in processing conflicting response tendencies. This can be seen in studies demonstrating that, in contrast to decreasing overall RTs, the RT cost of processing conflicting response information (conflict RT minus no conflict RT) does not decrease significantly even after weeks of practice (MacLeod, 1991). This result is not surprising if one considers that the processes needed to adjudicate conflicting response tendencies and inhibit non-selected responses are required for deceptive but not truthful responses.

To assess the effects of practice on the altered behavioral and ERP measures we found for Instructed and Self-generated Lies relative to Truthful responses, we had participants perform two 140-trial blocks of each condition (Johnson *et al.*, 2005). Catch trials requiring truthful responses were present in 20% of the trials in all blocks making any attempt to re-map the stimulus-response assignments in deception conditions evident, as well as ensuring a persistent task switch component in deception blocks. Behaviorally, our results for conceptually-based response conflicts replicated those for perceptually-based response conflicts. Comparing the two repetitions revealed that overall RTs decreased with practice in both truthful and deception conditions. Nevertheless, in accord with previous studies of perceptually-induced response conflicts (e.g., MacLeod, 1991) the RT cost associated with making deceptive responses (deceptive RT minus truthful RT) did not diminish for either Instructed or Self-generated Lies.

The concurrently obtained ERP measures also showed a differential pattern of practice-related effects for truthful and deceptive responses. For example, although practice resulted in increased PRP amplitudes and decreased MFN amplitudes for Truthful responses, the amplitude of neither of these ERP components was significantly altered in either deception condition. Thus, the lack of practice effects on medial frontal ERP indices of executive processes in the deception conditions is congruent with the lack of practice effects on the magnitude of the conflict-related RT costs in both deception conditions. Consistent with previous findings that practice strengthens episodic memories, thereby speeding retrieval and increasing LPC amplitudes (Johnson et al., 1985, 1998a), practice produced large LPC amplitude increases for Truthful responses, but only small increases for Instructed Lies and no increases for Self-generated Lies. This failure of practice to mitigate the effects of response conflict in either deception condition was striking given that participants had twice as much practice making deceptive responses as truthful responses. Importantly, both the ERP and behavioral results confirm that conceptually-based response conflicts show the same absence of practice effects as the much studied perceptual-based conflicts. Moreover, they also demonstrate that the inability to control the interference produced by executing incompatible responses is independent of the memory status of the words because the effects were the same for both self- and other-related lies. Although our participants made only about 500 deceptive responses, the lack of practice effects is similar to that in previous studies using thousands of trials or hours of practice (e.g., MacLeod, 1991).

Although the reasons why the processing of conflicting response tendencies should be so resistant to practice is not known, we suggested that the task switching component inherent in all deceptions is one possible explanation (Johnson et al., 2005). That is, the requirement to initially identify the truthful response before identifying an appropriate deceptive response always necessitates a task switch. Studies of task switching repeatedly find that, although the need for some types of control processes can be reduced by practice, the need for others is relatively less affected (see Monsell, 2003 for a review). For example, RTs following a task switch are delayed relative to non-switch trials, with the magnitude of these delays largely unaffected either by practice or even sufficient advance warning of an impending switch (Allport *et al.*, 1994; Rogers and Monsell, 1995). Further, Rogers and Monsell (1995) demonstrated that the executive processes that benefited most from practice were those that could be performed in advance of the stimulus, e.g., general task component processes, whereas those that benefited least could not be processed until the stimulus appeared. This finding is key because all deceptions depend on the specifics of the stimulus and thus cannot be prepared in advance unless the stimulus is entirely predictable. Also important for deception was their finding that, regardless of the participant's level of preparation for a given stimulus in one task, the stimulus-responses assignments associated with the other task appear to remain active, particularly if they were recently activated or were activated by irrelevant aspects of the stimulus (Allport *et al.*, 1994). These concurrently active and competing sets of stimulus-response assignments were shown to create significant response competition that also was not readily decreased through practice (Allport *et al.*, 1994; Rogers and Monsell, 1995).

Given that successful deceptions require the stimulus-response assignments for the pre-potent truthful response be kept active on every trial to ensure they are not selected, both truthful and deceptive sets of competing stimulus-response assignments must remain continuously activated. The presence of randomly occurring catch trials in our experiments further ensured that truthful stimulus-response assignments were loaded regularly, even if they were not loaded automatically following stimulus presentation. This constant refreshing of truthful response assignments reinforces their continued maintenance at high activation levels. Consequently, the conflicting response tendencies created by the pre-potent truthful response remains a powerful influence on response selection and execution processes that must always be overcome before a deceptive response can be made. Hence, the constant activation of the truthful response assignments is one possible explanation for the lack of practice effects on the efficiency with which deceptive responses can be executed. As suggested by our data and those of others, overcoming the activation of pre-potent stimulus-response contingencies would be a constant and unavoidable part of the cost of making deceptive responses. It is important to note that attempts to invoke cognitive strategies designed to reduce this conflict, if they were possible, would necessarily be conscious and therefore further increase task workload. Hence, any attempts to invoke such strategies would draw on the same limited resource pool as used for the other task components, which would result in even greater decreases in LPC amplitude.

Since our report on the effects of practice on CNS measures of deception-related processing (Johnson *et al.*, 2005), little research has been done. This is perhaps not surprising given the difficulty of conducting hemodynamic studies of practice effects. That is, most of the hemodynamic differentiation-of-deception studies reviewed above used blocked designs, making it very difficult to incorporate randomly occurring catch trials with a sufficiently high frequency to be of any use. Indeed, no hemodynamic study of deception or GKT has yet included catch trials, and without them it is impossible to be certain that any practice-related changes that are found over blocks are not due to participants surreptitiously reversing the stimulus-response assignments (cf., Bles and Haynes, 2008).

The few studies of practice effects that have appeared included only behavioral measures, i.e., RT and accuracy. For example, Vendemia *et al.* (2005) conducted a three-session study in which participants made self-generated random truthful and deceptive responses about a small set of personal semantic information, e.g., college major. Using the same instructions as in our studies, they replicated our findings of practice-related decreases in overall RT with no concomitant reduction in the RT cost of deceptive responses. In a group-design study, Hu *et al.* (2012) investigated the effects of practice on Instructed Lies about a few items of personal semantic information (name, birth date, hometown). Their three groups received either no instructions, instructions to speed their deceptive response, or training in speeding their deceptive responses. In a partial replication of our results, their no instruction and instruction groups continued to show a significant

RT cost for deceptive responses after practice. This RT cost was, however, absent in their training group, although this result appeared to be due entirely to a reduction in RT and error rate for deceptive responses only. In a result that is difficult to explain in the context of previous research, their training group failed to show any evidence of the typical general practice effects on RT or accuracy for truthful responses, raising the question of how this might occur or why practice effects should be present for deceptive but not truthful responses.

Taking a different tack, Verschuere and colleagues (e.g., Verschuere *et al.*, 2011; Van Bockstaele *et al.*, 2012) investigated how the relative probabilities of Truthful responses and Instructed Lies affect RT and found that the ease of lying about everyday activities increased with the frequency of lies. Despite the clear presence of a training effect in which the RT cost of deceptive responses disappeared, it did not carry over to the test session. This unexpected result led the authors to conclude that their training manipulation was insufficient to alter the pre-potent status of truthful responses (Van Bockstaele *et al.*, 2012). Nevertheless, the strength of the conclusions that can be drawn about the training effects in each of these studies is tempered by their failure to include supporting data from their catch trials. Consequently, based on the data presented, the possibility that the practice-related RT effects in these studies were actually due to participants reversing the stimulus-response assignments cannot be ruled out.

Had these studies recorded brain activity along with behavioral responses, it would have at least been possible to associate any practice-related behavioral changes with changes in cognitive processing and brain activity. In this way, these investigators might have been able to show that their practiced deceptions were executed with meaningful reductions in workload or in the use of executive processes. However, it is difficult based on behavioral measures alone to match the results of these studies with our overall pattern of changed and unchanged measures of behavioral and brain activity. Thus, their results serve to reinforce the idea that behavioral measures alone are not sufficiently multidimensional to permit researchers to completely characterize a behavior as complex and multi-faceted as deception.

Causal Results from Loss-of-Function Studies

As noted previously, ERP and hemodynamic functional neuroimaging studies only provide information about which brain activity is correlated with particular cognitive processes and not whether it is *necessary* for performing those processes. Historically, information on the causal role of various brain structures has been provided by neuropsychological researchers performing loss-of-function studies and, more recently, by the advent of studies employing TMS techniques. Although relatively few reports have been published thus far, a growing number of researchers are attempting to determine whether the changes in brain activity identified in hemodynamic and ERP studies reflect brain processes that are necessary for perpetrating a deception.

One finding evident from the studies reviewed above is that different types of deception are associated with the use of a variety of frontally-based executive and working memory processes. In a novel loss-of-function study, Abe and colleagues (2009) studied patients with Parkinson's disease because it has been suggested that they do not have a normal ability to be deceptive. To determine if this inability might result from their known impairments in frontal executive functions, Abe *et al.* (2009) performed resting state metabolic PET scans on 32 patients with Parkinson's disease while they performed a standard old-new recognition paradigm using picture stimuli. In addition to the truthful condition, a deception condition required participants to make Instructed Lies on one-fourth of the known and unknown pictures presented in a distinctive manner. Their results showed that, whereas there were no differences in performance between patients and controls for Truthful responses, patients with Parkinson's disease showed significantly worse performance on the Instructed Lies. Moreover, the magnitudes of the decreases in PET-derived measures of frontal lobe function, including the degree of hypo-metabolism in left DLPFC and right anterior prefrontal cortex, were positively correlated with the increased inability to lie. Given that these two frontal areas have been found repeatedly to be activated during Instructed Lies about episodic memories, these results provide good evidence that both these frontal areas are necessary for making Instructed Lies about episodic memories.

By contrast to the uncontrolled nature and extent of naturally occurring brain damage that produces loss of function, TMS techniques provide causal data on the role of particular brain areas by creating more controlled "temporary lesions" and a small number of TMS studies of deception has been conducted thus far. For example, Lubner's group (described in Luber *et al.*, 2009) performed a single-pulse TMS study in which stimulation was delivered over a series of intervals between 0 and 480 ms after stimulus presentation in a playing-card GKT paradigm. Based on previous results, they applied stimulation over left DLPFC, with stimulation of parietal precuneus cortex as a control. The results were contrary to their predictions because, whereas left DLPFC stimulation had no negative impact on the ability to make deceptive responses, precuneus stimulation did slow deceptive responses. Contrary to a host of results from hemodynamic studies, these findings suggest that DLPFC plays no role in deception-related processing deceptions while the precuneus does.

In another GKT study, which used a variation on the TMS technique known as Transcranial DC stimulation (TDCS), Karim *et al.* (2010) investigated the effects of stimulation on the ability to lie following a mock crime that involved stealing money. TDCS diminishes cerebral excitability by administering continuous weak cathodal currents through scalp electrodes, and consequently the investigators expected anterior prefrontal cortex stimulation to reduce the ease of lying by inhibiting prefrontal executive and working memory functions. Contrary to their predictions, the stimulation actually improved participants' ability to lie, as evidenced by their shorter RTs compared to the RTs obtained during no stimulation. However, a similar study by Priori *et al.* (2008), which applied both anodal and cathodal TDCS stimulation to DLPFC in different conditions, found the opposite pattern of results from that described in Karim *et al.* (2010). That is, Priori *et al.* reported that, although there was no effect of cathodal stimulation, anodal stimulation, which should increase cortical excitability, actually decreased the ability to lie.

Verschuere *et al.* (2012) investigated the role of the often reported findings of right VLPFC activity during deceptive responding by applying continuous stimulation to this brain area. Contrary to the results of most hemodynamic studies of deception, right VLPFC stimulation in their study failed to produce either RT slowing or any increase in error rates for Instructed Lies about memories for daily activities. Taken together, although limited in number and characterized by different stimulation parameters, the TMS results obtained to date are inconsistent and contradictory both with each other and with the results of virtually all the hemodynamic and ERP studies reviewed above. Hence, it appears too early to draw any meaningful conclusions from this limited sample of studies.

The TMS technique is relatively new, and one possible explanation for the inconsistent and unpredicted results is that the stimulation parameters may have been incorrectly selected. Because TMS creates temporary lesions in localized areas, both the spatial *and* temporal parameters of the stimulation must be selected correctly. Whereas the spatial parameters for stimulation can be identified readily using results from hemodynamic studies, those data provide no guidance regarding the temporal parameters of those activations. Although the ERP technique provides timing information, TMS researchers have yet to use it to identify the optimal stimulation intervals for their TMS pulses. This is particularly surprising given the sequential nature of processing in which deception-related processes follow the processing of truthful responses. For example, the longer duration of TDCS stimulation means that it affects both the initial processing of truthful responses as well as subsequent processing related to selecting a deceptive response, with no way to determine how TDCS stimulation affected either. Similarly, Lubner *et al.* (2009) delivered stimulation only between 0 and 480 ms post-stimulus, raising the distinct possibility that stimulation ended too early to affect much of the deception-related processing. By contrast, our ERP results suggest that TMS stimulation would be more effective if it were delivered later, between 500 and 1200 ms post-stimulus. Hence, an alternative to testing a prohibitive number of stimulation intervals in TMS studies is to merge the timing information from ERP studies with the spatial information from hemodynamic studies.

A less invasive method for producing temporary and reversible "loss of function" is to have participants perform a concurrent secondary task. Typically, this has been done in a non-targeted manner by presenting the stimuli associated with the secondary task at random intervals during the primary task.

However, Johnson *et al.* (2013) modified this procedure by precisely timing the presentation of the secondary task stimuli to disrupt processing during specific temporal intervals. The timing of the chosen intervals was based on when differences in ERP activity were seen between young and elderly participants during performance of an episodic encoding task. To test the assertion that the elderlies' episodic retrieval deficits are due to their altered ERP activity during encoding, a secondary task was introduced while healthy young controls encoded episodic memories. The secondary task intervals matched the time when the ERP activity was different in the elderly cohort over LIPFC. Using this procedure, episodic retrieval performance in the young adults was reduced to the decreased performance level of elderly adults, thereby providing evidence of a causal link between this altered ERP activity in the elderly and episodic encoding efficiency. Using this targeted secondary task method would provide another method for assessing potential causal linkages between the truthful-deceptive ERP differences and specific processes posited to be involved in deception. For example, presenting a secondary task during the pre-response interval could reveal whether the pre-response negativities elicited during Self-generated Lies are necessary for intention-based deceptions.

In sum, only a handful of loss-of-function studies have been conducted and, except for the findings of Abe *et al.* (2009), the results have failed to shed much light on the causal relations between the brain activations found in hemodynamic and ERP studies and deception-related processing. The reasons for these inconsistent results need to be resolved if TMS is to become a reliable method for providing causal information about brain-behavior relations in deception studies.

FORENSIC APPLICATIONS

While the majority of neurocognitive research on deception has been devoted to identifying the neural basis of different types of deception, a handful of researchers have attempted to move these basic findings into the realm of forensic applications by researching how well deceptive responses can be identified in individuals based on patterns of altered brain activity.

ERP Results

One of the main advantages of using the neurocognitive approach to studying deception has been the large number of ERP components that show significant T-D differences. More important, each of these T-D differences has its own unique spatiotemporal characteristics and, taken together, they are linked to the functioning of a wide variety of cognitive functions and brain areas, including multiple executive processes, episodic and semantic memory retrieval, intention-based processes, and valence-related processes. Another strength arising from this variety of ERP differences between the processing of truthful and deceptive responses is that credibility assessment tools based on these measures would presumably make the use of countermeasures difficult or impossible to conceal. While countermeasures might be attempted, it is unclear how or whether it would be possible to counter such a wide variety of different cognitive processes during the very brief temporal windows when they are active, i.e., all less than a second. In addition, any use of countermeasures would further increase the demands on limited controlled processing resources, thereby increasing workload and enhancing further the T-D differences in LPC amplitude. Moreover, at least some of the brain areas where these processes are performed, such as the ACC, are not under conscious control, rendering attempts to influence the processing there difficult or impossible to accomplish.

The large number of potentially available ERP deception markers could be used together, or in different subsets or clusters related to particular cognitive- and practice-related effects to create more powerful broad-based and/or targeted T-D classification algorithms, respectively. Alternatively, targeted T-D algorithms based on particular subsets of ERP activity could be developed to detect specific alterations in cognitive processing, such as alterations in tactical and strategic monitoring and workload. The variety and number of behavioral and neurocognitive measures of deception contrasts with early LPC-based approaches using the GKT procedure, a fact that should greatly enhance their usefulness. Preliminary efforts at using classification algorithms based on all the behavioral and ERP differences in our early studies produced T-D classification rates of 95% and above (Johnson *et al.*, 2002c). It is reasonable to expect that by using the increased information about deception-related processing gained in the interim, coupled with some crafting of test paradigms to optimally capture the T-D processing differences that have been identified, it should be possible to create better and more reliable deception detection and credibility assessment tools.

Hemodynamic Results

In an attempt to turn the fMRI technique into a replacement for polygraph, a few fMRI research groups have actively investigated how well T-D classifications can be made based on the hemodynamic activity obtained in GKT paradigms conducted after mock crimes. Kozel and colleagues (2004a, 2004b, 2005, 2009a, 2009b) have been particularly active in attempting to validate the ability of fMRI to detect deception in real-world settings. In one of the largest fMRI studies of deception to date, Kozel *et al.* (2005) created independent model-building and model-testing groups of around 30 participants each and scanned them after they committed a mock crime in which they stole a watch or ring. Data from the model-building group were subjected to a cluster analysis, which groups data in a way that minimizes the differences between data within a cluster while simultaneously maximizing the differences between clusters. Seven clusters of activated brain areas were identified, although the majority of participants' activations fell into three clusters, i.e., 1, 2, and 4. These investigators noted, however, that there was no cluster that contained data from every participant. Clusters 1, 2, and 4, which included activations in the four brain areas most commonly observed in mock crime scenarios (DLPFC, VLPFC, ACC, SMA) were chosen as the basis for the classification analysis. Classification was accomplished by computing the differential activation between the Lie contrasts (Lie minus Neutral, Lie minus Control) and True contrasts (True minus Neutral, True minus Control). This method accurately classified 27/29 deceptive participants for Cluster 1, 26/30 for Cluster 2, 23/26 for Cluster 4, and 28/30 for the combination of Clusters 1, 2 and 4. Using the same clusters in the Model-Testing group produced similar results, with correct classifications of 25/30 participants based on Cluster 1 and 28/31 using a combination of clusters 1, 2 and 4. Overall, correct T-D classification rates varied from roughly 83% to 93% across groups and methods. In a replication study using the same basic GKT procedure, Kozel *et al.* (2009b) reported highly similar T-D classification results, i.e., 25/29. Nose *et al.* (2009) also reported similar results in a GKT study involving knowledge of a particular playing card. Using a measure based solely on activation of right VLPFC, a location included in the Kozel *et al.* (2005) Cluster 2, Nose and colleagues correctly classified 32/38 (84%) of deceptive participants. In another playing card GKT, Monteleone *et al.* (2009) scanned 14 participants. Although they found no single T-D difference in brain activity that was present in every participant, activity in mPFC yielded the best classification rate (71%). Finally, in an attempt to enhance fMRI-based T-D classifications, Kozel *et al.* (2009a) tested whether simultaneously obtained SCR measures could increase classification accuracy. The results, however, failed to reveal any enhancement because there was no significant T-D difference in SCR activity.

The validity of these results was called into question by Ganis and colleagues (2011) based on their study of the impact of simple countermeasures on fMRI-based T-D classifications in a GKT paradigm. After their 26 participants performed a standard GKT, they were trained to hide knowledge of their birth date with the use of the covert countermeasure of executing an imperceptible movement of one of three fingers in the interval preceding their RT response. A comparison of the truthful and deceptive results from their standard GKT revealed two clusters of activated brain areas for probe stimuli that were highly similar to those identified in previous fMRI GKT studies and included VLPFC, ACC, and mPFC. Ganis *et al.* (2011) reported that using either cluster separately or both together produced perfect classification of deceptive responses, i.e., 12/12. However, the ability to classify deceptive responses correctly was seriously degraded in the countermeasure condition, i.e., only 4/12. As would be expected and in accord with their predictions, increased activation was found in contralateral motor cortex during the countermeasure condition as a consequence of the planning to make finger movements. Although Ganis and colleagues (2011) acknowledged that countermeasure-related brain activity was clearly present in their fMRI scans, they also pointed out that it could not serve as a general indicator of countermeasure use. This problem arises from the fact that any other, equally simple countermeasures task would produce a different and unknown pattern of hemodynamic activity, which would depend entirely on the particular processes utilized by the countermeasure task. It is important to note that, although theirs and likely all countermeasure tasks would increase overall workload during deceptions, as noted above there is no known fMRI-based measure capable of revealing increases in workload. Hence, without knowing the specific processing involved in the countermeasures, there is no way of knowing where to look for increased hemodynamic activity related to countermeasure use. Therefore, it appears that countermeasures will remain a substantial impediment to the widespread use of fMRI in deception detection and credibility assessment.

Finally, it should also be noted that all these forensic studies conducted to date were designed to determine whether fMRI can be successfully used to reveal the presence of concealed information. However, GKT/CIT procedures have been criticized repeatedly for their overall lack of applicability to the vast majority of forensic situations (cf., Honts *et al.*, 2005; Krapohl, 2011), and thus research needs to be done on a wider variety of deception scenarios.

FUTURE DIRECTIONS

The studies reviewed here demonstrate that research using both the ERP and fMRI techniques has provided new and complementary insights into the neurocognitive basis of deception. For reasons that are unclear, the majority of basic research and virtually all applied studies have employed the fMRI technique. It is probably not coincidental, therefore, that two commercial companies are already marketing fMRI-based lie detection services, i.e., No Lie MRI and Cephos Corporation, both claiming on their websites that they can "detect deception." Such claims are being made despite the fact that all peer-reviewed fMRI studies on the efficacy of T-D classifications about an individual's responses have employed GKT/CIT paradigms, with none having addressed the more difficult task of detecting when individuals are deceptive. Not surprisingly, the suitability of using fMRI in real-world deception detection and credibility assessment situations has been the topic of considerable debate in recent years. On a number of grounds, many deception researchers have questioned the feasibility, advisability, and even the ethics of using fMRI to detect deception or guilty/concealed information in forensic settings (Sip *et al.*, 2007; Bles and Haynes, 2008; Kozel and Trivedi, 2008; Spence and Kaylor-Hughes, 2008; Abe, 2011).

One basic criticism concerns the ecological validity of the deception research conducted to date, a criticism that applies equally to the extant ERP research.

While functional neuroimaging studies have provided much useful informa-tion, most studies were designed only to begin providing a cognitive framework of the processes used when individuals are deceptive. Consequently, most of the deception scenarios used thus far are relatively simplistic laboratory-based paradigms that were essentially collaborations between experimenter and par-ticipant. Not only are these conditions antithetical to real-world deceptions but they lack the subtlety, complexity, and dynamic nature of real-world decep-tions, thereby failing to incorporate many cognitive processes likely to play vital roles (cf., Abe, 2011; Bles and Haynes, 2008; Sip *et al.*, 2007).

Some important steps toward creating more realistic deception studies will come when investigators increase the emotional salience of stimuli and include a reward component in their experimental scenarios. The fact that many deceptions have an emotional component has largely been ignored by both fMRI and ERP researchers. It is essential, therefore, to move away from the emotionally neutral stimuli typical of most past research and toward the inclusion of positively- and negatively-valenced stimuli that permit the emotional components of deception to be identified and characterized. In addition, although reward is an essential component of most deceptions (cf., Vrij, 2008), it too has received little attention by deception researchers. Indeed, the lack of any substantial reward value in the extant deception literature presumably explains why, despite fMRI's unique ability to reveal brain activity in subcortical areas, no clear link-age has been established between deception and increased striatal activ-ity, an essential component of the brain's reward circuitry (cf., Liljeholm and O'Doherty, 2012). At least in this respect, fMRI has a clear advantage over ERPs because the latter technique is unlikely to detect any subcorti-cal components of reward. In sum, deception researchers need to create a more comprehensive understanding of all major cognitive, emotional, and reward components of deception before being able to fully justify the use of neuroimaging techniques in forensic settings. The possibility of mak-ing potentially damaging and life-changing judgments about individuals must be avoided.

Another question raised about the current suitability of fMRI for forensic appli-cations, which applies equally to ERP research, concerns the generalizability of the results to the populations most likely to be evaluated. This arises from the fact that all functional neuroimaging research to date has been conducted largely on relatively young, homogeneous, university-educated populations, which means that the results are probably not generalizable to many individuals and groups likely to be tested in forensic situations. Research is needed, therefore, to determine which deception-related processes and brain responses are affected by a wide range of demographic variables, such as race, ethnicity, culture, age, education, socio-economic status, and psychological profiles. Whereas the more controlled aspects of some deception-related processing, both cognitive and emotional, are likely to be affected by these demographics, as well as a variety of personality variables, more automatic processes such as response monitoring are likely to be relatively invariant. Nevertheless, which processes fall into the automatic and controlled processing categories needs to be firmly established.

One technology issue directly impacting the feasibility of using fMRI to detect deception reliably in forensic settings arises from the low levels of consistency and replicability of fMRI results seen thus far. Multiple investigators have noted the high levels of variability in the locations of activated brain areas across deception studies (e.g., Bles and Haynes, 2008; Spence and Kaylor-Hughes, 2008), as well as the uneven ability of investigators to replicate their own findings and those of other research groups (e.g., Spence and Kaylor-Hughes, 2008). The high levels of individual variability in brain activity, even during simple deceptions, were well documented in each of the fMRI GKT studies reviewed above, none of which was able to find a single T-D difference that was present in every participant. Sip *et al.* (2007) noted that this degree of individual variability further increases the difficulty and perils of using group differences as a guide for making T-D judgments about individuals. Consequently, various hemodynamic researchers have called for greater efforts at providing a more detailed characterization of individual responses (e.g., Kozel and Trivedi, 2008), a topic that has received even less attention in the ERP literature. Finally, it should be noted that these high levels of variability arose in simplistic, laboratory-based settings, and thus this problem can only be expected to worsen in more realistic scenarios, which will invariably interact with individual psychological profiles.

A surprising aspect of the extant hemodynamic research on deception has been its exclusive focus on identifying the anatomical correlates of deception. This has meant that fMRI investigators have been forced to rely on research conducted on other cognitive functions to explain the possible roles of deception-related brain activations. Consequently, it is not uncommon for different researchers to propose different, sometimes conflicting explanations about the role of a given brain area in deception processing. Putting this into context, the limited approach taken thus far is not typical of that used to study other complex cognitive functions, which generally include experimental manipulations designed to reveal the functional roles of activated brain areas. Thus, there is a real absence of empirical evidence showing how graded changes in a specific deception-related variable produces graded changes in hemodynamic activity for each of the brain areas activated during deception. Without functional information comparable to that in neurocognitive ERP studies of deception, fMRI studies are limited to creating static characterizations of a highly dynamic process.

In summary, many questions remain to be investigated about the cognitive and neural basis of deception-related processing using both the ERP and hemodynamic techniques. This is particularly true with respect to the use of more complex and realistic deceptions that mimic the emotional and reward components of most deceptions. One important step toward this goal will be the creation of more elaborate and refined models of the cognitive processes involved in deception that can lead to empirically-testable hypotheses. Considerably more research will be required to develop scientifically-valid methods for deception detection and credibility assessment that will work effectively across demographically diverse populations in a wider range of forensic applications. Nevertheless, research addressing these different issues should pay off in the creation of a greater variety of sophisticated and targeted credibility-assessment tools able to capture different aspects of deception-related processing. Moreover, learning to incorporate multiple, simultaneously, and sequentially obtained behavioral and/or brain-based measures in tests tailored to specific scenarios should ensure that the loss of any one, or even a few, measures in an individual will not lead to a failed assessment and also reduce the likelihood that the use of countermeasures would go undetected.

CONCLUSIONS

The studies reviewed here show that researchers using functional neuroimaging techniques have provided many new insights into the cognitive and neural processes in deception. Despite the fact that only a few dozen studies have been published to date, ERP and fMRI studies have firmly established that, compared to truthful responses, deceptive responses are characterized by significantly different patterns of behavioral and brain activity. Further, this truthful-deceptive disparity in processing increases with both the importance of the stimuli being lied about and the complexity of the deception. It is now well established that deception-related processing draws on a number of cognitive processes performed in the frontal lobes and is equivalent to performing a second task in addition to the task of identifying truthful responses. Consequently, deceptive responses are characterized by greater amounts of ERP and hemodynamic activity with much of this additional activity being related to the increased reliance on the executive processes used to implement cognitive control. Moreover, other cognitive processes used during deception such as strategic monitoring, working memory, and post-retrieval processing, while not unique to deception, are typically not required to make truthful responses under the same circumstances. In addition, ERP findings indicate that this additional processing has distinct temporal characteristics relative to truthful responding, particularly when real-time evaluations are used to formulate intention-based responses. Taken together, these findings suggest that more realistic deceptions will produce additional differences, a situation that bodes well for the future development of CNS-based deception detection and credibility assessment tools.

The results of both ERP and hemodynamic studies have confirmed Lykken's (1959) early insight that there is no specific lie response. Although Lykken reached this conclusion long before the advent of functional neuroimaging techniques, the available data indicate that there is no pattern of brain activity uniquely associated with deception. Whereas research on the neurocognitive basis of deception is still in the early stages and many relevant cognitive processes remain to be studied, it has already been established that deception is a complex and multifaceted function. Moreover, like virtually every other complex cognitive function, the specific processes engendered during deception vary in a flexible and dynamic manner in response to the circumstances and goals of the deception.

Finally, given the complementary information provided by the ERP and fMRI techniques, it appears certain that creating a detailed understanding of how deception-related processing is instantiated in the brain, as well as converting basic research findings into usable real-world deception detection and credibility-assessment tools, will be accomplished only by combining the temporal and spatial information provided by these two techniques. The dynamic nature of real-world deceptions means that it will continue to be difficult for fMRI to provide crucial insights into how different activated brain areas interact with one another in real time to allow a person to be deceptive. Thus, it is reasonable to conclude that only the ERP technique, with its millisecond resolution, has the ability to reveal the intricacies of the complex interplay of cognitive processes in various brain areas required by deception-related processing. This ability, coupled with the fact that there are no limitations on who or how often individuals can be tested, suggests that the ERP technique is more likely than fMRI to play the major role in deception detection and credibility assessment in the future.

REFERENCES

Abe, N., 2009. The neurobiology of deception: evidence from neuroimaging and loss-of-function studies. Current Opinion in Neurology 22, 594–600.

Abe, N., 2011. How the Brain Shapes Deception: An Integrated Review of the Literature. The Neuroscientist 17, 560–574.

Abe, N., Suzuki, M., Mori, E., Itoh, M., Fujii, T., 2007. Deceiving others: distinct neural responses of the prefrontal cortex and amygdala in simple fabrication and deception with social interactions. Journal of Cognitive Neuroscience 19, 287–295.

Abe, N., Fujii, T., Hirayama, K., Takeda, A., Hosokai, Y., Ishioka, T., et al., 2009. Do Parkinsonian patients have trouble telling lies? The neurobiological basis of deceptive behaviour. Brain 132, 1386–1395.

Abe, A., Okuda, J., Suzuki, M., Sasaki, H., Matsuda, T., Mori, E., et al., 2008. Neural correlates of true memory, false memory, and deception. Cerebral Cortex 18, 2811–2819.

Abe, N., Suzuki, M., Tsukiura, T., Mori, E., Yamaguchi, K., Itoh, M., et al., 2006. Dissociable roles of prefrontal and anterior cingulate cortices in deception. Cerebral Cortex 16, 192–199.

Allen, J.J.B., Mertens, R., 2009. Limitations to the detection of deception: True and false recollections are poorly distinguished using an event-related potential procedure. Social Neuroscience 4, 473–490.

Allport, D.A., Styles, E.A., Hsieh, S., 1994. Shifting intentional set: Exploring the dynamic control of tasks. In: Umilta, C., Moscovitch, M. (Eds.), Attention and Performance XV. MIT Press, Cambridge, MA, pp. 421–452.

Baddeley, A., 2000. The episodic buffer: a new component of working memory? Trends in Cognitive Sciences 4, 417–423.

Baddeley, A., 2012. Working Memory: Theories, Models, and Controversies. Annual Review of Psychology 63, 1–29.

Badre, D., 2008. Cognitive control, hierarchy, and the rostro–caudal organization of the frontal lobes. Trends in Cognitive Sciences 12, 193–200.

Barch, D.M., Braver, T.S., Sabb, F.W., Noll, D.C., 2000. Anterior cingulate and the monitoring of response conflict: Evidence from an fMRI study of overt verb generation. Journal of Cognitive Neuroscience 12, 298–309.

Bartholow, B.D., Pearson, M.A., Dickter, C.L., Sher, K.J., Fabiani, M., Gratton, G., 2005. Strategic control and medial frontal negativity: Beyond errors and response conflict. Psychophysiology 42, 33–42.

Ben-Shakhar, G., Furedy, J.J., 1990. Theories and Applications in the Detection of Deception: A Psychophysiological and International Perspective. Springer-Verlag, New York.

Bhatt, S., Mbwana, J., Adeyemo, A., Sawyer, A., Hailu, A., Vanmeter, J., 2009. Lying about facial recognition: An fMRI study. Brain and Cognition 69, 382–390.

Bles, M., Haynes, J.-D., 2008. Detecting concealed information using brain-imaging technology. Neurocase 14 (1), 82–92.

Botvinick, M.M., Braver, T.S., Barch, D.M., Carter, C.S., Cohen, J.D., 2001. Conflict monitoring and cognitive control. Psychological Review 108, 624–652.

Braver, T.S., Barch, D.M., 2006. Extracting core components of cognitive control. Trends in Cognitive Sciences 10, 529–532.

Browndyke, J.N., Paskavitz, J., Sweet, L.H., Cohen, R.A., Tucker, K.A., Welsh-Bohmer, K.A., et al., 2008. Neuroanatomical correlates of malingered memory impairment: Event-related fMRI of deception on a recognition memory task. Brain Injury 22 (6), 481–489.

Burianova, H., Grady, C.L., 2007. Common and unique neural activations in autobiographical, episodic, and semantic retrieval. Journal of Cognitive Neuroscience 19, 1520–1534.

Cabeza, R., St Jacques, P., 2007. Functional neuroimaging of autobiographical memory. Trends in Cognitive Sciences 11, 219–227.

Cabeza, R., Dolcos, F., Graham, R., Nyberg, L., 2002. Similarities and differences in the neural correlates of episodic memory retrieval and working memory. NeuroImage 16, 317–330.

Cabeza, R., Rao, S.M., Wagner, A.D., Mayer, A.R., Schacter, D.L., 2001. Can medial temporal lobe regions distinguish true from false? An event-related fMRI study of veridical and illusory recognition memory. Proceedings of the National Academy of Sciences USA 98, 4805–4810.

Cabeza, R., Prince, S.E., Daselaar, S.M., Greenberg, D.L., Budde, M., Dolcos, F., et al., 2004. Brain activity during episodic retrieval of autobiographical and laboratory events: An fMRI study using a novel photo paradigm. Journal of Cognitive Neuroscience 16, 1583–1594.

Carrión, R.E., Keenan, J.P., Sebanz, N., 2010. A truth that's told with bad intent: An ERP study of deception. Cognition 114, 105–110.

Carter, C.S., Braver, T.S., Barch, D.M., Botvinick, M.M., Noll, D., Cohen, J.D., 1998. Anterior cingulate cortex, error detection, and the online monitoring of performance. Science 280, 747–749.

Christ, S.E., Van Essen, D.C., Watson, J.M., Brubaker, L.E., McDermott, K.B., 2009. The contributions of prefrontal cortex and executive control to deception: Evidence from activation likelihood estimate meta-analyses. Cerebral Cortex 19, 1557–1566.

Cohen, N.J., Squire, L.R., 1980. Preserved learning and retention of pattern analyzing skill in amnesia: Dissociation of knowing how and knowing that. Science 210, 207–209.

Conway, M.A., Pleydell-Pearce, C.W., Whitecross, S.E., 2001. The neuroanatomy of autobiographical memory: A slow cortical potential study of autobiographical memory retrieval. Journal of Memory and Language 45, 493–524.

Cunningham, W.A., Zelazo, P.D., 2007. Attitudes and evaluations: A social cognitive neuroscience perspective. Trends in Cognitive Sciences 11, 97–104.

Curtis, C.E., D'Esposito, M., 2003. Persistent activity in the prefrontal cortex during working memory. Trends in Cognitive Sciences 7, 415–423.

Ding, X.P., Gao, X., Fu, G., Lee, K., 2013. Neural correlates of spontaneous deception: A functional near-infrared spectroscopy (fNIRS) study. Neuropsychologia 51, 704–712.

Doucet, C., Stelmack, R.M., 1999. The effect of response execution on P3 latency, reaction time, and movement time. Psychophysiology 36, 351–363.

Farwell, L.A., Donchin, E., 1991. The truth will out: Interrogative polygraphy ("lie detection") with event-related potentials. Psychophysiology 28, 531–547.

Folstein, J.R., Van Petten, C., 2008. Influence of cognitive control and mismatch on the N2 component of the ERP: A review. Psychophysiology 45, 152–170.

Friedman, D., Johnson Jr., R., 2000. Event-related potential (ERP) studies of memory encoding and retrieval: A selective review. Microscopy Research and Technique 51, 6–28.

Fullam, R.S., McKie, S., Dolan, M.C., 2009. Psychopathic traits and deception: Functional magnetic resonance imaging study. British Journal of Psychiatry 194, 229–235.

Furedy, J.J., Davis, C., Gurevich, M., 1988. Differentiation of deception as a psychological process: A psychophysiological approach. Psychophysiology 25, 683–688.

Gamer, M., Bauermann, T., Stoeter, P., Vossel, G., 2007. Covariations among fMRI, skin conductance, and behavioral data during processing of concealed information. Human Brain Mapping 28, 1287–1301.

Gamer, M., Klimecki, O., Bauermann, T., Stoeter, P., Vossel, G., 2012. fMRI-activation patterns in the detection of concealed information rely on memory-related effects. Social Cognitive & Affect Neuroscience 7 (5), 506–515.

Ganis, G., Morris, R.R., Kosslyn, S.M., 2009. Neural processes underlying self- and other-related lies: an individual difference approach using fMRI. Social Neuroscience 4, 539–553.

Ganis, G., Kosslyn, S.M., Stose, S., Thompson, W.L., Yurgelun-Todd, D.A., 2003. Neural correlates of different types of deception: an fMRI investigation. Cerebral Cortex 13, 830–836.

Ganis, G., Rosenfeld, J.P., Meixner, J., Kievit, R.A., Schendan, H.E., 2011. Lying in the scanner: Covert countermeasures disrupt deception detection by functional magnetic resonance imaging. NeuroImage 55, 312–319.

Garavan, H., Ross, T.J., Murphy, K., Roche, R.A.P., Stein, E.A., 2002. Dissociable executive functions in the dynamic control of behavior: Inhibition, error detection and correction. NeuroImage 17, 1820–1829.

Gehring, W.J., Knight, R.T., 2000. Prefrontal-cingulate interactions in action monitoring. Nature Neuroscience 3, 516–520.

Gehring, W.J., Willoughby, A.R., 2002. The medial frontal cortex and rapid processing of monetary gains and losses. Science 295, 2279–2282.

Gilboa, A., 2004. Autobiographical and episodic memory-one and the same? Evidence from prefrontal activation in neuroimaging studies. Neuropsychologia 42, 1336–1349.

Gilboa, A., Winocur, G., Grady, C.L., Hevenor, S.J., Moscovitch, M., 2004. Remembering our past: Functional neuroanatomy of recollection of recent and very remote personal events. Cerebral Cortex 14, 1214–1225.

Goghari, V.M., MacDonald 3rd., A.W., 2009. The neural basis of cognitive control: Response selection and inhibition. Brain and Cognition 71, 72–83.

Gratton, G., Fabiani, M., 2001. Shedding light on brain function: The event-related optical signal. Trends in Cognitive Sciences 5, 357–363.

Gratton, G., Coles, M.G.H., Donchin, E., 1992. Optimizing the use of information: Strategic control of activation of responses. Journal of Experimental Psychology: General 4, 480–506.

Greene, J.D., Paxton, J.M., 2009. Patterns of neural activity associated with honest and dishonest moral decisions. Proceedings of the National Academy of Sciences 106, 12506–12511.

Haggard, P., 2008. Human volition: Towards a neuroscience of will. Nature Neuroscience Reviews 9, 934–946.

Hakun, J.G., Ruparel, K., Seelig, D., Busch, E., Loughead, J.W., Gur, R.C., et al., 2009. Towards clinical trials of lie detection with fMRI. Social Neuroscience 4, 518–527.

Hakun, J.G., Seelig, D., Ruparel, K., Loughead, J.W., Busch, E., Gur, R.C., et al., 2008. fMRI investigation of the cognitive structure of the concealed information test. Neurocase 14, 59–67.

Henkell, H., Bercarich, L., Rodriguez, C., Zhu, J., Johnson Jr., R., 2010. Cognitive and neural bases of subjective and objective relational judgments: An ERP study. Paper presented at the 50th Annual Meeting of the Society for Psychophysiological Research. Psychophysiology 47, S76.

Herwig, A., Prinz, W., Waszak, F., 2007. Two modes of sensorimotor integration in intention-based and stimulus-based actions. The Quarterly Journal of Experimental Psychology 60, 1540–1554.

Honts, C.R., Raskin, D.C., Kircher, J.C., 2005. The scientific status of research on polygraph techniques: The case for polygraph tests. In: Faigman, D.L., Kaye, D., Saks, M.J., Saunders, J. (Eds.), Modern Scientific Evidence: The law and science of expert testimony. West Publishing, St. Paul, MN.

Hu, X., Chen, H., Fu, G., 2012. A repeated lie becomes a truth? The effect of intentional control and training on deception. Frontiers in Psychology 3: Article 488, 1–7.

Hu, X., Wu, H., Fu, G., 2011. Temporal course of executive control when lying about self- and other-referential information: An ERP study. Brain Research 1369, 149–157.

Ito, A., Abe, N., Fujii, T., Hayashi, A., Ueno, A., Mugikura, S., et al., 2012. The contribution of the dorsolateral prefrontal cortex to the preparation for deception and truth-telling. Brain Research 1464, 43–52.

Ito, A., Abe, N., Fujii, T., Ueno, A., Koseki, Y., Hashimoto, R., et al., 2011. The role of the dorsolateral prefrontal cortex in deception when remembering neutral and emotional events. Neuroscience Research 69, 121–128.

Jahanshahi, M., Frith, C.D., 1998. Willed action and its impairments. Cognitive Neuropsychology 15, 483–533.

Johnson Jr., R., 1986. A triarchic model of P300 amplitude. Psychophysiology 23, 367–384.

Johnson Jr., R., 1988. The amplitude of the P300 component of the event-related potential: Review and synthesis. In: Ackles, P.K., Jennings, J.R., Coles, M.G.H. (Eds.), Advances in Psychophysiology, vol. III. JAI Press, Greenwich, CT, pp. 69–138.

Johnson Jr., R., 1993. On the neural generators of the P300 component of the event-related potential. Psychophysiology 30, 90–97.

Johnson Jr., R., 1995. Event-related potential insights into the neurobiology of memory systems. In: Boller, F., Grafman, J. (Eds.), Handbook of Neuropsychology, vol. 10. Elsevier, Amsterdam, pp. 135–163.

Johnson Jr., R., Donchin, E., 1985. Second thoughts: Multiple P300s elicited by a single stimulus. Psychophysiology 22, 182–194.

Johnson Jr., R., Barnhardt, J., Singh, C., 2000. Neural Correlates of deceptive responding under monitoring instructions: An ERP study. Paper presented at the 40th Annual Meeting of the Society for Psychophysiological Research. Psychophysiology 37, S52.

Johnson Jr., R., Barnhardt, J., Zhu, J., 2002c. A comparison of three methods for discriminating truthful from deceptive ERP activity. Paper presented at the 42nd Annual Meeting of the Society for Psychophysiological Research. Psychophysiology 39, S44.

Johnson Jr., R., Barnhardt, J., Zhu, J., 2003. The deceptive response: Effects of response conflict and strategic monitoring on the late positive component and episodic memory-related brain activity. Biological Psychology 64, 217–253.

Johnson Jr., R., Barnhardt, J., Zhu, J., 2004. The contribution of executive processes to deceptive responding. Neuropsychologia 42, 878–901.

Johnson Jr., R., Barnhardt, J., Zhu, J., 2005. Differential effects of practice on the executive processes used for truthful and deceptive responses: An event-related brain potential study. Cognitive Brain Research 24, 386–404.

Johnson Jr., R., Nessler, D., Friedman, D., 2013. Temporally-specific divided attention tasks in young adults reveal the temporal dynamics of episodic encoding failures in elderly adults. Psychology and Aging 28 (2), 443–456.

Johnson Jr., R., Pfefferbaum, A., Kopell, B.S., 1985. P300 and long-term memory: Latency predicts recognition performance. Psychophysiology 22, 497–507.

Johnson Jr., R., Singh, C., Barnhardt, J., 2000b. The role of response conflict in deceptive responding: An ERP study. Paper presented at the 40th Annual Meeting of the Society for Psychophysiological Research. Psychophysiology 37, S52.

Johnson Jr., R., Henkell, H., Simon, E.J., Zhu, J., 2008a. The self in conflict: The role of executive processes during truthful and deceptive responses about attitudes. NeuroImage 39, 469–482.

Johnson Jr., R., Henkell, H., Simon, E.J., Zhu, J., 2010. Attitude complexity and the role of evaluative processes: An event-related potential study. Paper presented at the 17th Annual Meeting of the Cognitive Neuroscience Society. Published in the Supplement to the Journal of Cognitive Neuroscience. p. 139.

Johnson Jr., R., Kreiter, K., Russo, B., Zhu, J., 1998a. A spatio-temporal analysis of recognition-related event-related brain potentials. International Journal of Psychophysiology 29, 83–104.

Johnson Jr., R., Kreiter, K., Zhu, J., Russo, B., 1998b. A spatio-temporal comparison of semantic and episodic cued recall and recognition using event-related brain potentials. Cognitive Brain Research 7, 119–136.

Johnson Jr., R., Simon, E.J., Henkell, H., Zhu, J., 2011. The role of episodic memory in controlled evaluative judgments about attitudes: An event-related potential study. Neuropsychologia 49, 945–960.

Johnson Jr., R., Barnhardt, J., Adler, N., Simon, E.J., Zhu, J., 2002a. An ERP study of deception: Lying about personal facts. Paper presented at the 42nd Annual Meeting of the Society for Psychophysiological Research. Psychophysiology 39, S44.

Johnson Jr., R., Barnhardt, J., Adler, N., Simon, E.J., Zhu, J., 2002b. An ERP study of deception: Lying about personal experiences. Invited paper presentation at the 42nd Annual Meeting of the Society for Psychophysiological Research. Psychophysiology 39, S11.

Johnson Jr., R., Henkell, H., Rendel, D., Bitton, A., Schroeder, C., Zhu, J., 2008b. The brain processes underlying deceptions about personal traits: An ERP study. Paper presented at the 48th Annual Meeting of the Society for Psychophysiological Research. Psychophysiology 45, S100.

Karim, A.A., Schneider, M., Lotze, M., Veit, R., Sauseng, P., Braun, C., et al., 2010. The truth about lying: Inhibition of the anterior prefrontal cortex improves deceptive behavior. Cerebral Cortex 20, 205–213.

Koechlin, E., Summerfield, C., 2007. An information theoretical approach to prefrontal executive function. Trends in Cognitive Sciences 11, 229–235.

Kornhuber, H.H., Deecke, L., 1965. Hirnpotentialänderungen bei Willkürbewegungen und passiven Bewegungen des Menschen: Bereitschaftspotential und reafferente Potentiale [Brain potential changes during voluntary and passive movements in humans: The readiness potential and reafferent potentials]. Pflügers Archiv für die gesamte Physiologie des Menschen und der Tiere 284, 1–17.

Kozel, F.A., Trivedi, M.H., 2008. Developing a neuropsychiatric functional brain imaging test. Neurocase 14 (1), 54–58.

Kozel, F.A., Padgett, T.M., George, M.S., 2004a. A replication study of the neural correlates of deception. Behavioral Neuroscience 118, 852–856.

Kozel, F.A., Johnson, K.A., Laken, S.J., Grenesko, E.L., Smith, J.A., Walker, J., et al., 2009a. Can simultaneously acquired electrodermal activity improve accuracy of fMRI detection of deception? Social Neuroscience 4, 510–517.

Kozel, F.A., Johnson, K.A., Mu, Q., Grenesko, E.L., Laken, S.J., George, M.S., 2005. Detecting deception using functional magnetic resonance imaging. Biological Psychiatry 58, 605–613.

Kozel, F.A., Laken, S.J., Johnson, K.A., Boren, B., Mapes, K.S., Morgan, P.S., et al., 2009b. Replication of functional MRI detection of deception. Open Forensic Science Journal 2, 6–11.

Kozel, F.A., Revell, L.J., Lorberbaum, J.P., Shastri, A., Elhai, J.D., Horner, M.D., et al., 2004b. A pilot study of functional magnetic resonance imaging brain correlates of deception in healthy young men. Journal of Neuropsychiatry and Clinical Neurosciences 16, 295–305.

Krapohl, D.J., 2011. Limitations of the concealed information test in criminal cases. In: Verschuere, B., Ben Shakhar, G., Meijer, E. (Eds.), Memory Detection: Theory and Application of the Concealed Information Test. Cambridge University Press, Cambridge, UK, pp. 151–170.

Langleben, D.D., Loughead, J.W., Bilker, W.B., Ruparel, K., Childress, A.R., Busch, S.I., et al., 2005. Telling truth from lie in individual subjects with fast event-related fMRI. Human Brain Mapping 26, 262–272.

Langleben, D.D., Schroeder, L., Maldigian, J.A., Gur, R.C., McDonald, S., Ragland, J.D., et al., 2002. Brain activity during simulated deception: An event-related functional magnetic resonance study. NeuroImage 15, 727–732.

Lau, H.C., Rogers, R.D., Ramnani, N., Passingham, R.E., 2004. Willed action and attention to the selection of action. NeuroImage 21, 1407–1415.

Lee, T.M.C., Liu, H.-L., Chan, C.C.H., Ng, Y.B., Fox, P.T., Gao, J.-H., 2005. Neural correlates of feigned memory impairment. Neuroimage 28, 305–313.

Lee, T.M.C., Au, R.K.C., Liu, H.-L., Ting, K.H., Huan, C.-M., Chan, C.C.H., 2009. Are errors differentiable from deceptive responses when feigning memory impairment? An fMRI study. Brain and Cognition 69, 406–412.

Lee, T.M.C., Liu, H.-L., Tan, L.H., Chan, C.C.H., Mahankali, S., Feng, C.M., et al., 2002. Lie detection by functional magnetic resonance imaging. Human Brain Mapping 15, 157–164.

Levine, B., Turner, G.R., Tisserand, D., Hevenor, S.J., Graham, S.J., McIntosh, A.R., 2004. The functional neuroanatomy of episodic and semantic autobiographical remembering: A prospective functional MRI study. Journal of Cognitive Neuroscience 16, 1633–1646.

Liang, C.-Y., Xu, Z.-Y., Mei, W., Wang, L.-L., Xue, L., Lu, D.J., et al., 2012. Neural correlates of feigned memory impairment are distinguishable from answering randomly and answering incorrectly: An fMRI and behavioral study. Brain and Cognition 79, 70–77.

Lieberman, M.D., 2003. Reflective and reflexive judgment processes: A social cognitive neuroscience approach. In: Forgas, J.P., Williams, K.R., von Hippel, W. (Eds.), Social judgments: Implicit and explicit processes. Cambridge University Press, New York, pp. 44–67.

Lieberman, M.D., 2007. Social cognitive neuroscience: A review of core processes. Annual Review of Psychology 58, 259–289.

Liljeholm, M., O'Doherty, J.P., 2012. Contributions of the striatum to learning, motivation, and performance: An associative account. Trends in Cognitive Sciences 16, 467–475.

Luber, B., Fisher, C., Appelbaum, P.S., Ploesser, M., Lisanby, S.H., 2009. Non-invasive brain stimulation in the detection of deception: Scientific challenges and ethical consequences. Behavioral Sciences and the Law 27, 191–208.

Lykken, D.T., 1959. The GSR in the detection of guilt. Journal of Applied Psychology 43, 385–388.

MacDonald III, A.W., Cohen, J.D., Stenger, V.A., Carter, C.S., 2000. Dissociating the role of the dorsolateral prefrontal and anterior cingulate cortex in cognitive control. Science 288, 1835–1838.

MacLeod, C.M., 1991. Half a century of research on the Stroop effect: An integrative review. Psychological Bulletin 109, 163–203.

Magliero, A., Bashore, T.R., Coles, M.G.H., Donchin, E., 1984. On the dependence of P300 latency on stimulus evaluation processes. Psychophysiology 21, 171–186.

Maguire, E.A., Mummery, C.J., 1999. Differential modulation of a common memory retrieval network revealed by positron emission tomography. Hippocampus 9, 54–61.

Mandler, G., 1980. Recognizing: The judgment of previous occurrence. Psychological Review 87, 252–271.

McPherson, B., McMahon, K., Wilson, W., Copland, D., 2012. "I know you can hear me": Neural correlates of feigned hearing loss. Human Brain Mapping 33, 1964–1972.

Mertens, R., Allen, J.J.B., 2008. The role of psychophysiology in forensic assessments: Deception detection, ERPs, and virtual reality mock crime scenarios. Psychophysiology 45, 286–298.

Miltner, W., Braun, C., Johnson Jr., R., Simpson, G.V., Ruchkin, D.S., 1994. A test of brain electrical source analysis (BESA): A simulation study. Electroencephalography and Clinical Neurophysiology 91, 295–310.

Mohamed, F., Faro, S., Gordon, N., Platek, M., Ahmad, H., Williams, M., 2006. Brain mapping of deception and truthtelling about an ecologically valid situation: Functional MR imaging and polygraph investigation-Initial experience. Radiology 238, 679–688.

Monsell, S., 2003. Task Switching. Trends in Cognitive Sciences 7, 134–140.

Monteleone, G.T., Phan, K.L., Nusbaum, H.C., Fitzgerald, D., Irick, J.-S., Fienberg, S.E., et al., 2009. Detection of deception using fMRI: Better than chance, but well below perfection. Social Neuroscience 4, 528–538.

Moscovitch, M., 1992. Memory and working-with-memory: A component process model based on modules and central systems. Journal of Cognitive Neuroscience 4 (3), 257–267.

Mostofsky, S.H., Simmonds, D.J., 2008. Response inhibition and response selection: Two sides of the same coin. Journal of Cognitive Neuroscience 20, 751–761.

Nachev, P., Kennard, C., Husain, M., 2008. Functional role of the supplementary and pre-supplementary motor areas. Nature Neuroscience Reviews 9, 856–869.

Nee, D.E., Brown, J.W., Askren, M.K., Berman, M.G., Demiralp, E., Krawitz, A., et al., 2013. A meta-analysis of executive components of working memory. Cerebral Cortex 23 (2), 264–282.

Nose, I., Murai, J., Taira, M., 2009. Disclosing concealed information on the basis of cortical activations. NeuroImage 44, 1380–1386.

Nunez, J.M., Casey, B.J., Egner, T., Hare, T., Hirsch, J., 2005. Intentional false responding shares neural substrates with response conflict and cognitive control. NeuroImage 25 (1), 267–277.

Owen, A.M., Stern, C.E., Look, R.B., Tracet, I., Rosen, B.R., Petrides, M., 1998. Functional organization of spatial and nonspatial working memory processing within the human lateral frontal cortex. Proceedings of the National Academy of Sciences 95, 12061–12068.

Phan, K.L., Magalhaes, A., Ziemlewicz, T.J., Fitzgerald, D.A., Green, C., Smith, W., 2005. Neural correlates of telling lies: A functional magnetic resonance imaging study at 4 Tesla. Academic Radiology 12. 164–172.

Picton, T.W., Lins, O.G., Scherg, M., 1995. The recording and analysis of event-related potentials. In: Boller, F., Grafman, J. (Eds.), Handbook of Neuropsychology, vol. 10. Elsevier, Amsterdam, pp. 3–73.

Picton, T.W., Bentin, S., Berg, P., Donchin, E., Hillyard, S.A., Johnson Jr., R., et al., 2000. Guidelines for using human event-related potentials to study cognition: Recording standards and publication criteria. Psychophysiology 37, 127–152.

Priori, A., Mameli, F., Cogiamanian, F., Marceglia, S., Tiriticco, M., Mrakic-Sposta, S., et al., 2008. Lie-specific involvement of dorsolateral prefrontal cortex in deception. Cerebral Cortex 18, 451–455.

Renoult, L., Davidson, P.S.R., Palombo, D.J., Moscovitch, M., Levine, B., 2012. Personal semantics: At the crossroads of semantic and episodic memory. Trends in Cognitive Sciences 16, 550–558.

Ridderinkhof, K.R., Ullsperger, M., Crone, E.A., Nieuwenhuis, S., 2004. The role of the medial frontal cortex in cognitive control. Science 306, 443–447.

Rogers, R.D., Monsell, S., 1995. The costs of a switch in a predictable switch between simple cognitive tasks. Journal of Experimental Psychology: Human Perception and Performance 124, 207–231.

Rosenfeld, J.P., 2011. P300 in detecting concealed information. In: Verschuere, B., Ben Shakhar, G., Meijer, E. (Eds.), Memory Detection: Theory and Application of the Concealed Information Test. Cambridge University Press, Cambridge, UK, pp. 63–89.

Rosenfeld, J.P., Soskins, M., Bosh, G., Ryan, A., 2004. Simple, effective countermeasures to P300-based tests of detection of concealed information. Psychophysiology 41, 205–219.

Ruchkin, D.S., Grafman, J., Cameron, K., Berndt, R.S., 2003. Working memory retention systems: A state of activated long-term memory. Behavioral and Brain Sciences 26, 709–777.

Rugg, M.D., Curran, T., 2007. Event-related potentials and recognition memory. Trends in Cognitive Sciences 11 (6), 251–257.

Rugg, M.D., Johnson, J.D., Park, H., Uncapher, M.R., 2008. Encoding-retrieval overlap in human episodic memory: A functional neuroimaging perspective. Progress in Brain Research 169, 339–352.

Schacter, D.L., Loftus, E.F., 2013. Memory and law: What can cognitive neuroscience contribute? Nature Neuroscience 16, 119–123.

Scherg, M., 1990. Fundamentals of dipole source potential analysis. In: Grandori, F., Hoke, M., Romani, G.L. (Eds.), Auditory evoked magnetic fields and electric potentials. Advances in Audiology, vol. 6. Karger, Basel, pp. 40–69.

Scherg, M., Picton, T.W., 1991. Separation and identification of event-related potential components by brain electric source analysis. Electroencephalography and Clinical Neurophysiology (Suppl. 42), 24–37.

Sip, K.E., Lynge, M., Wallentin, M., McGregor, W.B., Frith, C.D., Roepstorff, A., 2010. The production and detection of deception in an interactive game. Neuropsychologia 48, 3619–3626.

Sip, K.E., Roepstorff, A., McGregor, W., Frith, C.D., 2007. Detecting deception: The scope and limits. Trends in Cognitive Sciences 12 (2), 48–53.

Smith, E.E., Jonides, J., 1998. Neuroimaging analyses of human working memory. Proceedings of the National Academy of Sciences 95, 12061–12068.

Smith, E.E., Jonides, J., 1999. Storage and executive processes in the frontal lobes. Science 283, 1657–1661.

Spence, S.A., Kaylor-Hughes, C., 2008. Looking for truth and finding lies: The prospects for a nascent neuroimaging of deception. Neurocase 14, 68–81.

Spence, S.A., Kaylor-Hughes, C., Farrow, T.F., Wilkinson, I.D., 2008. Speaking of secrets and lies: The contribution of ventrolateral prefrontal cortex to vocal deception. Neuroimage 40, 1411–1418.

Spence, S.A., Farrow, T.F.D., Herford, A.E., Wilkinson, I.D., Zheng, Y., Woodruff, P.W.R., 2001. Behavioral and functional anatomical correlates of deception in humans. NeuroReport 12, 2849–2853.

Spence, S.A., Hunter, M.D., Farrow, T.F., Green, R.D., Leung, D.H., Hughes, C.J., et al., 2004. A cognitive neurobiological account of deception: Evidence from functional neuroimaging. Philosophical Translations of the Royal Society London B Biological Sciences 359, 1755–1762.

Squire, L.R., 1992. Declarative and nondeclarative memory: multiple brain systems supporting learning and memory. Journal of Cognitive Neuroscience 4, 232–243.

Svoboda, E., McKinnon, M.C., Levine, B., 2006. The functional neuroanatomy of autobiographical memory: A meta-analysis. Neuropsychologia 44, 2189–2208.

Swick, D., Jovanovic, J., 2002. Anterior cingulate cortex and the stroop task: Neuropsychological evidence for topographic specificity. Neuropsychologia 40, 1240–1253.

Tardif, H.P., Barry, R.J., Fox, A.M., Johnstone, S.J., 2000. Detection of feigned recognition memory impairment using the old/new effect of the event-related potential. International Journal of Psychophysiology 36, 1–9.

Tian, F., Sharma, V., Kozel, F.A., Liu, H.-L, 2009. Functional near-infrared spectroscopy to investigate hemodynamic responses to deception in the prefrontal cortex. Brain Research 1303, 120–130.

Tu, S., Li, H., Jou, J., Zhang, Q., Wang, T., Yu, C., et al., 2009. An event-related potential study of deception to self preferences. Brain Research 1247, 142–148.

Tulving, E., 1983. Elements of Episodic Memory. Oxford University Press, New York.

Turken, A.U., Swick, D., 1999. Response selection in the human anterior cingulate cortex. Nature Neuroscience 2, 920–924.

Vallesi, A., Mapelli, D., Schiff, S., Amodio, P., Umilta, C., 2005. Horizontal and vertical Simon effect: Different underlying mechanisms? Cognition 96, B33–B43.

Van Bockstaele, B., Verschuere, B., Moens, T., Suchotzki, K., Debey, E., Spruyt, A., 2012. Learning to lie: Effects of practice on the cognitive cost of lying. Frontiers in Psychology 3: Article 526, 1–8.

Vendemia, J.M.C., Buzan, R.F., Green, E.P., 2005. Practice effects, workload, and reaction time in deception. American Journal of Psychology 5, 413–429.

Verschuere, B., Schuhmann, T., Sack, A.T., 2012. Does the inferior frontal sulcus play a functional role in deception? A neuronavigated theta-burst transcranial magnetic stimulation study. Frontiers in Human Neuroscience 6: Article 284, 1–7.

Vrij, A., 2008. Detecting Lies and Deceit, Second ed. John Wiley and Sons, Chichester, UK.

Walsh, V., Cowey, A., 2000. Transcranial magnetic stimulation and cognitive neuroscience. Nature Neuroscience Reviews 1, 73–79.

Waszak, F., Wascher, E., Keller, P., Koch, I., Aschersleben, G., Rosenbaum, D., et al., 2005. Intention-based and stimulus-based mechanisms in action selection. Experimental Brain Research 162, 346–356.

Wu, H., Hu, X., Fu, G., 2009. Does willingness affect the N2–P3 effect of deceptive and honest responses? Neuroscience Letters 467, 63–66.

Zysset, S., Huber, O., Ferstl, E., von Cramon, D.Y., 2002. The anterior frontomedian cortex and evaluative judgment: A fMRI study. Neuroimage 15, 983–991.

Theories in Deception and Lie Detection

Aldert Vrij, *Giorgio Ganis*[†]

*Psychology Department, University of Portsmouth, [†]Psychology Department, University of Plymouth

OUTLINE

Introduction   303

An Abstract Theoretical Framework
for Deception and Lie Detection   305

A Brief History of Lie Detection   307

Physiological Lie Detection   310
  Anxiety-Based Polygraph Tests   311
  Theoretical Assumptions of CQT   313
  Accuracy of CQTs   314
  Recognition-Based Polygraph Test   315
  Accuracy of CITs   318
  Summary of Physiological Lie Detection   318

Non-Verbal Lie Detection   319
  Multifactor Model   319
    Emotional Reactions   320
    Cognitive Load   320
    Attempted Behavioral Control   321
  Self-Presentational Perspective   322
  IDT   322
  Non-Verbal Cues to Deception: No
    Pinocchio's Nose   324
  Support for the Theoretical Perspectives   325

Reasons for Few Non-Verbal
  Cues to Deception   326
  Some Cues are Overlooked   326
  Individual and Situational
    Differences   329
Accuracy Rates in Non-Verbal
  Lie Detection   331
Specific Non-Verbal Lie Detection Tools   332
  Facial Emotional Expressions   332
  BAI   333

Verbal Lie Detection   336
  SVA   336
  Accuracy of CBCA   338
  Reality Monitoring   340
  Verifiable Details   342
  SCAN   343

Functional Magnetic Resonance
Imaging-Based Lie Detection   345
  fMRI Studies   346
  Accuracy of fMRI Methods   351
  Replicability of fMRI Methods   352
  Generalizability of fMRI Methods   353

Credibility Assessment
http://dx.doi.org/10.1016/B978-0-12-394433-7.00007-5

Comparison of Physiological,
Non-Verbal, Verbal, and Brain
Activity Lie Detection   354

Interviewing to Detect Deception
Through Non-Verbal and Verbal Cues   356

Imposing Cognitive Load   356
Asking Unanticipated Questions   359

Conclusions   361

References   362

INTRODUCTION

Deception, a deliberate attempt to convince someone of something the liar believes is untrue, is a fact of everyday life. DePaulo *et al.* (1996) asked participants to keep a diary for one week of all their social interactions that lasted for more than ten minutes and to note how often they lied during these social interactions. Almost all participants admitted that they had lied during the week that they kept the diary. They lied in one out of every four social interactions (resulting in 1.5 lies a day) and to 34% of all the people they interacted with.

The overwhelming majority of lies people tell are not serious (DePaulo *et al.*, 1996) and many lies told in daily life are social lies (e.g., "I like your hair cut"). Conversations could become awkward and unnecessarily rude, and social interactions, including friendships and romantic relationships, could easily turn sour if people were to tell each other the truth all the time. In order to maintain a good working relationship with colleagues it is better to pretend to be busy when invited for lunch than to admit that you find their company boring and would rather avoid them. Similarly, it may be kinder to respond with enthusiasm when receiving an expensive present from a friend even when you do not like the gift. Social relationships benefit from people giving each other compliments now and again because people like to be liked and like to receive compliments (Aron *et al.*, 1989).

Social lies are told for psychological reasons, and serve both self-interest and the interest of others. They serve self-interest because liars may gain satisfaction when they notice that their lies please other people, or because they realize that by telling such lies they avoid an awkward situation or discussion. They serve the interest of others because hearing the truth all the time (e.g., "The steak you cooked was really tough," "You look much older now than you did a few years ago," "I would be surprised if you succeed in what you want to achieve") could damage a person's confidence and self-esteem.

However, sometimes the situation is different. Sometimes the lies that are told are serious and we would like to detect them. Who would not have liked to have known earlier that Mohammad Atta and 18 others came to the United States with the intention to carry out four coordinated suicide attacks on the New York Twin Towers, Pentagon, and White House? Who would not have liked to have known earlier that the former American business man Bernard Madoff was lying? Madoff pleaded guilty to using a fraudulent investment operation that paid returns to its investors from their own money, or the money paid by subsequent investors, rather than from any actual profit. The amount missing from client accounts, including fabricated gains, was almost $65 billion, and the court-appointed trustee estimated actual losses to investors of $18 billion. On 29 June 2009, Madoff was sentenced to 150 years in prison – the maximum allowed.

In a similar vein, the police detective wants to know whether the suspect's alibi is reliable, the customs officer wants to know whether the traveler really has nothing to declare, the immigration official wants to know whether the asylum seeker's life in his/her native country is indeed in danger as he/she claims, and the employer wants to know whether the candidate is indeed as capable as the candidate says. Being able to detect these sorts of lies would benefit individuals or the society as a whole. For that reason, researchers have been examining how liars respond and how they could be detected. Although this applied goal has been the most direct drive for deception research over the years, it is important to remember that solid applications must rely on a body of theoretically justified basic science. Without such grounding, there is no clear direction to take to improve the accuracy of existing methods, and when a method underperforms or fails, there is no principled way to proceed to troubleshoot. Thus, it is worth visualizing deception research on a continuum (Figure 7.1). The applied end of this continuum aims at developing methods to detect deception with the kind of field validity just described. In contrast, the theoretical end focuses on more general principles and theories about mechanisms and processes important for deception (e.g., theory of mind, working memory, executive control, etc.). In the middle, there is research that attempts to bridge these two ends, focusing on ideas and paradigms with a theoretical basis that could become useful for understanding and detecting deception in some situations.

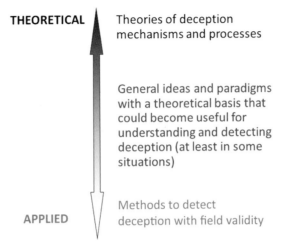

THEORETICAL — Theories of deception mechanisms and processes

General ideas and paradigms with a theoretical basis that could become useful for understanding and detecting deception (at least in some situations)

APPLIED — Methods to detect deception with field validity

FIGURE 7.1   Deception research continuum, from theoretical (top) to applied (bottom).

AN ABSTRACT THEORETICAL FRAMEWORK FOR DECEPTION AND LIE DETECTION

Deceptive mental states are not directly observable, which is the main reason why detecting deception is difficult. Thus, all lie detection approaches need to rely on an indirect route that attempts to find measurable internal processes thought to correlate with deceptive mental states. All approaches to detect lies can be described within a general theoretical framework with three core components (Figure 7.2): (1) one or more internal processes thought to correlate with deceptive mental states, (2) a set of variables used to measure or operationalize these internal processes, and (3) a set of analyses performed on these variables to infer that deception might have occurred.

Ideally, one would want to find an internal process (let us call it "process D") that correlates perfectly with a deceptive mental state such that a deceptive mental state is present if and only if process D is present. This internal process is a proxy for deceptive mental states that can be detected and measured by using a set of variables (e.g., behavior, skin conductance, neural activity in certain brain regions, etc.) and a set of analyses can be performed on these variables to infer the presence of a deceptive mental state. In practice, the

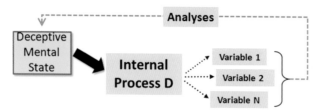

FIGURE 7.2   Theoretical framework for lie detection methods. Different methods postulate different internal process D, use different variables to measure process D, and perform different analyses on these variables to infer deception.

correlation between high-level mental states, such as deception, and internal processes that we can measure is far from perfect. On the one hand, typically there are non-deceptive mental states that also correlate with process D, resulting in false-positives (non-deceptive mental states incorrectly classified as deceptive). On the other hand, some deceptive mental states may correlate with other internal processes that we are not measuring, resulting in false-negatives (deceptive mental states classified as non-deceptive). Thus, the inference from the measured variables to deception is weakened. These are some of the theoretical reasons why the accuracy of lie detection methods is far from perfect.

There are four general approaches to detect lies, which differ on the details of the three core components just outlined: investigators could measure someone's physiological responses, observe his/her behavior, analyze his/her speech, or measure his/her brain activity. All four approaches share a common element – a response uniquely associated to deception, akin to Pinocchio's growing nose, does not seem to exist. In Pinocchio's case, his nose grew longer each time he lied and remained stable each time he told the truth. Such a response, that all liars show all the time and all truth-tellers never show, does not exist. However, differences between truth-tellers and liars may occur when analyzing physiological responses, behavior, speech, or brain activity, and the four ways to detect deceit have different theoretical underpinnings as to why this may happen.

For physiological lie detection approaches, process D is either anxiety or an orienting process, and the assumption is that liars are anxious and they respond more strongly to crime-related stimuli because they are familiar with them (but see also Honts in Chapter 4 of this volume). The variables used by this approach are peripheral ones, such as skin conductance, and the analyses are those typically used in psychophysiology. For approaches based on analyses of behavior, process D is also predominantly anxiety, but guilt and cognitive load are also important. Liars are assumed to be more anxious, to feel more guilty, and to have a higher cognitive load than truth-tellers. Typical variables include blink rates, voice pitch, gaze aversion, fidgeting, etc., and these variables are quantified using various coding methods. The basis of speech analyses is that liars experience cognitive load, try to make a convincing impression, or that their memory differs from that of truth-tellers.

The assumption of lie detection approaches based on brain activity is that some of the cognitive processes engaged by deception, such as response inhibition or recognition, are associated with sufficiently distinctive neural signatures that can be measured with techniques such as functional magnetic resonance imaging (fMRI) – the focus of this chapter. We will discuss all these theoretical approaches in this chapter together with the interview protocols nowadays used to detect deceit. By reading the physiological literature on lie detection it becomes evident that the interview protocol matters in lie detection. For example, the Relevant–Irrelevant Test (RIT) is considered to be unreliable simply because the examinee is not asked the correct questions. However, it is only in recent years that the idea that the interview protocol matters has been advocated in non-verbal and verbal lie detection research. Note, in our theoretical framework, interview protocol and related manipulations (e.g., increasing cognitive load) can be conceptualized as methods that increase the strength of the association between deceptive mental states and the postulated internal process, and reduce the chance that such a process may be engaged by other, non-deceptive mental states so as to enhance overall deception detection accuracy. We will outline the latest developments in this field. We will start this chapter with a brief history of lie detection.

A BRIEF HISTORY OF LIE DETECTION

Throughout history it has been assumed that lying is accompanied by physiological activity within the liar's body. The underlying assumption was that the fear of being detected was an essential element of deception (Trovillo, 1939a). Early lie detection attempts were based on the idea that fear is associated with a dry mouth (Ford, 2006). Therefore, the Chinese in 1000 BC, but also people in India and Western Africa, forced suspected liars to chew rice powder and then to spit it out. If the resultant powder was dry then the person was judged to have been lying (Kleinmuntz and Szucko, 1984; Trovillo, 1939a). Based on the same dry mouth assumption, the accused in north Bengal was told to prove his innocence by applying his tongue to a red-hot iron nine times. The full extent of this ordeal becomes clear if someone realizes that the accused was instructed to carrying the red-hot iron in his hands (Trovillo, 1939a).

Other techniques were based on the smell of fear. In Africa, the medicine man assembled all suspects in a circle and threw himself at the neck of each suspect to smell him (Trovillo, 1939a). In addition, early examples of the use of pulse (another fear indicator) have been recorded. During the Middle Ages, a European noble man suspected his wife of infidelity. At a dinner, one of his advisers casually laid his hand on the wife's wrist and conversed with her. When he mentioned the name of the man suspected to be the secret lover her pulse quickened, whereas the name of her husband resulted in no response (Trovillo, 1939a).

Another example of measuring fear is measuring blood pressure. Equipment to measure blood pressure "from the outside" was introduced in 1855 and one of the earliest observations of measuring the effect of fear on blood pressure was carried out in 1877 by the Italian physiologist Mosso (Trovillo, 1939a). In his book, *On the Witness Stand*, Münsterberg (1908) discussed the practical application of experimental psychology, including how to detect deceit. He proposed that courts utilize blood pressure tests for detecting deception (to date such tests are not accepted as evidence in most criminal courts throughout the world).

Physiological measurements of fear (through pulse and blood pressure, but also through respiration and galvanic responses) became more sophisticated and machines were developed to measure them all simultaneously. These machines were called "polygraphs" after the Greek words *poly* (many) and *grapho* (to engrave/write). In the 1920s and 1930s, Larson achieved a commanding position in this field (Trovillo, 1939b) and his efforts resulted in the

RIT (Larson, 1932) – the first widely used polygraph test. The test is disputed nowadays and Larson himself expressed doubts in his writings about the applicability of deception tests (Trovillo, 1939a).

Analyses of non-verbal behavior also have a long history which assumes fear underlies deception. A Hindu writing from 900 BC mentioned that liars rub the big toe along the ground and shiver, and that they rub the roots of their hair with their fingers (Rovillo, 1939a), and Münsterberg (1908) described the utility of observing posture, eye movements, and knee jerks for lie detection purposes (Trovillo, 1939b). Detailed analyses of non-verbal cues to deceit emerged in the second half on the twentieth century with Reid and Arther's (1953) analysis of the behavior of more than 800 suspects. Their observations, together with Horvath's (1973) work regarding non-verbal cues to deceit, resulted in the development of the Behavior Analysis Interview (BAI) (Horvath *et al.*, 1994, 2008; Inbau *et al.*, 2001, 2013) – a non-verbal lie detection tool still used to date.

In the late 1800s, the idea arose that liars could also be caught via word association tests. Galton (1879) experimented with the idea and Münsterberg (1908) advocated its forensic application. Examinees are presented with words that are either neutral or pertinent to a crime situation and asked to call out the first thing that comes to mind. A guilty suspect, who strives to reply to the target words with words that have no connection to the crime, will have a mental conflict that could be observed through measuring reaction times (Trovillo, 1939a). The concept was used less frequently than measuring physiological responses, because measuring reaction times was considered to be more difficult than measuring physiological responses (Trovillo, 1939a). With the availability of better technology, reaction times could be measured more easily and reaction time tests rapidly gained popularity in lie detection research (Verschuere, 2011).

Analyses of speech lack an extensive historical background. Indeed, the Hindu writing of 900 BC indicated that liars do not answer questions or are evasive (Trovillo, 1939a). The idea that liars are evasive remained popular and is incorporated in the BAI. The notion that the presence of speech can indicate deceit arose much later, and early systematic analyses of speech arrived in the 1950s in Germany (Undeutsch, 1982) and Sweden (Trankell, 1972). Köhnken and Steller (1988) took statement analysis a step further. They refined the available criteria mentioned by Undeutsch and Trankell and integrated them into a formal assessment procedure, which they called State-ment Validity Assessment (SVA) – a verbal veracity assessment tool still in use. Other verbal lie detection protocols followed, such as Reality Monitoring (Sporer, 1997).

The development of methods to monitor neural activity non-invasively in humans, such as electroencephalography (EEG), positron emission tomog-raphy (PET), magnetoencephalography (MEG), near-infrared spectroscopy (NIRS), and fMRI, has enabled researchers to examine variables more directly related to the brain that may detect deceit. The use of EEG to detect deceit dates back to the late 1980s (Rosenfeld *et al.*, 1988), whereas the first fMRI article on deception was published in 2001 (Spence *et al.*, 2001). The use of EEG (event-related potentials), PET, MEG, and NIRS to study deception is covered by Johnson in Chapter 6 of this volume. In this chapter, we focus on fMRI-based evidence.

PHYSIOLOGICAL LIE DETECTION

Modern physiological lie detection employs various physiological measures, such as circulatory measures (e.g., blood pressure), electrodermal measures (skin conductance produced by palmar sweat-gland activity), and respira-tory measures (Podlesny and Raskin, 1977, 1978). The polygraph accurately records these changes and is able to measure very small differences picked up from sensors attached to different parts of the body (for a detailed description of current techniques, see Raskin and Kircher in Chapter 3 of this volume).

Two theoretical approaches exist in polygraph testing. The underlying assumption in the *anxiety-based* approach is that guilty examinees show height-ened levels of arousal during key elements of the polygraph test because of a heightened threat that their deceit will be detected. The underlying assump-tion in the *recognition-based* polygraph approach is that guilty examinees will show orienting reflexes when they recognize crucial details of a crime. In this section, we first discuss anxiety-based polygraph tests, and then consider the underlying theoretical assumptions and their accuracy.

Anxiety-Based Polygraph Tests

The RIT was the first widely used polygraph test that is an anxiety-based test. In the RIT, two types of questions are asked: *crime-relevant* questions and *crime-irrelevant* questions. Crime-relevant questions refer to the crime under investigation, such as "Did you break into a black Mercedes last night?" All suspects, both innocent and guilty, will answer "No" to this question. Crime-irrelevant questions are unrelated to the crime and the examiner knows that the examinee will tell the truth when answering these questions. An example of a crime-irrelevant question is "Is today Tuesday?" The examiner then compares the physiological responses to both types of questions. The rationale behind the RIT is that the observed physiological responses are produced by detection anxiety (Raskin and Honts, 2002). Therefore, larger responses to the crime-relevant questions than to the crime-irrelevant questions are interpreted as signs of lying to the crime-relevant questions.

This rationale has been described as simplistic and naïve (Podlesny and Raskin, 1977). The crime-irrelevant questions are meant to control for interpersonal differences (i.e., differences in physiological responses naturally shown by different individuals). However, not only *interpersonal* differences, but also *intrapersonal* differences should be taken into account, which is the notion that the same person may respond differently to different questions due to the nature of those questions.

Suppose a woman is attached to a polygraph to discover whether she stole money from her employer's office. She is innocent, but she realizes that a large physiological response may imply that she will lose her job. Hence, the crime-relevant question "Did you steal the money?" has major consequences for her. Thus, it is possible that this crime-relevant question will result in a larger physiological response than a crime-irrelevant question about the color of her shirt, for example. There is agreement in the academic polygraph world that the RIT is an inappropriate polygraph test that should not be used (Honts, 1991; Iacono, 2008b; Lykken, 1998; Raskin, 1986; Raskin and

Honts, 2002; Saxe, 1994). The obvious problem is that the crime-irrelevant questions do not provide an adequate control for the emotional impact the crime-relevant questions can have on examinees (Iacono, 2000). Although the RIT technique was the dominant polygraph technique for many years, it is now infrequently used in criminal investigations (Raskin and Honts, 2002). However, it is still used in other settings, such as by insurance companies attempting to detect fraud in their clients' claims (Barkham, 2007).

In order to address the RIT criticisms, Raskin (1979, 1982, 1986) developed the Comparison (Control) Question Test (CQT). The CQT was originally developed by Reid (1947). Over the subsequent 20 years the CQT became the dominant forensic test in the United States. In the early 1970s, David Raskin and his graduate students used scientific methods to refine and provide validation data. Relevant questions (RQs) and comparison questions (CQs) are asked in such tests. RQs are specifically about the crime under investigation (e.g., "Did you shoot/stab/strangle Julie Appletoddler?").

CQs deal with acts that are related to the crime under investigation, but do not refer to the crime in question. They are always general in nature, deliberately vague, and cover long periods of time in the history of the examinee. The examiner formulates a CQ for which in the examiner's view a "No" answer would be deceptive. In a murder inquiry a CQ could be, "During the first 25 years of your life, did you ever hurt someone?" where the examiner believes that it is likely that the examinee did indeed hurt someone before age 26 (these are referred to in the profession as probable-lie comparisons). Under normal circumstances, some examinees may admit to this wrongdoing. However, during a polygraph examination they are unlikely to do this because the examiner will make the examinee believe that admitting to this would demonstrate that he/she is the type of person who would commit the crime in question and so will be considered guilty.

CQs are thought to result in stronger physiological responses than the RQs in the *innocent examinee*. Since the examiner puts so much emphasis on the CQs to which the innocent examinee will be deceptive, and because the innocent examinee knows he/she is answering truthfully to the RQs, the innocent examinee will become more anxious about his/her answers to the CQs than his/her answers to the RQs. However, the same CQs are expected to elicit weaker physiological responses than the RQs in the *guilty examinee*. A guilty suspect responds deceptively to both types of question, which in principle should lead to similar physiological responses to both types of question. However, RQs represent the most immediate and serious threat to the guilty examinee, which will make him/her more concerned about his/her lies to the RQs than to the probable lie questions.

Theoretical Assumptions of CQT

Several theories have been put forward by Davis (1961) to justify the CQT assumptions that guilty examinees will show the strongest responses to the RQs, whereas innocent examinees will show the strongest responses to the CQs. The *conflict theory* states that two incompatible reaction tendencies triggered at the same time produce a large physiological response. Lying to questions would trigger a conflict between "telling a lie" and "telling the truth;" the more serious the lie (e.g., the more serious the crime), the stronger the conflict between the two tendencies.

The *conditioned response theory* states that RQs that specifically address a certain transgression elicit a strong recollection of that transgression in guilty examinees, which creates strong physiological responses. The less-specific CQs will not elicit such a strong recollection in guilty examinees. The *threat of punishment theory* states that if the examinee fears serious negative consequences of being caught in the lie, the threat of punishment when lying will result in large physiological responses. Since the negative consequences for guilty examinees are thought to be larger in lying to RQs than in lying to CQs, the strongest physiological responses should be elicited by the RQs (National Research Council, 2003).

The National Research Council (2003, p. 213) describes these theoretical explanations as "… quite weak, especially in terms of differential fear, arousal, or other emotional states that are triggered in response to relevant or comparison questions." The problem is that none of the theoretical accounts rules out the possibility that innocent examinees show larger physiological responses to RQs than to probable-lie questions. Regarding the conflict theory, the

National Research Council suggested that a conflict between the examinee and examiner (e.g., an expectation of being falsely accused) could also evoke conflict tendencies in innocent examinees.

Regarding the conditional response theory, they suggested that RQs may evoke a variety of thought processes in innocent examinees, which could also create strong physiological responses. Consider the innocent suspect who is asked about the murder of his beloved wife. Mere mentioning of his wife may reawaken his strong feelings about her death, which will be recorded on the polygraph charts. Regarding the threat of punishment theory, the National Research Council suggested that innocent examinees may also associate serious negative consequences with not being believed when answering the RQs and that this could also result in strong physiological responses.

In sum, although several theoretical explanations for anxiety-based lie detection have been offered, they appear to be somewhat problematic, which raises doubts about the theoretical foundation of this type of lie detection.

Accuracy of CQTs

The accuracy of CQTs is difficult to establish. In laboratory experiments participants take part for the sake of the experiment. Examinees in such tests are not threatened by severe consequences of failing the tests and innocent examinees may therefore not reply as strongly to the RQs as they may do in real life. In field studies the polygraph examinations in real-life cases are examined. These studies typically suffer from a lack of "ground truth" – conclusive exonerating or incriminating evidence that can corroborate test outcome (Iacono, 2008a).

Ground truth is typically lacking since polygraph tests are carried out *because* there is no other evidence available. In field studies, because of the lack of conclusive evidence, confessions are used as ground truth. However, confessions are problematic as they are not independent from the test outcome (Iacono, 2008a; but see Honts, 1996). In fact, confessions and test outcomes are related to each other in the following way. Failing a polygraph test will lead to an interrogation. Confessions in such interrogations (including false confessions) will be considered as "hits." If a suspect does not confess, the case will not be included in the field study as only cases with confessions will be included. However, the suspects that are most likely not to confess in the post-polygraph interrogations are those who are actually innocent despite failing the test. Those incorrect polygraph outcomes will thus remain unnoticed. If an examinee passes a polygraph test, there will be no interrogation. If there is no interrogation there is unlikely to be a confession and the cases will not be included in the field study. Therefore, if an examinee was in fact guilty, this incorrect polygraph outcome will also remain unnoticed.

Vrij (2008) reviewed the accuracy rates reported in six published reviews of CQT laboratory research. Accuracy rates ranged from 74% to 82% in guilty examinees and from 60% to 66% in innocent examinees. Incorrect classifications of guilty examinees (incorrectly classified as being innocent) ranged from 7% to 10% and incorrect classifications of innocent examinees (incorrectly classified as being guilty) ranged from 12% and 16%. Vrij (2008) further reviewed the accuracy rates reported in six published reviews of CQT field research. (Seven reviews were included in Vrij's (2008) review, but we left Carroll (1999) out because, unlike all other reviews, inconclusive outcomes were not reported.) Accuracy rates ranged from 84% to 89% in guilty examinees and from 56% to 75% in innocent examinees. Incorrect classifications of guilty examinees ranged from 1% to 13% and incorrect classifications of innocent examinees ranged from 12% to 30%.

In summary, despite the uncertain theoretical underpinning, CQTs seem to be reasonably accurate, although errors are made particularly with innocent examinees. These errors occur when innocent examinees respond stronger to RQs than to CQs. When the National Research Council (2003) raised concerns about the theoretical foundation of anxiety-based polygraph testing, they had this problem in mind.

Recognition-Based Polygraph Test

The second approach in polygraph testing is the use of recognition-based polygraph tests. The theoretical foundation of such tests is the *orienting reflex* (Pavlov, 1927; Sokolov, 1963; Verschuere and Ben-Shakhar, 2011). An orienting reflex occurs when someone is confronted with a personally significant stimulus. The orienting reflex has its origin with Pavlov and it is described in psychophysiology as a response to novelty; the habituation of the orienting reflex is determined by personal significance. An orienting reflex probably occurs to facilitate an adaptive response by the individual to novel stimuli in the environment (National Research Council, 2003; Sokolov, 1963). Orienting reflexes result in physiological responses measured by the polygraph, such as an increase in electrodermal activity (EDA) (Nakayama, 2002) and a decline in heart rate (Raskin, 1979; Verschuere *et al.*, 2005), and also result in the occurrence of P300 brain waves measured via EEG (Rosenfeld, 2002).

The polygraph test based on this principle is called a Concealed Information Test (CIT) (Lykken, 1959, 1998; Verschuere *et al.*, 2011) and has the format of a multiple-choice test in which a critical item (often referred to as the probe) is presented together with several control items (often referred to as irrelevant items). Thus, in the Julie Appletoddler murder case described above, the examinee could be asked, "Julie has been found murdered. How was she killed? Was she drowned? Was she hit on the head with something? Was she shot? Was she beaten to death? Was she stabbed? Was she strangled?" If the guilty examinee recognizes the correct answer, an orienting reflex will occur. The innocent examinee, who does not know how Julie was killed, should show no orienting reflex to the probe compared with the irrelevant items during the test.

The theoretical foundation of the CIT receives more support among scholars than the theoretical foundation of the anxiety-based polygraph tests (Fiedler *et al.*, 2002). Yet, there are some concerns. The main concern expressed by the National Research Council (2003) is that reactions to familiar, personally significant probes and unfamiliar irrelevant items should be thought of as a continuum rather than a dichotomy. That is, suppose that the murderer used a revolver and suppose that the innocent examinee owns an unregistered pistol. That examinee may show responses to questions that mention handguns among the alternatives, even when he has no concealed knowledge about the murder weapon.

Honts' (2004) main concern about the CIT is related to the memory of guilty suspects. He argued that there is no scientific approach to predict what elements of a crime scene culprits are likely to remember and thus recognize during the test. For orienting reflexes to occur it is essential that culprits recognize the critical details during the test. Honts referred to eyewitness testimony research that shows that people generally have problems with accurately remembering details of the scene of crime, and that people's memory can be distorted by the remarks and comments of other people.

Apart from theoretical issues, there are some practical difficulties with designing a CIT. Selecting appropriate questions for a CIT is not an easy task. For a CIT to work, guilty examinees (i.e., culprits) should know the correct answers to the questions, otherwise they have no concealed knowledge; innocent examinees should not be able to figure out what the correct answers are, otherwise they will be mistakenly accused of having concealed knowledge. Culprits do not always know the correct answers; they may not have perceived the details the examiner is asking about or may have forgotten them by the time the test takes place.

One aspect that influences the culprit's memory is the time lapse between committing the crime and undergoing the CIT. The longer the period between the crime and the CIT, the more likely it is that the culprit has forgotten certain details; CIT examinations should be carried out as quickly as possible. Also, examiners may face particular difficulty in formulating appropriate questions for certain offenders. For example, serial offenders may have difficulty in recognizing details related to the specific incident under investigation (Nakayama, 2002). They may have committed so many crimes that they forgot exactly what happened during one particular crime they are asked about. With serial offenders, questions should be asked about items that are striking and uniquely associated with the crime under investigation (Nakayama, 2002), but this may be difficult to achieve.

Innocent examinees should not know the correct answers because if they do, they too could show a strong reaction. Innocent examinees do sometimes know the correct answers, because information about the critical items has been made available through the media, attorneys, or investigators. Regarding the latter, in many countries the police must inform suspects of the crime facts directly after arrest and this could include information that makes suspects aware of critical CIT items. Many suspects therefore could be aware of the critical items after being interviewed (Ben-Shakhar *et al.*, 2002). In addition, innocent examinees sometimes may guess the correct answer, such as when the correct answer is far more plausible than any of the alternatives.

Accuracy of CITs

Vrij (2008) reviewed the accuracy rates reported in six published reviews of CIT laboratory research. Accuracy rates ranged from 76% to 86% in guilty examinees and from 83% to 99% in innocent examinees. These accuracy rates compare favorably to CQTs. Only two CIT field studies have been published to date (Elaad, 1990; Elaad *et al.*, 1992), but they showed a different picture. Similar to laboratory studies, many innocent examinees were classified correctly (94% and 98%); however, the accuracy rates for guilty examinees were rather low (42% and 76%). Both field studies had limitations. For example, the number of questions asked was low (around two questions per CIT on average) and, as Ben-Skakhar and Elaad's (2003) review revealed, CIT examinations do increase in accuracy in correlation with the number of questions that are asked.

In summary, CIT polygraph tests have difficulty in pinpointing guilty examinees. This error occurs if a guilty examinee does not recognize the correct item in a multiple-choice test. Memory issues and a poor selection of items for the multiple-choice test have been given as an explanation for this problem.

Summary of Physiological Lie Detection

There are two major approaches in physiological lie detection: an *anxiety-based* approach and an *information-recognition* approach. The theoretical foundation for the anxiety-based approach (liars are more anxious) is weaker than the theoretical foundation for the information-recognition approach (liars show an orienting reflex), but research to date does not show that information-recognition tests are more accurate. The two approaches are vulnerable to different errors. Anxiety-based tests are vulnerable to a false accusation of an innocent examinee, which is an error that occurs if an innocent examinee is too anxious when responding to the RQs. Information-recognition tests are vulnerable to not identifying guilty examinees, which happens if a guilty examinee does not recognize the correct item in the test.

NON-VERBAL LIE DETECTION

Many different theoretical approaches exist to predict non-verbal cues to deception and three approaches in particular have been influential in lie detection research: the multifactor model (Zuckerman *et al.*, 1981), the self-presentational perspective (DePaulo, 1992; DePaulo *et al.*, 2003), and Interpersonal Deception Theory (IDT) (Buller and Burgoon, 1996). All three approaches have one important feature in common – the mere fact that people lie will not necessarily affect their non-verbal behavior. Sometimes, however, liars may show different behaviors than do truth-tellers and all three approaches emphasize that three factors could influence cues to deception. Compared with truth-tellers, liars may experience stronger emotions (particularly fear as a result of detection apprehension), liars experience higher levels of cognitive load, and liars are inclined to use more and different strategies to make a convincing impression on others.

In this section, we first discuss these three theoretical approaches and then discuss research that indicates non-verbal cues that are diagnostic cues to deceit. We provide some reasons as to why only a few cues appear to be related to deception and their relationship with deception is typically weak. We discuss the ability to detect deceit when people pay attention to someone's behavior. We then present two non-verbal lie detection tools promoted and used in real life, paying attention to "facial expressions of emotions including microexpressions" and the BAI.

Multifactor Model

According to Zuckerman *et al.* (1981), three factors may influence cues to deception: emotional reactions, cognitive load, and attempted behavioral control. Zuckerman *et al.* (1981) mentioned a fourth factor, "arousal;" however, as they acknowledge, arousal shows an overlap with the emotion factor. Each of these factors may influence a liar's non-verbal behavior and each emphasizes a different aspect of deception.

Emotional Reactions

Telling a lie is most commonly associated with three different emotions: fear, guilt, or delight (Ekman, 1985). Liars may feel guilty because they are lying, may be afraid of getting caught (which is also the basic assumption in the anxiety-based polygraph approach), or may be excited about having the opportunity to fool someone. The strength of these emotions depends on the personality of the liar and the circumstances under which the lie takes place (Ekman, 1985; Vrij, 2008). Importantly, the experience of guilt, fear, and excitement may influence a liar's behavior. For example, guilt may result in gaze aversion if the liar does not dare to look the target straight in the eye while lying. Fear and excitement may result in signs of stress, such as increases of movements, speech hesitations ("mm …" and "er …"), speech errors (stutters, repetition of words, omission of words), or an increased pitch. The stronger the emotion, the more likely that some of these behaviors will reveal deceit (Ekman, 1985).

Cognitive Load

Several factors may render lying cognitively more demanding than truth-telling. First, formulating the lie itself may be cognitively demanding. Liars must invent a story and monitor their fabrication so that it is plausible and adheres to everything the observer(s) know(s) or may find out. In order to maintain consistency, liars must remember what they have said to whom. Liars must also avoid making slips of the tongue and refrain from providing new leads (Vrij, 2008).

A second aspect of lying that adds to mental load is that liars are typically less likely than truth-tellers to take their credibility for granted (DePaulo et al., 2003; Gilovich et al., 1998; Kassin, 2005; Kassin et al., 2010; Kassin and Gudjonsson, 2004; Kassin and Norwick, 2004; Vrij et al., 2006c). As such, liars will be more inclined than truth-tellers to monitor and control their demeanor so that they will appear honest to the lie detector (DePaulo and Kirkendol, 1989). Third, because liars do not take credibility for granted, they may monitor the interviewer's reactions more carefully in order to assess whether they appear to be getting away with their lie (Buller and Burgoon, 1996; Schweitzer et al., 2002). Carefully monitoring the interviewer also requires cognitive resources.

Fourth, liars may be preoccupied by the task of reminding themselves to act and role-play (DePaulo *et al.*, 2003), which requires extra cognitive effort. The final three reasons relate to the fact that lies are more difficult to mentally access than truths, which adds to cognitive load. Deception requires a justification, whereas honesty does not (Levine *et al.*, 2010a), liars must suppress the truth while they are lying (Spence *et al.*, 2001), and whereas activating the truth often happens automatically, activating a lie is more intentional and deliberate (Gilbert, 1991; Walczyk *et al.*, 2003, 2005).

The extent to which lying is demanding often depends on the type of lie. Telling an outright lie may be more cognitively challenging than concealing information, and telling an elaborate lie may be even more demanding than providing short "Yes" or "No" answers. Lying may be more demanding when the lie is not well prepared or rehearsed.

People engaged in cognitively complex tasks make more speech hesitations (e.g., stutters) and speech errors, speak slower, pause more, and wait longer before giving an answer (Goldman-Eisler, 1968). Cognitive complexity also leads to fewer hand and arm movements (Ekman and Friesen, 1972), and to more gaze aversion, because looking the conversation partner in the eye can be distracting (Doherty-Sneddon *et al.*, 2002).

Attempted Behavioral Control

Liars may realize that observers use their behavioral reactions to judge whether they are lying and may, therefore, attempt to control their behavior in order to appear credible. To be successful, liars must suppress their nervousness while masking evidence of thinking hard to formulate an answer. They should also be able to show "honest-looking" behaviors and avoid "dishonest-looking" behaviors (Hocking and Leathers, 1980). These demands mean that liars may need to act, but they must also avoid displaying behavior that appears planned, rehearsed, or lacks spontaneity. According to this theoretical perspective, a liar's motivation and efforts to control behavior will increase when the stakes (negative consequences of getting caught or positive consequences of succeeding) increase (Ekman, 1985).

Self-Presentational Perspective

Zuckerman *et al.*'s (1981) perspective predicts that the more liars experience one or more of the three factors (emotion, cognitive load, behavioral control), the more likely it is that cues to deception will occur. These factors are present to a limited extent in the majority of lies that people tell (DePaulo *et al.*, 1996). In their self-presentational perspective, DePaulo *et al.* (DePaulo, 1992; DePaulo *et al.*, 2003) argue that emotions, cognitive load, and behavioral control may also influence the behavior of *truth-tellers*. Thus, liars may fear not being believed in high-stakes situations, but so will truth-tellers, because they also could face negative consequences if they fail to convince others. Given the similarities between liars and truth-tellers, this perspective predicts that clear, diagnostic non-verbal cues to deception are unlikely to occur.

According to DePaulo *et al.* (2003), liars and truth-tellers will succeed in their social interaction goals only if they appear sincere. The difference between lying and truth-telling is that the liar's claim to honesty is illegitimate and this lack of legitimacy has two implications: (1) Deceptive self-presentations may be less seen as truthful self-presentations and they may be presented less convincingly (e.g., because liars may have moral scruples, lack emotional investment in their false claims, or lack the knowledge and experience to back up their deceptive statements convincingly). (2) Liars typically experience a greater sense of awareness and deliberateness in their performances than truth-tellers, because they may take their credibility less for granted than truth-tellers. Deliberately trying to appear convincing may be counterproductive, however, as it may be viewed as rigid and over-controlled (DePaulo and Kirkendol, 1989).

IDT

A third perspective on deception, Buller and Burgoon's (1996) IDT, postulates that during face-to-face encounters, liars must accomplish numerous communication tasks simultaneously. They must produce a credible verbal message while projecting credible non-verbal behavior. They must also manage their emotions, attend to their conversation partner while keeping the dialogue running smoothly, send desired relational messages to their conversation partner and respond appropriately to what they say, and be discreet about any intentions to deceive their partner. IDT embraces Zuckerman *et al.*'s (1981) factors (emotion, cognitive load, and attempted behavioral control) as underlying reasons for cues to deceit (Burgoon *et al.*, 1999).

In addition, IDT emphasizes that when deception occurs in interactive contexts, it is not a unidirectional activity. Rather, both liar and receiver mutually influence each other (Burgoon *et al.*, 1996). According to IDT, receivers' behavior may influence senders' behavioral displays directly via synchrony, and indirectly by triggering behavioral adjustments (Burgoon *et al.*, 1999). Regarding the direct effects, when people communicate with each other, matching and synchrony may take place (Burgoon *et al.*, 1999; Chartrand and Bargh, 1999; Tickle-Degnen, 2006). People may mirror each other's posture or they may converge in how quickly and how loudly they speak. They may also reciprocate each other's gazing, nodding, accents, and smiling behavior (DePaulo and Friedman, 1998). This "chameleon effect" (Chartrand and Bargh, 1999) emerges even when strangers interact with each other and it typically occurs within a few minutes (Chartrand and Bargh, 1999).

The indirect effects are related to feedback from the receiver. When liars are exposed to negative feedback from the receiver, expressed through either verbal comments or through non-verbal behavior, liars may realize that their performance is lacking credulity. Consequently, liars may respond by making behavioral adjustments to diminish suspicions.

These three perspectives make clear that the relationship between lying and deceptive behavior is complex. Zuckerman *et al.*'s (1981) assumptions that liars may show signs of emotions and cognitive load seem straightforward, yet liars often do not experience emotions and high cognitive load (DePaulo *et al.*, 1996). DePaulo *et al.*'s (2003) self-presentation perspective stresses that such experiences are not the exclusive domain of liars – truth-tellers may experience them as well and may also display non-verbal cues associated with emotion or cognitive load.

The attempted behavioral control prediction is not straightforward given that the behaviors shown by deceptive senders, as a result of this deliberate control, will depend upon both their perceptions of what constitutes a credible non-verbal display and their acting skills in performing this display. Finally, the interactive approach of IDT implies that deceptive behavior may be influenced directly by the behavior of the receiver (a result of the chameleon effect) or indirectly influenced by the suspicions raised by the receiver (Burgoon *et al.*, 1999). The complex relationship between non-verbal behavior and deception makes it unlikely that clear, diagnostic, non-verbal cues to deception exist. Deception research, summarized in the next section, has supported this view.

Non-Verbal Cues to Deception: No Pinocchio's Nose

DePaulo *et al.*'s (2003) meta-analysis of cues to deception is the most comprehensive review assessing the consistency and strength of certain non-verbal cues indicating deception. Their meta-analysis includes 116 studies, although not all of these focus on non-verbal cues to deception, and includes 102 different non-verbal cues. Most of the studies were experimental studies where university students lied or told the truth for the sake of the experiment. Sometimes efforts were made to motivate the participants, such as by promising them a financial reward if they were convincing.

Significant findings emerged for 19 cues and these are listed in Table 7.1. Eight of those cues, listed in the bottom half of Table 7.1, were investigated in only a few studies and will not be discussed further. The cues are ranked in terms of their effect sizes (*d*). Cohen (1977) suggested that effect sizes of 0.20, 0.50, and 0.80 should be interpreted as small, medium, and large effects, respectively; the effect sizes in the meta-analysis were typically small. The highest effect sizes were found in the cues that were not often investigated (bottom half of Table 7.1), but if we concentrate on the cues that were investigated more often, the largest effect size was found for verbal and vocal immediacy, $d = -0.55$. The second highest cue, pupil dilation, obtained a *d*-score of 0.39 and most cues obtained effect sizes of around 0.20. In summary, one could conclude that non-verbal cues to deceit are typically faint and unreliable (for all effect sizes, information about the individual studies, definitions of the non-verbal cues, and the impact of several moderating factors on these cues, see DePaulo *et al.*, 2003).

TABLE 7.1   Non-Verbal Cues to Deception

Cue	d
Verbal and vocal immediacy	−0.55
Pupil dilation	0.39
Discrepant/ambivalent	0.34
Verbal and vocal uncertainty	0.30
Nervous, tense	0.27
Vocal tension	0.26
Chin raise	0.25
Pitch, frequency	0.21
Lip pressing	0.16
Illustrators	−0.14
Facial pleasantness	−0.12
Cues based on a small number of studies	
Changes in foot movements	1.05
Pupillary changes	0.90
Genuine smile	−0.70
Indifferent, unconcerned	0.59
Specific hand and arm movements	−0.36
Seems planned, not spontaneous	0.35
Intensity of facial expression	−0.32
Direct orientation	−0.20

Derived from DePaulo et al. (2003).

Support for the Theoretical Perspectives

The results of the meta-analysis provide general support for the theoretical perspectives discussed previously. Several cues (pupil dilation, nervousness, vocal tension, and pitch) indicate that liars may be more tense than truth-tellers. The findings that liars make fewer illustrators (movements tied to speech directly and serving to illustrate what is being said verbally; Ekman and Friesen, 1969) suggest that lying is somewhat more cognitively demanding than truth-telling. The remaining cues reveal that liars appear less immediate, more ambivalent, less involved, and more uncertain, and this fits well with the predictions that liars endorse their statements less convincingly than do truth-tellers (DePaulo *et al.*, 2003) and that liars often fail to control their behavior in a convincing manner (DePaulo *et al.*, 2003; Zuckerman *et al.*, 1981).

In the overwhelming majority of deception studies, however, no interaction took place between sender and receiver, making them inappropriate to test Buller and Burgoon's (1996) IDT. Studies that have employed an interactional interview style have provided mixed results regarding whether liars avoid displaying suspicious behaviors (Levine and McCornack, 1996). It may be that liars aim to suppress all behaviors that they believe are suspicious, but they often do not succeed (Buller *et al.*, 1996; Vrij, 2008).

Reasons for Few Non-Verbal Cues to Deception

The complex relationship between non-verbal behavior and deception, outlined above, already predicted that research would reveal only a few, and usually weak, relationships between non-verbal cues and deception. There are more explanations and this section highlights two of them.

Some Cues are Overlooked

One explanation for not finding consistent and reliable cues to deception is that some non-verbal cues are overlooked by researchers, sometimes because the scoring systems used to measure them are not detailed enough. Ekman (1985) has identified a number of different smiles, including a distinction between felt and false smiles. Felt smiles include smiles in which the person actually experiences a positive emotion, whereas false smiles are deliberately contrived to convince another person that a positive emotion is felt, when in fact it is not. Felt smiles are accompanied by the action of two muscles: the zygomatic major which pulls the lip corners upwards towards the cheekbone, and the orbicularis oculi which raises the cheek and gathers skin inwards from around the eye socket. The latter change produces bagged skin below the eyes and crow's-feet creases beyond the eye corners. In false smiles, the action of the orbicularis oculi muscle causing the effects around the eye is often missing (Frank *et al.*, 1993).

Ekman *et al.* found that truth-tellers make more felt smiles than liars, whereas liars make more false smiles than truth-tellers. When the distinction between felt and false smiles is not made, truth-tellers seem to smile as frequently as liars (Ekman *et al.*, 1988). Other differences between felt and false smiles include that false smiles are more asymmetrical, appear too early or too late, often last longer, and have a less consistent duration (Ekman, 1988; Ekman and Friesen, 1982; Ekman and O'Sullivan, 2006; Ekman *et al.*, 1990; Frank *et al.*, 1993). Similar patterns may occur with different behaviors. Non-verbal communication researchers have identified numerous types of hand movements (Bavelas *et al.*, 1995; Ekman and Friesen, 1969, 1972; McNeill, 1985, 1992). For example, based on the work of Efron (1941), Ekman and Friesen (1969) made a distinction between five movement categories: emblems, illustrators, affect displays, regulators, and adaptors. In their later writings (Ekman and Friesen, 1972; Friesen *et al.*, 1979), they restricted themselves to only three of these categories – emblems, illustrators, and adaptors – because "these three classes include all hand movement except for those times when the hand moves simply to establish a new position or rest" (Friesen *et al.*, 1979, p. 99). This three-class categorization is often used in deception research and all three categories appear in DePaulo *et al.*'s (2003) meta-analysis.

Ekman and Friesen (1972) make further distinctions into eight types of illustrators, but these subdivisions are typically not used by deception researchers. In one experiment, however, Caso *et al.* (2006) did differentiate between different types of illustrators. Truth-tellers described objects they had in their possession, whereas liars had to imagine that they had these objects in their possession. Liars made fewer deictic movements (pointing gestures) than did truth-tellers, perhaps due to the lack of real objects they could point at, but liars made more metaphoric gestures, which are typically made when people describe abstract ideas (McNeill, 1992). Illustrators as a whole entity (i.e., all the different types combined) were not linked to deception. Like smiles, it was only when specific types of distinctions were made among subclasses of behavior that deception cues were detected.

Hillman *et al.* (2012) examined a gesture that has never been examined before: speech prompting. People sometimes may find it difficult to "think of the right words" when they talk. This may result in gestures that occur when the person is trying to think of what to say next. Such speech-prompting gestures may accompany utterances such as "umm …" or "and then …," or occur during a pause in the dialogue. They may be small repetitive movements such as tapping, flapping, or small circular movements, or possibly large movements such as rehearsing the shape of an item of clothing before describing it verbally. Hillman *et al.* (2012) found that liars use more speech-prompting gestures than truth-tellers.

Recent research showed that even eye contact may reveal deceit. Eye contact is world-wide the most popular cue to deceit and the vast majority of people all over the world believe that liars look away. Charles Bond headed an ambitious "beliefs about cues to deception" project that was published under the name "The Global Deception Research Team" (Global Deception Research Team, 2006). Comprising an international team of researchers from 58 countries, each researcher collected data from 20 male and 20 female adult residents of their country. The participants were asked to write down their response to the question: "How can you tell when people are lying?" Respondents mentioned 103 different cues, of which nine were given by more than 15% of the participants. Of particular note was the notion that a liar cannot maintain eye contact and this belief was expressed by 64% of the participants; gaze aversion was the most frequently mentioned belief in 51 out of 58 countries.

To measure eye contact in deception research, researchers have measured extensively the number of seconds that the participant looks into the eyes of the interviewer (Vrij, 2008, discussed 45 such studies). No reliable pattern of findings emerged from that research (DePaulo *et al.*, 2003; Mann *et al.*, 2012, 2013; Vrij, 2008). However, significant differences between truth-tellers and liars emerged when it was examined whether participants made the impression of deliberately attempting to seek eye contact with the interviewer (Mann *et al.*, 2012, 2013). Liars showed more deliberate eye contact than truth-tellers. Deliberate eye contact focuses on the tendency to monitor ("check out") the interviewer and measures whether the interviewee made the impression of deliberately attempting to seek eye contact with the interviewer. Liars are more inclined than truth-tellers to do this for two reasons discussed above: to appear convincing and to monitor the interviewer.

"Deliberate eye contact" differs from traditional "eye contact" as it is not measured in terms of number of seconds. It is a subjective measurement and it can occur when someone looks into the eyes just a fraction longer than what would normally be expected in such a situation. This short, but vital, prolonged eye contact probably remains unnoticed when the total number of seconds that someone looks into the eyes of the interviewer during the entire interview is calculated. That is, in an interview that lasts several minutes, the few seconds of prolonged eye contact would not make much difference. Deliberate eye contact is a somewhat more subjective cue than traditional eye contact. However, although subjective, deliberate eye contact is often unmistakable. As in attraction, when a person holds the eye of the object of his/her desire for just a little longer than normal, such eye contact, while brief, is often noted by the receiver as deliberate. However, in an interview situation this is most likely interpreted (as intended) as a sign of candor. Deliberate eye contact grasps the theoretical concepts probably better than traditional eye contact measures. For example, if liars are inclined to monitor the interviewer they probably would like to do this in a subtle way.

Individual and Situational Differences

Another reason for the limited number of non-verbal indicators of deceit may be that a meta-analysis cannot capture signs of deceit at an individual level. That is, different individuals may give their lies away in different ways (DePaulo *et al.*, 2003) and such idiosyncratic cues do not become apparent when the focus is across studies. Similarly, cues to deception could be dependent on the situational context for the lie. A meta-analysis that accumulates findings across contexts would not apprehend those trends either.

Further, more cues to deception are likely to occur when the stakes are high rather than low. In high-stakes situations, liars may feel stronger emotions, may experience more cognitive load, and may be more motivated to manage their behavior in order to appear credible. In their meta-analysis, DePaulo *et al.* (2003) compared higher-stakes studies (e.g., studies where financial incentives were promised if the participant appeared credible) with lower-stakes studies. Some cues to deception, such as an increase in blinking, a decrease in leg and foot movements, and an increased speech rate appeared only in higher-stakes situations. The differences between liars and truth-tellers were still small, however, perhaps because a high-stakes situation will also affect truth-tellers or, alternatively, because the stakes were still not high enough in these laboratory-based higher-stakes studies.

What happens in situations where the stakes are really high, such as when guilty suspects lie in police interviews, when smugglers go through customs at airports, or when adulterous husbands are challenged by their wives? In order to examine how liars respond in high-stakes situations, one of few options is to analyze such real-life high-stakes situations. It is difficult, however, to capture such lies on tape and to establish the *ground truth* in such situations (i.e., to know for certain that someone was actually lying or telling the truth; Vrij and Mann, 2003), making such studies difficult to undertake.

Mann *et al.* (2002) published a comprehensive study about people's behavior in real-life high-stakes situations. They examined the behavioral responses of 16 suspects while they lied and told the truth during their police interviews. The police interviews were videotaped and the tapes were made available for detailed scoring of the suspects' behavioral responses. The suspects were interviewed in connection with serious crimes such as murder, rape, and arson, and were facing long custodial sentences if found guilty. Regarding the ground truth, clips of video footage were selected where other sources (reliable witness statements and forensic evidence) provided conclusive evidence that the suspect lied or told the truth.

Results revealed that, compared with when they told the truth, the suspects exhibited more pauses, fewer eye blinks, and fewer hand and arm movements (by male suspects) than when they lied. Indicators of being tense (such as fidgeting and gaze aversion) did not emerge. These indicators are the behavioral patterns that police officers typically expect in lying suspects.

Mann *et al.*'s (2002) results suggest that the suspects' cues to deception were more likely the result of increased cognitive load than of nervousness. The strongest evidence for this was the reduction in eye blinks during deception. Research has shown that nervousness results in an increase in eye blinking (Harrigan and O'Connell, 1996), whereas increased cognitive load results in a decrease in eye blinking (Wallbott and Scherer, 1991). The apparent predominance of cognitive load processes compared with emotional processes in those suspects is perhaps not surprising. Many of the suspects included in Mann *et al.*'s (2002) study had regular contact with the police and were probably familiar with the police interview situation, thereby decreasing their nervousness. Suspects in police interviews are typically of below average intelligence, however (Gudjonsson, 2003). There is evidence that less intelligent people will have particular difficulty in inventing plausible and convincing stories (Ekman and Frank, 1993). Alternatively, it may well be that the suspects were more tense when they lied, but that this was momentarily suppressed when they had to think hard. There is evidence that cognitive demand results in an automatic and momentary suppression of arousal (Leal *et al.*, 2008).

Accuracy Rates in Non-Verbal Lie Detection

Bond and DePaulo (2006) reviewed people's ability to detect deceit when paying attention to non-verbal behavior and their meta-analysis included 206 studies in which a total of 24,483 observers participated. These observers achieved an average accuracy rate of 54%, whereas just tossing a coin would lead to 50%. Vrij (2008) examined whether professionals, such as law enforcement personnel, were any better at this task than laypersons (typically college students). The results of 79 studies that included laypersons as observers and 28 studies that included professionals as observers were compared. There was no difference between the two groups. The laypersons achieved an accuracy rate of 54.27%, whereas the professionals achieved a 55.91% accuracy rate. The only difference between professionals and laypersons was that the professionals were more confident in their judgments than the laypeople (Vrij, 2008). As explained above, non-verbal cues of deceit may be more likely to occur when the stakes are higher. Based on O'Sullivan *et al.*'s (2008) selection of lie detection experiments, Vrij and Granhag (2012) compared accuracy rates in 13 low-stakes and 14 high-stakes samples. High-stakes truths and lies were indeed more easily detected (67%) than low-stakes truths and lies (55%).

There are, broadly speaking, two explanations for these generally poor accuracy rates (particularly in low-stakes studies): either observers rely on invalid non-verbal cues when attempting to detect deceit, or the non-verbal cues displayed by liars are too faint and unreliable. In their meta-analysis of lie detection research, Hartwig and Bond (2011) tested both explanations and found that poor accuracy rates were mainly attributable to the absence of clear-cut diagnostic cues to deceit.

Specific Non-Verbal Lie Detection Tools

Specific non-verbal lie detection tools have been developed to detect truth-tellers and liars, and we will discuss the two most well-known tools: examining facial emotional expressions and the BAI. Both tools are based on the emotion approach.

Facial Emotional Expressions

Over the years, Paul Ekman has argued that facial expressions of emotion betray liars (Ekman, 1985). According to Ekman, aspects of facial communication are beyond control and can betray a deceiver's true emotion via microexpressions (lasting 1/25 to 1/5 of a second) of that emotion. Ekman has claimed that his system of lie detection, which includes the observation of facial expressions of emotions including microexpressions, can be taught to anyone to achieve an accuracy of more than 95% (Ekman, 2006a, b).

Ekman has never published empirical data to back up this claim and he has never published data showing that observers achieve this accuracy. In fact, he has not published empirical data showing that facial (micro) expressions of emotions are diagnostic indicators of deceit. The latter has been investigated by a group of Canadian researchers. In an experimental laboratory study, Porter and ten Brinke (2008) found that microexpressions of emotions occurred in only 14 out of the 697 analyzed facial expressions and that six of those 14 microexpressions were displayed by truth-tellers. In a second experimental laboratory study, microexpressions occurred only in a minority of cases, and were again equally common in truth-tellers and liars (ten Brinke *et al.*, 2012). Those findings suggest that a lie detection tool based on microexpressions of facial emotions is largely ineffective.

Someone may argue that facial (micro) expressions of emotions only occur in high-stakes lies. In another research project, the same group of Canadian researchers examined a real-life high-stakes situation (ten Brinke and Porter, 2012; ten Brinke *et al.*, 2012). They examined the facial expressions (rather than microexpressions) of 52 individuals who pleaded on television to the public for the return of their missing relative. Half of the pleaders were later convicted of murdering that person. The "grief muscles" (corrugator supercilii and depressor anguli oris) were more often contracted in genuine pleaders than in deceptive pleaders and full contractions of the frontalis (failed attempts to appear sad) occurred more frequently in liars than in truth-tellers. However, based on these behaviors only a modest number of liars (around 56%) and more truth-tellers (around 82%) were classified correctly, resulting in a modest 69% overall accuracy (ten Brinke *et al.*, 2012).

In a second paper about this high-stakes situation, the facial expressions of 78 individuals (including the 52 individuals from ten Brinke *et al.*, 2012) were examined. More liars than truth-tellers expressed disgust, surprise, and happiness, whereas more truth-tellers than liars expressed sadness. However, the percentages were not impressive, as not many liars expressed disgust (40%), surprise (58%), or happiness (50%), whereas between 16% and 23% of truth-tellers also expressed these emotions. The same applied to sadness. Not many truth-tellers expressed sadness (52%), whereas a substantial amount of liars (26%) did. These findings do not support Ekman's claim that facial (micro) expressions of emotions can correctly classify more than 95% of truth-tellers and liars.

To complicate matters, facial (micro) expressions of emotions are difficult to spot even by trained observers, which raises the question whether there are easier ways to detect lies in these individuals. As a starting point, ten Brinke *et al.* (2012) reported that the genuine pleads were significantly longer (593 seconds) than the deceptive pleads (315 seconds), so perhaps speech cues (which are easier to spot than facial expressions) provide better clues to deception.

BAI

The second non-verbal lie detection tool is the BAI (Inbau *et al.*, 2001, 2013). Blair and Kooi (2004) claimed that over 150,000 police personnel have been trained in the use of BAI throughout the world and the tool is frequently used in the United States (Vrij *et al.*, 2006b). BAI investigators examine nervous behaviors and the BAI can therefore be classified as an emotion-based tool. However, there are other theoretical assumptions (Horvath *et al.*, 2008), such as liars' lack of understanding of how truth-tellers actually behave, and liars' reluctance to share much information out of fear that it will lead to deception detection.

The BAI protocol includes asking non-threatening questions, investigative questions, and behavior-provoking questions, the latter consisting of 15 questions, such as "Did you take the money?" (in the case of an alleged theft of money) and "Do you know who took the money?" In the BAI it is assumed that guilty suspects are more likely than truth-tellers to display nervous behavior, such as crossing their legs, shifting about in their chair, and performing grooming behavior while answering the question, whereas innocent suspects are more likely than guilty suspects to lean forward, establish eye contact, and use illustrators to reinforce their confidence in their statements. In addition, according to Inbau *et al.* (2001, 2013), guilty suspects are more likely to answer quickly and their answers will sound less sincere. Finally, guilty suspects are more likely to exhibit anxiety-reducing behavior such as shifting posture in their chair.

Horvath *et al.* (1994) tested the efficiency of BAI in a field study. Their study included 60 videotaped interviews with real suspects in which the BAI protocol was employed. When inconclusive outcomes were disregarded, an overall accuracy rate of 86% was obtained. This is an impressive accuracy rate, but the study had an important limitation. The ground truth in the study was unclear. That is, it could not be established with certainty that the innocent suspects were truly innocent and the guilty suspects were truly guilty. A lack of ground truth is a well-documented and widespread problem in deception field studies (Iacono, 2008a). In fact, Horvath *et al.* (1994) reported that the ground truth was established by "incontrovertible evidence" in only *two* of the 60 cases that they analyzed. They concluded that "If it were possible to develop ground truth criteria in a large number of cases such as occurred in these two instances, the interpretation of findings would be less problematic" (Horvath *et al.*, 1994, p. 805). This conclusion probably does not go far enough. The results of a study in which the ground truth is established in only 3% of the cases (two out of 60 cases) are simply unreliable.

We tested the working of BAI in a controlled laboratory experiment and our results directly refuted Inbau *et al.*'s (2001, 2013) predictions: liars were *less* likely to cross their legs and *less* likely to shift posture than truth-tellers (Vrij *et al.*, 2006b). In a subsequent lie detection experiment, we showed observers these videotaped BAI interviews. The observers were unable to distinguish the truth-tellers from the liars (Vrij *et al.*, 2007). Moreover, in Kassin and Fong's (1999) experiment half of the observers received training in the visual BAI cues. The trained observers' performance on a subsequent lie detection test was worse than that of untrained participants.

The finding that paying attention to the visual BAI cues *impairs* lie detection performance was supported by a field study where police officers judged the veracity of statements made by murder, rape, and arson suspects who told the truth and lied during their real-life (videotaped) police interviews (Mann *et al.*, 2004). The police officers were also asked which cues they pay attention to when they attempt to detect deceit. Mann *et al.* (2004) found a negative relationship between officers reportedly attending to the Inbau *et al.* cues (averting gaze, shifting posture, making self-adaptors, etc.) and accuracy in the lie detection task. That is, the more the officers endorsed Inbau *et al.*'s (2001, 2013) view on cues to deception, the worse they became at distinguishing between truths and lies. In other words, there is evidence that endorsing the information about visual cues to deception discussed in the BAI protocol is counterproductive and makes people worse lie detectors.

The three dominant theories about non-verbal cues to deception all assume that liars more than truth-tellers may experience emotions or cognitive load and attempt to make a convincing impression. Non-verbal cues to deceit have been extensively examined throughout the years, but the pattern that emerges from that vast body of research is generally pessimistic: non-verbal cues to deceit are typically faint and unreliable. Owing to the lack of diagnostic non-verbal cues to deceit, observers typically obtain poor accuracy rates when they attempt to discriminate between truth-tellers and liars on the basis of non-verbal behavior. Two non-verbal lie detection tools are sold to and used by practitioners, and they are both based on the premise that liars are more nervous than truth-tellers. There is no evidence that either of these tools actually works.

VERBAL LIE DETECTION

In non-verbal lie detection, the "emotion" approach appears to be dominant and anxiety-based tests are also the most frequently used tests in physiological lie detection. In contrast, verbal lie detection is not based on the emotion approach. Instead, the underlying assumptions in verbal lie detection are that liars have to think harder and that they try more than truth-tellers to make a convincing impression. Those two theoretical approaches are also used to explain behavioral cues to deception, whereas the non-verbal lie detection tools appear to focus more on emotion-related cues. In verbal lie detection research a third theoretical explanation is used – a memory-based approach, which is unique to verbal cues to deception.

The underlying assumption of this memory approach is that people remember experienced events differently from fabricated events and therefore talk about them in different ways. The lie detection tool based on cognitive load and impression management is called SVA, and the lie detection tool based on memory is called Reality Monitoring. In this section, we discuss how these tools work and how accurate they are. We then discuss recent research that sheds light on an alternative approach to lie detection – the verifiable detail approach. We conclude the section with a brief discussion of an atheoretical approach that appears to be very popular among practitioners: Scientific Content Analysis (SCAN).

SVA

SVA is a verbal lie detection tool designed to determine the credibility of *child* witnesses testimonies in trials for *sexual offences*. It is not surprising that a technique has been developed to verify whether or not a child has been sexually abused. It is often difficult to determine the facts in an allegation of sexual abuse, since often there is no medical or physical evidence. Frequently the alleged victim and the defendant give contradictory testimony, and often there are no independent witnesses to give an objective version of events. This makes the perceived credibility of the defendant and alleged victim important. The alleged victim is in a disadvantageous position if he/she is a child, as adults have a tendency to mistrust statements made by children.

SVA assessments are accepted as evidence in some North American courts and in criminal courts in several West-European countries, including Germany, the Netherlands, and Sweden (Vrij, 2008). The tool originates from Sweden (Trankell, 1972) and Germany (Undeutsch, 1982), and consists of four stages (Vrij, 2008): (1) a case-file analysis, (2) a semistructured interview; (3) a criteria-based content analysis (CBCA) that systematically assesses the quality of the transcribed interviews, and (4) an evaluation of the CBCA outcome via a set of questions (Validity Checklist).

The core of the technique is Stage 3, in which trained evaluators assess the presence of 19 different criteria in the transcribed interview (Köhnken and Steller, 1988; Steller and Köhnken, 1989). Each of those criteria is assumed to occur more frequently in truthful than deceptive accounts. According to CBCA theory, some criteria are likely to indicate genuine experiences because these criteria are typically too difficult to fabricate (Köhnken, 1996, 2004). Therefore, statements that are coherent and consistent (*logical structure*), whereby the information is not provided in a chronological time sequence (*unstructured production*) and which contain a significant amount of detail (*quantity of detail*), are more likely to be true. Moreover, possible indicators of truthfulness include if the child reports details that are not part of the allegation but are related to it (*related external associations*, e.g., a witness who describes that the perpetrator talked about various women he had slept with and the differences between them), when the witness describes his/her feelings or thoughts experienced at the time of the incident (*accounts of subjective mental state*), or when the witness describes his/her interpretation of the perpetrator's feelings, thoughts, or motives during the incident (*attribution of perpetrator's mental state*).

Other criteria are more likely to occur in truthful statements for motivational reasons. Truthful persons will not be as concerned with impression management as deceivers. Compared with truth-tellers, deceivers will be keener to construct a report that they believe will make a credible impression on others and will leave out information that, in their view, will damage their image of being a sincere person (Köhnken, 1996, 2004). As a result, a truthful statement is more likely to contain information that is inconsistent with the stereotypes of truthfulness.

The CBCA list includes five of these so-called "contrary-to-truthfulness-stereotype" criteria (Ruby and Brigham, 1998), including: *spontaneous corrections* (corrections made without prompting from the interviewer) and *admitting lack of memory* (expressing concern that some parts of the statement may be incorrect: "I think," "Maybe," "I am not sure," etc.). Although SVA is designed to evaluate children's testimonies in alleged sexual abuse cases, it has been argued that the technique can also be used to evaluate the testimonies of adults who talk about issues other than sexual abuse as the underlying factors of cognitive load and impression management also apply to adults (Köhnken, 2004; Porter and Yuille, 1996; Ruby and Brigham, 1997; Steller and Köhnken, 1989). Research findings have supported this view.

Accuracy of CBCA

CBCA has been widely researched and more than 50 empirical studies about this method have been published to date, mainly with adult participants (Vrij, 2008). Those studies demonstrate that CBCA analyses can be useful for lie detection purposes. In 20 studies, researchers computed total CBCA scores and compared these scores for truth-tellers and liars. The hypothesis that truth-tellers will obtain significantly higher total CBCA scores than liars was supported in 16 out of the 20 studies (80%). Only in one of the 20 studies (5%) did truth-tellers obtain lower CBCA scores than liars (Ruby and Brigham, 1998), but the protocol used in that study differed in several ways from the typical CBCA approach, including that assessments were based on watching videos rather than reading transcripts. In that respect, Ruby and Brigham's (1998) study is not a fair test of the CBCA method. Regarding the individual criteria, Criterion 3, *quantity of details*, received the most support.

The amount of detail was calculated in 29 studies and in 22 of those (76%) truth-tellers included significantly more details in their accounts than liars. Moreover, in not a single study did truth-tellers include significantly fewer details in their statements than liars. Finally, the extent to which CBCA analyses can discriminate liars from truth-tellers was examined in 24 studies. The average accuracy rate in these studies was 71% for detecting truths and 71% for detecting lies. In other words, there is evidence that CBCA can be effective in discriminating between truths and lies.

However, all these studies were laboratory studies and there are reasons to believe that the use of SVA is more difficult in real life. The problem is that CBCA scores are affected by factors other than the veracity of the statement. For example, older children produce statements that typically contain more CBCA criteria than younger children (Buck *et al.*, 2002), statements are unlikely to contain many CBCA criteria if the interviewer did not give the child enough opportunity to tell the whole story (Hershkowitz *et al.*, 1997), and highly suggestible children may give an inaccurate account when leading questions are asked (Bull, 2010; Fisher, 2010).

The fourth and final phase of the SVA method is to examine whether any of these alternative explanations may have affected the presence of the CBCA criteria in the transcripts. A checklist – the Validity Checklist – has been compiled for this purpose, which comprises 11 issues that are thought to possibly affect CBCA scores (Raskin and Esplin, 1991). By systematically addressing each of the issues addressed in the Validity Checklist, the evaluator explores and considers alternative interpretations of the CBCA outcomes. Each affirmative response that the evaluator gives to an issue raises a question about the validity of the CBCA outcome.

There are reasons to believe that applying the Validity Checklist is sometimes problematic. For example, some issues, such as *susceptibility to suggestion*, are difficult to measure. To examine a child's susceptibility to suggestion the interviewer is recommended to ask the witness a few leading questions at the end of the interview (Yuille, 1988). Interviewers should only ask questions about irrelevant peripheral information, because asking questions about central information could damage the quality of the statement. Being allowed only to ask questions about peripheral information is problematic, as it may say little about the witness' suggestibility regarding core issues of his/her statement. Children show more resistance to suggestibility for central parts than peripheral parts of an event (Dalton and Daneman, 2006).

It is difficult, if not impossible, to determine the exact impact that many issues have on CBCA scores. For example, in one study SVA raters were instructed to take the age of the child into account when calculating CBCA scores (Lamers-Winkelman and Buffing, 1996). Nevertheless, several criteria positively correlated with age. In other words, even after being instructed to correct the CBCA scores for age, the results still showed age-related effects, with older children obtaining higher CBCA scores than younger children.

Given these difficulties in measuring the issues and in examining the exact impact of these issues on CBCA scores, it is clear that the Validity Checklist procedure is more subjective and less formalized than the CBCA procedure. It is therefore not surprising that if two experts disagree about the truthfulness of a statement in a German criminal case, they are likely to disagree about the likely impact of Validity Checklist issues on that statement (Kohnken, personal communication, 1997). One field observation revealed that Swedish experts sometimes use the Validity Checklist incorrectly and this could be due to the difficulties with applying it (Gumpert and Lindblad, 1999). (1) Although SVA experts sometimes highlight the influence of Validity Checklist issues on children's statements in general, they do not always discuss how these issues may influence the statement of the particular child they are asked to assess. (2) Although experts sometimes indicate possible external influence on statements, they are inclined to rely upon the CBCA outcome, and tend to judge high-quality statements as truthful and low-quality statements as fabricated.

In sum, although SVA assessments are used as evidence in (criminal) courts to evaluate the veracity of child witnesses' testimonies in trials for sexual offences, the accuracy of these assessments is unknown. However, research has shown that CBCA-trained evaluators make mistakes in classifying truth-tellers and liars, and that the use of the Validity Checklist is problematic for a variety of reasons.

Reality Monitoring

A second verbal lie detection approach – Reality Monitoring – is only used by scientific researchers (and not by professionals) and has a strong theoretical underpinning. Reality Monitoring is based upon memory theory. The core of Reality Monitoring is that memories of experienced events differ in quality from memories of imagined events (Johnson and Raye, 1981, 1998). Memories of real experiences are obtained through perceptual processes and are therefore likely to contain, among other things, *perceptual information* and *contextual information.* Perceptual information may contain details of sound, smell, taste, touch, or visual details, whereas contextual information relates to spatial details (details about where the event took place and about how objects and people were situated in relation to each other, e.g., "He stood behind me") and temporal details (details about the time order of events, e.g., "First he switched on the video-recorder and then the TV," and about the duration of events). These memories are usually clear, sharp, and vivid.

Accounts of imagined events are derived from an internal source and are therefore likely to contain *cognitive operations*, such as thoughts and reasoning ("I must have had my coat on as it was really cold that night"). They are usually vaguer and less concrete. Although Reality Monitoring is not developed for lie detection purposes, it is used as such by researchers. Their claim is that "experienced events" reflect truth-telling, whereas "imagined events" reflect deception. Obviously, this is not always the case. A person who gives a false alibi by describing something he/she truly experienced, albeit at a different time than he/she claims to have done, is also describing an experienced event when he/she lies. Nevertheless, when Masip *et al.* (2005) and Vrij (2008) reviewed the Reality Monitoring deception research (all laboratory studies), they found that lie and truth accuracy rates were similar to those obtained with CBCA research. That is, in the ten studies in which Reality Monitoring was used to discriminate liars from truth-tellers, the average truth accuracy rate was 72% and the average lie accuracy rate was 66% (Vrij, 2008). In terms of individual criteria, the idea in particular that truth-tellers recall more perceptual information and contextual embeddings received support. In sum, research findings suggest that Reality Monitoring can be effective in discriminating between truths and lies.

There are restrictions in using a Reality Monitoring veracity assessment tool. For example, the tool cannot be used with young children. In some circumstances children do not differentiate between fact and fantasy as clearly as adults do, for several reasons including that children have a richer imagination than adults (Lindsay, 2002). Children may therefore be better than adults at imagining themselves performing acts.

It is probably also difficult to use the Reality Monitoring tool when people talk about events that happened a long time ago. Over time, cognitive operations may develop in memories of experienced events because they facilitate the remembering of events (Roediger, 1996). Someone who drove fast in a foreign country may try to remember this by recalling the actual speed the speedometer indicated; alternatively, he/she could remember this by logical reasoning and by deducing that he/she must have driven fast because he/she drove on the motorway. Imagined memories, on the other hand, can become more vivid and concrete over time if people try to visualize what may have happened (Manzanero and Diges, 1996).

Verifiable Details

An innovative approach in verbal lie detection is to examine whether details can be verified (Nahari et al., 2012b). Listeners use content qualities to distinguish between truths and lies and the richer an account is perceived to be in detail, the more likely it is to be believed. Liars may be aware that people will analyze their accounts in terms of richness in detail and therefore will try to provide false details in order to make an honest impression. However, although providing details helps to generate an honest impression, it also puts liars at risk, because investigators can verify such details and often do so. Liars are known to be aware of this danger (Masip and Ces, 2011; Nahari et al., 2012a) and thus may be inclined to avoid mentioning details. This puts liars in a dilemma. On the one hand, they are motivated to include many details so that they make an honest impression and, on the other hand, they are motivated to avoid providing details to minimize the chances of being caught.

A strategy that compromises between these two conflicting motivations is to provide details that cannot be verified. For example, it is much more difficult for the police to verify whether someone actually saw a black Audi driving by on a particular street than to verify whether someone actually made a phone call at a specific time. In alignment with this, Nahari et al. (2012b) found that, when attempting to make an honest impression, liars compared with truth-tellers provide more details that are difficult to verify and fewer details that are easy to verify.

The verifiability approach has benefits compared with the CBCA and Reality Monitoring approaches. It is more compatible with liars' strategic actions and gives liars a more difficult task to succeed in lying. Regarding liars' strategic actions, someone could argue that not all liars lack imagination (Merckelbach, 2004), which is one of the underlying assumptions of CBCA. Someone could also argue that not all liars talk about imagined events in their alibis (the underlying assumption of Reality Monitoring), but that many of them will refer to an event that they have actually experienced (albeit at another time that they claim they have). In theory, those explanations should nullify differences in detail between truth-tellers and liars (Gnisci *et al.*, 2010).

The verifiability approach should still be effective to discriminate between truth-tellers and liars even if liars have a rich imagination and even if they discuss previous experiences. Regarding giving liars a more difficult task, when liars realize that investigators use CBCA or Reality Monitoring to assess their credibility they may adjust their stories in order to sound convincing to such investigators. They will succeed if they include details that appear credible to CBCA and Reality Monitoring investigators but that cannot be verified, such as recalling a (made-up) conversation. They will succeed because their story becomes richer in quality in CBCA and Reality Monitoring terms, whereas it does not contain any more evidence. In contrast, if a liar knows that the investigator is after details that can be verified, the only way to convince the investigator is by including more detail that can be verified. In other words, the only option is to provide more evidence, which can subsequently be verified by the investigator. As such, the verifiability approach should be less open to countermeasures than using the more conventional CBCA and Reality Monitoring tools.

SCAN

A third verbal lie detection tool is SCAN, developed by the former Israeli police lieutenant and polygraph examiner Avioam Sapir. SCAN is very popular among practitioners but has not been researched much (Nahari *et al.*, 2012a). SCAN is atheoretical. It is assumed that truth-tellers and liars differ from each other on SCAN criteria (for a description of SCAN criteria, see Nahari *et al.*, 2012b) but no theoretical rationale is given for these assumptions.

In the SCAN procedure, the examinee is asked to write down in detail all his/her activities during a critical period of time in such a way that a reader without background information can determine what actually happened. The handwritten statement is then analyzed by a SCAN expert on the basis of a list of predetermined criteria. Sapir (1987/2000) claims that some SCAN criteria are more likely to occur in truthful than in deceptive statements (e.g., denial of allegations, use of self references), whereas other criteria are more likely to occur in deceptive than in truthful statements (e.g., change in language, missing information).

SCAN users refer to Driscoll's (1994) field study as evidence that SCAN works and, indeed, the accuracy rate obtained in that study was high at 83%. However, a serious limitation is that the ground truth could not be established. Nahari *et al.* (2012a) tested the efficiency of SCAN in a laboratory experiment. Truth-tellers truthfully wrote down their activities during the last half hour, whereas liars were asked to fabricate a story. The statements were analyzed with SCAN and, by way of comparison, also with Reality Monitoring. SCAN did not distinguish truth-tellers from liars above the level of chance, but Reality Monitoring did. With Reality Monitoring analyses 71% of truth-tellers and liars were correctly classified.

There is some overlap between SCAN and CBCA in the criteria that are examined. For example, the criteria "spontaneous corrections," "lack of memory," and "extraneous information" appear on both lists. Intriguingly, the predictions about how these criteria differ between truth-tellers and liars are contradictory. In CBCA the occurrence of these cues are perceived as indictors of truth, whereas in SCAN the same criteria are seen as indicators of deceit. Research regarding these individual criteria give support only to the CBCA assumptions (Vrij, 2008). In sum, although SCAN is popular among practitioners and widely used, there is no evidence that it actually works.

It is assumed that verbal differences between truth-tellers and liars are the result of liars having to think harder, trying more to make a convincing impression, or differences in memory. It is further assumed that liars more than truth-tellers avoid mentioning details that can be verified by investigators. Verbal veracity tools that are based on such theoretical principles (CBCA and Reality Monitoring) can distinguish truths from lies with around 70% accuracy. A third tool, SCAN, is popular among practitioners but is atheoretical. There is no evidence that SCAN actually works.

FUNCTIONAL MAGNETIC RESONANCE IMAGING-BASED LIE DETECTION

During the last decade, researchers have been using fMRI to monitor brain activity during deception (see also Johnson in Chapter 6 of this volume). Referring back to the logic described in Figure 7.2, the main assumption of this approach has been that brain measures may be better able to detect deception than peripheral psychophysiological measures (or behavioral measures) because the link between deceptive mental states and the measured variables is more direct: instead of going through a long inferential chain to infer deception, this approach postulates that process D is a brain process that can be measured directly with fMRI – after all, deception is a process that takes place in large part in our brain.

There are three classes of postulated neural processes engaged during deception:

(1) *Cognitive control processes* such as working memory, memory-retrieval conflict monitoring, and response inhibition. Those processes refer to the higher complexity of producing lies relative to telling the truth.
(2) *Memory-relate processes*, which refer to the fact that lies and truths may differ in how well they are encoded, and in the richness and quality of these memories.
(3) *Social cognitive processes*, referring to the idea that a successful liar needs to take into account the perspective of the target of the lie in order to be able to deceive that target.

It is not difficult to recognize that these processes are not new, but they are essentially neurocognitive versions of the processes already discussed by some of the purely cognitive theories described earlier.

fMRI measures the changes in regional cerebral blood flow due to neural activity taking place over the course of several seconds. Brain activation to specific classes of events (e.g., deceptive or honest answers) is typically measured by time-locking the fMRI time series to the onset of the events of interest and by averaging several tens of trials to achieve sufficient signal-to-noise ratio. The actual analyses of event-related fMRI time series are complicated by the fact that fMRI signals are due to slow hemodynamic changes and so there is substantial signal overlap between temporally adjacent trials that needs to be taken into account in the statistical models. fMRI has outstanding spatial resolution and so it can determine the location of brain processes in space with exquisite precision (on the order of a cubic millimeter). This would seem to imply that fMRI should be ideal to detect deception directly, since one should be able to probe the precise brain regions where deceptive mental states are implemented. However, as we will see below, to a large extent fMRI is just a tool that inherits the intrinsic limitations of the paradigms that it uses: not surprisingly, the inherent theoretical and practical limitations of CQT or CIT paradigms do not disappear simply by using fMRI, and flawed fMRI paradigms are still flawed paradigms.

fMRI Studies

Many fMRI studies on deception have been conducted over the last decade, using a variety of paradigms (e.g., Abe *et al.*, 2006, 2007, 2008; Bhatt *et al.*, 2008; Davatzikos *et al.*, 2005; Gamer *et al.*, 2007, 2009; Ganis *et al.*, 2003, 2009, 2011; Kozel *et al.*, 2004, 2005, 2009; Langleben *et al.*, 2002, 2005; Lee *et al.*, 2002, 2005, 2008; Mohamed *et al.*, 2006; Monteleone *et al.*, 2009; Nose *et al.*, 2009; Nunez *et al.*, 2005; Phan *et al.*, 2005; Spence *et al.*, 2001, 2004, 2008). Some of these fMRI studies used variants of the classic CIT paradigm described earlier, whereas others used variants of the differentiation-of-deception paradigm (Furedy *et al.*, 1988), in which participants are asked to lie half of the time and to tell the truth on the other half, ideally using the same questions or statements for the two conditions.

A few studies employed hybrid designs, such as by mixing elements of the CQT and differentiation-of-deception paradigms (e.g., Kozel *et al.*, 2005). (There were attempts to use this technique with autonomic measures, although they were not successful; Driscoll *et al.*, 1987.) Most fMRI studies have focused only on group data analyses, with only a handful reporting single individual accuracy rates. Unfortunately, numerous fMRI studies have been affected by design flaws (including basic ones such as absent or inadequate stimulus counterbalancing), which makes their interpretation difficult. This section will review a representative sample of fMRI studies, with an emphasis on studies that examined accuracy in single individuals.

The first published fMRI study used a differentiation-of-deception approach in which participants were asked questions about their daily activities and were told when to lie or tell the truth about them (Spence *et al.*, 2001). The main result of the study was that deceptive responses engaged ventral parts of the lateral prefrontal cortex more strongly than honest responses. These brain regions are often engaged in tasks that require the inhibition of motor response and so the pattern of results was interpreted as reflecting the need to inhibit a truthful response when producing a lie – a common interpretation of these kinds of findings. An additional brain region that was more engaged during deceptive than honest responses was the medial prefrontal cortex including the anterior cingulate, which is often engaged during tasks in which there is conflict between competing responses (among other things). These three brain regions were found to be related to deception in many subsequent studies. This is the first clear example showing that a cognitive control process (process D from Figure 7.1) monitored via brain imaging could be used to infer deception.

The study by Kozel *et al.* (2005) is an example of a hybrid paradigm. In this study, subjects took part in a mock-crime scenario during which they "stole" either a watch or a ring from a drawer. During the fMRI scan, four types of questions were asked: differentiation-of-deception parallel lie/truth questions about whether they had taken the ring (or the watch), neutral general questions with unambiguous "Yes" or "No" answers, and control questions like those used in the traditional CQT (e.g., "Have you ever cheated on a test?"). The lie versus truth comparison (data for the control questions were not reported) revealed activation in brain regions including the anterior cingulate, the orbitofrontal cortex, and the dorsolateral prefrontal cortex. These differences were generally attributed to the more demanding executive processes recruited during deception, including decision making and response inhibition (Kozel *et al.*, 2005). The first published fMRI work using a variant of the CIT paradigm employed playing cards as stimuli (Langleben *et al.*, 2002). Before the fMRI scan, participants were asked to pick one of three sealed envelopes. Unbeknownst to the participants all envelopes contained the same probe card, the Five of Clubs. The participants were told to look at the card inside the envelope in secret, to memorize it, put it in their pocket, and lie about possessing it during the following scan. During the scan, the probe card and many irrelevant cards were presented one at a time. On most trials, the question "Do you have this card?" was shown on top of each card, and participants had to respond by lying about the probe card and telling the truth about all other cards. There were also infrequent control cards during which the question "Is this the Ten of Spades?" was shown and to which the participants had to respond honestly. These trials were included to force participants to actually read the question on top of each card.

Comparing activation to the probe and irrelevant cards revealed activation in the medial prefrontal cortex, encompassing the anterior cingulate cortex, and sensorimotor regions in the left hemisphere (including the left inferior parietal lobule). There was no activation in the ventrolateral prefrontal cortex. Again, these results were interpreted in terms of response monitoring and inhibition processes required during deceit.

Interestingly, a subsequent CIT study with an almost identical card paradigm using the same stimuli found a somewhat different pattern of results (Phan et al., 2005). Importantly, and unlike the previous study (Langleben et al., 2002), the probe and irrelevant cards were counterbalanced across participants. In this study, stronger activation to the probe card than to the irrelevant card was found in the dorsal medial prefrontal cortex (not including the anterior cingulate cortex this time), ventrolateral prefrontal cortex, right superior temporal sulcus, and left parietal cortex. As for the other studies, these results were also interpreted as reflecting increased engagement of executive processes during deception, but no serious explanation was put forward for the discrepancy with the findings by Langleben and collaborators just described. Small differences in the paradigms, such as that 50 different cards were used as irrelevants in this study (as opposed to the 11 used by Langleben et al., 2002), differences in stimulus counterbalancing across subjects, or differences in the timing of the trials may have played a role.

Two subsequent studies (Gamer et al., 2007, 2009) also used variants of the CIT protocol with playing cards and bank notes. One card (Jack of Spades) and one banknote (20 euros) served as probes in the respective conditions. Four cards and four euro bank notes served as irrelevants. No counterbalancing of stimuli across participants was used, so the same probe and irrelevant cards were used for all participants. In the first study, the right insula and adjacent inferior frontal cortex and the right middle cingulate gyrus were more engaged by probes than irrelevants. Another region showing more activation to probes than irrelevants, discussed only in the conjunction analysis of the second study (Gamer *et al.*, 2009), was in the left inferior frontal cortex. No differences were found in the anterior cingulate cortex. This study also interpreted the right prefrontal activation as indexing response conflict monitoring and inhibition, but pointed out an alternative memory retrieval interpretation.

This alternative interpretation was tested in a subsequent study with the same stimuli, but with a different task in which participants pressed the same button to all items, thus minimizing the role of motor response interference and corresponding response inhibition processes. Contrasting probes and irrelevants revealed differential activation in the same left and right inferior frontal cortical regions found in the previous study, but also in two additional regions: the right supplementary motor area and the right supramarginal gyrus. Given that response selection processes were minimized in this study, the differences between probes and irrelevants in lateral prefrontal cortex were attributed mostly to memory-related processes, such as episodic retrieval. Unfortunately, as for other studies, it is difficult to know how much of these results were due to intrinsic stimulus differences between the probe and the irrelevant items since there was no counterbalancing of stimuli across participants and no formal control group using participants without concealed knowledge.

Another study (Nose *et al.*, 2009) also used a CIT protocol based on playing cards, but they did include a control group without concealed knowledge. The task was to detect a target card (the Eight of Diamonds) and not to disclose any information about the probe (Five of Clubs). The results showed stronger activation to probes than irrelevants in the concealed information group in the ventrolateral prefrontal cortex, bilaterally, left inferior frontal gyrus, right middle frontal gyrus, and right inferior parietal lobule. No differential activation was found in the anterior cingulate cortex and no differences were found in the group without concealed knowledge. The region that showed the most robust difference was the right ventrolateral prefrontal cortex. Again, the authors attributed differential activation in this region to the need to inhibit any external signs of recognition that may have revealed knowledge of the probe.

Finally, a recent CIT study used dates as stimuli (Ganis *et al.*, 2011). Participants were instructed to lie about knowing their date of birth (probe) and tell the truth about knowing irrelevant dates. Since the correct response to the probe and irrelevant was always "No" (which was a deceptive answer for probes, but a truthful answer for irrelevant), a target date was revealed to participants before the study that required an honest "Yes" response. This ensured that the participants did not simply press the "No" button mindlessly throughout the study. A no-knowledge control condition was included, within-subject, in which only irrelevant and target dates were presented. The results showed stronger activation in the concealed knowledge (relative to the no-knowledge) condition for probes than irrelevants in numerous areas, including the ventrolateral prefrontal cortex, bilaterally, the medial prefrontal cortex, including the anterior cingulate, the middle cingulate gyrus, and the inferior parietal lobule bilaterally. The most robust differences were found in the medial and ventrolateral prefrontal cortex. The interpretation put forward in this study focused on memory retrieval and novelty detection processes, emphasizing the high relative saliency of the probes.

Given the relatively small number of fMRI studies conducted so far on the topic and the design problems with many of these studies, it is hard to determine whether noise or systematic factors are responsible for differences between studies. For example, why is the anterior cingulate or the left ventrolateral prefrontal cortex not more active during deceptive than honest responding in all studies?

A meta-analysis encompassing all paradigms (Christ *et al.*, 2009) found stronger activation for deceptive than honest responses in some of the same regions described above, including the lateral prefrontal and insular cortex, bilaterally, the anterior cingulate, and the inferior parietal lobule, bilaterally. Many of these regions overlapped with those found in meta-analyses of executive processes such as working memory, inhibitory control, and task switching – all processes that are likely to be involved to some extent in deception tasks, but clearly suggesting that these regions are not specific for deception.

Perhaps the safer conclusion so far is that lateral and medial prefrontal cortices are engaged by a non-trivial combination of memory- and response-selection-related processes unfolding during deception tasks and that this information could be used to detect deception in suitable paradigms.

Accuracy of fMRI Methods

An important issue for the applicability of fMRI methods is whether they are sufficiently accurate in single participants. Although most studies have examined only group data, some have also estimated the accuracy of the methods in single participants. Davatzikos *et al.* (2005) re-analyzed the CIT data from a previous study (Langleben *et al.*, 2005) using high-dimensional non-linear pattern classification methods (support vector machines [SVMs]) to discriminate patterns of brain activation associated with producing deceptive and truthful responses. This method employs information from the entire brain simultaneously. In one analysis, single trials for all participants were modeled together, training a classifier on 99% of the trials and testing its performance on the remaining 1%. Results showed 87.9% accuracy (90% sensitivity, 85.8% specificity).

An additional cross-validation analysis trained a classifier on the average data for 21 participants (each participant providing two datasets: one for deceptive and one for honest responses) and tested it on the left-out participant. The results indicated that predictive accuracy at testing was 88.6% (90.9% sensitivity, 86.4% specificity). The single-participant analyses performed by Kozel *et al.* (2005) found accuracy rates of about 90%. Monteleone *et al.* (2009) performed one-out single-participant analyses on the CIT data collected in a previous study (Phan *et al.*, 2005), and found that the region that best discriminated between deceptive and honest cases was the medial prefrontal cortex, which could identify 71% of participants as lying without false alarms.

Nose *et al.* (2009) employed a one-out cross-validation analysis on activation data from the right ventrolateral prefrontal region, and found that they could discriminate individuals with and without concealed knowledge with 84.2% accuracy (the rate was identical for specificity and sensitivity). Ganis *et al.* (2011) used a one-out approach and linear SVMs applied to activation in three regions found in the main contrast between probes and irrelevants: the left and right ventrolateral prefrontal cortex, and medial prefrontal cortex. The results showed that these three regions could be used to discriminate concealed knowledge and no-concealed knowledge cases with 100% accuracy (the rate was identical for sensitivity and specificity).

Based on these few studies using different analytic methods, the average sensitivity and specificity is about 85%, but there is substantial variability across studies.

Replicability of fMRI Methods

A direct comparison of brain-imaging methods with other methods is difficult because of the different temporal and spatial resolutions and signal-to-noise levels associated with different methods. Nonetheless, one can ask the more limited question of whether the key results replicate across studies and laboratories. One replication of a study using exactly the same methods, procedures, and equipment is the study by Ganis *et al.* (2011). In this study, a different group of subjects (region-of-interest group) performed the same tasks as the main group for the purpose of defining regions of interest to be used in the main analysis. Seven out of 14 activation foci, the largest ones, overlapped between the two groups to an extent of more than 40 voxels. Some of these regions were summarized earlier. Since it was possible to classify participants at 100% accuracy in the main group using regions of interest defined in the second group, one could conclude that fMRI replicability may not be an issue, provided that the same stimuli, tasks, and equipment are used. Comparable results were found by a few other studies (e.g., Kozel *et al.*, 2005, 2009).

The seemingly large differences in results found even by the same group of researchers when using paradigms that appear to differ only slightly with each other is, however, potentially problematic. For example, Langleben *et al.* (2005) tried to replicate their own original work, with small changes to the paradigm, and found a very different pattern of results. On the one hand, the anterior cingulate and inferior parietal activations originally found were not replicated. On the other hand, the parietal lobes showed greater activation during honest than deceptive responses – the opposite of what was found in the first study (Langleben *et al.*, 2002). Although the dependence of brain-imaging results on small changes in paradigms may not necessarily be problematic, it may simply reflect the exquisite sensitivity of the technique. Currently, there is no clear understanding of how subtle changes in paradigms affect the precise pattern of brain activation. This is, of course, a relevant issue for application of the methods to complex real-life situations.

Generalizability of fMRI Methods

The extent to which the laboratory results can be generalized to field situations is currently unknown: (1) fMRI methods have to deal with the same problems that affect other methods, such as that our memories are not perfectly reliable and that memory is a constructive process, and (2) in addition to the important issue of the reliability of memory, in field situations, potential suspects are likely to use countermeasures – methods used to confound deception detection procedures.

Although traditional physical countermeasures would not work with neuroimaging techniques (other than by overtly disrupting fMRI data recording with head motion, which would be easy to detect), mental countermeasures may be highly problematic. Standard CIT paradigms using psychophysiological measures can be disrupted by countermeasures in which participants generate covert responses to the irrelevant stimuli. For example, one could imagine a specific motor reaction each time one sees a specific irrelevant item, effectively making these stimuli as salient as probes.

Similar effects of countermeasures previously shown to be effective with event-related potentials (Rosenfeld *et al.*, 2004) and peripheral physiological measures (Honts *et al.*, 1996) have been found recently in an fMRI study with a CIT using the participant's date of birth as the probe (Ganis *et al.*, 2011). The countermeasures used in this study entailed training participants in associating specific covert actions (e.g., imperceptibly moving the index finger of the left hand) with specific irrelevants. Deception detection rates were 100% without countermeasures, but only four out of 12 participants (33%) with concealed knowledge but also using these kind of mental countermeasures were classified correctly. Although more research on the topic is needed, the effect of these countermeasures is likely to be even stronger when using less salient probes (Rosenfeld *et al.*, 2006) and with participants motivated to beat the test, as in real situations.

The data summarized in this section suggests that fMRI methods currently are not obviously superior to more traditional methods for deception detection. This, together with the observation that they are much more expensive and difficult to administer than traditional methods, makes current fMRI methods rather unappealing for real-life applications. However, one should remember that research in this field is only around a decade old, and so it is likely that accuracy, reliability, and robustness against countermeasures will improve in the future by devising better paradigms and analyses and with progress in brain-imaging techniques. Nonetheless, it is clear from the evidence discussed here that much more research is needed before these methods can begin to compete with more traditional techniques and show potential for forensic applications.

COMPARISON OF PHYSIOLOGICAL, NON-VERBAL, VERBAL, AND BRAIN ACTIVITY LIE DETECTION

A comparison of the accuracy rates of the four methods of lie detection discussed in this chapter shows that fMRI and physiological lie detection achieve the highest accuracy rates (around 85% for both, mostly in laboratory-based CIT tests), followed by verbal lie detection (CBCA and Reality Monitoring, around 70%) and analyses of non-verbal behavior (around 55%). We can think of three reasons as to why fMRI and physiological lie detection yield the best results. First, they measure the underlying principles (i.e., process D, described in the Introduction) more directly. For example, the assumption that liars are more anxious than truth-tellers plays an important role in both physiological lie detection and non-verbal lie detection, but anxiety is more directly measured via physiological indices than through behavior. Similarly, the engagement of cognitive control processes during deception may be more directly measured via brain imaging than by observing behavior.

Second, fMRI and physiological lie detection occur under more controlled settings than non-verbal and verbal lie detection. For example, individual differences are better accounted for in fMRI and physiological lie detection (through the use of CQs or irrelevant items) than in non-verbal and verbal lie detection. Third, the understanding in physiological lie detection is that cues to deception can be elicited via specific paradigms and interview protocols. The idea that the questioning matters has long been neglected in non-verbal and verbal lie detection. In those domains the emphasis was on which non-verbal and verbal cues distinguish truth-tellers from liars, whereby no specific attention was paid to the questions that need to be asked to elicit such cues. This has changed recently, and the importance of questioning is now also acknowledged in verbal and non-verbal lie detection. The Strategic Use of Evidence (SUE) technique, discussed by Hartwig *et al.* in Chapter 1 of this volume, is a good example of this new approach, as are the approaches based on imposing cognitive load and asking unanticipated questions that are outlined in the next section.

In turn, verbal lie detection achieves better accuracy rates than non-verbal lie detection. It may be that non-verbal cues are simply not diagnostic enough to be used in veracity assessments (Hartwig and Bond, 2011; Levine *et al.*, 2010b) and, indeed, research has shown that non-verbal cues are typically less diagnostic of deceit than verbal cues (DePaulo *et al.*, 2003; Vrij, 2008). In part, this can be explained by taking the strategies of truth-tellers and liars into account. Two studies examining strategies revealed that truth-tellers and liars appear to use the *same non-verbal* strategies, but *different verbal* strategies (Hartwig *et al.*, 2010; Vrij *et al.*, 2010b).

Regarding non-verbal strategies, both truth-tellers and liars believed that signs of nervousness would appear suspicious. They therefore reported that they would try to suppress displaying signs of nervousness during the interview. Regarding verbal strategies, truth-tellers were mainly concerned with giving as much detail about what had happened as possible. In contrast, liars were keen not to give too much detail because to do so increases the chance of saying something that the interviewer knows or can find out to be untrue. The result of these different verbal strategies is that truth-tellers' stories are likely to be more detailed than liars' stories and research supports this claim (DePaulo *et al.*, 2003; Vrij, 2008).

Of course, not all verbal lie detection tools work and only those that are based on sound theory will do so (CBCA and Reality Monitoring). In other words, an essential element for cues to deception to occur is that they are based on sound theory.

INTERVIEWING TO DETECT DECEPTION THROUGH NON-VERBAL AND VERBAL CUES

In physiological lie detection it has been acknowledged for a long time that the type of questioning matters in lie detection. For example, as we reported above, the RIT is widely criticized for asking the wrong questions. Only in the last ten years has it been acknowledged that questioning also matters in non-verbal and verbal lie detection, and research about effective interview techniques has started to emerge. One interview approach is the SUE, which is discussed by Hartwig *et al.* in Chapter 1 of this volume. Two other approaches – the "imposing cognitive load" and "asking unanticipated questions" – are discussed here. Both approaches are embedded in cognitive load theory. The assumption is that it is possible to ask questions that raise *cognitive load* more in liars than in truth-tellers.

Imposing Cognitive Load

As we discussed above, lying can be more cognitively demanding than truth-telling (Vrij *et al.*, 2006a). First, formulating the lie may be cognitively demanding. A liar needs to invent a story, and must monitor his/her fabrication so that it is plausible and adheres to everything the observer(s) know or may find out. Moreover, liars must remember what they have said to whom in order to maintain consistency. Liars should also refrain from providing new leads (Vrij, 2008). Second, liars are typically less likely than truth-tellers to take their credibility for granted (Kassin *et al.*, 2010). As such, liars will be more inclined than truth-tellers to monitor and control their demeanor in order to appear honest to the investigator, and such monitoring and controlling is cognitively demanding.

Third, because liars do not take credibility for granted, they may monitor the *investigator's* reactions carefully in order to assess whether they appear to be getting away with their lie (Buller and Burgoon, 1996), which requires cognitive resources. Fourth, liars may be preoccupied with the task of reminding themselves to role-play (DePaulo *et al.*, 2003), which requires extra cognitive effort. Fifth, deception requires a justification, whereas honesty does not (Levine *et al.*, 2010a, b), and contemplating this justification adds to cognitive load. Sixth, liars also have to suppress the truth while they are fabricating, and this is also cognitively demanding (Spence *et al.*, 2001). Finally, while activation of the truth often happens automatically, activation of the lie is more intentional and deliberate (Walczyk *et al.*, 2003), and thus requires mental effort.

An investigator could exploit the differential levels of cognitive load that truth-tellers and liars experience to discriminate more effectively between them. Liars who require more cognitive resources than truth-tellers will have fewer cognitive resources left over. If cognitive demand is further raised, which could be achieved by making additional requests, liars may not be as good as truth-tellers in coping with these additional requests (Vrij *et al.*, 2010a, 2011).

One way to impose cognitive load is by asking interviewees to tell their stories in reverse order. This increases cognitive load because it runs counter to the natural forward-order coding of sequentially occurring events, and it disrupts reconstructing events from a schema (Gilbert and Fisher, 2006). Another way to increase cognitive load is by instructing interviewees to maintain eye contact with the interviewer. When people have to concentrate on telling their stories – like when asked to recall what has happened – they are inclined to look away from their conversation partner (typically to a motionless point), because maintaining eye contact is distracting (Doherty-Sneddon and Phelps, 2005).

In one experiment, half of the liars and truth-tellers were requested to recall their stories in reverse order (Vrij *et al.*, 2008); in another experiment, half were asked to maintain eye contact with the interviewer (Vrij *et al.*, 2010c). In both experiments no instruction was given to the other half of the participants. More cues to deceit emerged in the reverse-order and maintaining eye contact conditions than in the control conditions. Observers who watched these videotaped interviews could distinguish between truths and lies better in the reverse-order and maintaining eye contact conditions than in the control conditions. For example, in the reverse-order experiment, 42% of the lies were correctly classified in the control condition, well below that typically found in verbal and non-verbal lie detection research, suggesting that the lie detection task was difficult. Yet, in the experimental condition, 60% of the lies were correctly classified, which is more than typically found in this type of lie detection research.

An alternative way to impose cognitive load on liars is to ensure that in a given interview setting truth-tellers will provide more information. Talkative truth-tellers raise the standard for liars, who also need to become more talkative to match truth-tellers. Liars may be reluctant to add more information out of fear that it gives their lies away. They may also find it too cognitively difficult to add as many details as truth-tellers do, or if they do add a sufficient amount of detail the additional information may be of lesser quality or may sound less plausible. We recently successfully tested two ways of increasing the amount of detail truth-tellers generate. In one experiment two interviewers were used (Mann *et al.*, 2013). The second interviewer was silent, but showed different demeanors during the interview. In one condition he was supportive throughout (e.g., nodding his head and smiling), in a second condition he was neutral, and in a third condition he was suspicious (e.g., frowning). Being supportive during an interview facilitates talking and encourages cooperative witnesses (e.g., truth-tellers) to talk (Bull, 2010; Fisher, 2010; Memon *et al.*, 2010). Indeed, truth-tellers provided most detail in the supportive condition and only in that condition did they provide significantly more detail than liars (Mann *et al.*, 2013).

In a second experiment, half of the participants were primed and were asked before being interviewed to listen to an audiotape in which someone gave a detailed account of an event unrelated to the participant's interview (Leal *et al.*, 2013). Participants were informed that the purpose of the priming audiotape was to give them an idea of what a detailed account actually entails. The hypothesis was that if participants hear a model of a detailed answer, they are more likely to provide a more detailed answer themselves. The underlying assumption of this hypothesis was that interviewees' expectations about how much detail is expected from them is likely to be inadequate. Indeed, particularly when conversation partners do not know each other well, interviewees tend to give short answers (Fisher, 2010; Fisher *et al.*, 2011). Perhaps investigators can alter the participants' expectations about how much detail is required by providing them with a model answer. Leal *et al.* (2013) found that although truth-tellers and liars did not differ from each other in the non-primed condition, they did so in the primed condition, and primed truth-tellers gave more detailed answers that also sounded more plausible.

In sum, imposing cognitive load can be achieved in two different ways: (1) by using interventions that increase the difficulty to recall information (reverse order and maintaining eye contact) and (2) by using interventions that makes examinees more talkative.

Asking Unanticipated Questions

A consistent finding in deception research is that liars prepare themselves when anticipating an interview (Hartwig *et al.*, 2007). This strategy makes sense. Planning makes lying easier and planned lies typically contain fewer cues to deceit than do spontaneous lies (DePaulo *et al.*, 2003). However, the positive effects of planning will only emerge if liars correctly anticipate which questions will be asked. Investigators can exploit this limitation by asking questions that liars do not anticipate. Although liars can refuse to answer unanticipated questions, such "I don't know" or "I can't remember" responses will create suspicion and should therefore be avoided if the questions are about central (but unanticipated) aspects of the target event.

To test the unanticipated questions technique, pairs of liars and truth-tellers were interviewed individually about an alleged visit to a restaurant (Vrij *et al.*, 2009). The conventional opening questions (e.g., "What did you do in the restaurant?") were anticipated, whereas the request to sketch the layout of the restaurant was not. (Anticipation was established with the interviewees after the interview.) Based on the overlap (similarity) in the two pair members' drawings, 80% of the liars and truth-tellers were classified correctly (the drawings were less alike for the pairs of liars than pairs of truth-tellers), whereas on the basis of the conventional questions the pairs were not classified above chance level. A difference in overlap between anticipated and unanticipated questions further indicated deceit. Pairs of truth-tellers showed the same amount of overlap in their answers to the anticipated and unanticipated questions, whereas liars did not. They showed significantly more overlap in their answers to the anticipated questions than in their answers to the unanticipated questions.

Comparing the answers to anticipated and unanticipated questions can also be used to detect deceit in individual liars, as two recent experiments demonstrated. In the first experiment, truth-tellers and liars were interviewed about their alleged activities in a room (Lancaster *et al.*, 2012). Expected questions (e.g., "Tell me in as much detail as you can what you did in the room?") were followed by unexpected spatial and temporal questions. In the second experiment, truth-tellers and liars were interviewed about their alleged forthcoming trip (Warmelink *et al.*, 2012). Expected questions about the purpose of the trip (e.g., "What is the main purpose of your trip?") were followed by unexpected questions about transport (e.g., "How are you going to travel to your destination?"), planning ("What part of the trip was easiest to plan?"), and the core event ("Keep in mind an image of the most important thing you are going to do at this trip. Please describe this mental image in detail?"). Liars are likely to have prepared answers to the expected questions and may therefore be able to answer them in considerable detail. Liars will not have prepared answers for the unexpected questions and may therefore struggle to generate detailed answers to them. Indeed, in both experiments, compared with truth-tellers, liars gave significantly more detail to the expected questions and significantly less detail to the unexpected questions. This resulted in a larger decline in detail between anticipated and unanticipated answers in liars than in truth-tellers.

Another effective way to use the unanticipated questions technique when assessing individuals is asking the same question twice in different formats (Leins *et al.*, 2011). When liars have not anticipated the question, they have to fabricate an answer on the spot. A liar's memory of this fabricated answer may be more unstable than a truth-teller's actual memory of the event. Therefore, liars may contradict themselves more than truth-tellers. This approach works best if the questions are asked in different formats, as Leins *et al.* (2012)

have demonstrated. In Leins *et al.*'s (2012) experiment, truthful participants had visited a room, whereas deceptive participants did not. In the interview, however, all participants claimed to have visited the room. Participants were asked to verbally recall the layout of the room twice, to sketch it twice, or to verbally recall it once and to sketch it once. Liars contradicted themselves more than truth-tellers, but only in the verbal recall/drawing condition. Truth-tellers have encoded the topic of investigation along more dimensions than liars. They therefore find it easier than liars to recall the event more flexibly (along more dimensions).

CONCLUSIONS

In this chapter we demonstrated the importance of theory in lie detection. Only lie detection tools that are based on sound theory have the ability to elicit different responses from truth-tellers and liars, and only when the underlying theory is known can its strengths and weaknesses be identified. For example, anxiety-based lie detection tests are based on the assumption that liars, but not truth-tellers, will be anxious when discussing the crime. However, truth-tellers also can be anxious and, indeed, anxiety-based tests tend to classify some truth-tellers as liars. Recognition-based lie detection tests assume that liars, but not truth-tellers, will recognize details about the crime. However, liars do not always recognize these details and therefore recognition-based lie detection tests tend to classify some liars as truth-tellers.

A theoretical approach to lie detection demonstrates the importance of asking the right questions in lie detection interviews. If the questions relate to sound theoretical principles, they have the ability to elicit different responses from truth-tellers and liars, which facilitates the investigators' task of discriminating between them, as a recent wave of verbal and non-verbal lie detection research has shown. Questions that are not related to theory lack such an ability.

Since fMRI-based measures have the *a priori* advantage of monitoring more directly processes that are associated with deception, they could be critical for developing and testing deception theories. However, in terms of accuracy rates, fMRI lie detection has not been shown to be more accurate than the traditional lie detection measures to date. To fulfill their potential, fMRI researchers should pay closer attention to the research paradigms and ideas used in verbal and non-verbal deception research.

References

Abe, N., Suzuki, M., Mori, E., Itoh, M., Fujii, T., 2007. Deceiving others: distinct neural responses of the prefrontal cortex and amygdala in simple fabrication and deception with social interactions. Journal of Cognitive Neuroscience 19, 287–295.

Abe, N., Okuda, J., Suzuki, M., Sasaki, H., Matsuda, T., Mori, E., Fujii, T., 2008. Neural correlates of true memory, false memory, and deception. Cerebral Cortex 18, 2811–2819.

Abe, N., Suzuki, M., Tsukiura, T., Mori, E., Yamaguchi, K., Itoh, M., Fujii, T., 2006. Dissociable roles of prefrontal and anterior cingulate cortices in deception. Cerebral Cortex 16, 192–199.

Aron, A., Dutton, D.G., Aron, E.N., Iverson, A., 1989. Experiences of falling in love. Journal of Social and Personal Relationships 6, 243–257.

Barkham, P., 2007. Testing times. The Guardian, 18 September. Available from http://www.guardian.co.uk/science/2007/sep/18/sciencenews.crime.

Bavelas, J.B., Chovil, N., Coates, L., Roe, L., 1995. Gestures specialized for dialogue. Personality and Social Psychology Bulletin 21, 394–405.

Ben-Shakhar, G., Elaad, E., 2003. The validity of psychophysiological detection of information with the guilty knowledge test: a meta-analytic review. Journal of Applied Psychology 88, 131–151.

Bhatt, S., Mbwana, J., Adeyemo, A., Sawyer, A., Hailu, A., Vanmeter, J., 2008. Lying about facial recognition: an fMRI study. Brain and Cognition 69, 282–290.

Blair, J.P., Kooi, B., 2004. The gap between training and research in the detection of deception. International Journal of Police Science and Management 6, 77–83.

Buck, J.A., Warren, A.R., Betman, S., Brigham, J.C., 2002. Age differences in Criteria-Based Content Analysis scores in typical child sexual abuse interviews. Applied Developmental Psychology 23, 267–283.

Bull, R., 2010. The investigative interviewing of children and other vulnerable witnesses: psychological research and working/professional practice. Legal and Criminological Psychology 15, 5–24.

Buller, D.B., Burgoon, J.K., 1996. Interpersonal deception theory. Communication Theory 6, 203–242.

Buller, D.B., Stiff, J.B., Burgoon, J.K., 1996. Behavioral adaptation in deceptive trans-actions. Fact or fiction: a reply to Levine and McCornack. Human Communica-tion Research 22, 589–603.

Burgoon, J.K., Buller, D.B., Floyd, K., Grandpre, J., 1996. Deceptive realities: sender, receiver, and observer perspectives in deceptive conversations. Communication Research 23, 724–748.

Burgoon, J.K., Buller, D.B., White, C.H., Afifi, W., Buslig, A.L.S., 1999. The role of conversation involvement in deceptive interpersonal interactions. Personality and Social Psychology Bulletin 25, 669–685.

Caso, L., Maricchiolo, F., Bonaiuto, M., Vrij, A., Mann, S., 2006. The impact of decep-tion and suspicion on different hand movements. Journal of Nonverbal Behavior 30, 1–19.

Chartrand, T.L., Bargh, J.A., 1999. The chameleon effect: the perception–behavior link and social interaction. Journal of Personality and Social Psychology 76, 893–910.

Christ, S.E., Van Essen, D.C., Watson, J.M., Brubaker, L.E., McDermott, K.B., 2009. The contributions of prefrontal cortex and executive control to deception: evidence from activation likelihood estimate meta-analyses. Cerebral Cortex 19, 1557–1566.

Cohen, J., 1977. Statistical Power Analysis for the Behavioral Sciences. Academic Press, New York.

Dalton, A.L., Daneman, M., 2006. Social suggestibility to central and peripheral misin-formation. Memory 14, 486–501.

Davatzikos, C., Ruparel, K., Fan, Y., Shen, D.G., Acharyya, M., Loughead, J.W., Langleben, D.D., 2005. Classifying spatial patterns of brain activity with machine learning methods: application to lie detection. NeuroImage 28, 663–668.

Davis, R.C., 1961. Psychological responses as a means of evaluating information. In: Biderman, A., Zimmer, H. (Eds.), Manipulation of Human Behavior. Wiley, New York, pp. 142–168.

DePaulo, B.M., 1992. Nonverbal behavior and self-presentation. Psychological Bulletin 111, 203–243.

DePaulo, B.M., Friedman, H.S., 1998. Nonverbal communication. In: Gilbert, D.T., Fiske, S.T., Lindzey, G. (Eds.), The Handbook of Social Psychology. McGraw-Hill, Boston, MA, pp. 3–40.

DePaulo, B.M., Kirkendol, S.E., 1989. The motivational impairment effect in the communication of deception. In: Yuille, J.C. (Ed.), Credibility Assessment. Kluwer, Dordrecht, pp. 51–70.

DePaulo, B.M., Kashy, D.A., Kirkendol, S.E., Wyer, M.M., Epstein, J.A., 1996. Lying in everyday life. Journal of Personality and Social Psychology 70, 979–995.

DePaulo, B.M., Lindsay, J.L., Malone, B.E., Muhlenbruck, L., Charlton, K., Cooper, H., 2003. Cues to deception. Psychological Bulletin 129, 74–118.

Doherty-Sneddon, G., Phelps, F.G., 2005. Gaze aversion: a response to cognitive or social difficulty? Memory and Cognition 33, 727–733.

Doherty-Sneddon, G., Bruce, V., Bonner, L., Longbotham, S., Doyle, C., 2002. Development of gaze aversion as disengagement of visual information. Developmental Psychology 38, 438–445.

Driscoll, L.N., 1994. A validity assessment of written statements from suspects in criminal investigations using the SCAN technique. Police Studies 17, 77–88.

Driscoll, L.N., Honts, C.R., Jones, D., 1987. The validity of the positive control physiological detection of deception technique. Journal of Police Science and Administration 15, 46–50.

Efron, D., 1941. Gesture and Environment. King's Crown, New York.

Ekman, P., 1985. Telling Lies: Clues to Deceit in the Marketplace, Politics and Marriage. W. W. Norton, New York [Reprinted in 1992, 2001 and 2009.].

Ekman, P., 1988. Lying and nonverbal behavior: theoretical issues and new findings. Journal of Nonverbal Behavior 12, 163–176.

Ekman, P., 2006a. How to spot a terrorist on the fly by Paul Ekman. Washington Post, 29 October. Available from http://www.washingtonpost.com/wp-dyn/content/article/2006/10/27/AR2006102701478.html.

Ekman, P., 2006b. Cited in 'Looking for the lie by Robin Marants Henig'. New York Times Magazine, 5 February. Available from http://www.nytimes.com/2006/02/05/magazine/05lying.html?_r=1&sq=paul%20ekman&st=nyt&adxnnl=1&scp=1&pagewanted=1&adxnnlx=1332860440-pRQZGJjaz612yyPT1T4nkA.

Ekman, P., Frank, M.G., 1993. Lies that fail. In: Lewis, M. & Saarni, C. (Eds.), Lying and deception n everyday life. Guildford Press, New York pp. 184–201.

Ekman, P., Friesen, W.V., 1969. Nonverbal leakage and clues to deception. Psychiatry 32, 88–106.

Ekman, P., Friesen, W.V., 1972. Hand movements. Journal of Communication 22, 353–374.

Ekman, P., Friesen, W.V., 1982. Felt, false, and miserable smiles. Journal of Nonverbal Behavior 6, 238–253.

Ekman, P., O'Sullivan, M., 2006. From flawed self-assessment to blatant whoppers: the utility of voluntary and involuntary behavior in detecting deception. Behavioral Sciences and the Law 24, 673–686.

Ekman, P., Davidson, R.J., Friesen, W.V., 1990. The Duchenne smile: emotional expression and brain physiology II. Journal of Personality and Social Psychology 58, 342–353.

Ekman, P., Friesen, W.V., O'Sullivan, M., 1988. Smiles when lying. Journal of Personality and Social Psychology 54, 414–420.

Elaad, E., 1990. Detection of guilty knowledge in real-life criminal investigations. Journal of Applied Psychology 75, 521–529.

Elaad, E., Ginton, A., Jungman, N., 1992. Detection measures in real-life criminal guilty knowledge tests. Journal of Applied Psychology 77, 757–767.

Fiedler, K., Schmid, J., Stahl, T., 2002. What is the current truth about polygraph lie detection? Basic and Applied Social Psychology 24, 313–324.

Fisher, R.P., 2010. Interviewing cooperative witnesses. Legal and Criminological Psychology 15, 25–38.

Fisher, R., Milne, R., Bull, R., 2011. Interviewing cooperative witnesses. Current Directions in Psychological Science 20, 16–19.

Ford, E.B., 2006. Lie detection: historical, neuropsychiatric and legal dimensions. International Journal of Law and Psychiatry 29, 159–177.

Frank, M.G., Ekman, P., Friesen, W.V., 1993. Behavioral markers and recognizability of the smile of enjoyment. Journal of Personality and Social Psychology 64, 83–93.

Friesen, W.V., Ekman, P., Wallbott, H., 1979. Measuring hand movements. Journal of Nonverbal Behavior 4, 97–112.

Furedy, J.J., Davis, C., Gurevich, M., 1988. Differentiation of deception as a psychological process: a psychophysiological approach. Psychophysiology 25, 683–688.

Galton, F., 1879. Psychometric experiments. Brain 2, 149–162.

Gamer, M., Bauermann, T., Stoeter, P., Vossel, G., 2007. Covariations among fMRI, skin conductance, and behavioral data during processing of concealed information. Human Brain Mapping 28, 1287–1301.

Gamer, M., Klimecki, O., Bauermann, T., Stoeter, P., Vossel, G., 2009. fMRI-activation patterns in the detection of concealed information rely on memory-related effects. Social Cognitive and Affective Neuroscience 7, 506–515.

Ganis, G., Morris, R., Kosslyn, S.M., 2009. Neural processes underlying self- and other-related lies: an individual difference approach using fMRI. Social Neuroscience 4, 539–553.

Ganis, G., Kosslyn, S.M., Stose, S., Thompson, W.L., Yurgelun-Todd, D.A., 2003. Neural correlates of different types of deception: an fMRI investigation. Cerebral Cortex 13, 830–836.

Ganis, G., Rosenfeld, J.P., Meixner, J., Kievit, R.A., Schendan, H.E., 2011. Lying in the scanner: covert countermeasures disrupt deception detection by functional magnetic resonance imaging. NeuroImage 55, 312–319.

Gilbert, D.T., 1991. How mental systems believe. American Psychologist 46, 107–119.

Gilbert, J.A.E., Fisher, R.P., 2006. The effects of varied retrieval cues on reminiscence in eyewitness memory. Applied Cognitive Psychology 20, 723–739.

Gilovich, T., Savitsky, K., Medvec, V.H., 1998. The illusion of transparency: biased assessments of others' ability to read one's emotional states. Journal of Personality and Social Psychology 75, 332–346.

Global Deception Research Team, 2006. A world of lies. Journal of Cross-Cultural Psychology 37, 60–74.

Gnisci, A., Caso, L., Vrij, A., 2010. Have you made up your story? The effect of suspicion and liars' strategies on Reality Monitoring. Applied Cognitive Psychology 24, 762–773.

Goldman-Eisler, F., 1968. Psycholinguistics: Experiments in Spontaneous Speech. Doubleday, New York.

Gudjonsson, G.H., 2003. The Psychology of Interrogations and Confessions. Wiley, Chichester.

Gumpert, C.H., Lindblad, F., 1999. Expert testimony on child sexual abuse: a qualitative study of the Swedish approach to statement analysis. Expert Evidence 7, 279–314.

Harrigan, J.A., O'Connell, D.M., 1996. Facial movements during anxiety states. Personality and Individual Differences 21, 205–212.

Hartwig, M., Bond, C.F., 2011. Why do lie-catchers fail? A lens model meta-analysis of human lie judgments. Psychological Bulletin 137, 643–659.

Hartwig, M., Granhag, P.A., Strömwall, L., 2007. Guilty and innocent suspects' strategies during interrogations. Psychology, Crime, and Law 13, 213–227.

Hartwig, M., Granhag, P.A., Strömwall, L., Doering, N., 2010. Impression and information management: on the strategic self-regulation of innocent and guilty suspects. The Open Criminology Journal 3, 10–16.

Hershkowitz, I., Lamb, M.E., Sternberg, K.J., Esplin, P.W., 1997. The relationships among interviewer utterance type, CBCA scores and the richness of children's responses. Legal and Criminological Psychology 2, 169–176.

Hillman, J., Vrij, A., Mann, S., 2012. Um … they were wearing …: the effect of deception on specific hand gestures. Legal and Criminological Psychology 17, 336–345.

Hocking, J.E., Leathers, D.G., 1980. Nonverbal indicators of deception: a new theoretical perspective. Communication Monographs 47, 119–131.

Honts, C.R., 1991. The emperor's new clothes: the application of the polygraph tests in the American workplace. Forensic Reports 4, 91–116.

Honts, C.R., 1996. Criterion development and validity of the control question test in field application. Journal of General Psychology 123, 309–324.

Honts, C.R., 2004. The psychophysiological detection of deception. In: Granhag, P.A., Strömwall, L.A. (Eds.), Deception Detection in Forensic Contexts. Cambridge University Press, Cambridge, pp. 103–123.

Honts, C.R., Devitt, M.K., Winbush, M., Kircher, J.C., 1996. Mental and physical countermeasures reduce the accuracy of the concealed knowledge test. Psychophysiology 33, 84–92.

Horvath, F., 1973. Verbal and nonverbal cues to truth and deception during polygraph examinations. Journal of Police Science and Administration 1, 138–152.

Horvath, F., Blair, J.P., Buckley, J.P., 2008. The Behavioral Analysis Interview: clarifying the practice, theory and understanding of its use and effectiveness. International Journal of Police Science and Management 10, 101–118.

Horvath, F., Jayne, B., Buckley, J., 1994. Differentiation of truthful and deceptive criminal suspects in behavioral analysis interviews. Journal of Forensic Sciences 39, 793–807.

Iacono, W.G., 2000. The detection of deception. In: Cacioppo, J.T., Tassinary, L.G., Berntson, G.G. (Eds.), Handbook of Psychophysiology, second ed. Cambridge University Press, Cambridge, pp. 772–793.

Iacono, W.G., 2008a. Accuracy of polygraph techniques: problems using confessions to determine ground truth. Physiology and Behavior 95, 24–26.

Iacono, W.G., 2008b. Effective policing: understanding how polygraph tests work and are used. Criminal Justice and Behavior 35, 1295–1308.

Inbau, F.E., Reid, J.E., Buckley, J.P., Jayne, B.C., 2001. Criminal Interrogation and Confessions, fourth ed. Aspen, Gaithersburg, MD.

Inbau, F.E., Reid, J.E., Buckley, J.P., Jayne, B.C., 2013. Criminal Interrogation and Confessions, fifth ed. Jones & Bartlett Learning, Burlington, MA.

Johnson, M.K., Raye, C.L., 1981. Reality monitoring. Psychological Review 88, 67–85.

Johnson, M.K., Raye, C.L., 1998. False memories and confabulation. Trends in Cognitive Sciences 2, 137–146.

Kassin, S.M., 2005. On the psychology of confessions: does innocence put innocents at risk? American Psychologist 60, 215–228.

Kassin, S.M., Fong, C.T., 1999. "I'm innocent!": effects of training on judgments of truth and deception in the interrogation room. Law and Human Behavior 23, 499–516.

Kassin, S.M., Gudjonsson, G.H., 2004. The psychology of confessions: a review of the literature and issues. Psychological Science in the Public Interest 5, 33–67.

Kassin, S.M., Norwick, R.J., 2004. Why people waive their Miranda rights: the power of innocence. Law and Human Behavior 28, 211–221.

Kassin, S.M., Appleby, S.C., Torkildson-Perillo, J., 2010. Interviewing suspects: practice, science, and future directions. Legal and Criminological Psychology 15, 39–56.

Kleinmuntz, B., Szucko, J.J., 1984. Lie detection in ancient and modern times: a call for contemporary scientific study. American Psychologist 39, 766–776.

Köhnken, G., 1996. Social psychology and the law. In: Semin, G.R., Fiedler, K. (Eds.), Applied Social Psychology. Sage, London, pp. 257–282.

Köhnken, G., 2004. Statement Validity Analysis and the 'detection of the truth'. In: Granhag, P.A., Strömwall, L.A. (Eds.), Deception Detection in Forensic Contexts. Cambridge University Press, Cambridge, pp. 41–63.

Köhnken, G., Steller, M., 1988. The evaluation of the credibility of child witness statements in German procedural system. In: Davies, G., Drinkwater, J. (Eds.), The Child Witness: Do the Courts Abuse Children? (Issues in Criminological and Legal Psychology 13). British Psychological Society, Leicester, pp. 37–45.

Kozel, F.A., Padgett, T.M., George, M.S., 2004. A replication study of the neural correlates of deception. Behavioral Neuroscience 118, 852–856.

Kozel, F.A., Johnson, K.A., Mu, Q., Grenesko, E.L., Laken, S.J., George, M.S., 2005. Detecting deception using functional magnetic resonance imaging. Biological Psychiatry 58, 605–613.

Kozel, F.A., Johnson, K.A., Grenesko, E.L., Laken, S.J., Kose, S., Lu, X., Polina, D., Ryan, A., George, M.S., 2009. Functional MRI detection of deception after committing a mock sabotage crime. Journal of Forensic Sciences 54, 220–231.

Lamers-Winkelman, F., Buffing, F., 1996. Children's testimony in the Netherlands: a study of Statement Validity Analysis. In: Bottoms, B.L., Goodman, G.S. (Eds.), International Perspectives on Child Abuse and Children's Testimony. Sage, Thousand Oaks, CA, pp. 45–62.

Lancaster, G.L.J., Vrij, A., Hope, L., Waller, B., 2012. Sorting the liars from the truth tellers: the benefits of asking unanticipated questions. Applied Cognitive Psychology 27, 107–114.

Langleben, D.D., Loughead, J.W., Bilker, W.B., Ruparel, K., Childress, A.R., Busch, S.I., Gur, R.C., 2005. Telling truth from lie in individual subjects with fast event-related fMRI. Human Brain Mapping 26, 262–272.

Langleben, D.D., Schroeder, L., Maldjian, J.A., Gur, R.C., McDonald, S., Ragland, J.D., Childress, A.R., 2002. Brain activity during simulated deception: an event-related functional magnetic resonance study. NeuroImage 15, 727–732.

Larson, J.A., 1932. Lying and its Detection: A Study of Deception and Deception Tests. University of Chicago Press, Chicago, IL.

Leal, S., Vrij, A., Fisher, R., van Hooff, J., 2008. The time of the crime: cognitively induced bodily arousal suppression when lying in a free recall context. Acta Psychologica 129, 1–7.

Leal, S., Vrij, A., Warmelink, L., Vernham, Z., Fisher, R., 2013. You cannot hide your telephone lies: providing a model statement as an aid to detect deception in insurance telephone calls. Legal and Criminological Psychology Epub ahead of print. doi: 10.1111/lcrp.12017.

Lee, T.M.C., Liu, H.L., Chan, C.C., Ng, Y.B., Fox, P.T., Gao, J.H., 2005. Neural correlates of feigned memory impairment. NeuroImage 28, 305–313.

Lee, T.M.C., Liu, H.-L., Tan, L.H., Chan, C.C.H., Mahankali, S., Feng, C.M., Gao, J.H., 2002. Lie detection by functional magnetic resonance imaging. Human Brain Mapping 15, 157–164.

Leins, D., Fisher, R., Vrij, A., 2012. Drawing on liars' lack of cognitive flexibility: detecting deception through varying report modes. Applied Cognitive Psychology 26, 601–607.

Leins, D., Fisher, R.P., Vrij, A., Leal, S., Mann, S., 2011. Using sketch-drawing to induce inconsistency in liars. Legal and Criminological Psychology 16, 253–265.

Levine, T.R., McCornack, S.A., 1996. A critical analysis of the behavioral adaptation explanation of the probing effect. Human Communication Research 22, 575–588.

Levine, T.R., Kim, R.K., Hamel, L.M., 2010a. People lie for a reason: three experiments documenting the principle of veracity. Communication Research Reports 27, 271–285.

Levine, T.R., Shaw, A., Shulman, H.C., 2010b. Increasing deception detection accuracy with strategic questioning. Human Communication Research 36, 216–231.

Lindsay, D.S., 2002. Children's source monitoring. In: Westcott, H.L., Davies, G.M., Bull, R.H.C. (Eds.), Children's Testimony: A Handbook of Psychological Research and Forensic Practice. Wiley, Chichester, pp. 83–98.

Lykken, D.T., 1959. The GSR in the detection of guilt. Journal of Applied Psychology 43, 385–388.

Lykken, D.T., 1998. A Tremor in the Blood: Uses and Abuses of the Lie Detector. Plenum Press, New York.

Mann, S., Vrij, A., Bull, R., 2002. Suspects, lies and videotape: an analysis of authentic high-stakes liars. Law and Human Behavior 26, 365–376.

Mann, S., Vrij, A., Bull, R., 2004. Detecting true lies: police officers' ability to detect deceit. Journal of Applied Psychology 89, 137–149.

Mann, S., Vrij, A., Leal, S., Granhag, P.A., Warmelink, L., Forrester, D., 2012. Windows to the soul? Deliberate eye contact as a cue to deceit. Journal of Nonverbal Behavior 36, 205–215.

Mann, S., Vrij, A., Leal, S., Shaw, D., Hillman, J., Granhag, P.A., Fisher, R., 2013. Two heads are better than one? How to effectively use two interviewers to detect deception. Legal and Criminological Psychology 18, 324–340.

Manzanero, A.L., Diges, M., 1996. Effects of preparation on internal and external memories. In: Davies, G., Lloyd-Bostock, S., McMurran, M., Wilson, C. (Eds.), Psychology, Law, and Criminal Justice: International Developments in Research and Practice. Walter de Gruyter, Berlin, pp. 56–63.

Masip, J., Ces, C., 2011. Guilty and innocent suspects' self-reported strategies during an imagined police interview. Paper presented at the 4th International Congress on Psychology and Law, Miami, FL 3–5 March.

Masip, J., Sporer, S., Garrido, E., Herrero, C., 2005. The detection of deception with the reality monitoring approach: a review of the empirical evidence. Psychology, Crime and Law 11, 99–122.

McNeill, D., 1985. So you think gestures are nonverbal? Psychological Review 92, 350–371.

McNeill, D., 1992. Hand and Mind. University of Chicago Press, Chicago, IL.

Memon, A., Meissner, C.A., Fraser, J., 2010. The cognitive interview: a meta-analytic review and study space analysis of the past 25 years. Psychology, Public Policy and Law 16, 340–372.

Merckelbach, H., 2004. Telling a good story: fantasy proneness and the quality of fabricated memories. Personality and Individual Differences 37, 1371–1382.

Mohamed, F.B., Faro, S.H., Gordon, N.J., Platek, S.M., Ahmad, H., Williams, J.M., 2006. Brain mapping of deception and truth telling about an ecologically valid situation: functional MR imaging and polygraph investigation – initial experience. Radiology 238, 679–688.

Monteleone, G.T., Phan, K.L., Nusbaum, H.C., Fitzgerald, D., Irick, J.S., Fienberg, S.E., Cacioppo, J.T., 2009. Detection of deception using fMRI: better than chance, but well below perfection. Social Neuroscience 4, 528–538.

Münsterberg, H., 1908. On the Witness Stand: Essays on Psychology and Crime. Doubleday, New York.

Nahari, G., Vrij, A., Fisher, R.P., 2012a. Does the truth come out in the writing? SCAN as a lie detection tool. Law and Human Behavior 36, 68–76.

Nahari, G., Vrij, A., Fisher, R.P., 2012b. Exploiting liars' verbal strategies by examining the verifiability of details. Legal and Criminological Psychology Epub ahead of print. doi: 10.1111/j.2044-8333.2012.02069.x.

Nakayama, M., 2002. Practical use of the concealed information test for criminal investigation in Japan. In: Kleiner, M. (Ed.), Handbook of Polygraph Testing. Academic Press, San Diego, pp. 49–86.

National Research Council, 2003. The Polygraph and Lie Detection. National Academies Press, Washington, DC.

Nose, I., Murai, J., Taira, M., 2009. Disclosing concealed information on the basis of cortical activations. NeuroImage 44, 1380–1386.

Nunez, J.M., Casey, B.J., Egner, T., Hare, T., Hirsch, J., 2005. Intentional false responding shares neural substrates with response conflict and cognitive control. NeuroImage 25, 267–277.

Phan, K.L., Magalhaes, A., Ziemlewicz, T.J., Fitzgerald, D.A., Green, C., Smith, W., 2005. Neural correlates of telling lies: a functional magnetic resonance imaging study at 4 Tesla. Academic Radiology 12, 164–172.

Podlesny, J.A., Raskin, D.C., 1977. Physiological measures and the detection of deception. Psychological Bulletin 84, 782–799.

Podlesny, J.A., Raskin, D.C., 1978. Effectiveness of techniques and physiological measures in the detection of deception. Psychophysiology 15, 344–358.

Porter, S., ten Brinke, L., 2008. Reading between the lies: identifying concealed and falsified emotions in universal facial expressions. Psychological Science 19, 508–514.

Porter, S., Yuille, J.C., 1996. The language of deceit: an investigation of the verbal clues to deception in the interrogation context. Law and Human Behavior 20, 443–459.

Raskin, D.C., 1979. Orienting and defensive reflexes in the detection of deception. In: Kimmel, H.D., Van Olst, E.H., Orlebeke, J.F. (Eds.), The Orienting Reflex in Humans. Erlbaum, Hillsdale, NJ, pp. 587–605.

Raskin, D.C., 1982. The scientific basis of polygraph techniques and their uses in the judicial process. In: Trankell, A. (Ed.), Reconstructing the Past. Norsted & Soners, Stockholm, pp. 317–371.

Raskin, D.C., 1986. The polygraph in 1986: Scientific, professional, and legal issues surrounding acceptance of polygraph evidence. Utah Law Review 29, 29–74.

Raskin, D.C., Esplin, P.W., 1991. Statement Validity Assessment: interview procedures and content analysis of children's statements of sexual abuse. Behavioral Assessment 13, 265–291.

Raskin, D.C., Honts, C.R., 2002. The comparison question test. In: Kleiner, M. (Ed.), Handbook of Polygraph Testing. Academic Press, San Diego, CA, pp. 1–47.

Reid, J.E., 1947. A revised questioning technique in lie detection tests. Journal of Criminal Law, Criminology and Police Science 37, 542–547.

Roediger, H.L., 1996. Memory illusions. Journal of Memory and Language 35, 76–100.

Rosenfeld, J.P., Biroschak, J.R., Furedy, J.J., 2006. P300-based detection of concealed autobiographical versus incidentally acquired information in target and non-target paradigms. International Journal of Psychophysiology 60, 251–259.

Rosenfeld, J.P., Soskins, M., Bosh, G., Ryan, A., 2004. Simple, effective countermeasures to P300-based tests of detection of concealed information. Psychophysiology 41, 205–219.

Rosenfeld, J.P., Cantwell, B., Nasman, V.T., Wojdac, V., Ivanov, S., Mazzeri, L., 1988. A modified, event-related potential-based guilty knowledge test. International Journal of Neuroscience 42, 157–161.

Ruby, C.L., Brigham, J.C., 1997. The usefulness of the criteria-based content analysis technique in distinguishing between truthful and fabricated allegations. Psychology, Public Policy, and Law 3, 705–737.

Ruby, C.L., Brigham, J.C., 1998. Can Criteria-Based Content Analysis distinguish between true and false statements of African-American speakers? Law and Human Behavior 22, 369–388.

Sapir, A., 1987/2000. The LSI Course on Scientific Content Analysis (SCAN). Laboratory for Scientific Interrogation, Phoenix, AZ.

Saxe, L., 1994. Detection of deception: polygraph and integrity tests. Current Directions in Psychological Science 3, 69–73.

Schweitzer, M.E., Brodt, S.E., Croson, R.T.A., 2002. Seeing and believing: visual access and the strategic use of deception. The International Journal of Conflict Management 13, 258–275.

Spence, S.A., Kaylor-Hughes, C., Farrow, T.F., Wilkinson, I.D., 2008. Speaking of secrets and lies: the contribution of ventrolateral prefrontal cortex to vocal deception. NeuroImage 40, 1411–1418.

Spence, S.A., Farrow, T.F.D., Herford, A.E., Wilkinson, I.D., Zheng, Y., Woodruff, P.W.R., 2001. Behavioral and functional anatomical correlates of deception in humans. Neuroreport 12, 2849–2853.

Spence, S.A., Hunter, M.D., Farrow, T.F., Green, R.D., Leung, D.H., Hughes, C.J., Ganesan, V., 2004. A cognitive neurobiological account of deception: evidence from functional neuroimaging. Philosophical Transactions of the Royal Society of London. Series B: Biological Sciences 359, 1755–1762.

Sporer, S.L., 1997. The less travelled road to truth: verbal cues in deception detection in accounts of fabricated and self-experienced events. Applied Cognitive Psychology 11, 373–397.

Steller, M., Köhnken, G., 1989. Criteria-Based Content Analysis. In: Raskin, D.C. (Ed.), Psychological Methods in Criminal Investigation and Evidence. Springer, New York, pp. 217–245.

ten Brinke, L., Porter, S., 2012. Cry me a river: identifying the behavioural consequences of extremely high-stakes interpersonal deception. Law and Human Behavior 36, 469–477.

ten Brinke, L., Porter, S., Baker, A., 2012. Darwin the detective: observable facial muscle contractions reveal emotional high-stakes lies. Evolution and Human Behavior 33, 411–416.

ten Brinke, L., MacDonald, S., Porter, S., O'Connor, B., 2012. Crocodile tears: facial, verbal and body language behaviors associated with genuine and fabricated remorse. Law and Human Behavior 36, 51–59.

Tickle-Degnen, L., 2006. Nonverbal behavior and its functions in the ecosystem of rapport. In: Manusov, V., Patterson, M.L. (Eds.), The SAGE Handbook of Nonverbal Communication. Sage, Thousand Oaks, CA, pp. 381–399.

Trankell, A., 1972. Reliability of Evidence. Beckmans, Stockholm.

Undeutsch, U., 1982. Statement reality analysis. In: Trankell, A. (Ed.), Reconstructing the Past: The Role of Psychologists in Criminal Trials. Kluwer, Deventer, pp. 27–56.

Verschuere, B., Ben-Shakhar, G., 2011. Theory of the Concealed Information Test. In: Verschuere, B., Ben-Shakhar, G., Meijer, E. (Eds.), Memory Detection: Theory and Application of the Concealed Information Test. Cambridge University Press, Cambridge, pp. 128–148.

Verschuere, B., Ben-Shakhar, G., Meijer, E., 2011. Memory Detection: Theory and Application of the Concealed Information Test. Cambridge University Press, Cambridge.

Verschuere, B., Crombez, G., de Clercq, A., Koster, E.H.W., 2005. Psychopathic traits and autonomic responding to concealed information in a prison sample. Psychophysiology 42, 239–245.

Vrij, A., 2008. Detecting Lies and Deceit: Pitfalls and Opportunities, second ed. John Wiley, Chichester.

Vrij, A., Granhag, P.A., 2012. Eliciting cues to deception and truth: what matters are the questions asked. Journal of Applied Research in Memory and Cognition 1, 110–117.

Vrij, A., Mann, S., 2003. Deceptive responses and detecting deceit. In: Halligan, P.W., Bass, C., Oakley, D. (Eds.), Malingering and Illness Deception: Clinical and Theoretical Perspectives. Oxford University Press, Oxford, pp. 348–362.

Vrij, A., Fisher, R., Mann, S., Leal, S., 2006a. Detecting deception by manipulating cognitive load. Trends in Cognitive Sciences 10, 141–142.

Vrij, A., Mann, S., Fisher, R., 2006b. An empirical test of the Behavior Analysis Interview. Law and Human Behavior 30, 329–345.

Vrij, A., Mann, S., Fisher, R., 2006c. Information-gathering vs accusatory interview style: Individual differences in respondents' experiences. Personality and Individual Differences 41, 589–599.

Vrij, A., Granhag, P.A., Mann, S., Leal, S., 2011. Outsmarting the liars: towards a cognitive lie detection approach. Current Directions in Psychological Science 20, 28–32.

Vrij, A., Mann, S., Kristen, S., Fisher, R., 2007. Cues to deception and ability to detect lies as a function of police interview styles. Law and Human Behavior 31, 499–518.

Vrij, A., Mann, S., Fisher, R., Leal, S., Milne, B., Bull, R., 2008. Increasing cognitive load to facilitate lie detection: the benefit of recalling an event in reverse order. Law and Human Behavior 32, 253–265.

Vrij, A., Leal, S., Granhag, P.A., Mann, S., Fisher, R.P., Hillman, J., Sperry, K., 2009. Outsmarting the liars: the benefit of asking unanticipated questions. Law and Human Behavior 33, 159–166.

Vrij, A., Granhag, P.A., Porter, S.B., 2010a. Pitfalls and opportunities in nonverbal and verbal lie detection. Psychological Science in the Public Interest 11, 89–121.

Vrij, A., Mann, S., Leal, S., Granhag, P.A., 2010b. Getting into the minds of pairs of liars and truth tellers: an examination of their strategies. The Open Criminology Journal 3, 17–22.

Vrij, A., Mann, S., Leal, S., Fisher, R., 2010c. "Look into my eyes": can an instruction to maintain eye contact facilitate lie detection? Psychology, Crime, and Law 16, 327–348.

Walczyk, J.J., Roper, K.S., Seemann, E., Humphrey, A.M., 2003. Cognitive mechanisms underlying lying to questions: response time as a cue to deception. Applied Cognitive Psychology 17, 755–744.

Walczyk, J.J., Schwartz, J.P., Clifton, R., Adams, B., Wei, M., Zha, P., 2005. Lying person-to-person about live events: a cognitive framework for lie detection. Personnel Psychology 58, 141–170.

Wallbott, H.G., Scherer, K.R., 1991. Stress specifics: differential effects of coping style, gender, and type of stressor on automatic arousal, facial expression, and subjective feeling. Journal of Personality and Social Psychology 61, 147–156.

Yuille, J.C., 1988. The systematic assessment of children's testimony. Canadian Psychology 29, 247–262.

Zuckerman, M., DePaulo, B.M., Rosenthal, R., 1981. Verbal and nonverbal communication of deception. In: Berkowitz, L. (Ed.), Advances in Experimental Social Psychology, vol. 14. Academic Press, New York, pp. 1–57.

Index

Note: Page numbers with "f" denote figures; "t" tables.

9–11 attack, US Government's response at portals, 39–43

A
abstract theoretical framework of deception and lie detection, 305–307, 306f
ACC. *See* anterior cingulate cortex
accounts of subjective mental state, 337
accuracy
  Comparison Question Test, 314–315
  Concealed Information Test, 318
  criteria-based content analysis, 338–340
  deception detection judgments, 5–6
  functional magnetic resonance imaging, 351–352
  Future Attribute Screening Technology, 44–47
  non-verbal lie detection, 331–332
  polygraphs, 84–85
  reality monitoring, 341
  Scientific Content Analysis, 344
  Screening Passengers by Observation Techniques, 41
accuracy–confidence relationships, 5
adaptors, 327
additional processes, cognitive neuroscience, 235–236
administering polygraph tests, 70–74
admitting lack of memory, SVA, 338
advantages of laboratory research, 79
age effects, CBCA, 339–340
airports, 39–42
alcohol intoxication, 140
allocation strategies, reading behaviors, 170, 185–186
alteration of memories, polygraph countermeasures, 147–148

The American Polygraph Association Ad Hoc Committee on Polygraph Techniques, 84
amnesia, 140, 147–148
analyses, strategic use of evidence technique research, 26
analysis of variance (ANOVA), polygraph scoring, 105–106
anatomy, brain, 233f
anodal transcranial direct current stimulation, 276
ANOVA. *See* analysis of variance
ANS. *See* autonomic nervous system
anterior cingulate cortex (ACC)
  fMRI studies, 347, 348
  frequency of lying, 257
  intention-driven/instructed lies, 252
  tactical monitoring, 240
anti-countermeasure training, 149–151
anticipatory reactions, 74
anxiety-based approaches
  non-verbal lie detection, 49–50, 325–326
  polygraphs, 310–313
apparatus, reading behaviors studies, 189, 197, 200, 204
applied issues, polygraphs, 117–122
applied psychology
  forensic deception, 48–49
  strategic use of evidence technique, 15–23
area under the curve (AUC), polygraph scoring methods, 107–108
arm movements, 321
arousal, 161, 167–168, 319
attempted behavioral control, 321
attention, 175, 240

attitude misrepresentation, 281–282
attitude response LPCs, 262–263, 266
attribution of perpetrator's mental state, 337
AUC. *See* area under the curve
autobiographical memories, 237, 259, 266
automatic mode, polygraphs, 113–114
autonomic nervous system (ANS), 67, 164
autonomic nervous system inhibitors, 139
average blink rate, 170–171
aversive conditioning, 12–13
avoidance strategies, 9–10, 12–13, 19

B
back-calculation of event-related potentials,
        226–227
Backster procedures, 86
BAI. *See* Behavioral Analysis Interview
bank note probes, 348–349
base rates, 44–47
BDOs. *See* Behavior Detection Officers
behavior
    cognitive processes, 219–220
    deception correlates, 6–7
    self-regulation, 9–10
Behavior Detection Officers (BDOs), 41
Behavioral Analysis Interview (BAI), 8, 309,
        333–335
behavioral control, multifactor model, 321
behavioral strategies, threat avoidance, 10
belief in a just world, 13–14
belief misrepresentation, 281–282
BESA. *See* Brain Electrical Source Analysis
        program
bias, 111, 117–118, 314–315
bigger-is-better scoring, 90–92
birth date denial, 350
blinking
    average rates, 170–171
    cognitive load, 163–164, 170–172
    non-verbal lie detection, 330
    reading behaviors, 195–199, 202
blood flow dynamics, cognitive processing, 228
blood oxygen level-dependent (BOLD) fMRI,
        228
blood pressure, 308

body language, 39–40, 49–50. *See also*
        non-verbal lie detection
BOLD. *See* blood oxygen level-dependent fMRI
brain, anatomical regions, 233f
brain activity
    causal measures, 228–229. *See also* cognitive
        load
Brain Electrical Source Analysis (BESA)
        program, 225–227
buffer questions, polygraph tests, 72

C
cardiovascular reactions, polygraphs, 91
catch trials, instructed lie studies, 243
cathodal transcranial direct current
        stimulation, 276
causal measures, brain activity, 228–229
CBCA. *See* criteria-based content analysis
central executive brain activity, 234–280
central nervous system (CNS), 219, 231–238,
        233f
"chameleon effect", 323
characteristics, comparison question tests,
        66–67
check points, strategic use of evidence, 19
children, 336–339
circular fibers, pupil dilation, 164–165
closed-circuit silicon matrix cameras, 174–175
closed-ended questions, 18–19
coaching, countermeasure effectiveness, 141,
        143–144, 288–289
coding procedures, SUE technique, 25–26
cognitive control processes, 238–280, 345
cognitive load
    blood flow dynamics, 228
    causal measures, 228–229
    evoked pupillary responses, 162–163,
        168–170
    eye blinks, 163–164, 170–172
    interview techniques, 356–359
    multifactor model, 320–321
    neurocognitive studies, 284–287
    polygraph countermeasures, 151–154
    prepotent truth responses, 272–273
    reading behaviors, 185–186

response conflict, 288–289
SUE approach, 8–9
SVA, 336–338
task-switching, 272
valence, 268–269
cognitive neuroscience, 217–300
  additional processes, 235–236
  causal measures of activity, 228–229
  cognitive control, 238–280
  controlled processes, 235–236
  deception and credibility studies, 229–231
  differentiation-of-deception, 231, 270–271, 277–280
  diffusion tensor imaging, 228–229
  event-related potentials, 223–226
  executive processes, 234–280
  false memories, 238
  functional imaging, 222–228
  Guilty Knowledge Test, 231
  long-term memory, 237–238
  magnetoencephalography, 227
  near-infrared spectroscopy, 229
  positron emission tomography, 228
  principles, 220–222
  transcranial magnetic stimulation, 230–231
  working memory, 234–237. See also neurocognitive studies
cognitive operations, verbal lie detection, 341
cognitive processes, temporal coupling, 226
cognitive states, eye movements, 177–180
cognitive strategies, threat avoidance, 10
cognitive view of language processing, 178
coin flip studies, 256–257
Committee of Concerned Social Scientists, 82
Comparison Question Test (CQT), 312
  accuracy, 314–315
  common characteristics, 66–67
  conditioned response theory, 313
  conflict theory, 313
  theoretical assumptions, 313–314
  threat of punishment theory, 313
  use, 67–69
  Utah Probable-Lie Test, 69–78
  validity, 79–85

comparison questions (CQs), 68–69, 72, 101, 312
comparisons
  lie detection techniques, 354–356
  polygraph scoring methods, 94–117
    analysis of variance, 105–106
    data quantification, 97
    data transformations, 98–99
    datasets, 95–96
    effect sizes, 109–111
    multiple-issue decision rules, 100–101, 103–106, 104t
    number of charts, 99
    procedures, 95–101
    reduction in respiration line length, 97–98, 112
    scoring systems, 98, 101–109
    single-issue decision rules, 99–103, 102t
    two-stage rules, 100–101, 103–106, 104t
    validity of results, 111–117
complainants, polygraph tests, 121–122
computational neuroscience, 221
computerized interpretation, polygraphs, 92–94, 118–119
computerized polygraph system (CPS) algorithm, 92–93
  Law Enforcement Pre-Employment Test scoring, 105
  multiple-issue tests, 100
  single-issue decision rules, 99–100
Concealed Information Test (CIT)
  accuracy, 318
  countermeasures, 135–136, 144–147, 152–153
  event-related potentials, 280–284
  functional magnetic resonance imaging studies, 348
  misinformation, 146–147
  neurocognitive studies, 248
  "Oddball" paradigm, 232–233
  specific point countermeasures, 144–145
  theory, 152–153, 316. See also guilty knowledge test; polygraphs
concealment, critical information, 11–13
conceptually-driven response conflicts, 241–242, 244–245, 288–289
conditioned response theory, 313

conductance, skin, emotional arousal, 167
confidence, deception detection accuracy, 5
confidential tests, polygraphs, 119–121
conflict theory, 313
conflicting responses. *See* response monitoring
consolidation, episodic memory, 140, 147–148
constant voltage circuits, 113–114
contextual information, 340–341
continuum of deception research, 304, 305f
contraction
    pupils, 164, 167. *See also* dilation; pupil dilation
contradictions, elicitation, 19
contrary-to-truthfulness-stereotype criteria, 337
controlled processes, cognitive neuroscience,
        235–236
copy cues, 259
correlating behavior and cognitive processes,
        219–220
corrugator supercilii, 332–333
counter-countermeasures, polygraphs, 148
counter-interrogation strategies, 9, 14–15
countermeasure detectors, polygraphs, 148
countermeasures
    Concealed Information Test, 135–136,
        144–147
    detection, polygraphs, 148–149
    emotional recall, 145
    false memories, 136
    functional magnetic resonance imaging, 247
    future research, 154–155
    general state, 117, 134–136, 139–140
    information, 140–142
    mental disassociation, 144
    mental imagery, 143–144
    misinformation, 146–147
    physical, 143–144
    polygraphs, 117, 120, 131–158
        detection, 145, 148–149
        potential solutions, 148–149
        requirements, 135–136
        theoretical mechanism, 151–154
    practice efficacy, 141, 143–144, 288–289
    Relevant–Irrelevant Test, 136
    respiratory signatures, 149–151
    specific point, 134–140, 143–147

spontaneous, 137–139
Test for Espionage and Sabotage, 142
covariant behaviors, deception correlates, 6–7
CPS. *See* computerized polygraph system
        algorithm
CQs. *See* comparison questions
CQTs. *See* Comparison Question Test
credibility, 11–12
crime-relevant information, innocent suspects,
        146–147
criteria-based content analysis (CBCA),
        336–338
criterion bias, 111
critical information, concealment, 11–13
cross validation, polygraph test scoring
        methods, 105–106
crow's-feet, 326
CSD. *See* current source density analysis
cues of deception, 6–7
    elicitation, 7–9, 56–57
    non-verbal lie detection, 324, 325t
    at portals, 49–50
current source density (CSD) analysis, 226

D

data quantification, polygraph scoring method
        comparisons, 97
date stimuli, 350
data transformations, polygraph scoring
        method comparisons, 98–99
datasets, polygraph scoring method
        comparisons, 95–96
deception
    abstract theoretical framework, 305–307, 306f
    attitudes, 281–284
    beliefs, 281–284
    brain-based studies, 229–231
    continuum of research, 304, 305f
    cues, 6–7
    definitions, 4, 219–220
    detection
        general findings, 4–7
        human accuracy, 5–7
    evoked pupillary responses, 172–174,
        193–194, 199, 209

false memories, 238

forensic contexts, 48–49

high-stakes lies, 7

internal processes, 305–306

interpersonal, 47–48

investigative interviewing, 56–57

late positive component, instructed lie studies, 244

medial frontal negativity, instructed lie studies, 243–244

neurocognitive studies, 239–250

non-verbal cues, 325t

personal evaluations, 281–282

prerespose positivity, 244

reading behaviors, 159–216, 185t

stereotyped behaviors, 49–50

task-evoked pupillary responses, 173

theories, 301–374

Utah Probable-Lie Test, 75–76

Deception Indicated (DI) scores, 87–88

deceptive contexts, portals, 43–44

decision control, concept, 10

decision methods

  polygraphs

    computerized, 118–119

    multiple-issue tests, 100–101, 103–106, 104t

    single-issue tests, 99–103, 102t

    validity, 63–130

declarative memory, 237

defense attorney's confidential polygraph tests, 119–121

deictic movements, 327

deliberate eye contact, 328

demeanor, 39–40, 49–50, 320–321

demographic variables, 282–283

demonstration tests, polygraphs, 70–71

denial of birth date, 350

denial of self, 263

denial strategies, 19

Department of Defense Polygraph Institute (DoDPI), 87

Department of Homeland Security (DHS), FAST, 42–45, 45t

depressor anguli oris, 332–333

design, reading behaviors experiments, 188–189, 196–197

detection

  deception

    evoked pupillary responses, 172–174, 193–194, 199, 209

    general findings, 4–7

    human accuracy, 5–7

    ocular metrics during reading, 159–216, 185t

    polygraphs, 65

  plagiarism, 133

  polygraph countermeasures, 145, 148–149

DHS. *See* Department of Homeland Security

DI. *See* Deception Indicated scores

diagnostic techniques, polygraph comparisons, 84–85

differentiation-of-deception

  event-related potentials, 243–244, 258–259, 271–276

  functional magnetic resonance imaging studies, 347

  neurocognitive studies, 231, 270–271, 277–280

diffusion tensor imaging (DTI), 228–229

dilation

  pupils

    arousal, 161

    cognitive effort, 162–163

    pain habituation, 166–167

    physiology, 164

    slow followed by rapid constriction, 161–162, 172–173. *See also* evoked pupillary responses; pupil dilation; task-evoked pupillary responses

dilator pupillae, 164–165

direct current stimulation, 276

disassociative countermeasures, 144

disclosures

  manner, 22

  tactics, 17–18, 20–23

discourse processing, eye movements, 179–180

discriminant analysis, reading behaviors studies, 192–193, 198–199

DLPFC. *See* dorsolateral prefrontal cortex

DLT. *See* Utah Directed-Lie Test
DMPFC. *See* dorsal medial prefrontal cortex
dorsolateral prefrontal cortex (DLPFC)
    attitude responses, 266
    episodic memory, 275–276
    frequency of lying, 257
    functional magnetic resonance imaging
        studies, 347–348
    guilty knowledge test, 248
    postretrieval processing, 266
    simulated malingering, 255–256
    tactical monitoring, 240
    transcranial direct current stimulation, 276
    working memory, 234–237
dorsomedial prefrontal cortex (DMPFC), 348
drift, polygraph scoring, 91–92
drip-feeding disclosures, 21–22
drug countermeasures, 117, 120, 134–135, 139.
        See also general state countermeasures
dry mouth assumption, 307–308
DTI. *See* diffusion tensor imaging
dual-task situations, 238–239, 267–268, 277

E
early disclosures, 21–22
early processing, event-related potentials, 226
early studies of the central nervous system,
        231–238
Edinger–Westphal nucleus, 164–165, 171–172
EEG. *See* electroencephalography
efficacy, Information Gain Index, 46–47
efficiency, Behavior Analysis Interview, 334
electrodermal data, 91, 113–114, 310
electroencephalography (EEG), 310. *See also*
        event-related potentials
elicitation
    deception cues, 7–9, 56–57
    omissions and contradictions, 19
embarrassing incidents, 255
emblems, 327
emotional arousal, 167–168
emotional cues, 39–40, 49–50
emotional expressions, facial, 332–333
emotional impact of questions, 67
emotional reactions, multifactor model, 320

emotional recall, 145
emotionality, reading behaviors, 184, 185t
empirical scoring system (ESS), 90–92
    multiple-issue decision rules, 101, 103–105, 108
    single-issue decision rules, 100
    validity, 112
encoding, episodic memory, 238
episodic memory, 237
    consolidation, 140, 147–148
    dorsolateral prefrontal cortex, 275–276
    dual-task situations, 267–268, 277
    event-related potentials, 258–259
    hemodynamic monitoring, 245–246
    old–new differences, 258–259
    polygraph countermeasures, 136
    recall, 238
    reconsolidation, 147–148
ERPs. *See* event-related potentials
escape strategies, 12–13, 19
evaluation
    computational, 77–78, 92–94
    independent, polygraph results, 83
    numerical, 74–77, 86–88
    polygraph scoring methods, 94–117
    Utah Probable-Lie Test results, 74–78
        See also interpretation
event-related experimental designs, 226
event-related potentials (ERPs), 223–226, 310
    attitude responses, 262
    autobiographical memories, 259
    Brain Electrical Source Analysis program,
        225–227
    current source density analysis, 226
    differentiation-of-deception, 243–244, 251,
        258–259, 271–276
    early studies, 231–238
    familiarity/recollection, 258–259
    forensic applications, 280–284
    guilty knowledge/concealed information
        tests, 280–284
    instructed lie studies, 259–261
    intention-driven lies, 271–276
    late positive component, 232–233
    old–new differences, episodic memory,
        258–259

parietal episodic memory effect, 258–259
prerepsonse positivity, 244
scalp distributions, 226
tactical monitoring studies, 259–261
Evidence Framing Matrix, 22
evidentiary rules, polygraphs, 89
evoked pupillary responses, 161, 172–174
    autonomic nervous system, 164
    cognitive load, 162–163, 168–170
    deception detection, 172–174, 193–194, 199, 209
    sex effects, 161. *See also* task-evoked pupillary responses
excitement, multifactor model, 320
executive processes
    anterior cingulate cortex–dorsolateral prefrontal cortex circuit, 240
    cognitive neuroscience, 234–280
    posterror slowing, 240
    response monitoring, 240–241
    tactical monitoring, 251
experimental psychology, 220–221
explicit memory, 237
external validity, 7
eye blinks
    cognitive load, 163–164, 170–172
    non-verbal lie detection, 330
    reading behaviors studies, 195–199, 202. *See also* blinking
eye contact, 328
eye movements, 174–180
eye–mind assumption, 175
eye-tracking, 163, 175

F
facial emotional expressions, 332–333
facial microexpressions, 39–40, 50–51
false information, 11–12
false memories, 136, 147–148, 236–237, 341–342
false negatives, 75, 305–306
false positives, 305–306
false smiles, 326
familiarity, event-related potentials, 258–259
FAST. *See* Future Attribute Screening Technology

fatigue, 166
fear
    physiological measurements, 307–308
    smell of, 308. *See also* anxiety-based approaches
felt smiles, 326
fidgeting, 49–50
field studies
    polygraphs, 81–84
    reading behaviors, 199–207
        discussion, 202–203, 206–207
        methods, 200–202, 204–206
        procedures, 201–202, 205–206
        results, 202, 206
fight-or-flight responses, 65
finger plethysmography, 86
first fixation duration, 177
first-pass duration, reading behavior experiments, 189, 192
fixations
    durations, 177
    frequency, 177
    reading behaviors studies, 192, 194–195, 198
    reading studies, 175
        eye–mind assumption, 175
        immediacy assumption, 175
    semantic/syntactic content, 176
    word frequency, 179
    word lengths, 179
fMRI. *See* functional magnetic resonance imaging
forensic applications
    event-related potentials, 222
    hemodynamic studies, 235
    neurocognitive studies, 237
forensics, deception, 48–49
forward-calculation, event-related potentials, 226–227
foveal view, 175–176
"friendly polygrapher" hypothesis, 69, 119–121
frontal lobe
    direct current stimulation, 278
    Parkinson's sufferers, 277
frontalis muscles, 332–333
frontopolar cortex, 256

functional anatomy, 220–221
functional magnetic resonance imaging (fMRI),
      222, 228, 261–280, 345–354
   accuracy, 283–284, 351–352
   back-/forward-calculation with ERPs,
      226–227
   comparison to other techniques, 354–356
   concealed information tests, 348
   countermeasures, 247
   differentiation-of-deception, 347
   generalizability, 353–354
   replicability, 352–353
   spontaneous lies, 246
functional neuroimaging, 222–228. *See also*
      event-related potentials; functional
      magnetic resonance imaging;
      magnetoencephalography
funnel approach, strategic use of evidence, 19
Future Attribute Screening Technology (FAST),
      42–45, 45t
future research
   polygraph countermeasures, 154–155
   portals, 57–58

G
gaze aversion, 6, 320–321
gaze durations, 170, 177
general state (GS) countermeasures, 117,
      134–136, 139–140
generalizability
   functional magnetic resonance imaging
      studies, 353–354
   neurocognitive studies, 282–283
   polygraph testing, 118, 80
GKT. *See* Guilty Knowledge Test
go-past time, reading behavior, 177
goal setting
   reading behaviors, 180–181, 185t. *See also*
      standards of evaluation
good questioning technique, polygraphs, 68
governmental use of polygraphs, 122
grief muscles, 332–333
ground truth, 4–5, 314–315
GS. *See* general state countermeasures
guilt, investigative interviewing, 56–57

guilty examinees, 312–313, 320–321. *See also* liars
Guilty Knowledge Test (GKT)
   event-related potentials, 280–284
   neurocognitive studies, 231, 248. *See also*
      Concealed Information Test

H
habituation, pupillar pain responses, 166–167
hand movements, 321, 327
heart rate deceleration, 167
hemodynamic imaging
   cognitive neuroscience, 226–228
   forensic application, 280–284
   intention-driven responses, 257–258,
      277–280
   neurocognitive studies, 261–266
   spontaneous lies, 246
   validity, 279–280. *See also* functional
      magnetic resonance imaging
hierarchy of goals, reading behaviors, 181
high-frequency words, fixations, 179
high-pass filters, 113–114
high-stakes situations, 7, 329–330, 332–333
higher-order cognitive processing, eye
      movements, 179–180
history of lie detection, 307–310
Hotelling–Williams *t*-ratios, polygraph scoring
      methods, 108
human accuracy, lie detection, 5–7
hybrid designs, fMRI studies, 346
hypothalamus, pupil dilation, 164–165

I
idiosyncratic scoring, 91–92
IDT. *See* Interpersonal Deception Theory
IGI. *See* Information Gain Index
illusion of transparency, 13–14
illustrators, non-verbal lie detection, 325–326
immediacy assumption, eye-tracking, 175
implicit memory, 237
imposition of cognitive load, interview
      techniques, 356–359
impression management, SVA, 336–338
in vivo observations, passenger screening,
      39–40

inconclusive outcomes, Utah Probable-Lie Test, 75–76

increasing cognitive load, interview techniques, 356–359

incriminating evidence, escape and denial strategies, 19

independent evaluators, polygraphs, 83

individual differences, non-verbal lie detection, 329–331

individual variables, neurocognitive studies, 282–283

inferior frontal cortex, 348–349

inferior frontal gyrus, 349–350

inferior parietal lobule, 349–350

information control, concept, 10

information countermeasures, 140–142

information gain, 85

Information Gain Index (IGI), 46–47

information management strategies, 11–14
  liars, 11–12
  truth-tellers, 13–14

information processing, eye movements, 177–180

innocent examinees
  Comparison Question Test, 312–313
  Concealed Information Test, 317–318
  crime-relevant information, 146–147. *See also* truth tellers

instructed lies
  event-related potential studies, 259–261
  guilty knowledge tests, 248
  neurocognitive studies, 239, 251

instrumental detection, polygraph countermeasures, 148–149

insula, 348–349

intention-driven lies
  hemodynamic studies, 277–280
  late positive component, 252
  neurocognitive studies, 239, 270–271
  preresponse negativity, 252–253
  response times, 251–252
  working memory, 257–258

intention-driven responses to present events, 256

internal processes, deception, 305–306

internal validity, 4–5

Interpersonal Deception Theory (IDT), 47–48, 319, 322–324

interpretation
  polygraph tests
    computational, polygraph tests, 77–78, 92–94
    numerical, 74–77, 86–88
    scoring method comparisons, 94–117
  Utah Probable-Lie Tests, 74–78. *See also* evaluation

interview techniques, 356–361
  imposing cognitive load, 356–359
  psychology, 56–57
  unanticipated questions, 359–361

intrapersonal differences, polygraph tests, 311

intuition, 54

investigative interviewing, 56–57

investigative rules, 89

iParadigms LLC, 133

irises
  muscular control, 164–165. *See also* pupil

J

judgment accuracy, deception detection, 5–7

K

Kircher features, 92

knockout studies, transcranial magnetic stimulation, 276

L

laboratory studies
  advantages, 79
  polygraphs, use in the field, 112–113
  reading behaviors, 188–199
    discussion, 193–195, 199
    methods, 188–191, 196–197
    procedures, 190–191
    results, 191–193, 197–199
  Utah Probable-Lie Test, 80–81

lack of memory
  admissions, 338
  polygraph tests, 68. *See also* amnesia

Lafayette computerized polygraph systems, 113–114

language processing
   allocation strategies, 170
   eye–mind assumption, 175
   immediacy assumption, 175
   oculomotor view, 178
   task-evoked pupillary responses, 169
late disclosure, strategic use of evidence,
      21–22
late positive component (LPC)
   attitude responses, 262–263, 266
   autobiographical memories, 266
   differences between intention-driven and
      instructed lies, 252
   dual-task situations, 267–268
   event-related potentials, 232–233
   instructed lie studies, 244
   postretrieval processing, 266
lateral views, brain, 233f
Latin American Polygraph Institute (LPI),
      203–207
law enforcement officers, deception detection
      accuracy, 5
Law Enforcement Pre-Employment Tests
      (LEPETs)
   CPS scoring, 105
   multiple-issue scoring, 103–106, 104t
   scoring method comparisons, 94–117
left inferior parietal lobule, 348
left parietal cortex, 348
legal professionals, deception detection
      accuracy, 5
LEPETS. See Law Enforcement Pre-
      Employment Tests
lexical processing, eye movements, 179–180
liars
   cognitive load, multifactor model, 320–321
   Comparison Question Test, 312–313
   detection
      human accuracy, 5–7
      strategic use of evidence technique, 1–36
   event-related potentials, 259–261
   eye contact, 328
   hand movements, 327
   high-stakes situations, 7
   information management strategies, 11–12

medial frontal negativity, 243–244
polygraph spontaneous countermeasure
      effects, 138–139
reading behaviors, 194–195, 199, 209
self-regulation, 11
smiles, 326
social, 303
Utah Probable-Lie Test, 75–76. See also guilty
      examinees
lie detection
   theories, 301–374
      abstract framework, 305–307, 306f
      anxiety-based physiological approaches,
         310–313
      comparison of techniques, 354–356
      Concealed Information Test, 318
      functional magnetic resonance imaging,
         345–354
      history, 307–310
      interview techniques, 356–361
      non-verbal, theories, 319–335
      physiological, theories, 310–319
      reality monitoring, 340–342
      recognition-based physiological
         approaches, 310–311, 315–318
      Scientific Content Analysis, 343–344
      Statement Validity Assessment, 336–338
      verbal, 336–344
      verifiability approach, 342–343
lie detection "wizards", 5
light reflex, pupil dilation, 165
limbic system, 240–241
limitations
   malintent, 52
   strategic use of evidence technique, 29–30
   Utah Probable-Lie Test, 78
linguistic view, language processing, 178
literature search, strategic use of evidence
      technique research, 25
logical structure, SVA, 337
long-duration processes, 226
long-term memory, 237–238
loss-of-function studies, 277–280, 221
low base rates at portals, 44–47
low-frequency word fixations, 179

LPI. *See* Latin American Polygraph Institute
Lykken scoring system, 135–136, 145

M
Madoff, B., 303–304
magnetoencephalography (MEG), 227
malintent
    definition, 42
    FAST, 42–43, 45t
    investigative interviewing, 56–57
    limitations, 52
    physiological diagnostic approaches, 51–53
    science-based approaches, 54–55
manipulation checks, reading behaviors
        studies, 197–198
manner of disclosure, 22
matching, 323
materials, reading behavior studies, 189, 197,
        200, 205
measures, reading behavior studies, 189–190,
        197, 200, 205
mechanisms, polygraph countermeasures,
        151–154
medial frontal negativity (MFN), 243–244, 252,
        262–263
medial prefrontal cortex (mPFC), 263–264,
        347–348, 350
medial views of the brain, 233f
medical diagnosis versus polygraph accuracy,
        84–85
MEG. *See* magnetoencephalography
memory
    consolidation, 140, 147–148
    explicit/implicit, 237
    impairment, 255–256
    long-term, 237–238
    manipulation, 258
    polygraph tests, 68
    recall and reconsolidation, 147–148, 238
        See also episodic memory; semantic
        memory; working memory
memory-relate processes, 345
memory theory, reality monitoring, 336,
        340–342
mental disassociation, 144

mental imagery, 143–144
meprobamate, 139
meta-analysis, strategic use of evidence
        technique, 23–30
metaphoric gestures, 327
methods, reading behavior studies, 188–191,
        196–197, 200–202, 204–206
MFN. *See* medial frontal negativity
MGQT. *See* Reid Modified General
        Questions Test
microexpressions, 39–40, 50–51, 332–333
mid-frontal episodic memory effect, 258–259
midbrain, pupil dilation, 164–165
middle cingulate gyrus, 350
mirroring, 323
misinformation, 146–147
misspelled words, 180–181
mock thefts, 95–96, 346–351
modeling brain functions, 221
moderator analyses, strategic use of evidence
        technique, 27–28
modified yoga, 144
mPFC. *See* medial prefrontal cortex
multifactor model, non-verbal lie detection,
        319–321
multiple-issue decision rules, 72–75, 73t, 94
    comparisons, 100–101, 103–106, 104t
muscular control, irises, 164–165

N
National Center for Credibility Assessment
        (NCCA), 114
National Research Council (NRC), 83, 115
natural task switching, 243
NDI. *See* No Deception Indicated scores
near-infrared spectroscopy (NIRS), 229,
        248–249
nervousness, 49–50
neural anatomy, 233f
neurobiology, 221
neurocognitive studies, 217–300, 220–222
    cognitive workload, 284–287
    countermeasures practice, 288–289
    deception, 239–250
    future directions, 284–288

neurocognitive studies (*Continued*)
  generalizability, 282–283
  hemodynamic results, 261–266
  instructed lies, 239, 251
  intention-driven lies, 270–271
  loss-of-function, 277–280
  postretrieval processing, 282–284
  tactical monitoring, 251–259
  valence, 281–282. *See also* cognitive
    neuroscience
neuropsychology, 221
neuroscience, early studies, 231–238
neutral questions, 67, 72
NIRS. *See* near-infrared spectroscopy
NO. *See* No Opinion scores
No Deception Indicated (NDI) scores,
  87–88
No Opinion (NO) scores, 87–88
non-verbal behavior, 39–40, 49–50
non-verbal lie detection
  accuracy, 331–332
  blinking, 330
  comparison to other techniques, 354–356
  cues, 324, 325t
  eye contact, 328
  hand movements, 321, 327
  historical methods, 309
  individual and situational differences,
    329–331
  Interpersonal Deception Theory, 319,
    322–324
  interview techniques, 356–361
  microexpressions, 39–40, 50–51, 332–333
  multifactor model, 319–321
  self-presentational perspective, 319, 322
  smiles, 326
  specific tools, 332–335
  theories, 319–335
number of fixations per character, 190
number tests, polygraphs, 70–71
numerical evaluation
  polygraphs, 86–90
    seven-point scales, 86–87
    three-point scales, 87–88
  Utah Probable-Lie Test results, 74–77

O
object-relative sentences, 170
Objective Scoring System-1 (OSS-1), 93
Objective Scoring System-2 (OSS-2), 93–94
  compared to other scoring methods, 108–109
    multiple-issue tests, 100, 103–105
    single-issue decision rules, 99–100
Objective Scoring System-3 (OSS-3), 94
  multiple-issue tests, 101
ocular metrics
  deception detection, 183–188
  reading behaviors, 159–216, 185t
  reading behaviors studies, 191, 198
oculomotor deception tests, 183–184
oculomotor measurements, 163
oculomotor view of language processing, 178
"Oddball" paradigm, 232–233
Office of Technology Assessment of the US
  Congress, 82
old–new differences, event-related potentials,
  258–259
omissions, elicitation, 19
open-ended questions, 18–19
orbicularis oculi, 326
orbitofrontal cortex, 347–348
orienting reflexes, 310–311, 315–318
OSS-1. *See* Objective Scoring System-1
OSS-2. *See* Objective Scoring System-2
OSS-3. *See* Objective Scoring System-3
overall totals, Utah Probable-Lie Test, 76

P
P300 brain waves, 315–316
pain, pupil dilation, 166–167
parafoveal views, 175–176
parasympathetic nervous system (PNS), 164
parietal cortex, 256
parietal episodic memory effect, 258–259
Parkinson's disease, 275–276
PDD. *See* psychophysiological detection of
  deception
PDR. *See* pupil diameter responses
peak amplitude of electrodermal response, 97
peak amplitude of rise in diastolic point of
  cardiograph, 97

perceptual information, 340–341
perceptually-driven response conflicts, 241–242, 244–245
person variables, reading, 181–183
personal evaluation misrepresentation, 281–282
personal semantic memory, 237
personality factors, 119, 282–283
PET. *See* positron emission tomography
pharmacological amnesia, 147–148
physical assaults, 121–122
physical countermeasures, 143–144
physiological lie detection, 310–319
    anxiety-based approaches, 310–313
    comparison to other techniques, 354–356
    history, 307–309
    portals, 51–53
    recognition-based approaches, 310–311, 315–318
physiology, pupil dilation, 164–172
Pinnochio's nose, 306
placebo trials, 120
plagiarism detection, 133
plausible denials, 21–22
playing card probes, 346–351
PLT. *See* Utah Probable-Lie Test
plunging baseline prevention, polygraphs, 113–114
PNS. *See* parasympathetic nervous system
pointing gestures, 327
polygraphs
    accuracy, 84–85
    administering tests, 70–74
    anti-countermeasure training, 149–151
    anxiety-based approaches, 310–313
    applied issues, 117–122
    automatic mode, 113–114
    Backster procedures, 86
    basic principles, 65
    buffer questions, 72
    Comparison Question Test, 68–69, 79–85, 312
    computerized interpretation, 77–78, 92–94, 118–119
    confidential tests, 119–121
    countermeasures, 131–158
        detection, 145, 148–149

emotional recall, 145
future research, 154–155
general state, 117, 134–136, 139–140
information, 140–142
instrumental detection, 148–149
mental disassociation, 144
mental imagery, 143–144
misinformation, 146–147
physical, 143–144
potential solutions, 148–149
practice, 141, 143–144
requirements, 135–136
respiratory signatures, 149–151
specific point, 134–135, 137–140, 143–147
spontaneous, 137–140
statistical detection, 149
theoretical mechanism, 151–154
CPS algorithm, 92–93
decision-making, 63–130, 118–119
drug countermeasures, 117, 120
empirical scoring system, 90–92
episodic memory, 140, 147–148
evidentiary rules, 89
general state countermeasures, 117, 134, 136, 139–140
generalizability, 116, 80
good questioning technique, 68
governmental use, 122
high-pass filters, 113–114
history, 308–309
innocent suspects with knowledge of crimes, 146–147
interpretation, 74–78, 85–94
investigative rules, 89
laboratory research, 79
Lykken scoring system, 135–136, 145
multiple-issue decision rules, 100–101, 103–106, 104t
neutral questions, 67
number of charts, 99
number tests, 70–71
numerical evaluation, 74–77, 86–88
OSS-1, 93
OSS-2, 93–94
OSS-3, 94

polygraphs (*Continued*)
  personality factors, 119
  recognition-based approaches, 310–311, 315–318
  reduction in respiration line length, 97–98, 112
  Relevant Comparison Test, 116–117
  Relevant–Irrelevant Test, 311
  relevant questions, 66–68
  scoring systems, 94–117
  sensitivity, 91–92
  seven-point scales, 86–87
  single-issue decision rules, 99–103, 102t
  specific point countermeasures, 134–135, 137–140, 143–147
  spontaneous countermeasures, 137–140
  spot scoring rules, 75–76, 88
  strong emotional responses, 67
  subjects' state of mind, 68
  technique validity, 63–130
  test structure, 70–74
  theory, 310–319
  three-point scales, 87–90
  two-stage rules, 89–90, 100–101, 103–106, 104t
  Utah Directed-Lie Test, 78
  Utah Probable-Lie Test, 69–78
    accuracy in the field, 81–84
    accuracy in laboratory settings, 80–81
  validity, 63–130
  victim testing, 121–122
portals, 37–62
  deceptive context, 43–44
  Future Attribute Screening Technology, 42–45, 45t
  future research, 57–58
  investigative interviewing, 56–57
  microexpressions, 39–40, 50–51
  physiological approaches, 51–53
  related scientific literature, 47–54
  science-based screening approach, 54–55
  Screening Passengers by Observation Techniques, 39–42
  target base rates, 44–47
  time pressure, 47

unique aspects, 43–47
US Government's response to the 9–11 attack, 39–43
positron emission tomography (PET), 228
post-error slowing, 240
post-retrieval processing, 266, 282–284
practice of countermeasures, 141, 143–144, 288–289
prefrontal areas, near-infrared spectroscopy, 248–249
prefrontal cortex, 256
premovement potentials, 244, 251
prepotent truth responses, 272–273
prerespone negativity, 243–244, 252–253, 262–263
prerespone positivity, 244
present events, intention-driven responses, 256
pretest interviews, polygraph tests, 66, 70
prevention, plunging baselines on polygraphs, 113–114
probable-lie questions, 71
probe card studies, 346–351
proceduralization, 47–48
processing variability, 226
pronouns, fixation durations, 176
propranolol, 139–140, 147–148
psychological diagnosis versus polygraph accuracy, 84–85
psychological theory in interview tactics, 15–23
psychology
  experimental, 220–221
  investigative interviewing, 56–57
  pupil dilation, 164–172
  self-regulation, 9–10
psychophysiological detection of deception (PDD), 65, 152. *See also* polygraphs
pulse rates, 308
pupil constriction
  emotional arousal, 167. *See also* pupil dilation
pupil diameter responses (PDR), pain stimuli, 166–167
pupil dilation, 161
  autonomic nervous system, 164
  cognitive load, 162–163, 168–170

deception, 193–194, 199, 209
emotional arousal, 167–168
fatigue, 166
laboratory experiments, reading behaviors,
    189–190
light reflex, 165
pain, 166–167
parasympathetic nervous system, 164
physiological and psychological bases,
    164–172
reading behaviors studies, 192, 198
slow followed by rapid constriction, 161–162,
    172–173
startle response, 165–166
sympathetic nervous system, 167. *See also*
    evoked pupillary responses; task-evoked
    pupillary responses
pupil stability, 172–173

Q
quantity of detail, SVA, 337
questioning
    polygraph tests, 68
    strategic use of evidence technique, 17–20

R
radial fibers, pupil dilation, 164–165
RCT. *See* Relevant Comparison Test
reaction times (RT)
    attitude responses, 262
    cognitive neuroscience, 220–221
    historical perspective, 309
    instructed lie studies, 243–244
    intention-driven lie studies, 251–252
    ocular metrics, 191, 198
    postretrieval processing, 265–266
    pupil dilation, 164
reading behaviors
    deception detection, 174–183
    eye movements, 174–177
    field study 1, 199–203
    field study 2, 203–207
    fixation, 175–176
    goal setting, 180–181
    laboratory experiment 1, 188–195

laboratory experiment 2, 195–199
    linguistic/cognitive view, 178
    measures, 192, 198
    ocular metrics, 159–216, 185t
    oculomotor view, 178
    onset, 189–190
    regressions, 176
    Relevant Comparison Test, 184
    saccades, 175–176
    standards of evaluation, 182
    undoing negations, 186
real smiles, 326
reality monitoring, 336, 340–342
recall
    episodic memory, 238
    false memories, 238
recognition-based approaches
    event-related potentials, 258–259
    polygraph tests, 68, 310–311, 315–318
reconsolidation, episodic memory, 147–148
red-hot irons, 307–308
reduction in respiration line length (RLL),
    97–98
    computer-derived values, 112
    polygraph scoring, 92
    validity, 112
reflective evaluations, 261–262, 282–284
reflex factors, polygraph countermeasures, 144
reflexive evaluations, 261–262
regression latency, definition, 177
regressions, reading behaviors, 176
Reid Modified General Questions Test
    (MGQT), 85–86
related external associations, SVA, 337
Relevant Comparison Test (RCT), 116–117, 184
relevant questions (RQs), 66–68, 72, 312
Relevant–Irrelevant Test (RIT), 65, 85, 136, 311
repeated measures analysis of variance
    (RMANOVA), reading behaviors
    studies, 191
replicability, functional magnetic resonance
    imaging studies, 352–353
respiration, scoring, 75, 91
respiration line length. *See* reduction in
    respiration line length

respiratory signatures, 149–150
response monitoring
    anterior cingulate cortex, 240–241
    neurocognitive studies, 270–271
    right ventrolateral prefrontal cortex, 240–241
        See also conflicting responses
response times. *See* reaction times
response-synchronized event-related
        potentials, 226
review, strategic use of evidence technique
        research, 23–30
reward, cognitive processing, 219–220
rice powder, 307–308
right inferior parietal lobule, 349–350
right insula, 348–349
right middle cingulate gyrus, 348–349
right middle frontal gyrus, 349–350
right superior temporal sulcus, 348
right supplementary motor area, 349
right supramarginal gyrus, 349
right ventrolateral prefrontal cortex, 240–241,
        349–350
RIT. *See* Relevant–Irrelevant Test
Ritalin, 139–140
RLL. *See* reduction in respiration line length
RMANOVA. *See* repeated measures analysis
        of variance
robbery victims, 121–122
RQs. *See* relevant questions
RT. *See* reaction times

S
saccade latency, 177
saccades, 175–176
saccadic suppression, 175–176, 199, 209
sacrifice relevant (SR) questions, 72, 73t
sampling procedures, field-studies, 81
scalp distributions, event-related potentials, 226
SCAN. *See* Scientific Content Analysis
science-based screening approaches, portals,
        54–55
Scientific Content Analysis (SCAN), 343–344
scientific literature, portal studies, 47–54
SCIF. *See* Sensitive Compartmented
        Information Facilities

scoring
    polygraph tests, 74–78, 85–94
        comparison questions, 101
        computational, 92–94
        method comparisons, 94–117
            analysis of variance, 105–106
            data quantification, 97
            data transformations, 98–99
            datasets, 95–96
            effect sizes, 109–111
            number of charts, 99
            procedures, 95–101
            results, 101–106
            validity of results, 111–117
        multiple-issue decision rules, 100–101,
            100–101, 104t
        reduction in respiration line length, 97–98,
            112
        single-issue decision rules, 99–103, 102t
    Utah Probable-Lie Test
        computational, 77–78
        numerical, 74–77
scrambled sentences, 169–170
Screening Passengers by Observation
        Techniques (SPOT), 39–42
second-pass durations, 177, 190, 192
secondary tasks, 267–268, 277
self-generated lies, 270–271. *See also* intention-
        driven lies
self-presentational perspective, non-verbal lie
        detection, 319, 322
self-regulation
    avoidance strategies, 12–13
    decision control, 10, 12
    differences between liars and truth-tellers,
        11
    escape strategies, 12–13
    information control, 10–14
    psychology, 9–10
semantic memory, 237, 245–246
semantic processing, 169–170, 176, 179–180
Sensitive Compartmented Information
        Facilities (SCIF) cell phone violations,
        199–203
sensitivity, polygraph input, 91–92

sensors, polygraph countermeasure detection, 148–149

sensory processing, false memories, 238

September 11th, 2001, 39–43

serial offenders, Concealed Information Test, 317

seven-point scales, polygraph scoring, 86–87, 93

sex effects, evoked pupillary responses, 161

sexual assaults
  polygraph tests, 121–122
  SVA, 336–338

simulated malingering, 255–256

sincere smiles, 326

sincerity, 322

single-issue decision rules
  computational evaluation, 93–94
  method comparisons, 99–103, 102t
  Utah Probable-Lie Test, 72, 73t, 75

situational differences, non-verbal lie detection, 329–331

skin conductance, 167

slow pupillar dilation followed by rapid constriction, 161–162, 172–173

SMA. See supplementary motor area

smell of fear, 308

smiling, 326

social cognitive frameworks, 9–10

social cognitive processes, 345

social lies, 303

social psychology, deception, 47–48

SoE. See standards of evaluation

solutions, polygraph countermeasures, 148–149

SP. See specific point countermeasures

specific point (SP) countermeasures, 134–140, 143–147

specific tools, non-verbal lie detection, 332–335

speech analysis, historical perspective, 309–310

speech prompting, 327–328

speed of contraction, pupils, 164

speed of dilation, pupils, 164

sphincter pupillae, 164–165

spontaneous corrections, SVA, 338

spontaneous countermeasures, 137–139

spontaneous lies, fMRI, 246

SPOT. See Screening Passengers by Observation Techniques

spot scoring rules (SSR), polygraph tests, 75–76, 88

SR. See sacrifice relevant questions

SSR. See spot scoring rules

standards of coherence. See standards of evaluation

standards of evaluation (SoE), 182–188, 185t, 209

startle response, 165–166

statement analysis, historical perspective, 309–310

state of mind, polygraph tests, 68

statement–evidence consistency, 17, 27–28

Statement Validity Assessment (SVA), 309–310, 336–338

statistical detection, polygraph countermeasures, 149

stepwise discriminant analysis, reading behaviors studies, 193

stereotypes of deception, 6, 49–50

stimulus-synchronized event-related potentials, 226

strategic decisions, information management, 12

strategic level, strategic use of evidence technique, 17–18

strategic monitoring
  attitude responses, 262–263
  intention-driven lies, 270–271

strategic questioning, deception cue elicitation, 7–9

strategic use of evidence (SUE) technique
  check points, 19
  closed-/open-ended questioning, 18–19
  counter-interrogation strategies research, 14–15
  differences between liars and truth-tellers, 11
  disclosure tactics, 17–18, 20–23
  Evidence Framing Matrix, 22
  funnel approach, 19
  information management strategies, 11–14
  meta-analysis of research data, 23–30
  principles, 3

strategic use of evidence (SUE) technique
(*Continued*)
  psychological theory in interview tactics,
    15–23
  questioning tactics, 17–20
  self-regulation, 9–10
  state of the science, 1–36
  theoretical principles, 9–15
strategy variables, reading, 181–183
structure of polygraph tests, 70–74
subject-relative sentences, 170
subjective factors, polygraphs, 117–118
SUE. *See* strategic use of evidence
supplementary motor area (SMA), 244, 349
suppression, saccades, 175–176
supramarginal gyrus, 349
susceptibility to suggestion, children, 339
SVA. *See* Statement Validity Assessment
sweating, 167
sympathetic nervous systems (SNS), 161, 164,
  167
syntactic organization, 169–170, 176
systems-level analysis, 221

T
tactical disclosures, 17–18, 20–23
tactical monitoring, 240, 251, 259–261
target base rates, portals, 44–47
task variables, reading, 181–183
task-evoked pupillary responses (TEPRs),
  168–170, 173
task-switching, 272
TDCS. *See* transcranial direct current
  stimulation
temporal coupling, 226
temporal details, 340–341
temporal resolution, 228
temporary lesions, 276
TES. *See* Test for Espionage and sabotage
Test for Espionage and Sabotage (TES), 51–52,
  142
test structure, polygraph interviews, 70–74
theories, 301–374
  anxiety-based polygraph approaches,
    310–313

Behavior Analysis Interview, 333–335
Comparison Question Test, 313–314
Concealed Information Test, 316
criteria-based content analysis, 337
functional magnetic resonance imaging-
  based lie detection, 345–354
Interpersonal Deception Theory, 319,
  322–324
memory quality, 340–342
microexpressions, 332–333
multifactor model of non-verbal lie
  detection, 319–321
non-verbal lie detection, 319–335, 325t
physiological lie detection, 310–319
polygraphs, 310–319
reality monitoring, 340–342
recognition-based polygraph approaches,
  310–311, 315–318
self-presentational perspective of non-verbal
  lie detection, 319, 322
Statement Validity Assessment, 336–338
verbal lie detection, 336–344
verifiability approach, 342–343
threat avoidance, 9–10
threat of punishment theory, Comparison
  Question Test, 313
three-point scales, polygraph scoring, 87–90
time lapses, 317, 341–342
time pressure, portals, 47
TMS. *See* transcranial magnetic stimulation
total scores, Utah Probable-Lie Test, 75–76
training
  anti-countermeasures, 149–151
  countermeasures, 141, 143–144, 288–289
trait adjectives, event-related potentials,
  264–265
transcranial direct current stimulation (TDCS),
  276
transcranial magnetic stimulation (TMS),
  230–231, 276
Transport Security Administration (TSA), 39–42
truth-tellers
  Comparison Question Test, 312–313
  Concealed Information Test, 317–318
  crime-relevant information, 146–147

eye contact, 328
hand movements, 327
information management strategies, 13–14
polygraph spontaneous countermeasure
    effects, 138–139
self-regulation, 11
smiles, 326
Utah Probable-Lie Test, 75–76. *See also*
    innocent examinees
truthfulness stereotypes, 337
TSA. *See* Transport Security Administration
Turnitin, 133
two-stage rules, 89–90, 100–101, 103–106, 104t
types of smile, 326

U
UFT. *See* unreported foreign travel
unanticipated questions, 8–9, 359–361
undoing negations, reading behaviors, 186
unreported foreign travel (UFT) field study,
    199–203
unstructured production, SVA, 337
unsupported deception stereotypes, 6
US Army Military Police School Polygraph
    Branch, 86
US Government, 9-11 attack response at
    portals, 39–43
Utah Directed-Lie Test (DLT), 78, 138
Utah Probable-Lie Test (PLT), 69–78
    accuracy in the field, 81–84
    accuracy in laboratory settings, 80–81
    interpretation, 74–78
    laboratory accuracy, 80–81
    limitations, 78
    multiple-issue questioning, 72–75, 73t
    numerical evaluation, 74–77
    single-issue questioning, 72, 73t, 75
    spontaneous countermeasures, 138
    test structure and administration, 70–74
Utah scoring system, 86

V
valence, 263, 268–269, 281–284
validity
    comparison question tests, 79–85

criteria-based content analysis, 339
    hemodynamic studies, 279–280
    polygraph techniques and decision methods,
        63–130
Valium, 139–140
variable-duration processes, event-related
    potentials, 226
ventrolateral prefrontal cortex (VLPFC)
    concealed information tests, 349–350
    differentiation-of-deception studies, 347
    frequency of lying, 257
    functional magnetic resonance imaging
        studies, 347, 349–350
    intention-driven lies, 255
    response inhibition, 240–241
    simulated malingering, 255–256
    transcranial direct current stimulation, 276
    valence effects, 263–264
veracity, 3
verbal lie detection
    comparison to other techniques, 354–356
    interview techniques, 356–361
    reality monitoring, 340–342
    Scientific Content Analysis, 343–344
    Statement Validity Assessment, 336–338
    theories, 336–344
    verifiability approach, 342–343
verifiability approach, 342–343
victims, polygraph tests, 121–122
visual cortex
    autobiographical memories, 237–238, 259
    valence effects, 263–264
visual perception, language processing,
    177–180
VLPFC. *See* ventrolateral prefrontal cortex

W
Williams patterns, 149–151
"wizards", 5
word association tests, 309
word lengths, fixations, 179
working memory, 234–237, 257–258

Z
zygomatic major, 326